# SHERMAN

*Gen. William T. Sherman, 1865, soon after the death of President Lincoln.*

# SHERMAN

## Merchant of Terror, Advocate of Peace

### CHARLES EDMUND VETTER

**Pelican Publishing Company**
Gretna 1992

The word "Pelican" and the depiction of a pelican are
trademarks of Pelican Publishing Company, Inc., and are
registered in the U.S. Patent and Trademark Office.

**Library of Congress Cataloging-in-Publication Data**

Vetter, Charles Edmund.
    Sherman : merchant of terror, advocate of peace / by Charles
Edmund Vetter.
        p.   cm.
    Includes bibliographical references and index.
    ISBN 0-88289-860-4
    1. Sherman, William T. (William Tecumseh), 1820–
1891.   2. United States—History—Civil War, 1861–1865—
Campaigns.   3. Generals—United States—Biography.   4. United
States. Army—Biography.   5. Military art and science—United
States—History—19th century.
I. Title.
E467.1.S55V48 1992
973.7′092—dc20
[B]                                                                91–31713
                                                                        CIP

*Photographs courtesy U.S. Army Military History Institute.*

Manufactured in the United States of America

Published by Pelican Publishing Company, Inc.
1101 Monroe Street, Gretna, Louisiana 70053

*To Amy, whose perceptiveness of people and events is amazing; to Kimberly, whose energy and enthusiasm for life is wonderful; and to Kay, whose embrace and touch keeps the sea from engulfing us and the light from going out.*

# *Contents*

# Preface

THE VERY NATURE OF THE ISSUES addressed in this work have dictated the extensive use of *both* primary and secondary sources. This is not a biography of William Sherman, although I have dealt with his life from his entrance as a cadet at West Point to the surrender of Joseph Johnston in North Carolina. The presentation of biographical information provides the book with the necessary continuity for an adequate understanding of the major issues under consideration. This work is not a detailed history of Sherman's military exploits during the Civil War. In other words, the reader will not find in these pages a blow-by-blow or flanking-by-flanking account of the Army of the Tennessee's trek through Georgia and the Carolinas. There are a number of adequate biographies and military accounts of Sherman available, and I refer the reader to them if this is his area of interest.

My concern has been to examine five issues that I consider to be of importance to a better understanding of Sherman and his Civil War experience. These are issues which I submit have either been mistreated or totally ignored. Therefore, I have presented in the following pages a fresh and revised analysis of William Sherman, the person, and the impact he had on the American Civil War and on war in general. Specifically, these are the issues addressed:

1. An analysis of the complexities and diversities of the man
2. An examination of the evolutionary development of Sherman's philosophy of war

9

3. An understanding of the relationship between Sherman and Grant

4. An evaluation of Sherman's place in the context of American military history and of military history in general

5. A presentation of the sociological impact of Sherman's military actions

An adequate treatment of these issues has required that I consider of equal importance both primary and secondary sources.

Thus, I have relied heavily not only on the writings of Sherman himself, but of those who knew him intimately or had the fortune, or misfortune, of his acquaintance. I have made extensive use of the letters Sherman wrote to family members, friends, and colleagues. In addition, I have turned to the numerous diaries, journals, recollections, memoirs, articles, and histories written by eyewitnesses. I have also consulted newspapers and official documents. The available primary materials, both printed and in manuscript form, are rich, abundant, and diverse. A listing of these sources is presented in the primary sources section of the bibliography.

Because I refute many of the traditional and long-accepted conclusions made in the existing literature about Sherman, I have given equal treatment to secondary sources. Again, the material here is rich, abundant, and diverse. The controversial nature of his personality and his military actions has opened the door to a plethora of writings. An understanding of the analysis of secondary sources is a prerequisite for the type of work I have presented in this book. I have, therefore, done a thorough search of the secondary literature on this subject by examining biographies, interpretative works, and articles. They have been enlightening, frustrating, helpful, and necessary for a study of this nature. Again, I refer the reader to the secondary sources section of the bibliography.

# Acknowledgments

I WAS FIRST INTRODUCED to Gen. William T. Sherman by the late Dr. Jack Scroggs of The University of North Texas. As a professor for my master's thesis he suggested that I consider Sherman's theory of war as a possible topic. I followed his suggestion, and after a year and a half of work I completed what appears to me today to be a rather elementary analysis of Sherman. That was back in the mid-1960s.

For over twenty years my thesis gathered dust on my office book shelf. Then a few years ago I accepted an invitation to make a presentation on Sherman to the North Louisiana Civil War Round Table here in Shreveport. I pulled my thesis down, dusted it off, and made the presentation. After I had finished, Terry Jones, author of *Lee's Tigers*, asked me what I was going to do with my work on Sherman. I told him that it would probably be put back on my book shelf. Although I had kept up with the literature on Sherman and the Civil War as a whole, I had not thought in terms of writing a book. Terry, along with a number of the Round Table members, encouraged me to pursue the project. So, for over three years I got involved with Sherman once again and the result is *Sherman: Merchant of Terror, Advocate of Peace*. I will always be indebted to Dr. Scroggs, Terry, and the members of the North Louisiana Civil War Round Table. They have contributed more to the writing of this book than they will ever know.

Although I am a sociologist by trade, my love is history, particularly

11

Civil War history. My students know this and so do many of my colleagues here at Centenary College. As a result, I have been involved for the past five years in teaching an American Military History module. At the suggestion of the Military Science Department of Centenary I applied for admission to the United States Military Academy ROTC History Workshop. I was accepted and spent a full month at the academy in West Point studying under some of the finest military historians in the country. The experience has greatly enhanced my work on Sherman and I am deeply grateful for the training I received.

A very special expression of gratitude goes to Dr. Edwin Bearss, chief historian of the National Park Services. Dr. Bearss took the time from his very busy life to read, critique, and correct my manuscript. He is meticulous in his work and applied that standard to mine. I am honored that he shared his immense knowledge of the Civil War and of General Sherman with me. Although I take full responsibility for the final work, it has been enhanced by Dr. Bearss. I thank him for his tremendous assistance.

Ella Edwards, reference librarian, and Muzette Gallagher, interlibrary loan librarian of the Magale Library at Centenary College, have been marvelous. They were always available when I needed help and their professionalism is to be highly commended. Without their expertise and willingness to locate sources, this book would never have been written.

I also want to thank Marilyn and Gary Joiner for reading the manuscript. Gary's knowledge of the Civil War and military history in general is to be admired. He made numerous suggestions that improved my work. Marilyn is an English major and brought her knowledge of grammar to the manuscript. She also suggested the title. Both are Southerners, and I believe I have convinced them that Sherman was not a demon after all.

I am indebted to Paul Parks, former director of the Center for Learning Enhancement and Research, and Beverly McCracken, present director of the center, for relieving me of certain responsibilities so that I could concentrate on research and writing. They have been wonderful. A special thanks goes to Beverly's husband, Lowell, for taking me through the intricacies of the computer. He was always at hand, willing to help.

To Emily Veal, Karla Pinto, and Bettye Leslie, my secretaries, I say thank you for the many hours you spent in the library and in front of the copying machine. I appreciate the encouragement of Dan Garner and Polly Pickard of Cablevision of Shreveport, and I thank Centenary College for making available a sabbatical. Finally, I am indebted to my editor Nina Kooij of Pelican Publishing Company for her patience in guiding me through this my first book.

# Introduction

IN THE SOUTH, HE WAS CALLED a demon, a barbarian. In the North, he was a hero. Both views were heavily tainted with the bias of the times, but what more could be expected from those who directly and/or indirectly experienced William Tecumseh Sherman and the Army of the West? He was a person either hated passionately or admired with deep respect. Few could be found who were indifferent to him. He brought to the people of the South an unprecedented devastation that is still recalled and remembered. Unknowingly, Sherman made a significant contribution to the birth of the "Lost Cause" dialogue. To the North, he was the epitome of revenge, for it was said that he brought to the Confederacy that which it deserved. He taught Southerners the futility of secession and destroyed their will to fight.

Without a doubt, Sherman warranted such evaluations. To Northerners he *was* a hero, and in the eyes of most Southerners he *was* a barbarian. These descriptions, of course, are too simplistic; for Sherman was more, much more. Like all people, he was neither completely good nor totally bad, and like all people, he was complex and diverse. He could be mean and indifferent as well as good and compassionate. He experienced joys and sorrows, successes and failures. And like all people, he desired to find a place in his world that would provide him peace and fulfillment.

Eventually, like most people, he found that place—not as a hero, nor as a barbarian. He became that which he wanted more than

15

anything to be, a successful soldier in the United States Army. This was his core, his center, the thing that gave all else in his life meaning. Fulfilling this desire meant that he could have all the other trappings of success—occupation, family, status, respect from peers, recognition, security. Without the core, however, life for Sherman would have been incomplete.

Like so many others, Sherman did not find success, and therefore, fulfillment, easily. Indeed, there was a time in his life that he was convinced it would never come. He was slow in developing, late in blossoming. By age forty he could look back on his life and see a number of minor successes, some rather major failures, and an abundance of frustrated ambitions. Through it all he lived with the apprehension that all alternatives would be exhausted and that he would have to work for his father-in-law, a possibility abhorrent to him.

For all his life he had been dedicated to doing the right thing. He was responsible and ambitious. He worked hard and adhered to the values instilled in him since childhood. He had been taught to search out and fulfill the Great American Dream. Somehow in the beginning the search never led him to success. Things never seemed to be on his side. Thus, early in his life he came to view himself as a failure, and it had its effect. The self-esteem and self-confidence of his earlier years began to slip away. He developed feelings of inferiority that eventually led to moments of paranoia. He became overcautious and, particularly after First Bull Run and during his days in Kentucky and Missouri, saw things that really did not exist. Guilt began to take its toll.

Yet, in spite of his frustrations and feelings of failure, he never lost a deep faith in his abilities or vision. There was a very strong core to the man, a confidence inside that gave him an undying determination to keep trying. Plus, he liked himself, but he knew that he was not what he wanted to be. Events over which he had little control worked against him. Just as he would begin to feel settled and to foresee a future of stability before him, events would undo his life. Unseated by external occurrences, he eventually developed a sense of conflict with his environment. He became hypercritical, at times cynical, and extremely skeptical toward the normal avenues to success.

Early in life Sherman acquired a strong sense of right and wrong. Socialization in a prominent political family, one of upper-middle-class standing, had established certain basic principles in him. To be successful, to achieve recognition in a respectable position, and to gain independence were values instilled in him by various significant people in his life. A normal result of such socialization was a deep-seated need to please others. The members of his foster family, particularly the father, Thomas Ewing, became the "significant others" in his life. The Ewings were achievement-oriented and placed heavy emphasis on attainment of the American Dream. Thus, Sherman was surrounded with role models of that Dream. The pressure to succeed was ever present. Yet so many times, doing right, following the rules, only resulted in disappointment and disillusionment. Not an unfamiliar story. Who among us has not experienced similar emotions, disappointments, and frustrations?

However, there were influences and people in Sherman's life that made him determined to succeed. An intense drive had been planted and nurtured in him that made it impossible for him to give up or to quit trying. Actually, from the perspective of others, his failures were not that important. He always conducted himself well under the most trying circumstances. However, he believed they were major; thus, to him, they were.

In spite of such feelings he never gave up, he never broke under the weight of events. Perhaps it was his awareness of the Sherman family name in history, or the need to be seen favorably by his foster father-in-law that drove him on; perhaps it was his strong drive for recognition or the deep desire to be a good husband and provider for his family that kept him going. Or, perhaps it was his extreme dedication to the Protestant Ethic. Whatever it was (and more than likely, it was all of these), it worked.

Eventually, more specifically on the eve of the Battle of Shiloh, having just emerged with a struggle with himself and particular elements in his external world, he achieved a level of stability and fulfillment he had not experienced since his days at West Point. From that historic battle in 1862, to the time of his death some thirty years later, Sherman knew who and what he was. There would be problems and turmoil, but they would never control him. Shiloh was Sherman's moment of decision. It was his launching point to eventual fame and contentment. In a sense, the remainder of his life was simply a living out of the ideas developed prior to that event. From that point on, he polished his theory of war, adjusted to the husband and father roles circumstances would dictate, and found peace within himself. And he left a legacy that has yet to be fully comprehended.

Sherman's contemporaries and later historians have made numerous attempts to untangle the complexities of this man. The major personal characteristics that emerge from these attempts are intelligence, innovation, foresight, dedication, talent, and compassion. T. Harry Williams spoke of him as "an imaginative thinker and a political scientist and a social philosopher. . . ." James Merrill, author of one of the last full-length biographies of Sherman, found him to be dedicated and determined. He wrote, "[Sherman] assigned great importance to facing all situations with honesty and truth, meeting the demands of life head-on, no matter how unpleasant the consequences."

Others have made reference to these characteristics and, whether favorable or hostile in their complete analysis of Sherman, they all agree that his nature was one of diversity and complexity. Anyone who has studied Sherman with any intensity must agree with Basil Liddell Hart's summation. He sees Sherman as "the typical American," a man possessing extraordinary talents. He was restless, curious, and rebellious—truly American characteristics. Liddell Hart attributes this extraordinary quality to Sherman's paradoxical nature. So often, Sherman seemed contrary to what he was. To be sure, there were contradictions in his make-up, but the dominant feature was that of paradox. This is the reason Sherman was frequently misunderstood. Those around him failed to delve deeply enough to resolve the contradictions.

Liddell Hart captured better than any other writer this quality of Sherman's personality. Sherman, he wrote, had "a quickness of mind combined with minute exactness of observation." He possessed a "prophetic vision along with meticulousness about detail." He had "dynamic energy along with philosophical reflectiveness." He displayed "a discontent that at times sank into a melancholic depression and at other times rose to foaming crests of inspiration." Although Sherman held a strong "belief in his own vision," he also possessed "a doubt of his abilities that could only be dispelled gradually by the mentally registered facts of actual achievement." He acquired an "ardor in the pursuit of ideals that was accompanied by a sense of its futility." He possessed "democratic tastes and manners with a sardonic distrust of democracy," a "rebelliousness with a profound respect for law and order," and "a deep sense of loyalty coupled with an exceptional degree of moral courage and candor." He could be at one moment "logically ruthless" and in the next moment extremely compassionate. He was a man who mixed "warm affections with a coolly objective detachment."

Those who have studied Sherman also agree that he was selfish, prejudiced, at times politically naive, highly image-conscious, capable of arrogance, and quick to pass judgment. But, of course, this is what made Sherman human. Unfortunately, too much of what has been written about Sherman has either been in praise or degradation of the man. Such treatments are unjust, for no one, including Sherman, is without flaw. He, like all people, had his imperfections, his rough edges that were offensive to others. To understand Sherman it is imperative that his many sides be seen and appreciated. Such an understanding leads to a grasp of the whole. A major purpose of this book is to present the complexities and diversities of this man who has had such a terrific impact on the evolution of military history in the United States and, to a degree, in the world. Due to the enormous amount of both primary and secondary source material available, the task is difficult. It becomes even more so because, to most who knew him, he was a contradiction while, to those who understood him, he was a paradox. Contradictions are easy to understand; paradoxes require in-depth analysis. One wonders, did Sherman either consciously or unconsciously intend it to be this way?

William Tecumseh Sherman has come to be recognized as one of the original strategists to emerge from the American Civil War. To Liddell Hart he was "the most original genius of the American Civil War." James McDonough and James Jones, in their recent work on Sherman, speak of him in this manner: "[He] possessed one of the Civil War's finest military minds. He understood the totality of war." At the conclusion of their study, McDonough and Jones offer this observation: "In the final analysis, although Sherman more than once demonstrated tactical shortcomings in his military career, from the standpoint of strategy, logistics, and communications, the general had no superior on either side of the war; possibly no equal." Although this statement is somewhat exaggerated, there is no question that Sherman has left his mark on the development of strategic warfare. He understood soldiering and had a grasp of grand strategy, one that placed him on the forefront of a new era in warfare.

A second purpose of this study, one just as important as the first, is to examine the evolutionary development of Sherman's philosophy of war. Such an attempt is not new. Lloyd Lewis, Liddell Hart, Earl Miers, and Merrill, just to name a few, have produced detailed biographies on Sherman, intertwining throughout their narratives the growth of his ideas concerning war. The works are excellent and necessary for an understanding of Sherman. However, because of their purpose, basically biography, the works are cumbersome for an analysis of Sherman's philosophy. In addition, they have aged, and it is time for a new and fresh treatment.

A major publication by John Walters is the closest analysis in book form of Sherman's development of war. It is well researched and documented, but Walters' presuppositions concerning total war are biased and require caution on the part of the reader. His presentation is moralistic, which infringes on his objectivity and, thus, his analysis. Walters fails to see the paradoxical nature of Sherman, so he oversimplifies Sherman's complexities. In addition, he presents Sherman's methods of warfare in a historical vacuum, not recognizing the evolutionary development of warfare in its totality. To Walters, Sherman is a barbarian who threw open the doors to the madness of warfare and all its cruelties; thus he is responsible for the horrors of modern warfare. For Walters, Sherman is nothing more than a nineteenth-century merchant of terror, a man with a demented mind.

There is also an abundance of material that concentrates on the final product—that is, Sherman's theory of war and its implementation. Burke Davis, Joseph Glatthaar, John Barrett, William Scaife, and McDonough and Jones, have provided detailed accounts of troop movements, examples of economic and psychological warfare, and the implementation of total warfare. Although valuable works, they do not analyze the process Sherman went through to arrive at this theory. Attempts have been made to examine this process by such scholars as Stephen Ambrose and Albert Castel, but their treatments have been limited to articles in professional journals or popular periodicals. Lacking, therefore, is a thorough analysis of the various factors that influenced Sherman in his development of the type of warfare that, to some extent, revolutionized the theories and practices of warfare in his day.

Although referred to quite often, the full impact of Sherman's relationship with Grant has not been thoroughly researched. This relationship is a third major concern of this work. It can probably be stated with accuracy that Sherman's theory of war was due to Grant's ideas, influence, and example. Sherman's witnessing of Grant's operations at Vicksburg—specifically his decision to leave his base of supply—influenced him more than most writers seem to appreciate. Grant's coolness at Shiloh, when it appeared that defeat was at hand, left a lasting mark on Sherman's ideas. And Grant's encouragement of Sherman in the destruction of Jackson and Meridian in Mississippi and his final approval of the Georgia and Carolinas campaigns made it possible for Sherman to prove the worth of his ideas. Sherman would not have achieved the position of military genius had it not been for Grant. Likewise, Grant would have been less effective had it not been for Sherman's presence. While Grant achieved victory over the Confederates at Forts Henry and Donelson in Tennessee, it was Sherman who provided the necessary support and encouragement. And during the aftermath of Shiloh, when Henry Halleck made his attempt to bury Grant, it was Sherman who convinced Grant to be patient and allow the ill winds to pass. Both Grant and Sherman were dependent upon each other, and needed each other. Outwardly they were different—Grant always calm, Sherman forever nervous—yet, inwardly, they were very much alike. Interestingly, numerous works have been produced on Lee and Grant; Lee, Grant, and Sherman; and even McClellan, Grant, and Sherman; but nothing on just Grant and Sherman. This was an extremely important symbiotic relationship and, because of its importance, it must be given attention.

Militarily, Sherman lived on the outer edge of the nineteenth century. He was in the nineteenth century, but, in many ways, not of it. He was taught nineteenth-century principles of war; yet he realized that advances in technology were rapidly making those principles obsolete. He was taught the principles of gentlemanly warfare, the importance of professional armies fighting on a designated field of battle, the necessity of effective cavalry and its shock tactics, and the need for separating combatants from noncombatants. He understood clearly Napoleon, Jomini, and Clausewitz. Sherman's uniqueness, however, was his ability to see into the future and to summon the courage to act on what he saw. He knew, perhaps better than anyone else, that a new age had dawned, that the boundaries of the nineteenth century were expanding, and that warfare as it was currently conceived would never be the same. He was willing, indeed excited, to be the agent of such expansion. Thus, a fourth purpose of this study is to place Sherman in the context of military history, to determine his proper place in the development of warfare. What he thought and what his armies accomplished were the direct result of changes taking place in the nineteenth century, changes that were revolutionary from all aspects of society, not simply the military. Unfortunately, few attempts have been made to address this issue effectively.

Finally, the sociological impact of Sherman's actions has either been ignored or simply assumed. Emphasis has been placed on the economic and psychological results of his famous march to the sea and the following raid through the Carolinas. The previously mentioned authors refer to this type of warfare in their treatments of Sherman. Only one, however, comments on the sociological implications of Sherman's devastation, and even he fails to develop the idea. Liddell Hart briefly uses the term "sociology" in the introduction to his work on Sherman, but it appears almost as an afterthought. To be sure, Sherman's techniques brought economic and psychological disorganization to much of the South. But accompanying this disorganization was the sociological disruption of that region. Families were put in disarray, complete communities destroyed leaving the inhabitants adrift. Institutions were rendered dysfunctional, and local governments disorganized. Social cohesion, a necessity for human life, was seriously threatened and, in some cases, destroyed. Values, customs, rules were uprooted leaving hundreds of thousands of people adrift in a state of semi-normlessness. True, the old antebellum South was already in the process of demise, but Sherman pushed it over the edge. A final purpose of this book is to determine the nature of the sociological warfare of Sherman's marches through the South. It is important that the psychological terror be placed in a sociological context and that the economic devastation be seen as an attack on a culture, a way of life.

Without a doubt, Sherman was a great general. His greatness, however, did not come quickly. His concept of total war evolved over a period of twenty-five years. He was a man of superior intellect and, through practical observation and logical reasoning, he developed his theory of war. Then, with calculated risks, he put his theories into practice. To the astonishment of some and the chagrin of others, his venture, so new to the annals of war, was successful. The evolution began when Sherman first entered West Point at the age of sixteen and reached its climax and maturity after the Battle of

Shiloh in 1862. Indeed, Shiloh was the turning point. It was the testing ground for his stability, and he emerged, victorious. Shiloh gave him the needed self-confidence he had lacked for so long. At Shiloh, Sherman took control, not only of himself, but of his chosen profession.

# SHERMAN

# CHAPTER ONE

# "Destroy the Enemy's Supplies . . . and Break His Morale"

IN MAY 1836, A "TALL, slim, loose-jointed lad, with red hair, burned skin, and piercing black eyes"[1] boarded a stagecoach in Lancaster, Ohio. His ultimate destination was West Point, New York. Arriving at Zanesville, Ohio, he transferred to one of the coaches that transported passengers east and west along the National Road. After three days and three nights of continuous travel, he finally arrived at Frederick, Maryland, where he boarded a train and traveled by rail to Baltimore, Maryland. From Baltimore he continued his journey until he reached the nation's capital. Concluding a short stay with his foster father in Washington, D.C., the young boy traveled north to New York City where he visited his uncles. From that fascinating city he journeyed up the Hudson River to West Point, where at the age of sixteen, he enrolled as a cadet in the United States Military Academy.[2] His appointment had come from his adopted foster father, Sen. Thomas Ewing of Ohio.[3] Thus began the controversial military career of William Tecumseh Sherman.

Like many of the young men who had come to the Hudson Valley prior to him, and like those who would come later, Sherman was captivated by its beauty. Writing to Ellen Ewing, Thomas Ewing's daughter,[4] Sherman, with obvious enthusiasm, said, "Is not West Point worth visiting? Is not the scenery of the finest order in the world? Are there not incidents in its history that render it dear to us all? I might ask a hundred such questions which any individual who has ever been here would be compelled to answer in the affirmative."[5]

The natural beauty in which the academy was located would always bring positive feelings to Sherman; however, the same could not be said about the school itself. Concerning this issue, he had mixed feelings. Although he did well during his four years at the academy, graduating sixth in a class of forty-two,[6] the experience was unpleasant and distasteful in one respect. He grew to dislike the customs of the institution very quickly. Having already acquired an independent disposition, he had little use for such strictures as codes of dress, the demerit system, and unquestioned authority. Sherman never learned the value of "the niceties of dress in the approved West Point manner." He brought to the East "the Western frontier trait of evaluating a man by what he said and did rather than what he wore," and he never managed to change this attitude. As Lloyd Lewis says, "Elegance of clothes or manner had been . . . to the disadvantage of their wearer in the woodland regions [of the West] and it was this carelessness that now kept Sherman from the standing to which his intellect alone would have raised him." Lewis continues, "Judged on his academic record alone, he would have rated among the first five—honor men—of his class, but his errors in decorum had dragged him down."[7]

Nor did he think the demerit system worthy of the academy. Although he ranked sixth in his graduating class, Sherman was convinced the academy did not consider him "a good soldier." He wrote, "I was not a Sunday School cadet. I ranked 124 in the whole student body for good behavior. My average demerits, per annum, were about 150, which reduced my final class standing from Number 4 to Number 6."[8] He believed the demerit system was the reason, along with his lack of conformity to rules. "Neatness in dress and form, with a strict conformity to the rules, were the qualifications of office, and I suppose I was found not to excel in any of these."[9] Although not as deviant as some, Sherman was not a strict conformer and he felt he suffered unjustly as a result.

Learning the lesson of unquestioned authority did not come easily either. The United States Military Academy in the 1830s and 1840s was aristocratic in manners, ideals, and religion. It was an institution in which Southern mores and values were primarily predominate. The youth of the South, with their polished manner and easy confidence, enrolled in proportionately larger numbers than the men of the North and West. Thus, Sherman came under the influence of an army establishment basically Southern in character.[10] For the first time in his life, he was made aware of the existence of a class system in American society—a system founded on status, class, and authority. West Point, although an exaggeration, was a microcosm of that society, and it was here that Sherman learned of an authority that was intolerant of insubordination, even of the slightest form. "Nobody stopped to argue or to convince another person that a thing ought to be done." For an argumentative person like Sherman, this was a different concept. With a sense of amazement, on many occasions he must have cried, "A command was given and it was obeyed; if it was not punishment came swiftly."[11]

By the completion of his third year, Sherman had acclimated himself to what, to him, were the trivial and bothersome aspects of the academy and had grown to like the life of a cadet and soldier. "His distaste" was "for the meaningless customs and not for the profession itself."[12] He had internalized a deep respect for the army and developed a clear understanding of its role in a democratic society.

Liddell Hart writes, "The germ of soldiering [was] in his blood, and never [would] it loose its hold. All that [was] spiritual in the West Point tradition [had] been absorbed into his soul, as into his mind all that [was] profitable in the West Point education."[13] This became Sherman's dedication and his devotion. To Sherman, "duty," "honor," and "country" were more than mere words. They became an integral part of his being, the major themes to which he would give his life. Future events would necessitate an undying dedication to his country and its military institutions. There would be periods of doubt and confusion, yet he would remain true to his sworn duty. Honor would never be compromised. These three ideas, learned at West Point, became the foundation for Sherman's philosophy of war. As a confirmation of his determination, he wrote to Ellen, "Indeed, the nearer we come to that dreadful epoch, graduation day, the higher opinion I conceive of the duties and life of an officer of the United States Army, and the more confirmed [I am] in the wish of spending my life in the *service of my country*."[14]

There were a number of practical lessons Sherman learned at the academy that would prove to be of importance in later years. It was here that he was taught "artillery drills, . . . target-firing with long twenty-fours and thirty-twos, mortars, howitzers, etc., as also cavalry exercises. . . ."[15] This, along with lessons in engineering, natural

philosophy, chemistry, mathematics, drawing and French, contributed to the development of Sherman's young mind.[16] In addition to the routine course of study, Sherman was exposed to the
constructing of fortifications "as well as the manner of attacking and
defending them, Mineralogy and Geology, Rhetoric, Moral Philosophy, International and Common Law, Artillery and Infantry Tactics." Knowledge of such wide and varied information was important, not only to Sherman, but to all men in the military during the
nineteenth century because it was a prerequisite for being a scientific
officer.[17]

Basically, the lessons of warfare learned at the academy were theoretical and tactical and taught under highly controlled circumstances. Sherman was perceptive enough to understand the weak-
nesses and limitations of theory and the value of firsthand
experience. In discussions with his classmates about a possible war
with Great Britain over the Maine boundary, he displayed the eagerness of a young cadet to be commissioned and sent into battle. Such
an experience would "prove a better school for the soldier" than
West Point.[18]

The military texts of Antoine-Henri Jomini, chief strategist to
Napoleon, were not required reading for the cadets. They had been
at an earlier time but not during Sherman's four years of study.
Whether he was ever exposed to Jomini's writings is not known, but
because of nineteenth-century interest in the rudiments of artillery,
infantry, and cavalry, and because of Sherman's great curiosity, he
probably read them. Primarily, what Sherman learned at West Point
was obedience, regularity, tactics, and reverence for authority. There
were no lessons in great maneuvers or grand strategy, nor was Sherman exposed to military history or the art of war. The only military
theory he received came from the writings of Alfred Thayer Mahan,
and even that was elementary. West Point was mainly a school of
engineering and obedience. "By example, stern command, and punishment it taught cadets the things that a gentleman and an officer
did or did not do."[19] Thus, when Sherman graduated he was the
epitome of orthodox nineteenth-century militarism—a militarism
he would use and against which he would eventually rebel.

Although Sherman acquired a lasting respect for and a typical
cadet's knowledge of army life, he remained "restless and independent, full of energy," and grew "impatient with regulations and
bumbling superiors." As a means of coping with the frustration and

stress resulting from the need to adjust to a less than ideal situation, he was "occasionally inclined toward pranks" and minor violations of rules.[20] His intellectual achievements and periodic dalliances, however, went unnoticed, for he never advanced to the position of officer. In later years, after the Civil War was well behind him, he wrote of this lack of advancement: " . . . at no time was I selected for any office, but remained a private throughout. . . ."[21] In spite of this record, Sherman was a good student, bright and disciplined, and did well as a cadet. He believed he was always held in respectable esteem by his professors, " . . . especially in drawing, chemistry, mathematics, and natural philosophy."[22] He went through the regular course in the required time period and was graduated sixth in his class. This was no modest accomplishment by any standard, yet it seemed to rankle him that he never achieved recognition for his efforts. Although he makes no specific mention of it, this lack of recognition probably contributed to his future hypercritical stance toward the military and political establishments of his day. No doubt it also contributed to his determination to achieve renown for his actions in the future.

Among his fellow cadets he apparently found acceptance. They considered him an excellent conversationalist, genial and sociable. However, there were times when he displayed irritability and an overabundance of nervous energy. Many recall him as extremely outspoken and opinionated, sometimes to the point of being offensive. Never was he without words or ideas on practically any subject—but especially on the military and politics.

The controversial, and to some contradictory, nature of Sherman's personality began to appear during his days at West Point. Despite the frustrations with customs and his constant criticisms of the military, his feelings for the academy were strong and his dedication to the army unequaled. Yet he disliked having to sacrifice his individuality. West Point was not what he expected nor what he thought it ought to be. As Merrill says, "Its basic function was to turn out soldiers. It was a professional institution for professionals. Its product was an officer who would fight, who could submerge his individuality in prompt implicit obedience."[23] "Into his soul," Lewis writes, "the school tried to grind a trust in orthodoxy—orthodoxy in Christianity, in militarism, and in etiquette."[24] In his own way he fought the effort. True, he allowed himself to be assimilated enough to be graduated, but under the facade there was that constant struggle with the established and accepted views of the world. He wanted to be a soldier, but he was not sure the nineteenth-century techniques and methods were adequate. He wanted to see America grow and expand, but he had little confidence in the politicians at the head of state. He believed in a government of law, but held serious doubt as to the effectiveness of democracy. He was deeply entrenched in the ideas of the nineteenth century, but was acutely aware of a new era on the horizon.

It is difficult to determine the influence West Point had on the development of Sherman's philosophy of war because he never provided an in-depth evaluation of those years, and the letters he wrote while a cadet are limited. However, there is enough evidence to indicate a relationship with his later performance as a commander in the Civil War. It was during these years that he acquired a love for his country's military tradition and a desire to be part of that tradition. This would become the foundation of his philosophy, the ground upon which all else would be constructed. He learned the basic lessons of tactics, weapons, and authority; received training in fortifications; and came to an appreciation of the three branches of the army. When he graduated in 1840, his military thoughts were in tune with those of the typically trained soldier of his day. He left West Point with a respect for the orthodox doctrine which placed emphasis on geometrical warfare. War was a gentlemanly enterprise and deeply rooted in the Napoleonic tradition. How little he knew at the time that much of what he had learned would dramatically change in the days ahead.

It is possible to imagine the newly graduated cadet taking a final stroll along the wooded banks of the Hudson River—proud, relieved, optimistic about the future. In spite of the meaningless customs, West Point was a positive experience for Sherman. He did well. He had completed the first major step toward becoming a soldier. There were no indications of turmoil or conflict ahead. He had made a choice, to be a soldier, and was comfortable with his decision. Immediate barriers to future achievements were the furthest thing from his mind.

After graduation in June 1840, (Second Lieutenant) Sherman spent the summer on furlough in Ohio. The journey home must have brought to him a mixture of elation and concern. He was taking with him four years of accomplishment, yet he was facing a foster father-in-law who wanted him to seek a career in civilian life.

George H. Mead, a philosopher and social psychologist, in the early years of the twentieth century, constructed a theory of self-development that helps to explain this elation and concern. Mead, in his writings, deals with the creation of self and the mind, and with the social training process that produces them. Briefly, his theory states that there is no self until society, through parents and peers, creates one. Children, he submits, are not conscious of their own existence or their own minds except through interaction with others who teach them about themselves. At first the infant does not even realize that he/she is a distinct being. Later the child develops the concept of "other" as he/she recognizes that he/she is separate from those outside him/her. Parents become "significant others" who shape the mind and the concept of self. When the growing child begins to develop a general conscience, a general conception of "right" and "wrong," he/she is using as a reference some "generalized other." In other words, the child is beginning to understand how his/her whole society expects him/her to act. In this manner the child finally becomes socialized into the culture of society. Finally, Mead says, the social self is not entirely a passive "me" that accepts anything the society pours into it. The person also has an active, self-developing "I" that partially controls his/her destiny. Thus, every individual is a "me" that is shaped by society and an independent "I" that is self-controlling.[25]

Sherman's elation and concern were directly related to the "significant others" in his life. Heretofore these others had supported him and they had been in harmony with him. Thomas and Maria (Sherman's foster mother) Ewing had taken him into their home and made him part of their family. Thomas, for all intents and purposes, had become his father and had taken great care to provide for him. He had secured Sherman the appointment to West Point and constantly nurtured him through its four-year program. They had become father and son in all things except name. As a result, Sherman felt an obligation to the Ewings, particularly to Thomas. Therefore, as he traveled home for his graduation furlough he could look back on his performance at the academy with pride. At the same time, he could look forward to the reunion with elation. He had pleased a "significant other" in his life and he knew it.

As he traveled West, he also carried some concern and anxiety. Sherman knew that Thomas had wanted him to graduate in the Engineering Corps, but, as he said to Ellen in a letter, "This I can't do."[26] Thomas's reasoning for such a wish was wrapped up in his plans for Sherman's career. It was his desire that, once Sherman graduated from West Point as an engineer, he would resign his commission and enter civilian life.[27] For two reasons the dream did not become reality. First, Sherman did not rank high enough in his class to enable him to select the highly prized Engineering Corps, and, second, he wanted to see action as a soldier. Thus, he chose the artillery and, in doing so, knew he would cause conflict between himself and his foster father. The "me" part of his self told him what was expected of him, but the independent "I" demanded that he be his own person.

Thomas accepted Sherman's choice, at least for the moment. The conflict would arise again. Eventually Thomas would be joined by his daughter Ellen whom Sherman would marry, and the pressure would last for the biggest portion of his life. The significance of this event in Sherman's life is that it is the beginning of a conflict that would cause him to make a decision he did not want to make, and it would culminate in his loss of self-confidence and in acute feelings of failure.

Independence had come to be an important self-concept for Sherman. In various ways it had been instilled in him by his mother, sisters, brothers, and foster family. He had a strong sense of loyalty to the Ewings for all they had done for him, and he felt obligated to them. But he also knew he could never repay them for all they had done. As he grew older, dependence on them became an embarrassment and a burden. Independence was right, dependence wrong. Somehow, he had to make the break. More than likely, this explains Sherman's desire to stay in the army and to seek active duty that would take him away from Ohio.

While visiting in Lancaster, Sherman received orders assigning him to Company A, Third Artillery, in Florida. Saying his good-byes to the family, he traveled to Fort Columbus in New York harbor, where he reported for duty. From there he sailed to Savannah, Georgia, then to Fort Pierce, Florida.[28] For the next eighteen months he occupied posts along the east coast of Florida. He was assigned to troops that were responsible for gathering scattered groups of Seminole Indians. However, most of Sherman's time was spent in idleness, the heat and mosquitos making active exertion almost impossible.

His experiences with the Seminoles, although limited, did not prevent him from expressing his views about the Indian problem. As a result of the pillaging and burning by the Seminoles, the government had marched an army into the Florida territory to seek out and destroy them. Detachments of infantry and artillery had been used, but without success. The war against the Indians had dragged on for the past five years, and yet the Seminoles continued to pillage and burn. It was obvious to Sherman that the traditional techniques of warfare taught at West Point and advocated in the army manuals were ineffective. He was opposed to parleys and treaties, believing that confidence could not be placed in the Indians' promises.

To his foster brother Phil Ewing he wrote, "There is no use on earth talking with them. They'll break their word when it is to their interest—they will not acknowledge the authority of any self constituted chief to treat for the whole."[29] The entire military power of the territory, in combined operations, should be mobilized to put an immediate end to what he viewed as a menace.[30] For Sherman, the solution to the problem was to " . . . send a sufficient number of troops to literally fill the territory, declare martial law and then begin the war of extermination, this would be the most certain and economical method. The present method will not do—experience has shown it. . . ."[31] The overall strategy should be: "Destroy the enemy's supplies and . . . break his morale!"[32]

To implement such a strategy the army should establish and maintain a system of raiding villages, burning cabins, destroying corn, and killing cattle. These tactics would eventually break the Indians' morale and bring strategic success. Sherman's attitudes toward the Indians was like that of most whites in mid-nineteenth-century America. Indians were viewed as savages and a menace to progress; therefore, they should either cooperate with the expansion of civilization or suffer extermination. Thus, it was relatively easy for Sherman to recommend a type of warfare that would eventually lead to the destruction of a people's culture. To deviate from the accepted techniques of warfare against savages, nonhumans, was permissible. In this view Sherman was no different from the majority of military professionals in America. But the Seminole experience remained with Sherman and would influence him in ways different from others who fought the Indians. In the future Sherman would resolve the conflict between savagery and humanity, reach back to this experience, and apply the same techniques to the whites of the South. Herein lies the first hint of the type of warfare that led to his famous

"march to the sea." It appears he had grasped early in his career the
concept of culture. He understood the complexity of a people's culture and how it was intricately tied together—what sociologists today
would call "cultural integration." At the same time, he understood
its vulnerability—that is, destroy the various parts that make it a
whole and the whole crumbles, disintegrates.

After nearly a year and a half of "fighting" the Seminoles, Sherman was promoted to the rank of first lieutenant. Actually, the
closest he got to combat with the Indians was when he was ordered
to take a detachment of twelve mounted men and capture the Seminole chief, Coacoochee. With no difficulty, and without firing a shot,
he completed the assignment successfully.

Sherman's promotion meant a transfer from the war district, and,
at the close of 1841, he moved to Picolata, Florida, where he took
command of a detachment of Company G. His stay in Picolata was
brief and uneventful. In early 1842, the entire Third Artillery was
ordered to garrison the Gulf posts. Sherman's company, therefore,
was sent to Fort Morgan at the entrance to Mobile Bay, Alabama.[33]

Almost two years had passed since his leaving West Point and the
most exciting experience Sherman could claim was his participation
in a minor expedition against the Seminoles. Nothing glorious or
romantic—indeed, his life had basically been that of drudgery and
idleness. Yet, for Sherman, the few experiences he had had were
rewarding and meaningful. He continued to maintain his deep regard for the army as a profession, and, although not as idealistic, he
still remained committed to army life. While in Florida he had written to Phil with some disgust that "some old fogies . . . have demanded to be relieved from duty. . . ." Such action on behalf of a
soldier was beyond his comprehension. "A soldier to demand to be
relieved from the very spot where his duty calls him is an absurdity. . . ." He had made up his mind to "stay here until the end of the
war. . . ."[34] Sherman's first experience with active duty had not
shaken the foundation of his philosophy of war—that is, his strong
devotion to duty, honor, and country.

The few months Sherman spent at Fort Morgan provided him
with his first introduction to the life-style of Southern culture. "The
officer's uniforms were a passport to the best homes in Mobile," and
Sherman was invited to balls, the theater, art exhibits, balloon rides,
"and even temperance parades." Southern hospitality was opened to

him by a cousin who had married one of the most prominent cotton merchants in the city. Having access to such hospitality, Sherman did not hesitate to take advantage of the opportunity to socialize with the citizens and, in doing so, he began to understand this new and rather appealing world, a world quite different from that he had known in Ohio. His correspondence is filled with descriptions of the enjoyable moments he had attending balls, parties, "and moonlight rides into the Alabama countryside."[35] Again, as in Florida where he saw it for the first time, Sherman came into contact with slavery. He had no quarrel with the practice because to him slavery was constitutional, made legal by the government, and, therefore, an institution to be defended. Sherman's allegiance was not to the maintenance of slavery nor to its abolition. His allegiance was to the law, and as long as slavery was legal, he would defend it. He would never change his position on this issue.

On the whole, Sherman was enjoying himself. His life was full and satisfying; he was doing what he wanted to do and what he had been trained to do. Things could be better, but he had faith that with time and experience, they would improve. Promotions would come and events would avail him of opportunities for further achievement. He was young, optimistic, and a firm believer in the Protestant Ethic. Hard work would lead to success. In addition, he and Ellen were drawing closer. They had maintained a steady correspondence since he entered the academy and there was the prospect of a serious relationship developing. Happy, doing what he liked, hopeful of the future and the possibility of serious romance—what more could a young man want?

It was Ellen, however, that began to dampen his optimism. Sherman was probably unaware of the double-edged sword she represented. That knowledge would come to him later. Realizing her growing closeness to Sherman, she began to raise the issue of his career in the military. In response to her query as to why he remained in the army, he said:

> . . . But why don't I leave the Army? you ask. Why should I? It is the profession for which my education alone fits me, and as all appearances indicate the rapid approach of a time when the soldier will be required to do his proper labor, when a splendid field will spread before him, every reason exists why I should remain. Moreover, I am content and happy, and it would be

foolish to spring into the world and unprepared to meet its
coldness and trials.[36]

On this issue Sherman was very confident. To his brother John, he
wrote: "The Army is far better than diving into the world empty
handed or falling back into a state of dependency still more objec-
tionable, but there are advantages which an officer of the Army
enjoys that are very great as I myself have experienced, in having
this early in life seen so much of our own country and its people
whose principles can not be taught in books but must be learned
from experience and by mingling freely with it."[37]

Both Ellen and her father were beginning to pressure Sherman to
resign from the army and pursue a career in civilian life. Advancement would be more rapid and security more sure. In addition, a
civilian career would bring him back to Lancaster or settle him permanently in a desirable section of the country. Such an arrangement
would relieve him from suffering the whims of military transfers. In
the early years Sherman would counter their arguments by reiterat-
ing that he had studied for the military profession and was
"hold[ing] a place envied by thousands and for which hundreds of
the best young men of the country toil every year."[38] Besides, he had
met men who had resigned their commissions to seek wealth in the
civilian sector and all of them had confessed regret. In spite of his
unyielding attitude, the idea was planted. Realistically, he knew the
life of a soldier was not conducive to a successful marriage and
family. So began the process that eventually contributed to a period
of discontent and depression for him.

Sherman also addressed Ellen's interest in his personal religion.
She was Catholic and quite serious about her faith and the church.
She knew that for reasons of necessity rather than belief, Sherman,
while under the Ewing roof, had followed the pattern established by
the Ewing household. But now that he had been away from the
Ewing influence for a few years, she was curious as to his religious
beliefs. He told her that, since leaving home in 1836, he had followed no particular creed, nor had he professed any. He assured her
that he believed firmly "in the Doctrine of the Christian Religion,
the purity of its morals, the almost absolute necessity for its existence
and practice among all well regulated communities . . . ," for in this
manner peace and good will can be assured. Noting that his comments were the most he had ever written on this subject, he continued, "Yet I cannot, with due reflection, attribute to minor points

of doctrine or form the importance usually attached to them. I believe in good works rather than faith, and believe them to constitute
the basis of true religion, both as revealed in Scripture and taught by
the experience of all ages and common sense." He left the subject by
stating his ideas "were very general and subject to be moulded to a
definite shape by time, circumstances and experience. . . ."[39] In
sum, Sherman's "religion could be epitomized in the single word
'truth,' and his intellectual life was a research for it, in its varied
forms."[40]

In June 1842, Sherman's company was transferred to Fort Moultrie located on Sullivan's Island in Charleston Harbor, South
Carolina. Here he was to serve for two years, and it would be a time
of extreme importance in his further development and outlook both
professionally and privately.[41] During his hitch at Fort Moultrie,
Sherman traveled extensively throughout the South and became
even more acquainted with the people, the culture, and the problems of the region. In the summer, Moultrieville, situated on Sullivan's Island, was a place of fashionable resort for the wealthy families of Charleston and of South Carolina in general. Indeed, Fort
Moultrie was at that time "the toast of all who had ever served
there."[42]

It was here that the young redheaded lieutenant was ushered,
even more deeply than at Mobile, into a life-style completely new to
him. Along with other officers, he was overwhelmed with invitations
to experience the hospitality of the citizens of Charleston. Parties,
balls, and a variety of informal gatherings provided him with the
opportunity to make numerous agreeable and valuable acquaintances. His two summers at Fort Moultrie were filled with socializing
Southern-style, and he took full advantage of the opportunities.[43]

Besides the friends and acquaintances he made, Sherman also
cultivated an understanding and appreciation of Southern folkways
and customs. He participated in numerous discussions involving the
issues of slavery, states' rights, and secession. His views of the South
and its people were, no doubt, influenced significantly. In many
ways Sherman was a novice sociologist, for he saw things that others
simply took for granted. His mind was always active and he refused
to become static as a result of the endless routine of military duties
and mundane socializing with the Southern elite. The social strata of
South Carolina fascinated him and in his letters he provided some
rather interesting analysis. He noted, for example, that Sullivan's

Island was overflowing with men of high standing and "the worthless sons of broken down proud Carolina families."[44] His observations led him to conclude that the Carolinians were generally poor, did not have access to the comforts of life and were ignorant of major changes taking place in their world. Importance was placed on name and ancestry in spite of the fact that the Industrial Revolution was upon them. He saw in the Southern way of life the desire to maintain the old and a refusal to accept the new. As the collector of customs in Charleston said, "We like old things—old wine, old books, old friends, old and fixed relations between employer and employed."[45]

To Phil and John, Sherman expounded on the institution of slavery, providing greater elaboration of his views. He wrote to Phil, "The Negroes are well dressed and behaved, never impudent or presuming and so far as I can judge feeling very light indeed the chains of bondage. Servants are treated with remarkable kindness and in no instance would I see a difference in them and ours in the North were it not for the market place where they are exposed for sale."[46] Sherman blinded himself to this aspect of Southern culture and was convinced that, on the whole, slaves lived a good life. He did not see "the least sign of disaffection on the part of the negroes. . . ." He had seen them in the cities and "in the cotton fields and the rice ditches, met them hunting at all hours of the day and on the road at night. . . ." They always greeted him with, "How d'ye Massa? Please give me some bac [tobacco]."[47]

In response to abolitionists' talk of the horrors of slavery, Sherman stated, "I am no advocate of slavery as a means of wealth or national advancement, yet at the same time I know that the idea of oppression and tyranny that some people consider as the necessary accompaniment of slavery is a delusion of their own brain."[48] He refused to see reality on this issue. Granted, he feared the disruptive nature of slavery for the Union, but there was more to his position than that. Sherman viewed slaves as inferior to whites; they were by nature best suited for menial labor and subordination. He became an apologist for the institution of slavery. He did recognize it as being a serious national problem, but believed it would eventually die out. To John he wrote:

> If abolitionists suggest the removal of slaves from Maryland and Virginia, Kentucky and Missouri, just so surely will it not be done. But if they lie low common interest, the sole motive power

that can remove slavery, will cause the sending of slaves from those states to states further south, where white labor cannot be had. There is no doubt that in Maryland and Missouri labor is absolutely cheaper than slave, and so will it be in the southern states in succession as a poor white class enters, then negroes will go.[49]

Sociologists teach that there is a significant difference between attitude and behavior, and that it is a common error to assume the two are always in agreement. To make such an assumption in Sherman's case is erroneous. To automatically assume that Sherman's attitude toward slavery led to a corresponding behavior—that since he was prejudiced toward blacks he therefore acted out his prejudice in the form of discrimination—is to misunderstand him. The evidence does not support such a conclusion. Even when the ensuing war became a struggle to free the slave, Sherman continued to fight; and his treatment of blacks never took the form of discrimination. He was able to resolve this conflict, this contradiction, with his intense dedication to the idea of Union. If freeing the slaves meant the destruction of secession, then he would support freedom for the slaves. On the other hand, if the Union could be preserved by maintaining the institution of slavery, so be it. His responsibility was to his government, with or without slavery.

In the fall of 1843, Sherman took a leave of absence to visit his family in Lancaster. At the end of his furlough in December, he rejoined his company, making a detour on his return by way of the Mississippi River to New Orleans and then through Mobile and Savannah. He had grown to love travel and made it a policy never to return from a journey by the same route. After arriving at Fort Moultrie, army duties took him to other areas of the Southland that winter and spring. During the months of February, March, and April 1844, he was placed on a government investigating board and, as a result, sat in session in Marietta, Georgia, Bellenfoute, Alabama, and several other places in the central and northern sections of the Southern states.[50]

Always conscious of being a soldier and of the need to learn, Sherman took great care to make note of the topographical features of the country in which he was stationed or through which he traveled. Ever observant, he also made mental notes concerning the occupations, character, social organization, and sentiments of the inhabitants. But it was the value of geography that he particularly appreciated. Writing to Phil, he said, "Every day I feel more and more in need of an atlas, such as your father has at home; and as the knowledge of geography, in its minutest details, is essential to a true military education, the idle time necessarily spent here might be properly devoted to it."[51] This knowledge, of course, would stand him in good stead during the Civil War. Looking back on this period of his life after the war, Sherman wrote, "Thus . . . I was enabled to traverse on horseback the very ground where in after-years I had to conduct vast armies and fight great battles. That the knowledge thus acquired was of infinite use to me . . . I have always felt and stated."[52] Even after twenty years, the ground he traveled remained familiar. "I had a perfect conception of the character of the water, ground, soil, ranges of mountains, etc., that determine the character of roads on which an Army is so dependent."[53] To John, after having originally traveled the territory, he referred to how such knowledge could be used against the South in the event of war. Discussing the possibility of war with Great Britain, Sherman stated that a war would "at once crush their [the South's] prosperous rice and cotton trade . . ." and thus destroy the material strength of the region.[54] Later events would, of course, prove him correct. He perceived the vulnerability of the South, and it was to become one of the basic threads of his philosophy of war. The South's economy was too homogenous and dependent on the North. A blow at that economy would have a devastating effect.

With the adjournment of the investigating board, Sherman found himself back into the general routine of being a soldier. With more free time available, he turned his attention to the study of law, particularly those aspects that might be beneficial to him as a professional in the army. Specifically, he showed an interest in civil law. His interest was partially motivated by Ellen and Thomas, who were once again urging him to resign his commission. He had received a letter from his foster father that was "very kind but wound up with a hope that I was studying for 'Civil life.'" Thomas had been silent on this issue for several years and Sherman " . . . had thought he had long since relinquished that idea and his opposition to the army."[55] But, such was not the case. During Sherman's extended visit to Lancaster in 1843, he and Ellen committed themselves to each other and began to make plans for marriage. Out of concern for her, he began to use his leisure time studying law. In writing to John, he made mention of his interest in legal knowledge and explained his efforts in this area.

But he made it clear, "I have no idea of making law a profession, by no means; but as an officer of the army, it is my duty and interest to be prepared for any situation that fortune or luck may offer."[56]

Actually his understanding of law remained elementary. He avidly read Blackstone and other legal writers, but he never learned law well enough to even be a good lawyer.[57] Indeed, as will be seen, he failed miserably as a lawyer—not, it must be added, because of his intellectual ability but because of his lack of interest. The benefit of his study came as a soldier, for he used his understanding in the cities of Memphis, Atlanta, Savannah, and Raleigh. Handling the people in these captured cities was made more efficient simply because of his grasp of civil law. Law, just as much as geography and sociology, became an important factor in the development of his concept of war. War to Sherman was the result of citizens ceasing to adhere to a government's legal codes and cultural customs. Obedience to law and customs was the ultimate goal of war, and once obedience was achieved, war ceased.

Never could Sherman enter into anything without somehow relating it to the military and its role in society. To Ellen, he provided a justification for war. On many occasions he had made known to his friends and relations the great respect he had for his country and its government. Ellen had been exposed to this side of Sherman often, but he had never related it to war. Now, however, a justification for war was developing in his mind that was consistent with his respect for government. He told Ellen that he was convinced that war in and of itself should be avoided, " . . . but if it is necessary for the interests or honor of the country of course I . . . rejoice at the opportunity of being able to practice what in peace we can only profess."[58] War had come to be "an instrument of policy rather than . . . an impassioned drama or glorious adventure."[59] War's purpose was the reestablishment and maintenance of order in society. The cavalier approach to war, so often found in men from both the North and South, was intolerable to Sherman and he never understood it.

In a brief four years, the experiences began to accumulate. Indian expeditions, travel, exposure to the Southern way of life, observation of slavery, investigative experience, regular army duties, and the study of law had provided Sherman with a full and busy life. But what is significant is his response to those activities and experiences.

In his early socialization Sherman had learned the importance of curiosity. Things he saw and experiences he had were internalized and given meaning through serious analysis. As a result, Sherman began to develop a view of himself and of the world in which he lived. Even in times of idleness his mind was at work, evaluating, analyzing, and creating. This inevitably led to a concept of war.

At times during these early years it appeared as though he was possessed with a purpose that was single-minded in character—to become the complete soldier. This was his center, his core, around which all other things revolved. The internalization of basic ideas concerning war and warfare was the result. Although not fully developed at this point in his life, the tenets of psychological and sociological warfare, which he would implement some twenty years later, were beginning to form in Sherman's mind.

These were important times and somehow Sherman knew their importance. His intensity for learning, for success, and for independence most likely stemmed from the loss of his father while he was so young and the realization that he could never rely on that lost source. He knew he would have to make a life for himself without the assistance of a normal family setting. Or, at least in his own mind he felt he would have to do so. His strong drive and perhaps his nervous energy were related to the self-created high expectations he had placed on himself.

No doubt the Ewings had something to do with it also. The Ewing family, his adopted family, were respectable and highly successful. Thomas Ewing was nationally known. Sherman believed he should not fail in their eyes, especially Thomas's and Ellen's. He did not realize it at the time, but in spite of his present happiness and contentment, he was setting himself up for future self-identity problems. His increased involvement with Ellen, which would eventually lead to marriage, drew him even closer to the Ewing family. This situation would create difficulties he would never fully resolve. As will be more thoroughly explained, he began to move in the direction of believing many of the contradictions about himself. However, what he saw himself to be was in opposition to what the "significant others" in his life wanted him to be. But, the pressures were increasing and would eventually overcome him.

With the outbreak of the Mexican War in 1846, Sherman, like most soldiers across the country, had high expectations that he would participate. Now was the chance to achieve fame as a military hero. Immediately he sought orders to be transferred to Texas, but, much to his disappointment, the War Department assigned him to duty as a recruiting officer in Pittsburgh, Pennsylvania.

Hearing of Brig. Gen. Zachary Taylor's victory at Palo Alto and the American routing of the Mexican forces at Reseca de la Palma, Sherman said, "That I should be on recruiting service, when my comrades were actually fighting was intolerable. I wrote to the Adjunct-General asking him to consider me as an applicant for active service."[60] Restless to be reassigned, he repeatedly sent in applications for active service in the Mexican conflict. But nothing came. To John he wrote, "The recruiting service is progressing slow all over the country, and one half the companies are broken up so that officers may be sent out to reinlist new companies. Thus I feel that my efforts to get to Mexico must prove a failure for sometime to come."[61] At one point his enthusiasm overcame him. Without orders he gathered together some thirty recruits and transported them in person to Newport, Kentucky, in hopes that the superintendent of recruiting for the Western Department would order him West. Instead of being rewarded for his eagerness, he was submitted to a regular army cursing out and sent back to Pittsburgh.[62]

Finally orders came transferring him to California. Full of excitement, he wrote Ellen, "Ordered to California by sea around Cape Horn! Is this not enough to rouse the most placid? Indeed it is so great an event that I cannot realize it in its full force."[63] True, California was far from the major zone, but it was part of Mexico, and at least there was a greater chance of seeing action there than in Pennsylvania.

Sherman's company sailed from New York harbor the middle of July and after a long voyage landed in San Francisco.[64] The journey was rewarding and, except for a heavy storm sailing around Cape Horn, pleasant. He spent his time visiting with passengers, playing cards, angling for sea birds, writing letters, and sketching drawings of sights for Ellen.

He had applied for service in California with "hopes of glory and adventure."[65] California was not Mexico, but maybe the war would reach him. Like all young career soldiers, Sherman knew that he could not be fulfilled and accomplished in the military profession without experience in combat. However, thus far the opportunity to get that experience had not presented itself. The dream of glory through facing an enemy had been with him since he first set foot on the grounds of West Point. Now, perhaps, was his chance. The

Mexicans were foreigners, not savages. Maybe the opportunity had at last arrived. Combat, promotion, glory, adventure, fulfillment as a soldier—all at such an early age!

Unfortunately, the dream was not fulfilled. Contrary to his anticipation, the Far West proved to be uneventful. As with his duty in Florida and South Carolina, his desire for firsthand experience in war was not achieved. Instead, service in California turned out to be little different from the years he had spent on the East Coast, and for the first time a feeling of discontentment and disappointment came. Such emotions began to have an adverse effect on his general attitude. He repeatedly had hoped for service in the arena of national attention only to be either too late or too far away. War might flourish in Mexico and Texas, but in California the only targets on which Sherman could expend gunpowder were " . . . the ducks and geese in the plains, and the deer and bears in the mountains. . . ."[66]

After ten months' service, his disappointment worsened. Writing to Ellen he expressed his frustration, "I am so completely banished that I feel I am losing all hope, all elasticity of spirits. I feel ten years older than I did when I sailed, and . . . I do not feel that desire for exercise I formerly did. To hear of war in Mexico and the brilliant deeds of the army, . . . and my own old associates, everyone of whom has gained honors, and I out here . . . , banished from fame, from everything that is dear. . . ."[67] In April 1848, he had written, "I fear that I leaped the mark in search of glory by coming to California. . . ."[68] By August 1848, for the first time he was tempted to send his "resignation to Washington." He felt " . . . ashamed to wear epaulettes after having passed through a war without smelling gunpowder," and added, that " . . . God knows I couldn't help it and so I'll let things pass."[69]

In September 1848, Sherman received official news that the war with Mexico had ended.[70] "Reading of the promotions of his friends," he thought of his "one pathetic adventure in California— with ten men he had ridden into the town of Sonoma and arrested the illegally elected alcalde."[71]

He had every reason to feel depressed because he was still a first lieutenant, while service in the war had won Braxton Bragg and John F. Reynolds brevet majorities; U. S. Grant, a few years younger than he, a first lieutenant's post; Robert E. Lee and Joseph E. Johnston brevet colonelcies; Albert Sidney Johnston the position of inspector general; and George B. McClellan, who had graduated six years after him, the rank of captain. He was even falling behind his fellow soldiers in California. Joseph Folsom, a classmate at West Point, was a captain and Henry W. Halleck, private secretary to the military governor of California.[72]

The only activity that brought Sherman any real satisfaction was the role he played in the army's investigation of the discovery of gold in the Sacramento Valley. He was proud that the president made the investigation the subject of a special message to the people of the United States and that he had been part of the great migration that would eventually come. But he knew that such an investigation could have just as easily been conducted by a civilian body and that the recognition received was not equal to that given to a soldier as a result of combat. So, the satisfaction was short-lived. It was only a peripheral accomplishment, not the real thing.

The optimism Sherman brought with him to California was rapidly dying, and he began to take more seriously the thought of resignation. His thoughts increasingly turned to leaving the military for another profession. Constantly hearing of the American successes in Mexico and of the men who had gained glory depressed him. His pride took a serious beating. "These brilliant scenes nearly kill us who are far off, and deprived of such previous pieces of military glory."[73] To Phil he wrote, "I cannot reason myself into the belief that it is better that I should be clear of this war, for whether it is just or unjust it is the interest of every officer to gain experience in his profession and this can only be done in action, whilst I have been upon the ocean and here where all is peace others are gaining their experience that will make them our future generals."[74]

Instead of responding to events and experiences with enthusiasm and optimism as he had always done in the past, he began to react to them with dread and pessimism. Others who felt the isolation of service in California accepted the course of events in their lives and moved forward. Sherman, however, turned inward and blamed himself. He felt he had failed to meet the respect of his profession because he had not given himself in time of war. In later years he would write of his feelings, "I felt deeply the fact that our country had passed through a foreign war, that my comrades had fought great battles, and yet, I had not heard a hostile shot. Of course, I thought it the last and only chance in my day, and that my career as a soldier was at an end."[75]

The time spent in California had little to no influence on

Sherman's developing theory of war. His days were mostly passed in idleness and anticipation that either he would be ordered to Mexico or the war would come to him. This, of course, never happened. Acting as quartermaster and commissary, he did acquire experience in emergency supply problems "which was to stand him in good stead when, in later years, he had to approach problems, similar but greater, from a different angle."[76] However, even though Sherman's eagerness for success in the military waned during this period, they were important years. His concept of loyalty was tested and he emerged victorious. Feeling isolated and frustrated he could have imitated some of his fellow soldiers by deserting to the mines with the discovery of gold at Sutter's mill.[77] But, he refused to do so. He remained loyal to his oath as a soldier—to violate the sacredness of the military code was abhorrent to him and would remain so throughout his life.

Actually the significant development in these four years occurred not in his attitude toward theoretical warfare, but in his attitude toward himself and his future. Being bypassed by historical events proved traumatic. His socialization had taught him to work toward an honorable goal; yet, the approved means to achieve that goal were unavailable.

Robert K. Merton, through his theory of deviance, casts some light on Sherman's situation. In his essay, which first appeared in 1938 and was revised in 1949, Merton submitted that cultural goals and the institutionalized means to achieve those goals do not always, or for all people, bear a constant relation to one another. In other words, people at certain times in their lives internalize a goal of society, yet the approved means to achieve that goal are blocked, or the means, for whatever the reason, do not bring success. This dysfunction between goals and means thrusts a person into a state of "anomie" or normlessness, confusion, estrangement, even alienation. Merton states that persons experiencing anomie eventually adapt to their situation in one of five ways. They will conform by continuing to accept both the cultural goals and institutionalized means; they will innovate by accepting the goals and rejecting the means and, in so doing, create their own means; they will become ritualistic by rejecting the goals and accepting the means; they will retreat by rejecting both the goals and the means; or they will rebel by rejecting the prevailing values of society and substitute in their place new values of their own making.[78]

Sherman was a conformer. He adapted to his situation in California by a continual acceptance of the goal—success in the military—and the established means to achieve that goal. He was incapable of rejecting the values of his society, nor could he become an innovator by creating his own means. Although isolated geographically, he could not retreat either. The goals and means were too important to him. So, he conformed as was expected of a good soldier. His ambitions were too great, and he could not settle for the life of an average soldier. Eventually Sherman became a ritualist by burying the goal of military success and simply concentrating on the means. However, for him, conformity and ritualism could only be temporary. Such behavior was his way of adapting to an unpleasant situation until he could make a decision concerning his future.

A victim of circumstances, Sherman began to take his situation personally. He progressively experienced a deflation in his pride and ego. He had come to California with the hope of finding military fame and success. He had found neither. Since arriving in California, Sherman had been the obedient soldier who followed orders. He departed California with the firm belief that his military career had come to an end.

In 1850, Sherman returned to the Atlantic coast and on May 1, he married Ellen. The wedding took place in Washington, D.C., at the residence of her father, Thomas, who was serving as secretary of the interior under Pres. Zachary Taylor. Those in attendance were the president, his cabinet, and Senators Daniel Webster and Henry Clay.

In March of the following year Sherman received from the president a commission as captain, by brevet, to date from May 30, 1848, " . . . for meritorious services in California during the war in Mexico."[79] Two years later, on September 6, 1853, he yielded to his circumstances and the wishes of his wife and father-in-law. Hoping to find proper advancement in civilian life, he resigned his commission, and thus began a period of turmoil that was to last until 1861.

*Sherman as superintendent of the Louisiana State Seminary of Learning and Military Academy, ca. 1860.*

CHAPTER TWO

# *"War Is a Terrible Thing"*

IN 1849, BRIG. GEN. PERSIFOR F. SMITH arrived in California to assume command of the newly organized military Division of the Pa-
cific. This division was to be composed of the Departments of
California and Oregon. Shortly after Smith's arrival, Sherman asked
if he could return to the United States on furlough. He also let the
general know that he wanted to be reassigned. Smith's response was
a firm no, explaining that every man was needed in California and
that no requests for furloughs or reassignments would be considered, much less honored. Thinking this policy to be unfair, Sherman angrily retorted that he felt entitled to a furlough, that he had
been in California for more than two years and had gone beyond the
call of duty by serving as an acting adjutant without any increase in
pay or rank. His life and career, he submitted, had become static and
he was in need of a change. The answer, however, was still no.

A day later Smith asked Sherman if he would be his acting adjutant until the arrival of Maj. Joseph Hooker, who was to be his
regular adjutant. Realizing he had no other choice, Sherman consented and settled back into his usual routine. Then several weeks
later, much to his surprise, he was granted a sixty-day furlough.
Instead of traveling to Ohio, Sherman decided to use his time off to
improve his poor economic situation. Along with Lt. Edward O. C.
Ord, he took a surveying job near Stockton. Upon completion of this
work he then traveled to Sacramento and did some surveying for

Capt. John Sutter. Returning to Sonoma at the end of his leave, Sherman divided a $7,000 profit with Ord.

The furlough and money, however, did not help Sherman's attitude or mood. He remained restless and depressed. With the arrival of Major Hooker he was relieved as acting adjutant and his duties and responsibilities slackened greatly. Perhaps now would be the ideal time to leave the army. Writing to Thomas Ewing he expressed his belief that the army held no future for him. "I have had my share, and now want to look after my private interests."[1] Reviewing the roster of brevet promotions and seeing that his name was omitted, he wrote to General Smith, "I cannot conceal from myself in not receiving some mark of approval, or favor, at the same time, self respect compels me . . . to quit the profession, which in time of war and trouble I have failed to merit, and accordingly through you I must respectfully tender my resignation of commission as 1st Lieutenant I hold in the Army of the United States."[2] Refusing to forward the resignation to Washington, Smith asked Sherman to reconsider. This he did and withdrew the letter. Smith immediately appointed him his aide and Sherman "simply sank back into the dull routine of army-post life and remained there while the year 1849 passed."[3]

Then in December 1849, Sherman's long isolation from the civilized world came to an end. Due to an accident that prevented him from making the journey, Smith ordered Sherman to deliver a package of confidential dispatches to Washington, D.C. While there, he was also to report to Maj. Gens. Winfield Scott and Zachary Taylor concerning civil government in California. Sherman was delighted, and on January 2, 1850, he boarded the steamer *Oregon* and sailed for the East.

On arriving in New York, Sherman immediately reported to General Scott. He was glad to be back and a semblance of his old optimism returned, only to be destroyed as quickly as it had arisen. Being invited to dinner with General Scott was an honor, but the general's stories of his campaigns in Mexico simply increased Sherman's depression. The experiences only reminded him that he had missed his only chance to enhance his career as a soldier.

From New York, Sherman traveled to Washington where he completed his orders by delivering the dispatches to the War Department. Having done this, he looked forward to seven months' leave that would provide him time to make some decisions about his life.

He acted quickly by offering a formal proposal to Ellen, and, in May, they were married. Being a soldier was what Sherman knew, what he had been trained to do, and, deep inside, what he wanted. Yet he knew how precarious such a career was. But the pressure for civilian life intensified, coming from Ellen, Thomas, and now, John. In his brother's opinion, Sherman had done little with his life but roam the world "fixed in nothing but changeability."[4] He had been in the army for ten years and had basically nothing to show for it. Why not resign?

But, to Sherman, it was not that easy. Not only did he feel comfortable in the military, he was also getting different advice from California. Writing from the West Coast, General Smith urged him not to abandon his military career. He advised Sherman that he should not resign unless he could be sure of success in the civilian sector. To do so would be a mistake.[5]

So, Sherman bided his time. In September 1850, his leave ended, and he was ordered to report to Company C, Third Artillery, at Jefferson Barracks, St. Louis, Missouri. With optimism for the future and hope for a fresh beginning, Sherman headed West. Good news followed a month later with the receipt of his commission as captain in the Commissary Corps. He fell in love with St. Louis immediately and made preparations for Ellen to join him. Added to his optimism was the arrival of a daughter in late January 1851. Marriage, a family, service in a pleasant post, and a promotion— perhaps the future would be more favorable now.

But, there was a flaw. The "significant others" in his life did not view things as he did. Sherman had fully expected Ellen to accompany him in September to St. Louis, but because she was pregnant he was persuaded by the Ewings to leave her in Lancaster. Once the baby arrived, then they would join him.[6] Thus began the pattern of conflict and separation that would persist throughout their entire married life.

The pattern became even clearer after his arrival in St. Louis. Sherman learned there was a chance he might be ordered to Fort Vancouver in Oregon Territory. In an attempt to console her, he wrote, "Now my Dearest Ellen we must not act like children and be frightened at the first troubles we encounter, but must stand up manfully, make the best of the present, and depend more upon the future." He continued, "For the sake of argument, let us admit . . . I am ordered to Oregon. What would I do? Would I resign? No, because I have no other profession than the one I have thus far filled and which has now become one of responsibility. . . . To relinquish it for the chances of failure in another beginning would be a risk too great. . . ."[7] The Fort Vancouver assignment never came, and Ellen, along with Minnie, the new baby, moved to St. Louis. They were a family and there were pleasant times, but Sherman soon began to realize that his army salary was inadequate. His attempt at outside investments were unsuccessful. The fact that, for Ellen, money was of no consideration put them in a financial strain. In addition, pressure to resign was continuous. Writing to her daughter, Maria Ewing encouraged Ellen: "I hope you have not given up the idea of persuading Cump to resign his Post." She emphasized that the longer an officer stays in the army, the more reluctant he is to leave it.[8] Finally, the religious issue raised its head. Ellen began to pressure Sherman into joining the Catholic Church—if not for him, at least for her and his daughter. She was growing more and more uncomfortable about his status as a nonbeliever.

Briefly, the pattern was broken with Sherman's next assignment. Instead of being transferred to Oregon, Sherman, much to his pleasure, was sent to New Orleans. Even Ellen was more optimistic. She had given birth to their second daughter and looked forward to being with her husband. They settled in a comfortable house and were caught up in the cosmopolitan life of the city. Writing to her mother, she said, "We all like New Orleans very much. We have a pleasant house and I have good girls and so get along, finely."[9] But, the financial strain of living in a city like New Orleans was too great. Indeed, expenses were so high that Sherman began to worry about his future again. His goal was to stay in the service, provide a comfortable living for his family, and ensure a secure future. The experience in New Orleans was making it clear that such could probably not be done as long as he remained in the army.

In the process of inquiring about financial possibilities that would enhance his income, Sherman wrote to Maj. Henry S. Turner, a friend he had developed while in St. Louis. Turner was a partner in the banking firm of Lucas and Symonds. Although there was not an opening in the New Orleans branch, Turner informed Sherman of plans to open a branch in San Francisco, a branch to be named Lucas and Turner. He further encouraged Sherman to obtain a six-month leave and travel to California to look over the situation. With the assistance of both Lucas and Turner, the leave and travel were approved, and, early in 1853, Sherman once again sailed for the West Coast. Impressed with the prospect of the branch's success and satisfied with the compensation offered him, Sherman signed an agreement with Lucas and Turner promising to stay in San Francisco until January 1, 1860. Comfortable that he had found a promising future in civilian life, he submitted his resignation from the army on September 6, 1853, thus ending his first career in the military at the age of thirty-three.

Although, at the start, his banking career was a success, the venture eventually brought much misfortune and disappointment.[10] His family provided the first difficulty. Even before Sherman signed with the bank, from Lancaster, where she was staying while he was evaluating the prospects in California, Ellen wrote rather desperately:

> My hope . . . is now, that you will leave that Country entirely never again to be lured thither by promises of wealth or even by a certain prospect of gaining it. You do me justice in believing that I will cheerfully submit to any course you may determine upon, provided we are not to be separated for years, yet you will not forget to take into account the trial it would be for me to leave my parents, now growing old, with a certainty for not seeing them again for years and a probability of never meeting them again in this world. So . . . let this bring you home.[11]

But, Sherman's mind was set; he had made the break and was not about to turn back. If he returned to Lancaster, it would be without a job, and that would mean dependence on the Ewings. That he could not do and would not do.

Overcoming the protests of Maria and Thomas concerning Ellen and the girls moving to San Francisco, and compromising with them by leaving Minnie behind, the three Shermans headed West. From the beginning Ellen hated California and looked forward to returning to Lancaster. The frontier life-style was appalling to her. The geography with its vast acreage of sand was a discomfort and the rented house on Stockton Street was impossible to keep. To Sherman she complained, "If you prefer this outlandish place because of business advantages, that is no reason why I should be willing to give up home, parents, and friends for life."[12] And again, "I would rather live in Lancaster poor than to be a millionaire away from it."[13]

Although the bank did well at first, basically thanks to Sherman's business abilities, the good times did not last. This was the source of his second difficulty. The general panic in California, due to the exhaustion of the gold mines, rendered the banking business perilous. However, despite the rough times, Sherman managed to bring Lucas and Turner through without serious loss. While other banks were collapsing around him, Sherman held on and soon the danger passed. The owners, however, had had enough, and, early in 1857, the decision was made to close the San Francisco branch. In March of that year Sherman was instructed to conclude all affairs and return to New York City.

These were difficult years for Sherman and would have a lasting impact. As Merrill writes, "Throughout these years Sherman was still searching for a road to security, financial stability, and a position in life of which not only he but the Ewings would be proud. He had a great desire to succeed and to succeed quickly, and he firmly believed this was possible." Merrill continues, "His belief in a man's duty to his family and associates, to his community, and to his nation was strong. He assigned great importance to facing all situations with honesty and truth, meeting the demands of life head-on, no matter how unpleasant the consequences."[14] He placed high expectations on himself and others which resulted in an enormous amount of stress. Working in a profession that was not his first choice, the discontent of his wife, the precarious nature of banking in California, and the inability to make progress toward financial security all took their toll. He became irritable, short-tempered, and experienced fits of depression. In addition, his asthma attacks, which he had experienced periodically all his life, came more frequently. He would go for months never enjoying a night of uninterrupted sleep.

So, for the second time, Sherman was departing from California with a sense of failure. He had returned there with hopes that this time he would find a place in the world that would bring him peace and fulfillment. But, for the second time his hopes were shattered. He was personally in debt, had increased his family with a third child, Willy, and had no real prospects for the future. Perhaps, he must have thought, his fate was to be ever dependent on the Ewings after all.

After a brief visit in Lancaster, Sherman reported to New York City where he assisted in opening a branch office for Lucas and Turner. In October 1857, it failed. Just a few months earlier he had written to Ellen, "Of all lives on earth a banker's is the worst, and no wonder they are specifically debarred all chances in heaven."[15] And in September, he wrote, "If I were a rich man—of which there is not the remotest chance—I would as soon try the faro table as risk the chances of banking."[16] The closures he had experienced were the result of the economic state of the country, a series of panics making business ventures risky. Yet, as with the Mexican War, Sherman took them personally. To his brother John he wrote, "It seems that I am the Jonah of Banking, wherever I go there is a breakdown."[17] His disappointment was made even more intense because of the necessity to accept financial aid from his father-in-law. Deeply humiliated, he wrote to Ellen, "I'm beginning to lose what little self-respect I ever had."[18] And, to be expected, his thoughts turned to the military. To Ellen he said, "Our fate has been cast in the wrong time and I regret I ever left the army. . . ."[19]

While in St. Louis, the location of the home office of Lucas and Symonds, he finished some last-minute business concerning the branch banks. It was then that Sherman came into brief contact with the "bearded unkempt face of a wood-peddler." After considerable searching in his mind, he placed the face with a fellow cadet during his days at West Point. "The fellow had won honors in the Mexican War, arisen to a captaincy, then had resigned in discouragement and in hope that he could in industry earn a better living for his family." The two defeated soldiers, U. S. Grant and W. T. Sherman, spoke to each other, then separated. As Sherman watched the shabby and dejected little man walk away, he said to himself, "West Point and the Regular Army aren't good schools for farmers, bankers, merchants, and mechanics."[20] His evaluation, of course, was not totally accurate. There were numerous West Point graduates who had left the military to pursue more lucrative careers in the civilian sector. Most had done quite well. Sherman's statement upon seeing Grant, however, was indicative of his state of mind.

It was Sherman's intention to remain aloof from anything remotely related to the military. His desire was to give everything he had to his new direction in life—to make a clear break with his past. But, because of his military training, this was not always possible. For example, while banking in California, he was asked by San Francisco city officials to give aid in maintaining law and order among the thousands of somewhat lawless goldseekers. He agreed to assist and immediately clashed with the aims and actions of the established

Vigilance Committee. On one rather riotous evening Sherman sum-
moned the militia to arms, much to the disappointment of the committee. The vigilantes protested, pointing to the possibility of war
breaking out in the streets. Sherman explained that he sympathized
with the committee's wishes for a peaceful city—he too opposed the
behavior of the rabble and thugs that infected San Francisco—but
the law was the law. The regular process of government must be
preserved, and no matter how good their intentions, the possibility
of mob action was anarchical.[21]

Unable to obtain arms for his troops, Sherman, facing a determined group of vigilantes, made the decision to withdraw. Granted,
the law was the law, but it was also important to know when battles
can be won. Of this incident Liddell Hart says, " . . . the soldier-
banker based his action on the ultimate moral danger of condoning
the power of the mob, however moral the particular mob might be.
But he was sufficiently a statesman to reject aims which were, practically, unrealizable and to seize any chance of gaining the end along
the line of least resistance. Thus in California may be traced one
more link in the chain of causation of his strategy."[22] No matter how
sophisticated it is put, Sherman knew when to fight and when to
retreat. In this case, he retreated.

Upon completion of his responsibilities in St. Louis, Sherman
went home to Lancaster. After a rather unhappy Christmas, he,
experiencing periodic moods of melancholy, departed for Leavenworth, Kansas. There, under the tutelage of his two brothers-in-law,
he read law, passed the bar, and, in a rather half-hearted manner,
entered the legal profession.

Although most of Sherman's time was spent in study, he, like
everyone throughout the country, was preoccupied with the burning
issues of slavery, secession, and possible war. He relied heavily on his
brother John to keep him informed on these issues and in turn
freely voiced his opinions. He doubted that civil war would come
and wagered that, if it did, the South could not win. Viewing the
situation with a military mind he concluded that the South did not
possess "the physical and political power to oppress the free
States. . . ."[23]

It took only one case in the courtroom to convince Sherman that
he was not destined to be a lawyer. After defeat in the only case
he was ever to try, he was ready to leave Kansas and the legal

profession. This was an extremely low period in Sherman's life. Dejected, he looked back on his past and concluded that he had accomplished nothing of importance. His life, since leaving Fort Moultrie in 1843, had been marked by frustration, failure, and the ever-increasing reliance on his foster father's generosity. Being at Leavenworth made it worse because he was in contact with the army. Leavenworth was a garrison post, and "it reminded him too strongly of the life he loved but no longer shared, the career he had sacrificed. . . ."[24] To Ellen, he wrote, "I am doomed to be a vagabond, and shall no longer struggle against my fate. . . . I look upon myself as a dead cock in the pit, not worthy of further notice and will take the chances as they come."[25]

His pride and ego were taking a serious beating. He saw himself sinking deeper and deeper into obscurity, and, for one possessing his high level of ambition, this situation was devastating. He had failed to achieve a sense of usefulness in Florida and the Mexican War; his banking experience had ended in failure; and, as a lawyer, little could be said of his efficiency and efforts. He had mounting family responsibilities and a wife who was tied tightly to her father. Almost twenty years had passed since graduation from West Point and he felt he had nothing to show for his efforts. Indeed, there was ample reason for Sherman to feel deflated and conquered by hostile circumstances. Nearing age forty, when, as he well knew, a man of his abilities should have found himself established in some definite and honorable place, he must have seemed hardly more successful to many of his contemporaries than he appeared to himself. So confident of his abilities years ago, so sure of himself, now the doubt was overpowering. What had happened? What had gone wrong? What should he do?

Finally, with Sherman seeing nothing else on the horizon and desiring nothing else, the inevitable occurred. In the summer, of 1859, Sherman wrote his old friend, Assistant Adjutant General Don Carlos Buell, inquiring about the chances of getting back in the army. Buell replied that at present there were no openings, "that in these times everything turns on political or other influences." But, he added, " . . . I enclose . . . a paper which presents an opening that I have been disposed to think well of." The paper carried an announcement of a new military college to be started by the state of Louisiana, to be called the Louisiana Seminary of Learning and

Military Academy. He encouraged Sherman to apply, "If you could secure one of the professorships and the superintendency, as I think you could, it will give the handsome salary of $3,500."[26] Happy recollections of his days in the South, as well as economic necessity, led Sherman to submit his application immediately. Shortly afterward he received notice from Gov. W. T. S. Wickliffe that he had been selected. So, in the autumn of 1859 Sherman once again left his family in Lancaster, this time to assume the new duties as superintendent of the seminary.[27]

Of all the years in Sherman's life, the short one spent at the college in Louisiana was probably the most influential in developing his attitudes toward administration and command. In addition, it was also the happiest twelve months he had experienced in a number of years. Besides acquiring a strong belief in the need for a centralized head,[28] an increased respect for law,[29] and a greater dedication for strict individual discipline,[30] he was placed in the position of having to prove his love for the Union.

Upon his arrival Sherman immediately set to work learning his fourth profession. Although it was not the United States Army, the military training of young men had a positive effect on his attitude. With hope and enthusiasm he plunged into his duties. A fine organizer and capable executive, he had the school ready for operation after only a few weeks, and on January 2, 1860, it opened its doors to fifty-three cadets. That same month, with renewed optimism, he wrote his oldest daughter Minnie:

> I will soon have a good house, so next year you and Mama, [and the children] will all come down . . . where, maybe, we will live all our lives. I think you will like it very much. There is no snow here now. We had snow only two days this winter, and there is plenty of wood. . . . The grass is beginning to grow and the trees begin to look as though we would soon have flowers. . . .
>
> Your Mama tells me that you all expect me this winter, but I am counting on staying here, and bringing you all down next winter.[31]

As the year progressed, Sherman proved to be very popular with both faculty and students. He took great pleasure in mingling socially with his staff, and, when possible, he made it a point to talk personally with each of the cadets every day. Such attention, of course, brought respect and affection to him. David French Boyd, the seminary's professor of ancient languages, wrote, "He made every professor and cadet . . . keep his place and do his duty. At the same time he was the intimate, social companion and confidential friend of the professor's and a kind loving father to the cadets. All loved him." Boyd continued, " . . . often I have seen his private room full of boys, listening to his stories of army or western life which he loved so well to tell. . . . Nothing seemed to delight him so much as to mingle with us socially; and the magnetism of the man riveted us all to him very closely, especially the cadets."[32]

Sherman held firm command and there was never any doubt as to who was in charge. He demanded high standards from both faculty and cadets; he was seriously concerned about the happiness and health of his people and placed a heavy emphasis on military discipline and drill. He had no patience with poor teaching and took a personal interest in the academic progress of each cadet.

In the brief span of a year, Professor Boyd grew close to Sherman and has provided some highly perceptive insights into his personality. Although he was a man with high standards, Boyd observed, Sherman was not a professional scholar. He possessed no "literary and scientific acquirements" and, on the whole, was not a "general reader." As Boyd put it, "He was rather a tough, unpolished diamond, made great by nature of deep discernment, needing little the ideas of other men. But brilliant and original as he was in thought, he had not the usual accompaniment of genius—want of practicality. Sherman was eminently practical." It was this combination of brilliance, originality, and practicality that set Sherman apart from many other people of his day. It was this combination of characteristics that made it possible for him to break with the past and forge a path into the future. Unlike a Henry W. Halleck or a George B. McClellan, for example, he was not so entrenched in theory that he became its slave. Nor was he like an Ambrose E. Burnside or a John Pope who were willing to toss theory to the wind and rely solely on irresponsible practicality. Sherman managed to balance the two, and, in doing so, made effective use of his originality. The brilliance of Sherman lay in his ability to retain a respect for theory and, at the same time, when the need called for it, to demonstrate the ability to free himself from theory and allow practicality to take over.

Although the world would not see this combination of abilities in Sherman for three more years, Boyd glimpsed it as early as 1860. He wrote, "When the world knew but little of him, I looked up to Sherman as a singularly gifted man, his mind so strong, bright, clear, original, and quick as to stamp him as a genius; and his heart under his stern, brusque, soldierly exterior, the warmest and tenderest."[33] In essence, William Sherman was a complex man who abhorred complexities.

In addition, he was a happy man by nature and thus "he strove to make all around him happy." He was fluent and eloquent in speech, and, as one cadet has said, "made the impression of an ardent, powerful man, governed by a sense of devotion to his country and humanity."[34]

Finally there is this from Boyd's pen, " . . . his mind leaped so quick from idea to idea that he seemed to take no account of the time over which it passed and if he was asked to explain how he came by his conclusions it confused him. This weakness, if weakness it can be called, was due to his genius. His mind went like lightning to its conclusions. Such minds have no patience with the slow, short steps by which the less gifted must plod along to their laboriously reached conclusions. . . ."[35]

Sherman had a mind that processed information rapidly; he could select relevant information from irrelevant information with lightning speed and achieve a conclusion long before others had hardly begun to place ideas in logical sequence. Add to this ability the tremendous faith he held in his convictions, and there emerges a dynamic and inspiring person.

Such a combination of character traits, however, often leads to difficulties. They make it possible for an individual to transcend the present and become one who is ahead of the times. So became the fate of Sherman, and herein lies a seed of his theory of war. Who and what he was made it possible for him to revolutionize warfare. Eliminate these traits and Sherman's story would have little significance in the sweeping scope of warfare.

T. Harry Williams portrays this quality of Sherman in the following statement: " . . . a nature of explosive nervous energy and almost manic elation; a mind playing restlessly on all manner of subjects, military and otherwise; an appearance not martial but like a man of business; and a type unique but peculiarly American. Together they tell us a great deal about Sherman the man and Sherman the general." And Williams concludes: "Nobody would have thought of writing such things about George B. McClellan"[36]—or, it could be added, Ambrose E. Burnside, John Pope, P. G. T. Beauregard, or even Robert E. Lee.

As the first year of school progressed, it appeared that Sherman's wanderings had come to an end. He was proving himself "a fine organizer and splendid executive officer,"[37] and was developing a close attachment to the seminary. In February 1860, he wrote home to Ellen, " . . . if Louisiana will endow this college properly, and is fool enough to give me $5000 a year, we will drive our tent pins and pick out a magnolia under which to sleep the long sleep."[38] At last, maybe, he had found his place.

Unfortunately, however, the "significant others" in his life did not agree. Prior to taking the position as superintendent, Sherman had been offered a banking position in London. Both Ellen and Thomas had urged him to accept it, but Sherman had refused. The position remained open and, even though Sherman was showing signs of contentment and happiness in Louisiana, the pressure to go to London persisted. But Sherman was determined this time. To Ellen he wrote:

> . . . I am going to take the bit in my mouth, and resume my military character, and control my own affairs. Since I left New Orleans, I have felt myself oppressed by circumstances I could not control, but I [now] begin to feel [a] footing and will get saucy. But if I go to England I shall expect universal panic, the repudiation of the great National Debt, and a blow up generally. I suppose I was the Jonah that blew up San Francisco, and it took only two months' residence in Wall Street to bust up New York, and I think my arrival in London will be the signal of the downfall of that mighty empire.

In Louisiana he could not do much harm and maybe, if he were careful, he could do a little good. He said, " . . . here we have solitude and banishment enough to hide from the misfortunes of the past."[39]

To Thomas he wrote that granted "it is dull . . . here in the Pinewoods. . . ." But his salary was regular, more than he had earned in Kansas, and, more important, "I am content."[40]

The pressure from home continued, however, and became so great that at one point he described his situation as that akin to an antelope. He wrote, "The hunter hides himself and ties a rag to the rammer of his gun. The antelope runs off as far as possible, but fate brings him back. Again he dashes off in a new direction, but curiosity or his Fate lures him back, and again off he goes but the hunter knows he will return and bides his time."[41] He had to make a decision between $5,000 more in salary as a banker in London or "an honorable position, and pleasant future for my family and children" in Louisiana.[42] His deep mistrust of finance and financiers, his desire to be part of the military, and his great need for inner peace eventually prevailed. He chose the "honorable position" and remained at the seminary. He had grown tired of wandering and failure. The "I" in him took control.

While advocating the cause of the seminary before the state legislature, Sherman necessarily spent much of his time in Baton Rouge, the capital. There he was drawn into the political discussions of the day. Since most Southerners considered John Sherman, William's brother in Congress, an abolitionist, some of the members of the school's board of supervisors feared that their new superintendent might be of similar mold. At a dinner given by Gov. Thomas O. Moore, Sherman dispelled their fears. He declared that his brother was not an abolitionist in the radical sense of that word, that he was opposed to slavery but did not advocate any use of force against the existing institution of the South.[43] As for himself, Sherman had known when applying for a position in the South that his opinions on slavery would be good enough for the region. He elaborated by stating that he believed the institution of slavery to be completely constitutional and that it was the proper place for the black in society. He added, however, that he would advocate prohibition of the separation of families in the sale of slaves and that he would favor abolishing laws which forbade slaves from learning to read and write.[44]

On another occasion he was swept into a discussion of slavery and the abolitionist movement that led him to present his position concerning a possible civil war. Sherman stated that "it would be wise if northern people would confine their attention to the wants and necessities of their own towns and property, leaving the South to manage slavery." If that could be accomplished, war would not come. The abolitionist movement was a serious problem. If allowed to run its logical course, the result would be disunion, civil war, and anarchy.[45] If that were to happen, he informed his listeners, then he would have no choice. He was willing to aid the Southern states if they were forced to protect themselves against the blacks and abolitionists, but he could not do so if they proposed to leave the Union. His loyalty then would be to the North, or, more specifically, the Union.[46] This issue was firmly settled for Sherman. He wrote to

Ellen, "If the southern states should organize for the purpose of leaving the Union I could not go with them."[47] And to his brother John, he said, " . . . You may assert that in no event will I forego my allegiance to the United States as long as a single State is true to the old Constitution."[48]

Sherman's concern and growing disgust with the national situation in 1860 seemed to him to parallel "the vigilante disorders in San Francisco in the 1850's." According to Merrill, Sherman had concluded that "the United States had become so democratic that mere popular opinion stood above the law. Men had discarded constitutions, lawbooks, and statutes to follow the popular clamor of the barrooms and newspapers."[49] Concerning the refusal by the people of Kansas and Nebraska to accept slavery, Sherman said to Boyd, "If we go to Civil War for a mere theory, we deserve a monarch and that would be the final result, for you know perfectly well the South is no more a unit on that question than the North. . . ."[50] Actually, the more he pondered the events that were leading the country into seemingly irreversible crisis, the less he blamed the institution of slavery. To G. Mason Graham, president of the seminary's board of supervisors, he wrote that the cause could be found in "a tendency to anarchy."[51] He had seen it in the vigilantes of California, the Jayhawkers of Kansas, and the underground railroad of Ohio. To him, it appeared that every group thought it was sovereign. To Thomas he angrily wrote, "I think the People have done as they d___n please so long that they think their sovereign will is the law— Every state, country, village, family is the sovereign, and can defy all mankind."[52]

Traditionally Sherman's biographers have seen in his views on anarchy a call for monarchy. For example, Lloyd Lewis dedicates a full chapter in his work to this aspect of Sherman's thinking and even entitles it "We Deserve a Monarch."[53] And James Merrill makes the statement, "On several occasions Sherman announced a preference for monarchy over democracy."[54]

The evidence does not warrant such a conclusion. Sherman's criticisms were directed, not against democracy as a means of governing people, but against the people who were misusing democracy. Sherman, as has been noted, was dedicated to the Union and the Constitution. He believed in the legal process as established by that constitution and felt that process was being flaunted.

Such a view was in accord with his upbringing and not at all unusual for his day. He was a Westerner and had been taught that the national government and the union of the states were of greater significance than individuals or individual states. Highly influenced by his foster father, Sherman had come to revere the Union, and he would do anything within the law to maintain it. In his youth he had seen Thomas Ewing support Andrew Jackson for president, and then again, Jackson's stand against the nullificationist John C. Calhoun. The law, created by the people, established in the Constitution, should be supreme. A monarchy would have gone against all he had been taught and all he had become. It was out of disgust that he said "we deserve a monarch." Sherman knew well the thin line separating democracy and anarchy, and he believed that line had been crossed. People were flaunting the Constitution and therefore, the supreme law of the land, and they were doing it all in the name of democracy. To Graham he gave this timely evaluation:

> The law is or should be our king; we should obey it, not because it meets our approval but because it is the law and—because obedience in some shape is necessary to every system of civilized government. For years this tendency to anarchy has gone on till now every state and county and town through the instrumentalities of juries, either regular or lynch, makes and enforces the local prejudices, as the law of the land. This is the real trouble, it is not slavery, it is the democratic spirit which substitutes mere opinions for law.[55]

The "democratic spirit" to which Sherman referred was anarchy, for it was built on prejudice rather than law. The process was breaking down and threatening the true meaning of a democratic society. To Ellen, he wrote:

> Our country has become so democratic that the mere popular opinion of any town or village rises above the law. Men have ceased to look to the constitutions and law books for their guides, but have studied popular opinion in bar rooms and village newspapers, and that was and is law. The old women and grannies of New England, reasoning from abstract principles, must defy the Constitution of the country. The people of the South, not relying on the Federal Government, must allow people to favor filibustering expeditions against the solumn treaties of the land, and everywhere from California to Maine any man could do murder, robbery or arson if the people's prejudices lay in that direction.[56]

No, it was not democracy Sherman questioned; it was defiance of law, the guide to governing people in a society, that disturbed him. Defiance was leading to anarchy.

The efficiency which Sherman displayed at the seminary convinced the board of supervisors that the right man had been elected as superintendent. They knew he was the man to keep at any cost; thus, every effort was made to sway his deep-seated loyalty and staunch attachment and fidelity to the Union. But, their efforts were in vain. As described by one biographer, "Surface opinions change with the wind, it is useless to argue against fundamental beliefs."[57]

A determination existed in the make-up of Sherman, sometimes bordering on stubbornness. Granted, for the past ten years his life had not gone the way he had expected or wished. And, true, he was at a very vulnerable stage in his life. One failure after another, the need to find a career that would give him security and fulfillment, struggles with his family, and an unrealized desire for national recognition as a soldier were still very much with him. His present situation in Louisiana had helped greatly to begin the process of healing the wounds of the past. But, he knew history loomed in the wings and might destroy his present direction. Yet, despite this situation, one thing he knew above all else—the Union must be preserved. Even if it meant another failure, he knew he would hold to that fundamental belief. But, he was troubled by it all. From the very beginning of his brief tenure as superintendent, the threat of secession and war was present. He believed the Constitution was not "a mere rope of sand that would break with the first pressure."[58] Secession was treason, was war. It could not succeed because the government of the United States was a reality and would defend its flag, property, and civil servants. Even though it would lead to bloodshed, Sherman justified the use of force to maintain the Union. After all, that is what his military training was all about.

During the Christmas season of 1860, Sherman remained in Louisiana. His wife and children were in Ohio and all the cadets were away for the holidays. It was a quiet time but a fearful time. Across the country, every festive celebration was tainted with discussion of secession and possible war.

Sherman spent Christmas Eve with his friend and admirer, Professor Boyd, and, on that day, he received the news that South Carolina had officially withdrawn from the Union. The news brought tears to Sherman's eyes, and for an hour or more he paced the floor pouring his heart out to his friend. The words he spoke are quite revealing, not only about his feelings, but about his views on the war as a whole. He said:

> You, you, the people of the South, believe there can be peaceable secession. You don't know what you are doing. . . . If you will have it, the North must fight you for its own preservation. Yes, South Carolina has by this act precipitated war. Other Southern states will follow through sympathy. This country will be drenched in blood. God only knows how it will end. Perhaps the liberties of the whole country, of every section and every man will be destroyed, and yet you know that within the Union no man's liberty or property in all the South is endangered. Then why should any Southern state leave the Union? Oh, it is all folly, madness, a crime against civilization.

Speaking as if he had a vision of the devastated South five years hence, he continued, "You speak so lightly of war. You don't know what you are talking about. War is a terrible thing. I know you are brave fighting people but for every day of actual fighting, there are months of marching, exposure, and suffering. More men die in war from sickness than are killed in battle. At best war is a frightful loss of life and property, and worse still is the demoralization of the people. . . ."

With an astute awareness of the impact of the Industrial Revolution on war, he said:

> Besides, where are your men and appliances of war to contend against them? The Northern people not only greatly outnumber the whites of the South, but they are a mechanical people with manufactures of every kind, while you are only agriculturists—a sparse population covering a large extent of territory, and in all history no nation of mere agricultrists ever made successful war against a nation of mechanics. . . .
>
> The North can make a steam-engine, locomotive or railway car; hardly a yard of cloth or a pair of shoes can you make. You are rushing into war with one of the most powerful, ingeniously mechanical and determined people on earth—right at your door.

Finally, with a prediction of how such a conflict would end, he said, "You are bound to fail. Only in your spirit and determination are you prepared for war. In all else you are totally unprepared, with a bad cause to start with. At first you will make headway, but as your limited resources begin to fail, and shut out from the markets of Europe by blockade as you will be, your cause will begin to wane . . . if your people would but stop and think, they must see that in the end you will surely fail."[59]

In this one brief outcry, Sherman spoke from his head and his heart. It grieved him deeply to see the course his country was taking. With these words, spoken with great passion, he brought together the basic precepts of his life and what would eventually become the major tenets of his philosophy of war. Loyalty to the Union, the absurdity of secession, the seriousness of war and its devastation, the losses in life and property that would come, economic warfare, psychological warfare, and sociological warfare, all flowed from his mouth as though they had been pent up for years.

His foresight was phenomenal! How right it is for Lewis to call Sherman "the fighting prophet." He had the ability to put facts and ideas together that enabled him to predict with a high level of accuracy the events of the future. In essence, he was responding to the spirit of the times. Whether he liked it or not, he was being forced to step into the mainstream of historical developments. He was in tune with what had gone before him and with what was in front of him. And it was this quality that helped to make Sherman great.

Sherman now realized that events beyond his control were bringing his career as an educator to an early end. The nation he loved so deeply was falling apart and with it went his plans to make a home in the South for his long-neglected family. Another job, the fourth in four years, was disappearing before his eyes, and there was nothing he could do about it. As Lloyd Lewis so aptly put it, "He had been the Jonah of banking, now he was the Jonah of school teaching—he was the Jonah of everything."[60]

The withdrawal of South Carolina created a dilemma for the Federal authorities in Washington. Should Fort Sumter be reinforced against a possible attack from the Southerners? Sherman had no problem himself as to what should be done. In command of the Federal garrison was his former instructor at West Point and friend from Fort Moultrie days, Maj. Robert Anderson. Sherman's answer to the problem was simple. "Let them hurt a hair of his head in the execution of his duty, and I say Charleston must [be] blotted from existence."[61] He believed that Fort Sumter should be reinforced "if it cost ten thousand lives."[62]

The letters Sherman wrote to his family during these tumultuous weeks portray clearly his views of the conditions that had engulfed him. Immediately his thoughts turned to the Mississippi River. Always the strategist, he grasped the significance of that body of water, and predictions flowed from his pen. In January 1861, he wrote " . . . South Carolina will soon drop far astern, and the battle will be fought on the Mississippi."[63] He knew that under no circumstances could the North permit the Mississippi River to pass out of its control.[64] To Thomas Ewing, Jr., he wrote, "The Mississippi, source and mouth, must be controlled by one government. . . ."[65] Peace, he submitted, could not be maintained between two governments while one owned the source of this great river and the other the mouth. The laws of trade and commerce would force the two nations into war. Little did he know as he expounded these views that in a matter of two years he would be on that river defending what he considered to be the key to the war. Thus, in 1860, another thread was woven into his understanding of the coming war and how it should be fought.

The year 1861 found events moving swiftly toward Louisiana's withdrawal from the Union. On January 18, Sherman submitted his resignation to Governor Moore, and reminded the chief executive that he had accepted the position of superintendent of the seminary while " . . . Louisiana was a State in the Union, and when the motto . . . was . . . 'By the liberality of the General Government of the United States. The Union—*esto perpetia.*'"[66] He could not and would not remain in his position once Louisiana seceded. "I prefer to maintain my allegiance to the Constitution as long as a fragment of it survives." It would be wrong for him to stay, thus he requested of the governor, "I beg you to take immediate steps to relieve me as superintendent . . . ; for on no earthly account will I do any act or think any thought, hostile to or in defiance of the old Government of the United States."[67]

Near the end of February, Sherman turned over all property, records, and money belonging to the seminary. He then returned to Ohio, far poorer in prospects than when he had arrived in Louisiana, but far richer in knowledge of the Southern people and the nature of the problems to be solved by the dreaded process of war. He carried with him the realization that in only a matter of time his country would be plunged into the worst conflict of its history. Such a realization was perhaps more acute for Sherman than many others because he also carried with him the experiences of warm personal friendship. He had grown to love the South and its people, and the pain upon leaving must have been overpowering. In addition to friends, he was also leaving what he had hoped to be a stable future professionally. Boyd, who returned to the school after having served in the Confederate army, wrote to Sherman in 1875. He said warmly and affectionately, "I remember well how it grieved you to leave us, and how sorry were we to see you go, and how great an influence was brought to bear on you to keep you at your post at the head of our school. Moore and Bragg and Beauregard and Dick Taylor all wrote you most urgently to stay."[68]

When the day for his departure arrived, the cadets were formed in his honor on the parade grounds. He passed down the line bidding each officer and cadet good-bye. At the end of the last column Sherman attempted to deliver the speech he had prepared, but emotion choked his efforts. Finally, after a long silence, he simply placed his hand over his heart and said, "You are here." Turning on his heel, he quickly disappeared.[69]

By no means was it hatred of the South that forced Sherman to leave. It was his respect and devotion to the Constitution and the Union of all the states that made the South his enemy. Torn between respect for the Union and affection for the South, Sherman actually had no desire to take part in the coming war. He wrote at this time, "I would prefer to hide myself, but necessity may force me to another course."[70]

Sherman's brief tenure at the seminary was productive and extremely satisfying. Indeed, the time spent in Louisiana was probably the most fulfilling he had known since leaving West Point twenty years earlier. An established position in a semi-military institution held promise of security for himself and his ever-growing family. To Minnie he tried to explain matters:

> I know you would all like the house so much, but dear little Minnie man proposes and God disposes. What I have been planning so long and patiently and thought we were on the point of realizing—the dream and hope of my life, that we could all be together once more in a home of our own, with peace and quiet and plenty around us—all, I fear, is about to vanish and again I fear I must be a wanderer, leaving you all to grow up at Lancaster without your Papa.

> Men are blind and crazy. They think all the people of Ohio are trying to steal their slaves and incite them to rise up and kill their masters, I know this is a delusion, but when people believe a delusion they believe it harder than a real fact, and these people in the South are going, for this delusion, to break up the government under which we live.[71]

Although still feeling the instability of the failures of the past, Sherman had felt he was finally moving in the right direction. He had a goal, one he could live with. He was involved in activities that brought him satisfaction and a hope for security. Now it had all come to an end.

The depression and disillusionment must have been overpowering. As Earl Schenck Miers puts it, " . . . the man . . . was virtually a nobody, who saw his life following a blind, discouraging pattern." For so long he had hoped, dreamed, and planned only to have it all end in disaster.[72] Liddell Hart provides this rather poetic summary:

> Thus it was in a mood of extreme depression that Sherman made his way north. He had gone south with high hope that at last his weather-beaten fortune had reached a fair haven. Professionally and personally, these hopes had been justified. In the South he had at last found a secure anchorage. And then a cataclysm of nature—human nature—had not merely disturbed the surface of the water but changed the whole face of the land. His career was adrift once more. Adrift because where there had been a harbour there was now no longer one—blotted out by the earthquake. It was a crowning irony of fate, after surviving so many local storms in which his bark had merely floundered.[73]

A close examination of this brief period in Sherman's life indicates that a number of important ideas had taken shape in his thinking about war. He became convinced more than ever that authority was a necessary ingredient for groups performing tasks. One master must be in control, especially in the military. This ingredient was even more important in time of war. He continued to hold firmly to the concept of law and order, believing that in time of war soldiers must be obedient if law and order were to be achieved and maintained. Of greater significance, however, was the development of his attitude toward secession and the importance of the Mississippi River. Secession could not go unchallenged, and, strategically, the Mississippi River was the key to its defeat. He had grasped clearly the need for unity and the value of important waterways. True, Sherman was still the orthodox soldier he had been in earlier years. Who was not, on the eve of the Civil War? However, with Sherman, something was beginning to change in his attitude toward traditional warfare. Perhaps a clue to this change can be found in part of the statement he blurted out to his friend Boyd on receiving word of South Carolina's secession. He had said, "Only in your spirit and determination are you prepared for war." Although he may not have been consciously aware of what he was actually saying at the time, this was the beginning of Sherman's break from the belief that numerical superiority was of greater value than surprise and that geometrical warfare was superior to psychological and sociological warfare. The last twenty years of his life had posed a serious threat to his own spirit and determination. He had come to identify with an individual's vulnerability. Now he began to transfer his own experiences onto the entire earth. He saw the relationship between personal troubles and public issues. Such an exercise enabled him to see clearly the South's weakness. What he was slowly developing was what would eventually come to be called psychological warfare. Sherman would not implement it until he had experienced a major crisis in his life, but, ultimately the destruction of that "spirit and determination" would bring him military fame.

In early March 1861, Sherman returned to Lancaster. After spending a few days with his family, he traveled east, supposedly to see his brother John. Actually he was going to Washington to establish some type of connection with the War Department. On his journey from Louisiana after resigning from the seminary, he had noticed that the people in the South were " . . . earnest, fierce and angry, and were evidently organizing for action; whereas, in Illinois, Indiana, and Ohio, he saw not the least sign of preparation."[74] He was amazed at what appeared to be apathy throughout the North. The South had already committed "a hundred acts of open war and treason. . . ." Southerners had seized "forts, mints, arsenals, revenue cutters, and whatever . . . government property they could lay their hands on. . . ." Yet the North seemed to pay no attention. Everybody was attending to his business as in time of peace. To Sherman it appeared that secession was going to go unchallenged.[75] Arriving in Washington, he witnessed utter disorganization and neither saw nor heard of any immediate plans of preparation. "Even in the War Department and about the public offices there was open, unconcealed talk, amounting to high-treason."[76]

While his brother was in Washington, John arranged an interview for Sherman with the newly inaugurated president, Abraham Lincoln. As they entered the president's office, John looked at Lincoln and said, "Mr. Lincoln, my brother is just up from Louisiana and may be able to give you some information you want." Turning to Sherman the president asked, "Ah! how are they getting along down there?" to which Sherman replied, "They think they are getting along swimmingly—they are preparing for war." Lincoln's response was not what Sherman wanted to hear. "Oh well!" the president said, "I guess we'll manage to keep house." Sherman remained silent throughout the remainder of the interview, but once he and John departed and they were alone, he, in complete and utter disgust, blurted to his brother, "You have got things in a hell of a fix, and you may get them out as best you can." Sherman felt he knew the Southern people and that neither the administration nor the people of the North in general did. In his view "the country was sleeping as a volcano that might burst forth at any minute."[77] He felt the time had come when the laws of the Constitution must be backed up with force, "and the longer the postponement, the more severe must be the application."[78] Following the war, he recalled his impressions of the situation in Washington.

> After the election of Mr. Lincoln in 1860, there was no conceal-
> ment of the declaration and preparation for war in the South. In
> Louisiana . . . men were openly enlisted, officers were ap-
> pointed, and war was actually begun in January, 1861. The forts
> at the mouth of the Mississippi were seized, and occupied by
> garrisons that hauled down the United States flag and hoisted
> that of the State. The United States Arsenal at Baton Rouge was
> captured by New Orleans militia, garrison ignominiously sent
> off, and the contents of the arsenal distributed. These were as
> much acts of war as was the subsequent firing on Fort Sumter,
> yet no public notice was taken thereof; and when months after-
> ward I came North, I found not one single sign of prepara-
> tion.[79]

There was no doubt in his mind, " . . . the Northern leaders surely ought to have foreseen the dangers and prepared for it."[80] Needless to say, Sherman found it difficult to understand the lax attitude among the leaders of the country.

Meanwhile, in need of money (Ellen was pregnant for the sixth time), he packed his bags and traveled to St. Louis to become president of the Fifth Street Railroad, a position he had secured from a friend. It only paid $2,500 a year but it would have to do.[81] He departed for St. Louis troubled, disturbed, and disgusted. Not only was he a man with a large and growing family to support, but what he had seen going on around him he thought to be absurd and sheer folly. How would he manage in a country that was, in his opinion, headed for ruin and destruction? The confidence he had begun to regain and build while in Louisiana was rapidly disintegrating. Slowly but surely, his personal perception of the world in which he lived, and the flow of historical events, would clash. The confrontation would be traumatic for Sherman and would come close to ending any hope of a successful military career.

Sherman's ability to weigh and measure circumstances and events and draw conclusions about their outcome was phenomenal. Although little real preparation for war was taking place, a martial enthusiasm was rapidly gaining hold, but Sherman refused to be part of it. ". . . Sherman was no ardent cavalier, to be swept away in a surge of martial enthusiasm and popular excitement to a gallant but useless sacrifice." His love for his Union was rational and pragmatic, not emotional. He would provide services to his country, but the services must be of value. His mind told him always to take the long view, to see beyond immediate circumstances and events.[82] In addition, experience had taught him to be cautious and realistic. Thus, he waited. Although life had not gone the way he had hoped, and although failure had created distress for him, he did understand his abilities and limitations.

In April, with the president's call for 75,000 men to serve three months, Sherman was urged by his friends to return to Ohio and raise one of the state's regiments. He declined the offer to do so. He did not believe the three months' recruits would be effective. This disturbance was not a riot but a revolution. It was not a mob incident but a war that would have to be fought by a well-trained army. Three months' service did not permit enough time to prepare a command for effective performance. An army's success depended on preparation—good preparation—and that would take time. Besides, he argued, he did not feel he could throw his family "on the cold charity of the world."[83] This was not going to be a three-month war. Sherman saw, as so many others did not, that this war would be long—long, confused, and disorganized.[84] He would serve if the call was changed to three years and only then.[85]

Other offers for service came, but he declined. For example, soon after getting settled in St. Louis, he received a telegram from Postmaster General Montgomery Blair requesting that he accept the chief clerkship in the War Department. "We will make you assistant secretary [of war] when Congress meets."[86] He rejected the offer, explaining that he had made certain commitments in St. Louis and could not turn away from them.

A few days later, Frank Blair, a powerful political figure in Missouri, offered Sherman a brigadier generalship, commanding the Department of Missouri. To this offer, Sherman responded, "I told him that I had once offered my services and they were declined; that I had made business engagements in St. Louis which I could not throw off at pleasure; that I had long deliberated on my course of action, and must decline his offer, however tempting and complimentary."[87]

Although desirous for military employment, Sherman held back; he refused to rush into a situation he perceived as unstable. As a result of past failures, he had grown to be cautious. This time he had to be sure. He could not afford to jeopardize his family a fifth time.

Also, he had no confidence in the military policy of the Lincoln administration. Granted, he approved of the president's determination to use force to defend and maintain Federal authority, but he knew that 75,000 volunteers for three months would not succeed. To John he said, "volunteers and militia never were and never will be fit for invasion, and when tried, . . . will be defeated." In a matter of time, he added, Lincoln will drop them "like a hot potato."[88] He concluded with this prediction, "The time will come in this country when professional knowledge will be appreciated, when men that can be trusted will be wanted, and I will bide my time. I may miss the chance; if so all right; but I cannot and will not mix myself in the present call." He continued, "The first movements of the government will fail and the leaders will be cast aside. A second or third set will arise, and among them I may be, but at present I will not volunteer as a soldier or anything else. If Congress meets, or if a National Convention be called and the regular army be put on a footing with the wants of the country, if I am [then] offered a place that suits me, I may accept. But in the present call I will not volunteer."[89]

This period in Sherman's life is difficult to understand and easily misunderstood. Some writers simply choose to pass over his attitude toward presenting his talents for service to his country, offering little or no explanation or interpretation.[90] Others go to the extreme and portray a predictability in Sherman that makes him superhuman. He becomes a prophet, a seer.[91] Still others see his hesitancy to rush into the crisis as an act of unmitigated selfishness.[92]

Actually, the truth is complex and is wrapped up in a combination of circumstances and influences. First, it cannot be denied that Sherman had a rather unique ability to grasp information and make fairly accurate predictions concerning future events. He knew the war would last for years; he knew the South could not emerge victorious. Second, despite the turmoil in his life since leaving the army, Sherman knew his capabilities as well as his shortcomings. He knew best how he could serve his country effectively and refused to be shuttled into any areas where his talents would not be used. Third, he had grown cautious and realistic. In addition, he had learned the value of being practical. As a result, Sherman had come to be an opportunist, though not in the complete sense of that term. A true opportunist is a person who takes advantage of opportunities or circumstances with little regard for principles or ultimate consequences. Sherman saw in the events taking place around him the opportunity to achieve his lifelong goal and dream of military success and glory. But, such an emphasis on self which, according to one writer, "usually indicates pronounced egocentrism,"[93] did not permit Sherman to disregard principles or ultimate circumstances. To draw such a conclusion is to indicate a lack of understanding of Sherman. His life up to this point was abundant with examples of dedication to high and admirable principles. Fourth, Sherman had a large family, and he accepted willingly the responsibility to care for it. Looking back over his life, he concluded that his efforts thus far had been rather unsuccessful. His life had been a record of small successes and dramatic failures. Had it not been for his father-in-law, the chances were good that his family would have fallen to pieces. He resented this dependence and needed to be free from it. Sherman had worked his way into a dilemma; "he was deeply indebted to Thomas Ewing, but at the same time, he looked upon his father-in-law as an antagonist. . . ."[94] Now was his chance to settle this issue once and for all, but it would require taking the proper step at the appropriate time. Fifth (and this is closely related to the fourth influence) was his tremendous need to be accepted by the "significant others" in his life. Not only did he want to be a success in his own eyes, but he wanted to be seen as successful by those in his immediate and extended family. Yet he wanted to be accepted by them for what he wanted to be, not for what they wanted him to be. Part of his dilemma was knowing he could have had that acceptance early in his married life if only he had been willing to live out his days in Lancaster working for his father-in-law. Sixth, Sherman was dedicated to the principle of Union and held a strong loyalty to his country. He wanted to be a part of preserving that Union now that it was being threatened, but he wanted to make his contribution in an area for which he was best trained. Further, he believed firmly in speed and efficiency, and to serve as a war clerk was not, in his opinion, the most effective way to speedily and efficiently get the United States through this present crisis. He was convinced that to accept a position in the army not suited to his abilities or training would lead not only to another failure in his personal life, but would ultimately hamper the resolution of the present national crisis. Thus, he was determined to keep himself in the background, at least for a while, because "I saw [that] the controlling powers underrated the measure of hostility which I reasoned would lead to the sacrifice of the first [military] leaders."[95] For his sake, and for the sake of his country (he really seems to have believed that), he did not want to be sacrificed.

To attempt to explain Sherman's behavior at this critical stage in his life by providing simple reasons in the form of extreme patriotism or pronounced selfishness is inadequate. Nor can this period be passed over. Sherman was a highly complex and diverse individual, and he defies simple explanations. He was sensitive to the influences in his life, and the decisions he made always took them into account.

Liddell Hart offers a partial explanation of Sherman's behavior that is credible in the light of the above analysis. He does not deny that Sherman had a "calculating spirit at a time of national emergency." It would be difficult to find anyone who did not in one manner or other. But, he adds, "Calculating, yes; but not in the ordinary sense of self-interest or self-esteem. It would, of course, be absurd to contend that Sherman entirely forgot self. That is not the way those who rise to high position in any army, and he who cherishes romantic beliefs to the contrary will be disillusioned if he studies history and historical diaries. The best that can be said is that the best men place self second to country." He continues, "But, if self was not omitted from Sherman's calculations, their foundation was a realistic grasp of the problem—the balanced opinion that the best service could be rendered by the man who served in the place for which he was best fitted." Liddell Hart concludes, "Other men, many others, have shared Sherman's reluctance to serve in a post inferior to their self-estimated capacity. Where Sherman was exceptional was in the exactness of his estimate. And still more in his equal reluctance to occupy any post which in his judgment was higher than his capacity at any period warranted."[96] Students of Sherman must remember that, at a later period in his life, the general refused to accept positions he knew were not suited to his abilities and that he was even willing to waive rank for the success of a cause.

Remaining in the background did not mean severing his mind from strategical thoughts. His letters, particularly to John, were at this time abundant with military advice that was sound and perceptive. Realizing that war ultimately meant invasion by the enemy, he queried his brother, "I take it for granted that Washington is safe; that Pickens can beat off all assailants; that Key West and Tortugas are strong and able to spare troops for other purposes; that, above all, Ft. Monroe is full of men, provisions, and war materials, and that the Chesapeake is strongly occupied." And what of the avenues of travel to the South? "Baltimore must be made to allow the free transit of troops without question," he said, "and the route from Wheeling to the Relay House kept open."[97]

He understood the strategic importance of the approach via Harpers Ferry and the upper Potomac to Pennsylvania and urged that both be guarded. Fort Smith should be occupied as well as an island off the city of Mobile. These were vital areas to be used not only for offensive operations but for the establishing and maintaining of a blockade of the South.

Further, Sherman knew the important relationship between military and political policy. Each influences the other and the two must be kept as separate as possible, or, at least, in accord with each other. Thus, he urged, "The question of national integrity and slavery should be kept distinct, for otherwise it will gradually become a war of extermination—a war without end." "This," says Liddell Hart, "rose above strategy to grand strategy. . . ." It was vital that a clear definition of what the war was about be established. In doing so, the proper means could be determined to successfully achieve the desired ends.[98]

Sherman also understood the importance of the border states, control of the Mississippi River, and economic factors. His insight told him that all three would be key elements in defeating the South.

But most of all, he knew that this war would be different from other wars of the past. Not only would it involve military might, but it also would be highly political; not only would it be conducted by professionals, but it would also require the mobilization of the civilian population. It would be a war fought with nineteenth-century tactics and twentieth-century innovations. And it would not be brief. In this he felt alone—"Only I think it is to be a long war—very long—much longer than any politician thinks."[99]

And so, he waited.

# CHAPTER THREE

# "We Must Fight and Subdue Those in Arms Against Us"

FINALLY, THE RIGHT OPPORTUNITY ARRIVED. In May 1861, Sherman received a telegram from his brother John in Washington, telling him to come at once, that he had been appointed colonel of the Thirteenth Regular Infantry and was wanted in Washington immediately.[1] Sherman took from a trunk, where they had been stored since 1853, the saddle, sash, and sword he had used in his earlier days as a soldier, and headed East.[2]

The men of the Thirteenth Infantry were yet to be recruited, but Sherman accepted the commission in preference to a brigadier generalship of volunteers because it meant a permanent position with regular army rank. He arrived in Washington and received the commission from the general-in-chief, the aged Gen. Winfield Scott. Sherman had hoped to return West to enlist his men at Jefferson Barracks near St. Louis, but Scott assured him that his lieutenant colonel could accomplish this task and made him part of his own staff. So, much to Sherman's disappointment, he remained in Washington and was given the job of inspecting recruits as they flooded into the capital.

This experience simply added to his depression. As Lloyd Lewis writes, "He wanted to be out of the bureau-ridden capital. . . . All around him were politicians who were loud with baseless confidence, and army officers who were morose with anticipation of defeat."[3]

Of the troops crowding into the city Sherman said, they came

81

wearing uniforms "as various as the States and cities from which they came." These citizen-soldiers were so loaded down "with overcoats, haversacks, knapsacks, tents, and baggage" that it would take twenty-five to fifty wagons to move a single regiment. And the cooking and baking facilities of the camps "would have done credit to Delmonico."[4]

Nor was he pleased with the continued talk of disloyalty so evident on the streets of Washington. Present at a gathering in John's room, a group of congressmen discussed the war, saying how public sentiment had changed in Washington and that they were confident the conflict would be ended quickly. To which, Sherman tersely interjected, "The sentiment of the people of Washington is such that they will cut the throats of our wounded in the hospital or on the sidewalk with table knives if our army should meet with disaster. . . ."[5] Nothing he had seen could convince him otherwise. Indeed, his brief experience in the capital simply solidified his earlier feelings about the ongoing conflict. To Ellen, on the eve of the Battle of Bull Run, he wrote, "I still regard this as but the beginning of a long war, but I hope my judgment therein is wrong, and that the people of the South may yet see the folly of their unjust rebellion against the most mild and paternal government ever designed for men."[6] And just one week before the Union forces attacked the Confederates at Bull Run, Sherman tried to construct a picture of the situation and what lay in the future. To his daughter Minnie, he wrote, "War is a terrible thing, especially when, as now, we are fighting . . . others whom I used to know as kind, good friends, and they thinking they are defending their country, their houses and families against foreign invaders. So, my dear child, don't get in the habit of calling hard names, of rebels, traitors, but remember how easy it is for people to become deceived and drawn on step by step till war, death and destruction are upon them. . . ."

Of war itself, and the destruction of armies, he added, "All around for miles fences are torn down and hogs, horses and cattle roam at will through clover and wheat and corn fields. No matter how much officers may wish to protect, soldiers will take rail fences for their campfires, and it is miraculous how soon a fence disappears and yet nobody did it. Thus, wherever an army goes there will be destruction of property. . . ." And, finally, words of compassion, "We must fight and subdue those in arms against us and our government, but we mean them no harm. This is a strange war, and God grant it may never be felt near you all."[7]

Fortunately, at least from Sherman's perspective, he remained on duty with General Scott for only ten days. In less than a month he would be in battle. The Confederates had placed two armies in front of Washington, one at Manassas Junction under the command of Brig. Gen. P. G. T. Beauregard and the other near Winchester under Gen. Joseph E. Johnston.[8] Urged on by popular clamor, General Scott hurried his preparations for an advance, and, on July 12, ordered his armies forward. Brig. Gen. Irwin McDowell was to attack Beauregard and Maj. Gen. Robert Patterson was to move against Johnston. Sherman was in command of the Third Brigade of the First Division of McDowell's army at Fort Corcoran, Virginia.[9]

Sherman took command of the brigade on July 1 and immediately set about preparing the troops for service in the field. Here, for the first time but not the last, he was faced with utter confusion. To his mind such confusion would inevitably lead to disaster. Privates disobeyed orders, rambled about at will, stole oats and corn for their horses and apples for themselves, and fired at houses for sheer sport.[10] Years later he would recall, "With all my personal efforts I could not prevent the men from straggling for water, blackberries, or anything in the way they fancied.[11] Immediately, with the single-mindedness he had always possessed, he labored to reorganize his brigade and restore discipline, keeping his men's minds occupied and their bodies fit with exercises.

On July 16, McDowell's divisions moved forward and on the 18th had a skirmish at Blackburn's Ford, near Centreville in which four or five of Sherman's men were killed.[12] This engagement assured the Federal commander that the Confederates were indeed in strong force just beyond Bull Run and that a serious full-scale battle was imminent. It came on July 21, and Sherman personally led his brigade into combat. So often in the past he had longed for fighting, now the time had arrived. Bull Run (Manassas) was his baptism of fire and he handled it well. Although nervous and anxious, he displayed remarkable control and steadiness and made a good showing. As one correspondent reported, "His coolness and efficiency surprised friends familiar with his excitable temperament."[13]

Sherman entered the action in the late forenoon and pursued the retreating Rebel forces for more than a mile. Then he had to assume the defensive and, after a determined struggle, his brigade was beaten in detail as Sherman committed his four regiments in piecemeal and was forced to retreat.[14] Immediately, Sherman formed his men in a hollow square and marched them from the field. Slowly the square retreated, falling apart as danger disappeared. In a matter of minutes he had successfully brought his men to safety, "disorganized, but not scared," and bivouacked at their Centreville camp.[15] For four hours Sherman was in combat and was grazed by enemy fire in the knee and shoulder.

What at one point appeared to be a victory for McDowell's forces was suddenly transformed into retreat and defeat, then became a rout. One congressman present as a spectator wrote of the retreat, "There was never anything like it for causeless, sheer, absolute absurd cowardice, or rather panic, on this miserable earth before.

"Off they went, one and all; off down the highway, over across fields, towards the woods, anywhere, everywhere, to escape. To enable them better to run, they threw away their blankets, knapsacks, canteens, and finally musket, cartridge-boxe, and everything else."[16] Sherman had read of retreats and he had witnessed the panic and confusion of men at fires and shipwrecks, "but nothing like this."[17]

It was a tragedy, and what made it even more tragic was the fact that the battle had been well-planned. In Sherman's view, "It was one of the best-planned battles of the war, but one of the worst fought."[18] To his wife, he wrote, "The battle was nothing to the absolute rout that followed and yet exists."[19]

In his official report Sherman stated, "This retreat was by night, and disorderly in the extreme. The men of different regiments mingled together, and some reached the river at Arlington, some at Long Bridge, and the greater part returned to their former camp at or near Fort Corcoran."[20] The loss in his brigade was 109 killed, 208 wounded, and 264 missing. A total in casualties of 581. The loss in killed and wounded in Sherman's brigade alone was nearly one-fourth that of the army.[21]

In the aftermath of the battle Sherman wrote Ellen of his reactions to the blood and death of war: " . . . for the first time I saw the carnage of battle, men lying in every conceivable shape, and mangled in a horrible way; but this did not make a particle of impression on me, but the horses running about riderless with blood streaming from their nostrils, lying on the ground hitched to guns, gnawing their sides in death."[22] It seems Sherman had prepared himself for the horrors of slaughtered men, "but he had not fortified himself against the butchery of animals."[23]

The Union defeat confirmed for Sherman that the war would be a long one and, perhaps, one that could not be won easily. The overwhelming defeat affected him deeply. In the past when things had gone against him, Sherman's typical response had been to blame himself, even when conditions had not warranted such a response. For one who already possessed a nervous, perhaps hyperactive, personality, the experience at Bull Run (Manassas) thrust him into spells of irritability and acute depression. But this time, instead of turning in on himself he began to blame those around him, not only for his own defeat, but for the entire fiasco. He openly criticized the conduct of some of his officers and men in his brigade as well as the administration in Washington. Although misplaced and highly inappropriate for his rank, Sherman had a foresight that was accurate and would eventually be justified. His problem was that he did not know how to keep his mouth shut.

Despite his lack of poise and diplomacy, and although his criticisms and evaluations were making him enemies, certain elements were on his side. The vigor he displayed on the battlefield did not go unnoticed, and with the influence of his brother John, the Ohio delegation in Congress recommended he be promoted. In addition, General McDowell[24] and Colonel Burnside[25] in their official reports made honorable mention of Sherman's brave services. Thus, on August 3, 1861, he was commissioned as a brigadier general of volunteers.[26]

The experience at Bull Run, Sherman's first taste of war, influenced his thinking in a number of ways. Probably most noticeable was the blow to his fundamental instinct for law and order. Telling Ellen of the disorder he witnessed on the way to Bull Run, he wrote, " . . . I always feared the result, for everywhere we found people against us. No curse could be greater than invasion by a volunteer army. No Goths or Vandals ever had less respect for the lives and property of friends and foes, and henceforth we ought never to hope for any friends in Virginia."[27] Defeat seemed to be less shameful than the abuses he witnessed. The experience would never leave him. He wrote these words at a time when he still held a slim hope that a violent confrontation might be avoided. Perhaps the North and the South could achieve a common ground based on friendship. But with the horrible destruction that occurred at Bull Run, such hope died. Sherman had crossed his own Rubicon, and he realized that to hope was now useless. So he let go and plunged forward. In two years he would be prepared to carry the cause of war to the lives and property of Mississippi, Georgia, and the Carolinas. Southerners would become friends again once they laid down their arms and rejoined the Union, but only then.

Also, Sherman was more sure than ever that there had to be organization in time of war. The disorganization he witnessed was the result of inadequate leadership due to the lack of a proper chain of command.

After observing the effects of the Union volunteer army during the first encounter with the enemy, he realized even more the need for regular recruits. "They did as they pleased . . . ," stampeded, fled, and with no regard for their army or country.[28] Each private had the habit of thinking and acting on his own, thus there was no unity of purpose. Volunteers were constantly complaining and refusing to follow orders. To Ellen again, he gave this evaluation, " . . . and our soldiers are the most destructive men that I have ever known. It may be that other volunteers are just as bad, indeed the complaint is universal, and I see no alternative but to let it take its course. Now I suppose that there is not a man, woman or child but would prefer Jeff Davis or the Czar of Russia to govern them rather than an American Volunteer Army. My only hope now is that a common sense of decency may be inspired into the minds of their soldiers to respect life and property."[29] In time Sherman would have to make adjustments in his attitude toward volunteers because of the enormous armies required during the Civil War. The adjustment would be made by the use of regulars in training and disciplining volunteers. At this point in his thinking, Sherman was not willing to accept the totality of war and the demand it would make on civilians, combatants as well as noncombatants. In 1861 he was in tune with the average professional soldier when it came to the rules of war. Influenced by both Jomini and Mahan, he saw war "as a kind of game played by experts off in some private sphere . . . ,"[30] and "unquestionably at this stage Sherman was prejudiced against citizen soldiers and did not want to be associated with them."[31]

Now he knew that the North had a long and tedious road ahead. With great emotion, he wrote, "Nobody, no man, can save the country.

The difficulty is with the masses. Our men are not good soldiers. They brag, but don't perform, complain sadly if they don't get everything they want, and a march of a few miles uses them up. It will take a long time to overcome these things, and what is in store for us in the future I don't know."[32] Sherman knew the South; he knew its culture, and, therefore, he knew what could be expected. He perceived a unity of purpose among Southerners that did not exist among Northerners. He wrote, "In all the Southern states they have succeeded in impressing the public mind that the North is governed by a great mob (of which unfortunately there is too much truth) and in the South that all is chivalry and gentility."[33] To bring this war to an end, unity had to be established while simultaneously the cohesiveness of the South would have to be destroyed. This would not come quickly or easily, and it would have to begin by demanding of the army strict obedience and discipline.

Further, the Bull Run experience taught Sherman the importance of mobility; indeed he was coming to see it as "the mainspring of war." He had been exposed to the principle of mobility at West Point and had gotten a glimpse of its importance in Florida against the Seminoles. Bull Run (Manassas) implanted it in his mind.[34]

Finally, Sherman's first experience in combat had an impact on the manner in which he viewed himself. Self-analysis had always been important to him; he constantly evaluated his ideas and actions and was always deeply interested in and sensitive to the evaluations of others. Over the years, this process had created much turmoil in his life. Always pressuring himself to do better, he never managed to be completely pleased with his achievements. The failures he had experienced he had blamed on himself. In most cases he was unfair to himself. History, circumstances, and events had always seemed to put him in the wrong places at the wrong times. Just as he had apparently found a stable life in Louisiana, catastrophe in the form of secession took it away. But now, instead of blaming himself and his own shortcomings, he directed his criticisms and frustrations outward. Officers were incompetent, volunteers incapable, and the administration inept. In the wake of the Bull Run debacle, as he listened to those around him and as he analyzed his own performance, he began to realize, "Maybe I'm not as confused as I had thought." Two months after the battle he wrote to his brother, "There is no time to be lost and I will not spare my individual efforts, though I still feel as one groping in the dark. Slowly but surely the public is realizing what I knew all the time, the strong vindictive feeling of the whole South."[35] Perhaps Bull Run had awakened among the people of the North the realization that this was going to be a long war, that the South was seriously determined to achieve its independence and would go to extremes to succeed.

Yet, despite these fleeting moments of stability, doubt still prevailed. Granted, his ideas were beginning to be recognized as true. He had finally taken active part in the service of his beloved Union, and a clear and systematic philosophy of war was beginning to emerge, but the doubts lingered and continued to take their toll. Also, he was finding himself caught between the traditional ideas he held concerning war and the innovations he saw this particular war would demand. This war, he sensed, although he was not quite willing to admit it as yet, was to be one of ideas and unlimited objectives.

After being commissioned a brigadier general in August 1861, Sherman for a short time commanded a brigade in the Army of the Potomac and was stationed in Washington. His letters indicate a growing feeling of security while at the same time a desire to take things slow and easy. The sense of stability was tentative and precarious. After all, he had been optimistic before and the result had always been disastrous. So, Sherman became even more guarded. He did not want to accept any great responsibilities that would prevent future advancement and security. He did not want to fail again; thus he became extremely cautious and calculating. Writing to his wife on August 3 from his new post, he said, "This will keep me where I want, in a modest position till time and circumstances show us daylight."[36] Once his mind was cleared and he could feel firm ground under his feet and " . . . see some end to this muddle,"[37] then, and only then, would he accept a full command. So, until that moment arrived he proposed to " . . . go on as heretofore, to endeavor to fill my place as well as possible, to meddle as little as possible with my superiors, and to give my opinion only when asked for. . . ."[38]

In mid-August Sherman was asked by Maj. Gen. Robert Anderson to meet him at the Willard Hotel. Upon his arrival Sherman found Anderson dining with Sen. Andrew Johnson of Tennessee. Johnson informed Sherman that President Lincoln had decided to provide assistance to the pro-Union people of Kentucky and Tennessee and had appointed General Anderson to command the troops that would make up the Department of the Cumberland.[39] Anderson had selected Sherman to be his second in command.[40]

This new assignment impressed and excited Sherman. At last, proper steps were being taken by the administration to meet the national crisis. To Ellen, he wrote, "How few realize the stern fact I too well know. Unless we can organize a large party in Kentucky and Tennessee there is a danger that our old Govt. may disintegrate and new combinations formed. . . ." Maybe this was the beginning of a proper strategy. To Sherman it had become clear that there "should be only three [armies] East, Center, West. . . ."[41] Now Lincoln was moving in that direction.

But, there still remained a lack of confidence. To Ellen, he continued, "I hardly know my sphere in Kentucky, but it will be political and military combined. I think Anderson wanted me because he knows I seek not personal fame or glory, and that I will heartily second his plans and leave him the fame. Most assuredly does he esteem my motives. Not till I see daylight ahead do I want to lead."[42]

Before leaving Washington for his new assignment, Sherman received a promise from President Lincoln that in no event would he be asked to take a high command. He was not ready for such responsibility.[43] This was a rather unusual request coming from a man in the military but understandable coming from one with Sherman's present state of mind. William Sherman was a frightened man.

Encouraged with the change to the Western region, Sherman's attitude improved. He was glad to be leaving the confusion of the Virginia theater and was hopeful that things in Kentucky and Tennessee would be different. Also, this would mean he would be located in a strategic position. He had always held the strong conviction "that in Kentucky and Tennessee lay the key to the immediate future, and in the Mississippi lay the key to ultimate victory."[44]

Upon his arrival in Cincinnati on September 1, "the mercury of Sherman's emotions fell,"[45] for the West proved to be no different from the East. Here too, he found an atmosphere of confusion and disorganization. What he had hoped to be a new beginning for himself and the Union effort turned out to be a near tragedy.

In less than two months Sherman's hopes slipped into despair. He grew even more nervous than usual and his perception of his surroundings was adversely affected. In the unfolding events he saw little of a positive nature. Not only did recruits have to be begged from the governors of Indiana and Illinois, they came to the department ill-trained and poorly equipped. At every point he witnessed inefficiencies and procrastinations. But, he had made a commitment, was following the career for which he had been trained, and knew he could not reverse his direction. Tragically, he believed in his ideas about war and the present condition of his troops, yet there must have been that doubt and fear that maybe he was wrong, that perhaps his perceptions were misguided. The more he allowed this inner conflict to go unresolved, the more it enslaved him, and the more it influenced his overt behavior.

Believing the Confederates were on the verge of occupying Kentucky as a springboard for an offensive into Indiana and Ohio, Sherman began writing Washington for more regiments, only to be turned down. To John he wrote, "We ought to have here a well appointed Army of a hundred thousand men,"[46] and predicted, "If the Confederates take St. Louis and get Kentucky this Winter you will be far more embarrassed than if Washington had fallen into their possession, as whatever nation gets control of the Ohio, Mississippi, and Missouri Rivers will control the Continent. This they know and for this they labor. You of the North never fully appreciated the energy of the South."[47] Fearing personal failure and the loss of a strategically vital area of the country, and witnessing the lack of understanding on behalf of the administration in Washington lead Sherman to overestimate the force and intentions of the enemy. Brooding over the tragedy of sending young untrained boys into battle, Sherman grew more morose, and worry about the lack of discipline and the absence of equipment made him even more nervous.

Then, of all possible things, General Anderson fell ill from exhaustion, and circumstances thrust Sherman into full command of the Department of the Cumberland! He had no alternative but to assume the position "though much against the grain, and in direct violation of Mr. Lincoln's promise. . . ."[48] Immediately, Sherman reminded the president of the promise and received assurance that Brig. Gen. Don Carlos Buell would relieve him as soon as he arrived from California.[49] To Garrett Davis, a friend and resident of Paris, Kentucky, Sherman wrote, "I am forced into the command of this department against my will."[50]

The situation he inherited from Anderson was worse than it had been upon their arrival in Kentucky. There was no staff to carry on the routine duties of the department. Local citizens were complaining daily about the disruptive behavior of soldiers. Brig. Gen. George H. Thomas who had come to Kentucky with Sherman was calling for reinforcements. And politicians began at once to remind him of President Lincoln's desire that East Tennessee be delivered from the grasp of the Confederacy.[51]

With energy Sherman set to work to organize his department and prepare his troops for the task before them. However, the duties and responsibilities, and the lack of support from Washington, were overpowering. Fearing failure again and believing the Confederate troops who had entered the southern portion of the state were far superior to his, he began to call Washington for men and arms far in excess of the need. As the result of an inadequate intelligence system, he believed as true the rumors concerning the size of the enemy's armies. He was prepared to believe the worst and, therefore, credited the Southerners with not only huge forces but plans for an all-out offensive.[52] To Adj. Gen. Lorenzo Thomas, he wrote, "You know my views—that this great center of our field was too weak, far too weak, and I have begged and implored till I dare not say more." He continued, "I again repeat that our force here is out of all proportion to the importance of the position. Our defeat would be disastrous to the nation, and to expect of new men, who never bore arms to do miracles is not right."[53]

The situation reached a climax when Sec. of War Simon Cameron stopped off in Louisville on his return to Washington from St. Louis. Seizing the opportunity to speak to someone in direct authority, Sherman met with the secretary and his party at the Galt Hotel. During the course of the conversation Sherman argued that for the purpose of defense 60,000 men would be needed and "for offense, before we were done, 200,000." Such figures startled Secretary Cameron and his party. "Great God!" he exclaimed, "Where are they to come from?"

Unfortunately for Sherman, among the civilians in the party accompanying Cameron was Samuel Wilkerson, a correspondent of the New York *Tribune*. Sherman had already captured the ire of correspondents prior to the secretary's visit. Because of his distrust of reporters and editors, he had become unpopular with them. On numerous occasions he had accused them of publishing too much information that he felt assisted the enemy. In an attempt to correct this situation, he had acted to place restrictions on their access to military plans and troop movements. On one occasion he had a reporter of the Cincinnati *Commercial* imprisoned. As a result, the word passed among correspondents and editors that Sherman was an enemy of the press. So, by the time the Cameron incident took place, the reporters were ready to pounce. And pounce they did. Wilkerson confided to another correspondent that Cameron regarded Sherman as "unbalanced and that it would not do to leave him in command."[54] It was not long until the newspapers across the country were carrying a report of the conference, duly noting the fact that the requests for reinforcements by Sherman were insane. An article in the Chicago *Tribune* said, "I know not whether it is insanity or not but the General . . . indulged in remarks that made his loyalty doubtful. He even spoke despondingly; said the rebels could never be whipped; talked of a thirty-years' war."[55] A number of other newspapers were giving similar reports stating that Sherman was mad and in need of care and sympathy. Even Secretary Cameron, referring to Sherman's call for 200,000 troops to defend the Mississippi Valley, held him up to public ridicule and branded him a "crazy man."[56]

Coupled with his mental condition and distaste for such an early position of responsibility, the negative publicity devastated Sherman. It was simply one more in a long line of incidents that would culminate in a major crisis for Sherman. In spite of his efforts to achieve stability, his own attitude, along with forces beyond his control, worked against him. His military career was now in jeopardy, and he knew it.

On November 12, 1861, General Buell relieved Sherman of his command. Sherman was ordered to report to Maj. Gen. Henry Halleck in Missouri.[57] Due to his " . . . fidgety manner and toscin-shrill dispatches" all the suspicions appeared to be true. He appeared thoroughly demoralized, "stampeded" (the description used by Halleck), while McClellan expressed it more pointedly, saying, "Sherman's gone in the head."[58]

On reaching St. Louis, Sherman reported to General Halleck. A friend of his at West Point and in California, Halleck received Sherman kindly and with encouragement. Overlooking the ridicule Sherman was being bombarded with by the newspapers, Halleck immediately assigned him to active duty in Sedalia, Missouri, where he was to inspect the condition of troops stationed there. Although

Halleck made no reference to Sherman's difficulties, Sherman complained that the newspapers continued to "harp on my insanity and paralyze my efforts."[59] For example, the Cincinnati *Commercial* congratulated Kentucky on escaping from "the peevishness, prejudice and persecution" of a man who "is a perfect monomaniac. . . ." With sarcasm, the story stated that Sherman's " . . . favorite often proclaimed plan for the successful management of the war is the suppression of every newspaper in the country—a theory which he advocates the more strongly since the comments of the press on his requisition of only 200,000 men."[60]

The press would continue to haunt Sherman in the days ahead. A lesson he should have learned but never did was to cooperate with and accommodate the media. The wounds inflicted by newspapers and correspondents in Kentucky and Missouri were too deep. Instead of accepting the media's rightful place in a democratic society, even in time of war, Sherman carried on a constant battle with editors and reporters. He could never grow to trust them and, as they were to many military figures of world history, they were always a menace to Sherman as well. True, this experience and subsequent ones demonstrated that he had at least partial justification for his distrust; it was a characteristic that influenced his future military strategy. Yet, he never realized that he was fighting a losing battle. He never gave up, however, and continued to believe that the press was a serious detriment to the Union cause. He expressed his sentiment best during the Vicksburg campaign: "I know they will ruin me, but they will ruin the country too. Napoleon himself would have been defeated with a free press."[61]

By now Sherman was almost a completely other-directed person. Extremely concerned about his image in the eyes of others, he grew even more nervous and hyperactive. Instead of relaxing and approaching his new duties calmly, he set a frantic pace. Inspecting, planning, and training filled most of his working hours. Burning the candle at both ends, he attempted to compensate for the negative things people were reading and saying about him. Instead of improving his situation, he worsened it. To John, he wrote, "Some terrible disaster is inevitable. . . . Could I now hide myself in some obscure corner I would do so, for my conviction is that our Government is destroyed. . . ." He was sure that " . . . no human power could restore it."[62] One newsman who observed him in St. Louis reported that "his eyes had a half-wild expression," and he smoked cigars continuously. "Sometimes," the reporter continued, "he works for twenty consecutive hours. He sleeps little. Nor do the most powerful opiates relieve his terrible cerebral excitement."[63]

Finally, the inevitable happened. On November 29, Sherman received a dispatch ordering him to return to St. Louis to begin a twenty-day leave. Halleck, who had been treating Sherman with courtesy and consideration, wanted him to return to his home in Lancaster, hoping that a rest might restore his stability. Arriving in St. Louis, Sherman was met by Ellen, who after considerable persuasion, convinced him to go to Ohio. She felt the period of respite would provide time to " . . . allow the storm to blow over somewhat." Sherman finally relented and returned with his wife to Lancaster, "where I was born, and where I supposed I was better known and appreciated."[64] Leaving, he informed Halleck that he wanted to waive his right to command a division when he returned.

Halleck wrote to Maj. Gen. George McClellan in Washington that Sherman had not done well with his assignment in and around Sedalia. Therefore, "I am satisfied that General Sherman's physical and mental system is so completely broken by labor and care as to render him for the present entirely unfit for duty." He continued, saying that "perhaps a few weeks' rest may restore him. I am satisfied that in his present condition it would be dangerous to give him a command here."[65]

The newspapers had a heyday. Learning of Sherman's recall from Sedalia and return to Lancaster, correspondents eagerly carried the news across the country. On December 11, the Cincinnati *Commercial* carried the following story under the bold headline, GENERAL WILLIAM T. SHERMAN INSANE:

> The painful intelligence reaches us, in such form that we are not at liberty to disclose it, that Gen. William T. Sherman . . . is insane. It appears that he was, at the time while commanding in Kentucky stark mad. We learned that he at one time telegraphed to the War Department three times in one day for permission to evacuate Kentucky and retreat into Indiana.
>
> He has, of course, been relieved altogether of command. The harsh criticisms that have been lavished on this gentleman, provoked by his strange conduct, will now give way to feelings of deepest sympathy for him in this great calamity. It seems providential that the country has not to mourn the loss of any army through the loss of the mind of a general into whose hands were

committed the vast responsibilities of the command of Kentucky.[66]

Thus, William Tecumseh Sherman, distraught and melancholy, a man who now had experienced failure in both civilian and military life, temporarily turned his back on the war. He had lost that confidence he knew so well twenty years earlier as he left West Point headed for a successful career as a soldier. He must have had a sense that history had passed him by. For the sake of individual pride, he had been determined to make good, but that determination had only led him to further failures and rejections. Scared, cautious, bitter, and depressed, he had performed his duties in Missouri mechanically, but to no avail. "I could not hide from myself that many of the officers and soldiers . . . looked at me askance and with suspicion."[67] So, reluctantly, Sherman returned home. "Once more life had thrown him like a weed on his father-in-law's doorstep."[68] Dejected and confused, he began the process of collecting his thoughts and searching for stability. Unknown to him at the time, a foundation had been built for his life and, ultimately, for his concept of war. Much that he had learned in defeat would shape the course of his later military triumphs.

Obviously, this was an extremely trying and critical time in Sherman's life, and it is difficult to evaluate. He had left Washington with the hope that things would be different in the West, only to discover that in many ways they were much worse. This situation disturbed him greatly, perhaps more so than it did others. As a result, his response got him into trouble. Indeed, his response almost ended his military career.

The interpretation accepted by most historians concerning Sherman's behavior during this period is that he suffered a collapse[69] or a nervous breakdown.[70] Some have even labeled him a manic-depressive psychotic.[71] Such interpretations are too simplistic and do not provide an accurate understanding of the man. Such interpretations are lacking in foundation and represent a failure to consider the total social setting in which Sherman functioned. The evidence, when considered as a whole, indicates that here was a man experiencing a high level of stress responding in a quite normal way. The evidence also indicates that Sherman was a victim of labeling, not only by his contemporaries, but by many historians who have written about him.

Sherman's difficulties were the result of a number of factors. First, he took his past with him to Kentucky. As has been noted, his failures in civilian life had made him cautious and reluctant to assume a position of great responsibility. He did not want to fail again, especially as a soldier. Thus, he was hypersensitive to his environment. No doubt, this state of mind caused him to draw conclusions about his circumstances that were not totally accurate. But such a mental state does not warrant the label insane or psychotic. If these are the criteria to be used in support of the thesis that Sherman suffered a nervous breakdown, then a number of other Civil War officers must be included in the list with him. Nor can it be concluded that his fear of failure lead to a collapse. This fear did not make him dysfunctional or irrational, it simply made him overly cautious. Second, he knew the South well and had witnessed its preparation for war firsthand. He knew how serious its people were about secession. Also, he knew the strategic importance of the Cis-Mississippi area. Thus, it was logical that he would be extremely concerned about the lack of Federal preparations in the West and the reality of aggressiveness on behalf of Southerners. In light of what he knew, his call for 200,000 troops does not seem absurd and, therefore, does not justify the label insane. Indeed, as has been pointed out on several occasions, "when the government put into the Western theater total forces approximating those demanded by Sherman in 1861, it appeared that he had been right."[72] Further, it is interesting that McClellan did not undergo a similar experience in Virginia as a result of his overestimating the enemy in that sector and his constant call for up to 273,000 troops. Third, Sherman refused to accept the role of the press in a free society during time of war. His mind was that of a soldier. Information and secrecy were vital for victory and to lose the element of surprise by allowing the enemy to have access to important tactical and strategical knowledge was abhorrent to him. He held a professional contempt for journalists and let it surface. Had he learned to handle the press like Ulysses Grant or cater to their every need as did George B. McClellan, things probably would have been much different. But he did not and was attacked by them viciously. Fourth, Sherman was extremely animated in his behavior. He was filled with emotional energy and, on many occasions, wore people out simply by being in their presence. Those who had the opportunity to observe him leave these descriptions: It appeared "as if his superabundant energy had consumed his flesh . . ." and "his whole face [was] mobile as an actor's. . . ."[73] A reporter remarked that Sherman "walked, talked or laughed all over. He perspired thought at every pore." A general depicted him as one who talked constantly and smoked cigars incessantly, and an officer said, "At his departure I felt it a relief and experienced almost an exhaustion after the excitement of his vigorious presence."[74] Sherman's physical presence left him open for negative evaluations. It seems people automatically conclude that there is a correlation between physical behavior and mental stability. Such a correlation, of course, is not always true. In Sherman's case, it was not. Fifth, Sherman had an active, quick mind. "His manner [was] pronounced, his speech quick, decided, loud." Adam Badeau, Grant's biographer, continues with, "His words were distinct; his ideas clear, rapid, coming indeed almost too fast for utterance, but in dramatic, brilliant form, while an eager gesticulation illustrated and enforced his thought simultaneously with speech itself. Boiling over with ideas, crammed full of feeling, discussing every subject and pronouncing on all; provoking criticism, and contradiction and admiration by terms; . . . starting new notions constantly in his own brain, and following them up, no matter how far or whither they led; witty, eloquent, sarcastic, logical; every peculiarity fascinated or commanded the attention."[75] And finally this from Col. Henry Stone. Sherman was "quick-eyed, ingenious, nervously active in mind and body, sleeplessly alert on every occasion, with a clear idea of what he wanted and an unyielding determination to have it, he made himself and everybody around him uncomfortable till his demands were gratified. . . ."[76] Sherman's problem was his quickness and bluntness. He said what he felt at the time, and he said it without fear of consequence. This opened him up to being misunderstood and misinterpreted, and he never took the time nor made the effort to clarify exactly what he meant. He simply assumed that others were on the same thought wave as he was. This, of course, got him into trouble. Sixth, and last, as E. Merton Coulter points out, Sherman "believed in rapid and thorough work—he was impatient in the extreme with what he considered half-way measures."[77] War, for Sherman, was the final instrument society must use to re-establish law and order. When all else failed, war must be implemented, and because of its horror, war must be implemented quickly and efficiently. Once law and order are restored, war ceases. This was a passion with Sherman and "it was the working of this passion to carry a task efficiently to a conclusion that led his compatriots in 1861 to declare that he was insane. . . ."[78] He wanted speed and efficiency in war preparations, and he saw neither; so he struck out at those around him, placing blame, hoping to motivate.

In the light of these factors—his past history of failure; his knowledge of the South, and his understanding of the strategic importance of the Mississippi River area; his battle with the press; his animated behavior; his active, quick mind; and his desire for efficiency and results—it is clear why some would conclude that Sherman had indeed gone crazy, that he had suffered a nervous breakdown, a mental collapse. His perception of the situation was total, whereas those around him saw it only in part. Thus, his behavior was open to misunderstanding. But those who have drawn the conclusion of mental illness have failed to mention that he remained functional, carried out his duties, and, on the whole, was quite rational in thought. Nor do they give much credence to the fact that most of his "outlandish" statements were correct. They see his behavior as deviant. After all, he did not speak like normal people, nor did he behave normally according to them. He was given to moods, was extremely nervous in conversation, and was hypercritical. Therefore, it has been concluded, these must be indications of mental disorders. People saw what they wanted to see. So, they labeled him—first as insane, then as one experiencing a nervous breakdown.

There is no denying that Sherman made mistakes in judgment— what Civil War commander did not? But he was not psychotic nor did he suffer a nervous collapse. He was a man who responded to a difficult set of circumstances in a very normal manner. Had others held Sherman's perception of the Western situation, more than likely their response would have been similar. His unique characteristics and his understanding of contemporary events caused him to behave in the only way he knew, and that behavior was seen as deviant. Sherman, therefore, became the victim of negative labeling by those who could not or would not understand. Sherman's problem was, to use the social psychologist Erving Goffman's phrase, in his "presentation of self."[79] He could not "blend with his environment,"[80] thus his presentation of self was offensive. But, as Stephen Ambrose puts it, " . . . Sherman was no psychotic. He was an intensely emotional man who had a highly developed imagination. His quickness of mind, his ability to see in a flash all the possibilities, eventually led him to greatness. . . ."[81] Sherman's major mistake was not in his perception of what ought to have been done, but in his manner of expressing what ought to have been done. Militarily speaking, his strategy was sound, his tactics horrible.

Finally this. It is amazing how quickly this supposedly manic-depressive psychotic recovered from his supposed mental breakdown. He returned to duty in less than twenty days.

CHAPTER FOUR

# "The Very Object of War Is . . . Death and Slaughter"

SHERMAN MADE EXCELLENT USE of his twenty-day leave. With the assistance and support of his wife, family, and friends, he began to sort out his life and gain a healthy perspective. To his brother John he admitted just how low he had fallen, "I am so sensible now of my disgrace from having exaggerated the force of our enemy in Kentucky that I do think I should have committed suicide were it not for my children."[1] He confessed to Ellen that a major cause of his despondency was related to the loss of a number of East Tennesseans to whom he felt responsible. While he was in command in Kentucky, these Tennesseans received word that Sherman was moving to their rescue. Hoping to assist him, they began harassing the local Confederates by burning bridges in the area. A number of them were killed, and Sherman failed in his rescue attempt.

Concerning this incident and the impact it had on Sherman, Ellen wrote to John, "I find that the keenest source of trouble to Cump is in the fact that he could not go to the relief of the East Tennesseans at the time the bridges were burned." She pleaded, "Can you not bring him to the belief that he is in no way responsible for that?"[2]

Although the barrage of newspaper stories continued, Sherman knew he was not insane. He had lost his confidence, was ashamed of having made mistakes, and was frustrated with what he believed to be incompetence on the part of the administration and politicians. His ideas were stable (he felt confident of that) and mostly accurate; the difficulty was in their lack of acceptance and in his method of

101

*Gen. William T. Sherman, 1865.*

presenting them. The gulf between what he knew had to be accomplished in order to defeat the South and what was actually being done was, in his view, quite distant. So, instead of being patient, he criticized, and instead of using the system to implement his ideas, he fought it. The resulting confrontation, along with his list of failures, weakened him. Thus, frustration led to impatience, and impatience lead to self-doubt. If this crisis were to pass, there was much Sherman had to learn, and he had to learn it quickly. He had to learn that when fighting an adversary—either on the battlefield or in life—the battleground must be selected wisely. The successful path to victory is to make sure battles are fought that can be won and to know the differences between battles and wars. He also had to learn to recognize and delineate personal mistakes and blunders from the circumstances of history. To blame oneself for personal failures that are the result of forces beyond one's control is to perceive life in a distorted manner. On this account, Sherman was guilty. Further, Sherman had to grasp the meaning and significance of power. His naivete on this issue had continually gotten him into trouble. He had to see that the system was all-powerful and that if changes were to occur, he had to work within the system and make it work for him. Sherman knew that to achieve success and to realize the national recognition in the one profession he loved above all others, he had to change. This would be his last chance.

So, with the undying faith of his wife, his own self-determination, the lessons he had learned rather painfully over the past forty years, the support of John Sherman and Thomas Ewing (both speaking on his behalf in Washington), and the willingness of Halleck to assist him, Sherman achieved a level of stability that enabled him to return to duty.

Against Ellen's wishes (she had wanted him to remain in Lancaster until early spring), Sherman left home on December 18, bound for St. Louis. Although sympathetic and understanding, Halleck decided that Sherman was still not prepared for command in the field and assigned him instead to command the camp of instruction at Benton Barracks. His orders were to instruct 12,000 recruits in the art of war and to prepare the troops for "service at a moment's warning."[3] Sherman had left Lancaster on somewhat of a high note. After all, he was returning to duty rather than slowly slipping into obscurity, and the Louisville *Journal* had published laudations of him: "His [Sherman's] mind is probably unsurpassed in power and comprehensiveness by that of any military man of our country. . . . In his dauntless heroism he is equal to Richard the Lionheart. His deportment at the Battle of Bull Run, as we have heard it described by eye-witnesses, was worthy of the greatest hero of any age. He has been deemed insane only to those individuals who could not comprehend him . . . his intellect, we are happy to learn, is as calm and firm as it ever was."[4] The high note, however, was tempered with reality. He was still insecure and depressed as he set out to do his duty. The disgrace of having surrendered his command continued to weigh heavily on his mind. But, he was back and was determined to survive. Perhaps the obscurity at Benton Barracks would buy him some time. So, training, discipline, supplying food and equipment, and planning for future battle became his primary concerns.

Although willing to conform to the demands expected of him, Sherman did not relinquish his individuality nor his ideas concerning the South. In letters to his brother he expressed concern that although the Union forces had possession of St. Louis and the railroads in northern Missouri, the situation was bleak and even dangerous. It was taking all of Halleck's command in the West to effectively watch a country swarming with secessionists. They were scattered all over the countryside, making it necessary for Halleck to do the same with his army.

This type of warfare was disturbing to Sherman and, apparently, its implications were not understood by the political and military authorities. To John he said:

> Now Halleck has in Missouri about 80,000 men on paper, and they are not in organized shape [with] more than 10,000 or 20,000 opposed to him, yet the country is full of Secessionist, and it takes all of his command to watch them. This is an element that politicians have never given full credit to. The local Secessionist are really more dangerous than if assembled in one or more bodies, for then they could be traced out and found, whereas now they are scattered about on farms and are very peaceable, but when a bridge is to be burned they are about. . . .

He wished he could take another view of his surroundings and of the war, "but I cannot. It thrusts itself up at me from every side and yet I hope that I am mistaken. . . ."[5] For Sherman this was a "national war" in the Jominian sense; a war "waged against a united people, or a great majority of them"; a people "filled with a noble ardor and determined to sustain their independence." Thus, "every step [of the invading army] is disputed" even by guerrillas if necessary. Such a war of invasion creates serious difficulties for the invader. It requires the division of large forces for the purpose of protecting lines of communications. Not only must the invading army destroy the defending armies, but "the country should be occupied and subjugated."[6]

Sherman would have had Carl von Clausewitz on his side as well, for in his work, *On War*, Clausewitz had observed that "at the end of a victorious campaign, when lines of communication have begun to be overstretched," the invading army must expend valuable resources to protect its rear. "Often," he stated, "the finest victory has been robbed of its glory as a consequence of this problem."[7]

Sherman saw clearly the implications of this problem and was beginning to question the policy of occupying cities and using valuable troops to hold vital lines of communications. In addition, what most military professionals were calling unfair tactics performed by mobs and thugs, Sherman saw as outright guerrilla warfare. Part of his West Point training, based on the concept of two large armies maneuvering into favorable positions then attacking in mass with cavalry and infantry, was being questioned. He had witnessed the futility of such action at Bull Run (Manassas) and again at Shiloh. That type of warfare was perhaps appropriate in the eighteenth century, but this enemy was different. War was no longer the domain of kings and professional warriors paid by the state. No, the rebellion of the Southern states was a rebellion of all the people—professional soldiers, civilians, women, and children. It was supported and encouraged by all the basic institutions of the South.

Sherman was coming to understand that war was total. The battlefield was expanding, and, eventually, he believed, would take in the entire South. To most soldiers in 1861–62, these ideas, at best, were only vague notions. They were contrary to the orthodox theories of warfare. Most military men were unaware that they were straddling the end of an old era and the beginning of a new one. Warfare was on the brink of dramatic change, and they were part of that change; they would be the very agents to usher it in. In a sense, the Industrial Revolution, which could not be turned back even on the battlefield, had made them all pawns in a new game of chess with different rules. Few, at least at the beginning of the conflict, would be willing to abide by the new rules, much less understand them, and, therefore, would make mistake after drastic mistake. Careers would be ruined and thousands of lives would be lost. Others would be pulled reluctantly into the modern age where nations would fight nations, while still others would cast off much of the old and willingly embrace the new. Sherman, as a result of his knowledge of the South, his understanding of history, and his refusal to relinquish his individuality, was of the latter group. As a pawn, he became a master of total warfare and earned the title "the first modern general."

Sherman was growing keenly aware of the transitional nature of this conflict and more than likely would have agreed with Walter Millis's analysis that rejects the conclusion that the Civil War was "the first modern war." Instead, after careful analysis, Millis concludes that "the great struggle was less 'modern' than transitional." He writes, "Much of the bloody past still clung to its operations and to the concepts which energized them; and it was not until the later years of the war that the new weapons and logistics began to draw the outlines of a different if not less bloody, future." Concerning the attitudes of the fighting men, Millis says, "The enthusiastic volunteering of the young, still fired by the romantic nineteenth-century ideas of glory and honor, made it unnecessary to face until well on in the war the hard problems of conscription and of the military obligation in a democracy." Millis continues, "The Civil War began at Bull Run with what was already, no doubt, the anachronism of men standing up in ordered ranks in the open to fight each other with ball, bayonet and butt; not until it was reaching its end in the trenches before Petersburg was the killing being brought down to the engineering operation which it was increasingly to become." It took 200,000 lives before "the more romantic concepts of war" were laid to rest. And with those lives went war's glory and honor, "its respect for the weak, its rewards for the valorous. . . ." Millis concludes, "When it was over the war of the 'fight' was already deeply overlaid by the beginning of the war of organization and the machine, the war against civilians and resources as well as the uniformed soldiery of the enemy, the war of conscripted peoples rather than of volunteer armies."[8]

In the midst of all the turmoil of the present, Sherman was getting a glimpse of the future, and it disturbed him. He was seeing the history of warfare unfold before him and he hoped "that I am mistaken."

But this was to come later. These impressions would eventually be used in his development of a new concept of warfare. At the moment, however, there were more pressing things on his mind. He had to undo the mess of his life by proving to those around him, particularly his men and superiors, that he was a good soldier. So, he concentrated his efforts on getting his troops ready for "service at a moment's warning." Yet as he concentrated on the routine and mundane aspects of soldiering, his mind continued to work. The rudimentary elements of total war were becoming lenses in eyeglasses that influenced all he observed. He saw the importance of railroads for communications and supplies, but more important was the problem of using them effectively while in a hostile country surrounded by a hostile people. Like others, although not many, he held the conviction that the real key to the war was located in the West—the Mississippi River. As early as First Bull Run (Manassas), Sherman saw that in Kentucky and Tennessee lay the door to immediate victory.[9] His idea was to cut off the outer roots of the Confederacy and then sever the deeper roots beneath the trunk so that the tree, its foundation undermined, would collapse. To cut the outer roots, Sherman looked to battles between two hostile armies; the deeper roots would be cut in a more revolutionary manner. As yet it was not clear how that would be done, but he knew it would most likely be revolutionary. It could not be done by the orthodox manner of warfare. New strategy using a combination of both old and new tactics and logistics would have to be implemented.

By the end of December, Sherman informed Halleck that he had ready for action four infantry and two cavalry regiments. Halleck was pleased with the rapid progress Sherman was making and slowly took him into his confidence. He observed him closely and gradually included him in a number of strategy conferences. The change in Sherman impressed Halleck to the extent that he wrote General McClellan that Sherman was recovering and would soon be fit for duty as a field commander. Then Halleck wrote Sherman explaining why he had assigned him to Benton Barracks. He said, "When you came here . . . your health was so broken and your nervous system so shattered by hard labor, anxiety and exposure, as to unfit you for field service. . . ." Thus, he added, " . . . I thought that Benton Barracks was, under the circumstances, best suited to your health." He emphasized that he " . . . did not consider it a subordinate one [position], but one of the most important in this Dept." He concluded, "I believe you can and will render important service in this

Department, and the time may soon come when we must all take the field. When it does come there is no one who I had rather have with me than yourself."[10]

The time was soon coming for on February 6 word was received by Halleck that Grant had captured Fort Henry. Ten days later Grant succeeded in compelling the unconditional surrender of Fort Donelson. To keep him supplied was of paramount importance, and Halleck had selected Sherman for the job by assigning him to command the District of Cairo, a part of Grant's rear zone, with headquarters at Paducah, Kentucky.[11] This was the regulating center not only for supplies and reinforcements to Grant, but also for the water connections with Halleck in Missouri and Buell in Kentucky. Sherman's responsibility was to keep Grant supplied. Immediately, Sherman approached his task with enthusiasm, energetically providing Grant with men, food, and encouragement. In addition, he cared for the wounded and processed prisoners. "At last things were beginning to move."[12]

The experience was exactly what Sherman needed. New life entered his veins as he went about the task of providing support for Grant. The old self-doubt and fear of failure were no longer visible. He was part of an action that he viewed as vital and necessary if the war were to be won. A born quartermaster, he had a sure grasp of the important factors of supply and transport, and he used them well. Grant succeeded, at least in part, because he knew Sherman was supporting him with the essentials of battle. The experience for Sherman proved to be valuable in another way. Later in the war, his reputation as a commander and master strategist would be grounded in his knowledge of supply and transport. Such knowledge would ensure the security of his moves through Georgia and the Carolinas. Indeed, Sherman became a master strategist because he was a born quartermaster.[13]

Sherman's observations of Grant's victories at Forts Henry and Donelson taught him a lesson in warfare that would remain with him throughout the Civil War. Upon hearing the details of Grant's victory at Donelson, Sherman, as well as other strategists, was surprised, almost shocked. "Grant had violated an orthodox rule by besieging a fort that held as many as or more men than he commanded." Military texts, particularly the one written by Jomini, had established a firm guideline when attacking fortifications—the attacker must possess a five to one advantage.[14] Sherman, throughout his military career, would never encounter a similar situation. The lesson was in the boldness of the act. Grant had taken a risk, but due to his determination, he had succeeded. The man who had committed the act also impressed Sherman, and, from Fort Donelson on, his admiration for Grant never ceased and a trusting friendship developed that would never die.

After the capture of Donelson, Halleck, fearful and probably a bit envious of Grant's success, began to find fault with the future commander of the Union forces. Besides providing improper reports to Halleck, Grant traveled to Nashville without explaining the purpose of the trip. He was, therefore, out of touch with his superior for a number of days. Although the trip was for military purposes, Halleck assumed that Grant, who had a long and well-known record of drinking heavily at times, was away celebrating his victory. He sent word to Washington of his suspicion and in less than two weeks after the victory at Donelson, Grant was restricted to his tent without a command. Dejected and doubtful of his position, Grant asked to be relieved. Due to Lincoln's intervention, however, the request was not granted and on March 13, he was restored to command.

In this period of difficulty, Grant was encouraged not only by Sherman's words but by the memory of how Sherman had supported him during the Donelson battle. He appreciated the speed with which Sherman had kept him supplied. Years later Grant would write in his memoirs of this period:

> During the siege of Donelson General Sherman had been sent to Smithland . . . to forward reinforcements and supplies to me. At that time he was my senior in rank and there was no authority of law to assign a junior to command a senior of the same grade. But every boat that came up with supplies or reinforcements brought a note of encouragement from Sherman, asking me to call upon him for any assistance he could render and saying that if he could be of service at the front I might send him and he would waive rank.[15]

Sherman was anxious to grow close to Grant because he saw in him a man unafraid to act. All around him Sherman had observed nothing but hesitancy on the part of commanders. This man was different; he was in the middle of action, and Sherman wanted to be part of it even if he had to waive his rank in the process. Both probably perceived in each other a number of similarities that drew them together. Although Grant had fallen further into the humility of failure than Sherman, each had been tried and tested; and although their temperaments were quite different (Grant was basically calm, quiet and withdrawn, while Sherman was nervous, vocal, and outgoing), they must have sensed a commonality, an identity with each other. Instant trust became a characteristic between them that would develop and last throughout their lives. This was just the beginning of a relationship that would bring them both fame and military glory. As T. Harry Williams so aptly put it, "Now began the great partnership of Grant and Sherman, the association that would profoundly influence Sherman's whole personality and later career."[16]

Sherman's eagerness to work with and for Grant did not extend however to getting involved with the dispute with Halleck. Encouraging Grant privately was one thing, but trying to intervene directly with Halleck was another matter. Had the Grant-Halleck dispute occurred three months earlier, Sherman more than likely would have done so, and such action would have probably had regrettable consequences. It would have destroyed the friendship and support Halleck had displayed for Sherman during a time he really needed it. But, not this time. Sherman was achieving the stability he had sought for so long, and his perception of when to speak and when to remain silent was clear. So, instead of attempting to intervene on behalf of Grant, he steered clear of the conflict and busied himself with strategy. At last "his mind was functioning clearly; intense apprehension had turned into acute penetration." Instead of brooding "over himself as a wronged man"[17] and striking out at the least provocation, he studied the enemy, prepared for any eventuality, and encouraged Grant quietly and in ways that would not embroil himself in the conflict. He had at last achieved maturity as his social setting defined maturity. He would never be comfortable with the ridiculous actions of the system, but he had learned to give it respect and use it to his own gain.

In March, Sherman and his division left Paducah, steamed up the Tennessee River just beyond Fort Henry, and encamped with the forces of Brig. Gen. C. F. Smith. He was to participate in the southward movement of Halleck's forces to capture Corinth, Mississippi. This city was a central supply depot and base of operations for Confederate armies in the Mississippi Valley. Three days after Sherman's arrival, Smith ordered him to move forward and destroy the

Memphis and Charleston Railroad between Tuscumbia, Alabama, and Corinth, Mississippi. Due to high waters and a downpour of rain, the attempt failed and Sherman returned to Pittsburg Landing. In spite of the failure, the experience was profitable for Sherman. This attempt to break the "vertebrae of the South"[18] impressed on his mind more than ever Napoleon's truth that "the whole secret of war lies in being master of the communications."[19]

Joining forces with Grant, Sherman encamped on the banks of the Tennessee River near a small log church called Shiloh. Here he would remain until he was engulfed in the largest battle of his military career. While there he made himself "familiar with all the ground inside and outside my lines."[20] He must have sensed that something spectacular was on the horizon, that at last things were beginning to move. He was sure that the West was where the Union could weaken the Confederacy. "A stab in the back is as fatal as one in the breast,"[21] thus he acted on the supposition that he was leading an invasion force to break the back of the South.[22] Just four months earlier Sherman was at home in Lancaster, convinced he would never experience command in the field. Now he was making preparations for war. No longer was he afraid. No longer did he exaggerate the size of his enemy.[23] He had achieved peace within himself and confidence in his abilities, and he had a clear understanding of what must be done to wage war against the South.

Externally, he still looked the same, but "his moodiness had all but disappeared." Merrill has constructed a graphic picture of Sherman on the eve of the Battle of Shiloh that is worthy of repeating here. The "nervous energy, the rich imagination" were still evident and his mind continued "running restlessly on all sorts of subjects." Merrill states, "Sandy-haired and gaunt, with a grizzled, short-cropped beard, Sherman still had that 'wild expression in his eyes.'" One observer stated, "I never saw him but I thought of Lazarus." He was described in the following manner, "His shoulders twitched, and his hands were never still, always drumming on a table or fiddling with his beard or fidgeting with the buttons on his coat." And he probably sensed that "The men under his command, most of them just out of training camp, did not relish tasting combat for the first time under a man who had been, but a short time ago, suspected of 'insanity' and 'emotional imbalance.'"

In spite of his physical appearance and the probable suspicion he knew existed among his troops, Sherman was ready. Although still somewhat insecure, he had a clear grasp of himself and his place in the total scope of things. Merrill continues with a report of a visit to Sherman's headquarters by S. M. Dayton, a friend of Thomas Ewing's. Dayton "came away from the interview believing that the general was the most self-effacing man he had ever met." He said, "Sherman discussed in detail the war and his own status in the army. He indicated that he was entirely satisfied with his present command and that he desired nothing more from Washington except to be left alone. 'I aspire to nothing and will ask for nothing.'"

Shortly after Dayton's visit, Sherman, in a letter to Ewing wrote, "Give my love to everybody, and all I ask is to be allowed to fill a subordinate place in this war. The issues involved are too great to be the subject of personal ambition."[24]

During the late days of March, all was serene and quiet around the sleepy little church near the west bank of the Tennessee River. However, the peace was not to last. Two Union armies—the Army of the Tennessee and the Army of the Ohio, with combined forces of 60,000—were converging on the area. By the end of March these young Federals, most untried in battle, were gathering with naive confidence and strong assurance that victory would soon be at hand. Beyond the low hills these novices of warfare could see Southern cavalrymen in reconnaissance. One private wrote his girlfriend, "I gazed from a lofty eminence, my darling sweetheart, and looked upon the Rebels with vigor and contempt."[25]

A similar naive confidence ran through the Southern ranks twenty-two miles southwest of Pittsburg Landing at Corinth. "One Southerner can whip three Yankees" was a statement often heard among the men of the Confederate army gathering at that small Mississippi town.[26] The Confederate generals were planning a surprise attack—the one thing Grant felt they would not do. With 44,000 men under his command, Gen. Albert Sidney Johnston was making preparations to attack the Union forces and, with a victory, redeem his losses of Kentucky and Tennessee.[27] " . . . You can but march to a decisive victory over agrarian mercenaries, sent to subjugate and despoil you of your liberties, property and honor," Johnston told his men on April 3. "The eyes and hopes of 8,000,000 . . . people rest upon you."[28]

Thus it was that through the early days of April 1862, these two great armies drew close together like "two herds of apprentice killers, pathetically eager to learn their trade in what Sherman, then and later, frankly reminded his men was 'horrid war.'"[29]

On Sunday morning, April 6, the Battle of Shiloh began, and for two days the two armies were involved in heavy engagement. When it ended on the evening of April 7, the blood and gore of human violence was evident in every corner of the battlefield. Nothing like this had happened before in the Western hemisphere. It was also evident that people's view of war would never be the same. Shiloh, and the horrible acts committed there, created significant changes in attitudes, not only of its participants but of those who heard of its sickening details. Wiley Sword, in his introduction to the reprint of *Shiloh: Bloody April*, writes of these changes. He says, "Originally, from the standpoint of the participants, Shiloh contributed to a significant metamorphosis—if only in the attitude of the common soldier. Beyond the grisly horrors endured, the battle largely reflected a maturing of perspective—a toughening in posture of and a commitment of inner resolve—that provided the tenacity to endure all that the Civil War was—the crossroads of our destiny." Not only were the fighting men affected, but so too were their leaders. Sword continues, "As a vital personal influence Shiloh also provided an enormous impetus. From the fiery conflict . . . emerged the fighting qualities that were to sustain many of the war's most important leaders. The tenacious, bull dog determination of U. S. Grant, the icy calculating nerve of 'Billy' Sherman, and the furious combative ardor of Bedford Forrest and Pat Cleburne, were perhaps first evident at Shiloh." Sword explains, "Yet, most of all, the Battle of Shiloh had a profoundly sobering effect upon the nation. The Civil War, initially thought of in mostly idealistic and patriotic terms, was finally revealed to be a terrible, drawn out ordeal of indeterminable tragedy. Beyond the already grim loss of life and limb, the dreadful prospect that many thousands more of America's sons would be sacrificed before the fighting ended loomed in full perspective. If before there had been thoughts of a quick, almost bloodless termination of the conflict, there belatedly remained only the prospect of dire, unrelenting warfare."[30]

The battle's outcome was disappointing to both sides, though both claimed victory. It gave rise to intense and sustained controversy between supporters of rival leaders on both sides. In the North, Grant and Sherman were violently assailed for being surprised by

the Confederates on the first morning of fighting and for not pursuing them the next afternoon. On the Southern side, there was almost
universal belief that nothing but the death of General Johnston had
prevented the capture and annihilation of the Federal army on the
first day and that Beauregard faltered by calling the fighting to an
end on the second.

A re-enactment of Shiloh is not necessary for the purpose of this
study. The reader is encouraged to turn to the numerous works
available for details. What is important for the present analysis are
the lessons learned by Sherman, the manner in which he conducted
himself, and the impact Shiloh had on him and his development. It
was here on the banks of the Tennessee River that Sherman was able
to restore his broken pride with what some have called heroic action.
Shiloh proved to be a type of spiritual tonic, a tonic for new life.

During the heat of the battle, Sherman was everywhere: encouraging his troops, rallying the stragglers, directing the batteries, con-
ferring with other commanders, superintending every movement in
person. He fought with great skill and energy and had much to do
with saving the Union army from destruction. Although surprised
on that first morning (a situation he never admitted), he did not
panic and was successful in preventing a rout from developing. His
ability to switch at a moment's notice, both mentally and physically,
from the offensive to the defensive, partially saved the day.[31] As a
result, those who had earlier seen him as crazy did not deny his
energy, coolness, courage, skill, and perseverance after his performance at Shiloh.

He was wounded twice; one bullet passed through his hand and a
second tore his shoulder strap, scratching his skin. A third bullet
barely missed his head, traveling through his hat. Before the end of
the action three horses had died under his saddle.[32]

The men who fought beside him remarked after the battle that
"all around him were excited orderlies and officers, but though his
face was besmeared with powder and blood, battle seemed to have
cooled his usually hot nerves." Still others remarked that he had not
waved his arms when he talked, and had not talked as much as in the
past. Indeed, it appeared "Sherman had found something to make
him forget himself, completely, utterly."[33] His behavior gained for
him the trust and confidence of his men. Sherman was an entirely
different person when in battle. Said an officer who had known him

for years, "At such times his eccentricities disappeared, his grasp of the situation was firm and clear, his judgment was cool and based upon sound military theory as well as upon quick practical judgment; and no momentary complication or unexpected event could move him from the purpose he had based on full previous study of contingencies. His mind seemed never so clear, his confidence never so strong, his spirit never so inspiring, and his temper never so amiable as in the crisis of some fierce struggle. . . ."[34] The young lieutenant, John T. Taylor, Sherman's aide-de-camp, remarked: "General Sherman's conduct soon instilled . . . a feeling that it was grand to be there with him."[35] And Lt. Patrick White of Company B, First Illinois Artillery, concluded that Sherman was "the coolest man I saw that day."[36] Sword gives this account of Sherman's behavior, "Sherman would remain with his handful of men, 'struggling to maintain this line,' unmindful of personal danger. Indeed, he may have considered that his troops no longer could influence the outcome of the battle. Yet Sherman's presence counted for much. His leadership on the field of battle fired men's souls. It inspired bravery and it steadied their nerves. When the fighting was over, they would speak in awe of Sherman's valor. He was the genius born of crisis."[37]

This was his first important battle command, yet so ingrained were the details of war upon his mind that his spirit leaped at once beyond the novelty of the situation and wore the new experience like an old habit. He experienced the strange joy of profound selflessness that is necessary for a successful military commander in combat. Here amid the clash of human flesh, William Tecumseh Sherman came into his own. This was the turning point. Shiloh was the testing ground for his stability, and he emerged victorious. Shiloh gave him the needed self-confidence he had lacked for so many years.

Sherman knew that he had performed well and that, at last, the crisis of his life was over. To Ellen, with apparent satisfaction, he wrote, "I won't attempt to give an account of the battle, but they say I accomplished some important results, and General Grant makes special mention of me in his report, which he showed me."[38] The one man whose approval he had rapidly come to respect recognized his contribution. That, of course, was Grant. At Donelson, Sherman was drawn to Grant because of his boldness and willingness to act. At Shiloh, not only did he see firsthand that boldness in action, specifically in the form of the importance of the offensive in war, but he also learned from Grant the need to remain cool and in control when apparent defeat was imminent. During the fighting on Sunday, April 6, Grant passed from one part of the field to another. In later years he left this recollection of that eventful day: "During the whole of Sunday I was continuously engaged in passing from one part of the field to another, giving directions to division commanders. In thus moving along the line, however, I never deemed it important to stay long with Sherman." He felt that Sherman was in control and even though he commanded troops who had never "seen the elephant," he "by his constant presence with them, inspired a confidence in officers and men that enabled them to render services on that bloody battlefield worthy of the best veterans." Sherman's division was experiencing some of the hardest fighting of the day. Grant spoke further of the importance of his new-found friend, "A casualty to Sherman that would have taken him from the field . . . would have been a sad one for the troops engaged at Shiloh. And how near we came to this! On the 6th Sherman was shot twice. . . ."[39] After the fighting, in his official report, Grant said, "I feel it a duty . . . to a gallant and able officer, Brig. Gen. W. T. Sherman, to make a special mention. He not only was with the command during the entire two days' action, but displayed great judgment and skill in the management of his men. Although severely wounded in the hand the first day his place was never vacant."[40]

Such praise would not end at Shiloh, for the ability and untiring energy displayed by Sherman during the siege of Corinth elicited the applause of Grant. Afterwards, in an official dispatch, Grant would write, "His service as division commander in the advance on Corinth, I will venture to say [was] appreciated by the now general-in-chief [General Halleck] beyond those of any other division commander."[41]

A few days after the Battle of Shiloh, Sherman's friend and supporter, Halleck, arrived on the field and observed, " . . . it is the unanimous opinion here that Brigadier General W. T. Sherman saved the fortunes of the day on the 6th, and contributed largely to the glorious victory on the 7th. . . . I respectfully recommend that he be made a major general of volunteers to date from the 6th instant."[42] In urging Sherman's promotion as a major general, Grant wrote to the War Department: "At the battle of Shiloh, on the first day, he held, with raw troops, the key point of the landing."

Grant went on to say, "It is no disparagement to any other officer to say, that I do not believe there was another division commander on the field who had the skill and experience to have done it. To his individual efforts I am indebted for the success of that battle."[43]

But perhaps the greatest satisfaction Sherman received was in the form of vindication. After the battle, a New York reporter interviewed Sherman and remarked on how different he was from when he had last talked with him in Missouri. The reporter said, "Since I first saw him, his eyes had grown much calmer, and his nervous system healthier."[44] Even the highly belligerent Cincinnati *Commercial* "shifted its anti-Sherman posture." Its publisher "acknowledged to Tom Ewing the gross wrongs the newspaper had inflicted on his now famous brother-in-law."[45]

Shiloh brought a marriage of two men who would ultimately play key roles in healing the ruptured Union. Grant and Sherman were meant for each other militarily. Although historians have generally emphasized the contrasts between them, actually they were quite similar. Both were from the Midwest, and only two years separated them in age, with Sherman the older of the two. Both had graduated from West Point. Neither had been willing to sacrifice his individuality and, therefore, was never viewed as an outstanding cadet. Sherman was noted for his sloppiness and nervous energy, Grant for his proficient horsemanship. Both had gone on to various military posts where they had reaped nothing but obscurity and disappointment. Although the Mexican War had not passed Grant by as it did Sherman, it gained him little recognition. Eventually, due to personal problems, both had left the army to seek a life in the civilian sector. Each had failed following attempt after attempt and regretted having ever left the military. Grant sank the lowest economically and lived many of his days in abject poverty. Sherman was affected the most psychologically, being thrust by circumstances and himself into a serious state of self-doubt. The war provided both with opportunities to pull themselves from their respective doldrums. Grant acted first, Sherman more cautiously. Both had re-entered the military with the hope of achieving stability and success. They wanted it for themselves and their families. These similarities almost automatically drew these two men together. Indeed, almost in a mysterious manner, they knew each other well. They became fast friends and colleagues and grew to have great admiration for each other—Grant for Sherman's intelligence and skill, Sherman for Grant's confidence, determination and fighting abilities. Although opportunities arose, they never saw each other as rivals.

Granted, there were also contrasts. Sherman was tall and thin with sharp features, sandy-red hair and gray eyes. His speech was rapid and his gestures highly animated. As already noted, his mind was full of ideas which were expressed with great rapidity. Grant was short and of modest build. His hair and beard were darker than Sherman's and much fuller. His eye "seemed formed rather to resist than aid the interpretation of his thought and never betrayed . . ." his ideas.[46] Grant had a heavy-set jaw, a square brow and slightly stooped shoulders. He spoke slowly, yet always to the point, and there was nothing of the flamboyant about him. His entire demeanor spoke of simplicity. However, as Badeau put it:

> In battle . . . the sphinx awoke, the riddle was solved. The outward calm indeed was even then not entirely broken, but the utterance was prompt, the ideas were rapid, the judgement was decisive; the words were those of command; the whole man became intense as it were with a white heat. His nature indeed seemed like a sword, drawn only in the field or in emergencies. At ordinary times a scabbard concealed the sharpness and temper of the blade; but when this was thrown aside, amid din of battle, the weapon flashed and thrust and smote—and won.[47]

"Never were two so dissimilar men ever associated in a great military enterprise," writes C. E. Macartney. "Grant was charmed, interested, and fascinated by Sherman. Sherman relied confidently in the strength and judgment of his superior."[48]

Maj. Gen. Oliver O. Howard, during the conflict at Chattanooga, provided an interesting and perceptive study of the two generals. He wrote, "It was a privilege to see these two men, Grant and Sherman, together. Their unusual friendship—unusual in men who would naturally be rivals—was like that of David and Jonathan. It was always evident, and did not grow from likeness, but from unlikeness. They appeared rather the complements of each other—where the one was especially strong, the other was less so, and vice versa. It was a marriage of characters, in sympathy, by the adjustment of differences." Howard seemed to have captured the essence of this relationship. There were differences, in some cases drastic ones, yet instead of creating dissention and conflict, they drew the two men together. The differences complemented each other, thus a symbiotic relationship was established where each became dependent on the other. These two dissimilar organisms found it mutually beneficial to live together. Howard continues his analysis: "Grant in command was . . . habitually reticent. Sherman was never so. Grant meditated on the situation, withholding his opinion until his plan was well matured. Sherman quickly, brilliantly, gave you half a dozen." And further:

> Grant appeared more inclined to systematize and simplify; bring up sufficient force to outnumber; do unexpected things; take promptly the offensive; follow up a victory. It was a simple, straightforward calculus which avoided too much complication. It made Grant the man for campaign and battle. Sherman was always at his best in campaign—in general manoeuvers—better than in actual battle. His great knowledge of history, his to-pographical scope, his intense suggestive facilities seemed often to be impaired by the actual conflict. And the reason is plain; such a mind and body as his, full of impulse, full of fire, are more likely to be perturbed by excitement than is the more ironbound constitution of a Grant. . . .

Howard concludes with, "Sherman, patriotic all through, was very self-reliant. He believed in neglecting fractions and was not afraid of responsibility. Grant, probably much influenced by his earliest teachings, relied on Providence than simply on himself; he gathered the fragments for use, and was also strong to dare, because somehow, without saying so, he struck the blows of a persistent faith."[49]

In October 1864, with the perspective of two years of fighting, Sherman, visiting with Brig. Gen. James H. Wilson, contrasted his generalship with Grant's. He said:

> Wilson, I am a damn sight smarter than Grant. I know a great deal more about war, military history, strategy, and grand tactics than he does; I know more about organization, supply, and administration, and about, everything else than he does. But I tell you where he beats me, and where he beats the world. He don't care a damn for what the enemy does out of his sight, but it scares me like hell. . . . I am more nervous than he is, I am more likely to change my orders, or to countermarch my command than he is. He uses such information as he has, according to his best judgement. He issues his orders and does his level best to carry them out without much reference to what is going on about him. And, so far, experience seems to have fully justified.[50]

This new and unique relationship, a perfect blending of similarities and differences, was cemented even further as a result of Halleck's actions. After the Battle of Shiloh, Halleck took steps to reorganize the armies of the West. In addition, for political reasons and due to the criticisms Grant was receiving in the newspapers concerning his handling of the troops at Shiloh, Halleck relegated Grant to the empty post of second-in-command, with Halleck as his superior in the field. This immediately threw Grant into a state of depression. He asked for and received a thirty-day leave and voiced feelings about leaving the army. Upon hearing this, Sherman sought Grant out. He found him in his tent sitting on a stool, sorting letters. Immediately Sherman beseeched him to stay, "illustrating his case as my own." The words Sherman said to Grant are important not simply because of the positive influence they had, but also because they reveal the place at which Sherman had arrived in his own development. Sherman recalled the comments in his *Memoirs*. He said to Grant:

> Before the battle of Shiloh, I had been cast down by a mere newspaper assertion of 'crazy'; but that single battle had given me new life, and now I was in high feather; and I argued with him that, if he went away, events would go right along, and he would be left out; whereas, if he remained, some happy accident might restore him to favor and his true place. He certainly appreciated my friendly advice, and promised to wait awhile; at all events, not to go without seeing me again, or communicating with me. Very soon, after this, . . . on the 6th of June, I received a note from him saying that he had reconsidered his intention, and would remain.[51]

The past and the present were drawing the two together. Sherman was feeling for Grant that powerful emotion which one feels for a person whom he has befriended and considered to be important to him. Through the confidence Grant gave Sherman, Sherman's own confidence grew. Now, by helping Grant, Sherman displayed that long-needed spiritual awakening. T. Harry Williams describes accurately the meaning of Grant's relationship for Sherman. He writes, "Sherman blossomed under Grant's supervision. He became sure of himself. He was deft and decisive on the field and able and fertile in counsel. In some way the stolid and apparently prosaic Grant gave the mercurial and seemingly more brilliant Sherman a poise and a balance theretofore lacking." According to Williams, and he is right,

Sherman was quite cognizant "of the transformation and of Grant's part in it, and he analyzed it with a realism that reflected his growing sense of security." Williams attributes Sherman's growth to "a simple faith in success"[52] that he observed in Grant, and the realization that no longer was he alone. Writing to Grant, Sherman summed up his feelings in this way, " . . . when you have completed your best preparations you go to battle without hesitation . . . no doubts, no reserve; and I tell you that it was this that made me act with confidence. I knew wherever I was that you thought of me, and that if I got in a tight place you would come—if alive."[53]

The bond created at Shiloh would last and continue to be cultivated by both men. At Vicksburg, Sherman strongly opposed Grant's final plan against the Confederates, yet Sherman followed orders to the letter, and when it proved successful it was Sherman who made public his opposition. To a group of civilians, he said, "Grant is entitled to every bit of credit in the campaign. I opposed it; I wrote him a letter about it."[54] After Sherman's successful march to the sea, it was Grant who gave Sherman full credit for devising the move. He said, "The question of who devised the plan of march from Atlanta to Savannah is easily answered: it was clearly Sherman, and to him belongs the credit of its brilliant execution."[55] When a bill was introduced in Congress to raise Sherman to the rank of lieutenant general and perhaps even general-in-chief, Sherman wrote Grant: " . . . I have written to John Sherman to stop it. . . . I would rather have you in command than anybody else. . . . I should emphatically decline any commission calculated to bring us into rivalry; and I ask you to advise your friends . . . to this effect."[56] And finally, when Grant was ordered to North Carolina to inform Sherman of the government's rejection of the peace treaty terms Sherman had negotiated with Joseph E. Johnston, instead of publicly humiliating his friend, Grant slipped secretly into Raleigh. After advising Sherman to demand the immediate surrender of Johnston's army, Grant slipped quietly away, declining Sherman's invitation to meet with him and Johnston. The relationship they had created did not provide room for jealousy or rivalry. They were of one accord and one purpose.

Just as uplifting for Sherman's morale was the greeting he received from the rank and file of his troops. In an advance during the battle, Sherman met the same Kentucky troops who six months earlier had disliked him so much at Muldraugh's Hill, thirty-six miles south of Louisville. Now when they saw him with his hat in tatters, black powder on his face, and his hand bandaged, they cheered with "such shouting you never heard." A few days later he visited their camp and "never before received such marks of favor."[57] Praise was also lavished on him by his fellow officers as well. In later years Lovell H. Rousseau would say, "Sherman gave us our first lessons in the field in the face of the enemy" and A. D. Nelson would add, "During the eight hours the fate of the army depended on the life of one man; if General Sherman had fallen, the army would have been captured and destroyed."[58]

Sherman would always remember these cheers and words of praise for they were the first he had received since the beginning of the war, and they came at a most appropriate time. The memory of them would remain with him and continue to supply him with confidence as he waged total war on the South.

Shiloh further hardened Sherman's prejudices toward politicians and the press. But this time he kept his comments private. Never a lover of either since his California days, his dislike was greatly intensified by his Kentucky and Missouri trials. As a result of their attack on Grant's handling of the battle at Pittsburg Landing, Sherman continued his fight against them in Tennessee. To Ellen he wrote, "The very object of war is to produce results by death and slaughter, but the moment a battle occurs the newspapers make the leader responsible for the death and misery, whether of victory or defeat. If this be pushed much further officers of modesty and merit will keep away, will draw back into obscurity and leave our armies to be led by fools or rash men."[59]

Concerning both politicians and editors he wrote these harsh words to his wife: " . . . I do feel for the thousands that think another battle will end the war. I hope that the war won't end until those who caused the war, the politicians and editors, are made to feel it. The scoundrels take good care of their hides, run up after a fight and back again before there is a chance for another. . . ."[60]

To his father-in-law he angrily wrote, "We all knew we were assembling a vast army for an aggressive purpose. The President knew it. Halleck knew it, and the whole country knew it, and the attempt to throw blame on Grant is villainous. The fact is, if newspapers are to be our government, I confess, I would prefer [Braxton] Bragg,

[P. G. T.] Beauregard, or anybody as my ruler, and I will persist in my determination never to be a leader responsible to such power."[61]

Even as late as June, almost a full two months after the Battle of Shiloh, Sherman had not dropped the matter. From Corinth he wrote Ellen, "I will get even with the miserable class of corrupt editors yet. They are the chief cause of this unhappy war. They fan the flames of local hatred, and keep alive those prejudices which have forced friends into opposing hostile ranks. [N]o sooner does an officer rise from the common level, but some rival uses the press to malign him, destroy his usefulness, and pull him back to obscurity or infamy. Thus it was with me, and now they have nearly succeeded with Grant."[62] Disgustedly, he tried to conclude the issue with this: "Let them scramble for the dead lion's paw. It is a barren honor not worthy of contending for. If these examples and a few more will convince the real substantial men of our country that the press is not even an honest exponent of the claims of men pretending to serve their country, but the base means of building up spurious fame, and pulling down honest merit. I feel that I have my full reward in being one of the first to see it and suffer the consequences."[63]

Later, while stationed at Memphis, Sherman would once again attack the politicians and editors by accusing them of being greater enemies to the country than the men who had taken up arms against the government.[64] Unfortunately for Sherman, this battle was a long, but futile one. He would eventually have the power to make the South bend its knee at his presence, but he would never manage to win against his two greatest enemies, not even the smallest skirmish. But, never again would either come close to defeating him as at one time they almost did.

Sherman's experience at Shiloh bolstered his belief that the "very object of war is to produce results by death and slaughter." Writing to Ellen he drew a vivid picture of the scene and aftermath of battle: "The scenes on this field would have cured anybody of war. Mangled bodies, dead, dying, in every conceivable shape, without heads, legs; and the horses! I think we have buried 2,000 since the fight, our own and the enemy's; and the wounded fill houses, tents, steamboats and every conceivable place. All I can say [is] this was a battle, and you will receive so many graphic accounts that my picture will be tame."[65] The scenes of death and suffering horrified Sherman, and as he surveyed the aftermath of the bloodiest battle ever fought to

that point on the North American continent, he grew in his determination to do all in his power to bring the war to an end as quickly
as possible.

Immediately after Shiloh, while waiting for Halleck to decide how
best to pursue the Confederate army to Corinth, Sherman set to
work teaching his division the rules of soldiering. He became a
painstaking drill instructor, talking, writing, and explaining every
detail. He placed sentries himself, galloped along picket lines, taught
his men how to fell trees for fortifications, and how to clear under-
brush. Sherman took the time to lead his men on lateral movements
and taught them the art of marching effectively. He showed them
how and where to dig sinks and how to improve sanitation while
encamped. He explained to cannoneers how to cut hay for their
horses the moment a march ends, and he worked to put a halt to the
malingering of officers and men around tents and hospitals. He
issued a general order which stated, "If the men are unable to bear
arms, they will form on the left of the company unarmed. If not in
the hospital, but suffering from diarrhea, they can be hauled to the
drill-ground by the colonel's order and there must be silent and
observe the movements of the division."[66] Constantly concerned
about the carelessness of officers, sentinels, and troops, it was his
purpose to establish new habits of behavior by persistent drill and
training.[67]

As early as the days following Bull Run, Sherman set an example
for his officers and men. He would not permit his wife to visit him in
1861 because he felt it would have a negative impact on his troops.[68]
After the Battle of Shiloh he was determined to continue this pattern. Although stricken by malaria while building bridges in swamp
land, he scorned shelter and lay by the roadside and directed the
work. Eventually, he had to be placed in an ambulance, but stayed at
the scene of activity so that he could see and hear the men working
and, when necessary, send orders.[69]

In his official report of the Battle of Shiloh, Sherman commented
on a number of important aspects concerning the morale and training of troops. Advancing his troops to the Corinth road, he saw the
well-ordered and compact columns of General Buell's Army of the
Ohio forces. This formation not only impressed Sherman, but also
"gave confidence to our newer and less disciplined men."[70] He also
made reference to the importance of a regiment holding its ground.

As he put it, "to retire a regiment for any cause, has a bad effect on them."[71]

The most difficult problem Sherman faced was training his hungry men how to forage for their brigades without pillaging civilians. In this, he was like other officers of the time. Foraging should be done with complete respect for private property and in accordance with military law. Like other officers, Sherman had on occasion to bring the force of that law down on violators. He issued orders giving quartermasters authority to submit receipts to civilians with the promise that they would eventually receive payment from the United States government on proof of loyalty. Writing later concerning this period of the war, Sherman would say that he "had personally beaten and kicked men out of yards for merely going inside." It would not be long, however, until he would change his views concerning foraging. The attitudes of Southerners and their constant efforts to hamper the movement of troops would make him realize the absurdity of fighting an enemy in traditional ways. Sherman was coming to realize that the army ought to act in ways that would effectively wean noncombatants from allegiance to their flag. If this could be done by taking from them their means of subsistence, then well and good. At this point, however, Sherman still held to the traditional attitude toward foraging and continued to lecture his officers and men that their mission "is to maintain, not to violate, all laws human and divine."[72] But, he was only a few months away from making a radical change, a change that would make him the power defining what the laws of war meant.

Overall, the time spent working with his troops from Shiloh to Corinth was productive in Sherman's mind. Concerning the march itself, he wrote in his *Memoirs*, "I esteemed it a magnificent drill, as it served for the instruction of our men in guard and picket duty, and in habituating them to outdoor life: and by the time we had reached Corinth I believe that army was the best then on this continent, and could have gone where it pleased."[73]

Although the Union forces had collapsed at Shiloh, the causes were intriguing to Sherman. Fully expecting to be on the offensive, the Union troops were surprised at having to stand on the defensive. They were prepared to hit and never dreamed of having to guard. The experience taught Sherman that if it is to be successful an army must not settle into a single mode. It must always be prepared to execute any plan which promises success. The unexpected is the key. An army must be flexible. Shiloh taught him that surprise is much more effective than numerical superiority. He learned this well on the first day when Johnston's forces attacked his division, and he witnessed it again when Grant, seemingly defeated, surprised the Confederates by turning a retreat into an offensive action.

On May 26, 1862, Sherman received from the War Department his commission as major general of volunteers.[74] He readily and proudly accepted the promotion and wrote to Ellen, "I received today the commission of Major General, but, I know not why, it gives me far less emotion than my old commission as 1st Lieutenant of Artillery. The latter, I know, I merited; this I doubt, but its possession completes the chain from cadet up, and will remain among the family archives when you and I repose in eternity."[75]

So, Shiloh was the turning point for Sherman; it was the testing ground for his stability and from it he emerged victorious. Not only did he prove to others that he had the ability to perform, he proved to himself that he was capable of being a soldier. Shiloh gave him the needed self-confidence he had lacked for so long. At Shiloh, Sherman took control not only of himself but of his profession. Finally he was confident he could take any position he wished among his peers.[76]

# CHAPTER FIVE

# *"War Is Destruction and Nothing Else"*

IN MID-JULY 1862, Henry Halleck was promoted to general-in-chief of all the armies of the United States and ordered to report to Washington. Grant was given command of the forces in western Tennessee and northern Mississippi, while Sherman was placed in command of the District of West Tennessee. Before leaving for Washington, Halleck sent words of thanks and encouragement to Sherman, saying, "I am more than satisfied with everything you have done. You have always had my respect, but recently you have won my highest admiration. I deeply regret to part from you"[1] Sherman could not have been more pleased than to have received such praise from his commander, and he expressed his appreciation by telling Halleck, "I thank you for the kind expression to me. . . . You cannot be replaced out here. . . . We are all the losers. . . ."[2] So, as his friend and supporter headed east to the nation's capital, Sherman, deeply grateful for Halleck's sustenance and patronage, traveled west to Memphis where he was ordered to be the military administrator of that recently captured Confederate city. And thus began the final stage in his evolutionary development of warfare.

At the beginning of the war Sherman's notions on conducting warfare were similar to those of most professional soldiers of the day. As John Barrett puts it, "He understood and accepted the sanction that the noncombatant population, as well as private property generally, should be free of molestation except where military

127

necessity prevailed."[3] A few months in Memphis, in contact with the civilian enemy, changed his mind. Ironically, Sherman would forever be indebted to this Southern city for teaching him the need for total war.

When Sherman arrived in Memphis on July 21, he found the city "dead; no business doing, the stores closed, churches, schools, and every thing shut up."[4] The citizens who remained after the Confederate army was forced to evacuate the city were Southern sympathizers and were far from pleased to see Sherman and his troops. Most remained indoors, while a few were bold enough to venture on the streets to show their displeasure at being citizens of an occupied city.

For Sherman, such conditions were intolerable, and he set out at once to bring Memphis back to life. In his view, a dead and hostile captured city would eventually become a serious drain on the Union forces. He, therefore, ordered all the stores opened and churches, schools, theaters, and places of amusement and recreation to be reestablished. He even organized a program to aid the poor and destitute. Because the city was a Union base of operations, Sherman put his men to work on fortifications. When he had to destroy a number of buildings for this purpose, he authorized compensation for the owners. He also restored the mayor to his position and started city government on the road to functioning again. Although he took no action to close down the houses of prostitution, he did reorganize the local police force and assisted them in clearing the streets of thugs and other malcontents. Determined to show the citizens that he wanted to work with them rather than against them, "he issued an order permitting trade, without military or Treasury Department passes, over the five roads leading into the city from the surrounding areas."[5] He informed the mayor that he would not, unless necessary, interfere with the function of civil courts and would provide assistance in helping the city council collect taxes.[6] As a result of such actions, it was not long before the city resumed an appearance of an active, busy, prosperous place.[7] Sherman understood well the need for organization in peoples' lives; it provided stability and predictability, so he made sure he and his troops "displayed . . . regard for the rights of citizens and . . . concern for their welfare."[8] Yet the underlying purpose in all the steps he took to establish a state of normalcy in Memphis was of a military nature. He was a soldier, and his duty was to fight his country's enemy as effectively as possible so as to bring the war to an end. By establishing normalcy through organization, he felt he could "teach Southerners that war was terrible and peace beautiful, that rebellion meant ruin, while obedience to law meant, in the end, prosperity."[9] His hope was that "by a policy of justice and mercy he might nurture in the citizens of Memphis a renewed loyalty to the Union."[10]

Despite these acts of leniency, Sherman constantly held before the citizens of Memphis the fact that the city was a military garrison and would be treated as such. He would not let them forget that this was war, a war to determine which people, "that of the North or South, shall rule America."[11] There was no doubt in his mind as to who should rule, and his actions and words gave clear evidence of his position. He made it understood that it was his responsibility to put the city in a thorough state of defense. To do this he ordered that, when the head of a family headed South, the entire family must follow. The quartermaster was to seize all buildings left vacant and belonging to disloyal owners, and such buildings were to be leased when possible. All blacks working for the United States were to be registered and an account of their time kept so that payment could be made for their services.

Hundreds of slaves were being sent into Memphis from the surrounding occupied territory, and Sherman saw in them a weapon to be used against the South. A staunch anti-abolitionist, he did not favor giving them their freedom, yet he was not adverse to using them for military purposes. Neither Congress nor the president had as of that time provided a clear policy as to how they should be treated by the army. Different generals had issued orders according to their own political sentiments ranging from complete freedom to returning them to their owners. Generals Grant and Halleck regarded the blacks as slaves. They had stated, "The labor of the slave belonged to his owner, if faithful to the Union, or to the United States, if the master had taken up arms against the Government. . . ."[12] Sherman chose to follow their pattern, "Therefore, in Memphis we received all fugitives, put them to work on the fortifications [at Fort Pickering], supplied them with food and clothing, and reserved the question of payment of wages for future decision. No force was allowed to be used to restore a fugitive slave to his master . . . but if the master proved his loyalty, he was usually permitted to see his slave, and, if he could persuade him to return home, it was permitted."[13] In short, Sherman saw the fugitive slave as a means to an end, i.e., the destruction of the enemy. When he learned of the issuing of the preliminary Emancipation Proclamation, he expressed his disapproval, saying, "Are we to feed all the Negroes? Freedom don't [*sic*] clothe them, feed them, and shelter them."[14] It disturbed him that Washington had freed the slaves without providing any mechanism for them to make the transition into the mainstream of society. To John he said, "You cannot solve this Negro question in a day."[15]

Sherman felt that all persons who remained in Memphis were bound to bear allegiance to the United States, and that they must at once make their choice between the South or the North. If they stayed and gave assistance to the enemy in any way, they were to be treated as spies. He held that Memphis had been a camp of the Confederate army, had been captured by the United States navy and army, and now was a military post. Under such circumstances there was to be no law but the law of war, and, this meant, in Sherman's mind, the will of the commander. He was to be accountable to no one except his superiors, and nothing would exist within the limits of his command but that which he approved. With respect to his army, Sherman believed he was governed by the Articles of War and the army regulations; with regard to all others his power was unlimited, except to the extent that it might be abridged or controlled by instructions of his government.[16] There could be no neutrality; there could be no laws but the laws of war—these were the rules the people of Memphis must adhere to during the city's occupation and until the war ended.

In addition to placing strict controls on the citizens of Memphis, Sherman also attempted to put an end to the Federal government's cotton-buying activities. Supposedly, to give encouragement to the local planters of the border states, Union officials permitted open trading of cotton with the Confederates. The United States, particularly the New England textile industries, needed the South's cotton. Sherman understood this need, but what disturbed him was the lax manner in which the Federal government permitted such trading to occur. Among the many Northern buyers and Southern sellers who flocked to Memphis were speculators and profiteers intent on getting rich off the war. Also, because gold and supplies were used as major means of exchange, Sherman was convinced that much, if not most, of the profits made provided aid to the Confederate cause.

Such activity was contrary to his view of conducting war against an enemy.

On August 11, he wrote to Secretary of the Treasury Salmon P. Chase concerning this situation, saying that the government's policy of buying cotton without investigating the seller was a mistake. He felt that much of the profit made from this enterprise went to the Confederate armies in the field. He told Chase, " . . . I have no doubt that Bragg's army at Tupelo, and [Earl] Van Dorn's at Vicksburg, received enough salt to make bacon, without which they could not have moved their armies in mass; and that from ten to twenty thousand fresh arms, and a due supply of cartridges have also been got, I am equally satisfied."[17] Sherman believed that Bragg and Van Dorn were the direct beneficiaries of the cotton-trading activities in Memphis. He also believed that the government's policy was providing assistance to groups of guerrillas in the area by supplying them with materials. To the secretary he emphasized, "This is no trifle; when one nation is at war with another, all the people of the one are enemies of the other; then the rules are plain and easy of understanding." For Sherman, the events of the past year made it clear that this war was going to be total, that it would involve the military as well as the civilian population. Again to the secretary, he explained, "The Government of the United States may now safely proceed on the proper rule that all in the South are enemies of all in the North; and not only are they unfriendly, but all who can procure arms now bear them as organized regiments, or as guerrillas. There is not a garrison in Tennessee where a man can go beyond the sight of the flag-staff without being shot or captured."[18]

In an attempt to stop such activity Sherman enforced an embargo forbidding a large amount of trade to take place.[19] His action, however, was disapproved by Washington and he was informed that the government would not sanction his embargo and ordered him to permit open trading. He regarded the rebuke as sheer folly and ignorance. To him, trade and commerce with the enemy was merely a means of destroying "the flag and the Government whose emblem it is."[20] He held that commerce and war were mortal foes and that wherever they met or crossed paths, one of them had to be eliminated. His developing concept of total war included politics and economics, but not this kind. This type of activity to him was politically unwise, economically unsound, and militarily unjustifiable.

However, despite his strong feelings—and it was rare for Sherman not to have strong feelings—he obeyed his government's order and lifted the embargo. He took care "not to heckle the Washington authorities"[21] as he had done in Kentucky and Missouri. He was determined not to get involved in a quarrel that might bring destruction to his newly acquired fame. At last, Sherman had learned which battles to fight and which ones he should let go.

Of even more concern than questionable cotton trade was the guerrilla activity and unorganized civilian resistance in and around Memphis. As Merrill puts it, such activity "deeply affected the general, and he began to realize the difficulty faced by a conquering army operating in a hostile country."[22] Confederate units were able to move with greater flexibility and rapidity and not be hampered by the civilian population. Surprise was to the enemy's advantage. Such activity was intolerable to Sherman and he did not hesitate to take stern action. The persistence of raiders in firing upon nonmilitary steamboats along the Mississippi caused him to take firm action against the citizens of Memphis. On September 27, he issued Special Orders No. 254, which, in part, stated:

> Whereas many families of known rebels and of Confederate in arms against us having been permitted to reside in peace and comfort in Memphis, and whereas the Confederate authorities either sanction or permit the firing on unarmed boats carrying passengers and goods for the use and benefit of the inhabitants of Memphis, it is ordered that for every boat so fired on ten families must be expelled from Memphis.
>
> The provost-marshal will extend the list already prepared so as to have on it at least thirty names, and on every occasion when a boat is fired on will draw by lot ten names, who will be forthwith notified and allowed three days to remove to a distance of 25 miles from Memphis.[23]

Just three days prior to the issuing of this order, Sherman retaliated against a band of guerrillas who had fired on the packet *Eugene*. Believing that "partisans were not entitled to the protection of the laws of civilized warfare,"[24] he issued the following orders to Col. Charles C. Wolcutt of the Forty-Sixth Ohio: "The object of the expedition you have been detailed for is to visit the town of Randolph [30 miles upstream from Memphis] where yesterday the packet *Eugene* was fired on by a party of guerrillas. Acts of this kind must be promptly punished, and it is almost impossible to reach the actors, for they come from the interior and depart as soon as the mischief is done. But the interests and well-being of the country demands that all such attacks should be followed by a punishment that will tend to prevent a repetition." His order continued, "I think the attack on the *Eugene* was by a small force of guerrillas from Loosahatchie, who by this time have gone back, and therefore that you will find no one at Randolph; in which case you will destroy the place, leaving one house to mark the place."[25]

Despite the harshness of the order, Sherman was not a cruel or vengeful person. He wanted to set an example. A guerrilla was careless as to the means employed and the persons attacked. In his opinion, partisans were wild beasts and should be hunted down and destroyed. Such lawless activity combined with civilian resistance disgusted Sherman; thus, it had to be stopped. Sherman was driven to such extremity "when the guerrilla turned from firing on troops to firing on noncombatants." He, therefore, "tried by one swift lesson to check this ominous extension of guerrilla methods."[26] To Grant he explained his actions, "I caused Randolph to be destroyed, and have given public notice that a repetition will justify any measures of retaliation, such as loading boats with their captive guerrillas as targets (I always have a lot on hand), and expelling families from the comforts of Memphis, whose husbands and brothers go to make up those guerrillas. I will watch Randolph closely, and if anything occurs there again I will send a brigade by land back of Randolph and clean out the country."[27] Two weeks later he wrote Maj. John A. Rawlins, Grant's chief of staff, concerning partisans along the river, saying, "We will have to do something more than merely repel these attacks. We must make the people feel that every attack on a road here will be resented by the destruction of some one of their towns or plantations elsewhere."[28] Retribution and retaliation had become not personal characteristics for personal revenge but basic tenets of his philosophy of war. They were means to an end, and that end was a rapid close to the war. Sherman had come to the realization that " . . . when one is at war with another all the people of one are enemies of the other."[29]

The experiences with the citizens of Memphis were responsible for the final fashioning of Sherman's theory of war. He had come to regard the rebellion in terms of a "collective responsibility"[30] rather than as a war of professionally armed men in uniforms. From West Point to Bull Run, and from Bull Run to Shiloh, Sherman had believed that it was only necessary for two nations to send their armies against each other, and the victor on the battlefield would be the victor at home. While at Memphis, however, as he evaluated the knowledge and experiences he had accumulated over the years, he realized that a change had taken place in himself and in his view of warfare. Further, he began to understand clearly that due to changes beyond him (the Industrial Revolution, humanism, social evolution, etc.) a new spirit of war had made its entrance on the stage of contemporary life. Whereas many of his contemporaries were still deeply entrenched in the ideas and attitudes of an agrarian social order, Sherman was on the cutting edge of change. At Memphis, he became aware of his place in history. Perhaps herein lies the principal source of many of his earlier troubles—the fact that he refused to be rooted in the past yet did not have the power or position to move into the new era. While many thought in narrow terms—McClellan, both Johnstons, John B. Hood, Robert E. Lee, Ambrose E. Burnside—Sherman saw the future, and, in seeing it, had no choice but to move toward it.

At first Sherman had opposed the war and hoped for another solution to the crisis, but now he realized that the only way to put an end to it was to change the nature and character of warfare. His adversaries had to be made to hate the very thought of war and regret having started it. Defeating the enemy army on a specific battlefield had become archaic. He had concluded that the time when the enemy's armies could be destroyed in battle had come to an end. The enemy's will must be destroyed.

To Grant, Sherman wrote the following on October 4: "We cannot change the hearts of those people of the South, but we can make war so terrible that they will realize the fact that, however brave and gallant and devoted to their country, still they are mortal and should exhaust all peaceful remedies before they fly to war."[31] Sherman had ceased to look upon war as a chivalrous part-time activity with a scent of romance. It had become an anarchical state of the mind. Having a strong instinct for government and order, he believed that, when laws were abused, the end result could only be war. Sternly he lectured P. A. Fraser, a resident of Memphis:

> Would to God ladies better acted their mission on earth; that instead of inflaming the minds of their husbands and brothers to lift their hands against the Government of their birth and stain them in blood . . . and thereby avoid "horrid war," the last

remedy on earth . . . when the time comes . . . we will see which
is more cruel—for your partisans to . . . shoot down the passengers and engineers, or for us to say the families of such men
engaged in such hellish deeds shall not live in peace where the
flag of the United States floats.[32]

Law and anarchy were seen as two opposing forces, and war began
when law broke down. Sherman realized and accepted the fact that
people created war, and that armies were merely the means of ending it. War was a way of expressing a difference in ideas and a means
of proving which group had superior or inferior might; war, however, could not prove which was the possessor of truth. While in
Memphis, Sherman understood that his fight was against anarchy
and that his enemy could appear in either the North or the South;
he would fight it under either flag. To his brother in Congress,
Sherman made the following remarks concerning the revolt of the
South: "It is about time the North understood the truth. That the
entire South, man, woman and child are against us, armed and
determined. It will call for a million men for several years to put
them down. . . . My opinion is there never can be peace and we must
fight it out. . . . The greatest danger North is division and anarchy. . . ."[33] Just a few days later in another letter to John, he spoke of
the need to establish new rules. He wrote:

> I rather think you now agree with me that this is no common
> war, that it was not going to end in a few months or a few years.
> For after eighteen months [of] war the enemy is actually united,
> armed and determined, with powerful forces well handled, dis-
> ciplined and commanded on the Potomac, the Ohio, the Mis-
> souri. You must now see that I was right in not seeking promi-
> nence at the outstart. I knew, and know yet that the northern
> people have to unlearn all their experience of the past thirty
> years and be born again before they will see the truth.[34]

Although Sherman had arrived at a revolutionary concept—
revolutionary for the North American continent—it was simply an
extension of Jomini. Concerning an invading army, Jomini had
said: "The invader has only an army, and his adversaries have an
army, and a people wholly in arms, and making means of resistance
out of everything, each individual of whom conspires against the
common enemy; even the non-combatants have an interest in his
ruin and accelerate it by every means in their power." He also said,
" . . . [the invader] holds scarcely any ground but that upon which

he encamps; outside the limits of his camp everything is hostile and multiplies a thousandfold the difficulties he meets at every step of the way."[35]

Sherman in west Tennessee, north Mississippi, and now in Memphis knew what Jomini was describing. For the past nine months seemingly he had operated in territory where every house was filled with enemies.[36] Southern tactics would eventually bring defeat if allowed to continue. As long as the Union armies had to contend with protecting their rear with enormous numbers of men, and as long as guerrillas and noncombatant warfare were left unpunished, the North could never achieve victory. Union lines of communication were threatened by such activities. Sherman believed that the entire male population of the South was armed. But, he had developed a solution. He was convinced that the South could be defeated by superior numbers. However, the numbers had to be free, so that full combat strength could be used in the fighting of battles. For this to happen, the people of the South would have to have their will broken. Once this was accomplished, then the Union armies could freely move against the Confederate armies. In essence, Sherman concluded that since the first hostile shot, the people of the North had no option; they must conquer or be conquered.

For sure, by October 1862, Sherman felt confident that it was impossible to stop the growing conflict by changing the minds of the people of the South. Their minds could not be changed. Thus, he arrived at the conclusion that Southern men and women would cherish peace. He deduced that the resisting power of a modern democracy depended more on the strength of the popular will than on its armies' fighting abilities. To interrupt the life of the people of the South and destroy hope for its redemption would be more effective than any military victory. This is what he meant when he wrote his wife, "The North may fall . . . into anarchy first, but if they can hold on the war will soon assume a turn to extermination, not of soldiers alone, that is the least of the trouble, but the people."[37] Personal contact with the hostile forces was necessary to awaken the enemy and shock them into surrender. Although some students of Sherman have attempted to place the cause of his attitude on his desire for revenge, it was not a hatred of the South that lay at the bottom of his concept of war.[38] It was his deep respect and devotion for the Constitution and the Union that made the South his enemy. And it was his extreme distaste for war that compelled him to work in a way that he felt would bring the war to a rapid end. If this meant "a new set of rules—rules which were not in accord with the accepted viewpoint," then so be it.[39]

Bluntly, yet accurately, Sherman said, " . . . generally war is destruction and nothing else."[40] To his daughter Minnie he attempted to explain war. He wrote, "I have been forced to turn 'families' out of their houses and homes and force them to go to a strange land because of their hostility, and I have today been compelled to order soldiers to lay hands on women to force them to leave their homes to go to join their husbands in hostile camps. Think of this, and how cruel men become in war when even your papa has to do such acts. Pray every night that the war may end."[41] Yet, despite the cruelty and horror, the key to ending the war was to make it what it really is. The North had to strike at the Confederacy in its weakest possible parts and thus destroy the opponents' means of livelihood. In that way the enemy would be weakened morally and materially. To Grant, Sherman said, the Southern people " . . . cannot be made to love us, but may be made to fear us, and dread the passage of troops through their country."[42]

By the fall of 1862, Sherman's philosophy of war had reached maturity. All that was left was its implementation, and the opportunity would come soon. He considered the people of the South enemies of the Union. These people had, by choice, rejected the laws of the Constitution, and in doing so, provided justification for Sherman's use of military force against the civilian population. Such action, ugly as it might be, cruel in the eyes of most, would demoralize the noncombatants, and in turn, have a negative effect on the soldiers of the Confederate armies. Sherman knew that men were basically willing to fight for two reasons—their country and their families. In 1862, for most, both were the same; in many cases, they were inseparable. If a division between the two could be created, then choices would have to be made. Sherman was confident that of the two, family would be selected over country—especially a country that had little or no history. By his attack on the civilian population, he believed the Confederate armies in the field, even those in the East, would be shattered. So, the new rule was to destroy the morale of the Southern soldier by striking at his heart. The psychological effect, Sherman believed, would be devastating.

Yet there was more to Sherman's concept than psychological warfare. Not only was the enemy's morale ever present in Sherman's mind, the sociological principle was of utmost importance also. By paralyzing the basic social institutions of the South, the enemy's ability and will to supply its fighting forces in the field would be destroyed. Although the perspective was not developed by sociologists until after World War I, Sherman had an excellent grasp of the social disorganization approach to the understanding of a society undergoing rapid change.

According to this perspective, society is organized by a set of expectations or rules. Social cohesion is established and maintained as institutions and individuals adhere to social expectations. The society is organized. People know what to expect and what is expected of them. This cohesiveness, however, can be disrupted by change. For example, immigration, urbanization, and industrialization increased during World War I and disrupted the organization of society. The old order experienced varying degrees of disintegration and disorganization; the old rules and expectations no longer applied. Society became disorganized.

In addition, the stress experienced by individuals because of social disorganization often produces personal disorganization. Although Sherman did not articulate it in this manner, in essence, his decision to make war on noncombatants was for the purpose of creating social disorganization in the lives of Southerners. Families were to be uprooted, communities devastated, institutions made dysfunctional, and local inhabitants set adrift. By his actions he intended to disturb the social cohesion of the South in such a way as to destroy the Southerners' will to continue the war. It became his intention so to disrupt the rules and expectations of their lives that they would be thrust into varying degrees of normlessness. Not only would the social system of the South be disorganized, but individual citizens would experience personal disorganization as well. Liddell Hart has written, "Sherman had an uncommon appreciation of the truth that military power rests on a civil foundation [social expectation]. If he shared the common professional incomprehension as to how this public support could be tactfully developed on his own side (although seeing the need) he had exceptional insight into the ways of weakening the war-will and undermining the civil foundation [social expectations] of the other side not only psychologically, but economically."[43] And, it must be added, sociologically.

The oft-quoted phrase for which Sherman is best known, "War is hell," he could not recall as having ever said. The closest he came to using the statement was in an address he made on August 12, 1880, before a G.A.R. convention at Columbus, Ohio. He said, "There is many a boy here today who looks on war as all glory, but boys, it is all hell." But, he agreed with its message. In September 1864, he stated, "You cannot qualify war in harsher terms than I will. War is cruelty, and you cannot refine it; and those who brought war into our country deserve all the curses and maledictions a people can pour out."[44] To Sherman the people of the South were collectively responsible for disunion and the war, and they should be punished collectively. In a sense, this war was to be fought not simply to bring the Union together again, but to make sure that the idea of secession would never enter the minds of Southerners in the future. The effect of this type of warfare would be "a certain disregard for human rights and dignity."[45] But, for Sherman, that did not matter. War had changed; it had become ruthless. Those of the old military tradition would call his concept barbaric, but to such abuses Sherman would reply that "war is war, and not popularity-seeking."[46]

Yet, behind this firmness, this ruthlessness, this drive for efficiency, there always remained an element of humanity. And herein lies not a contradiction, but a paradox. The core of the man was his tremendous desire for and dedication to peace through union and law. When all else failed to resolve differences and order became disorder, he felt it appropriate to resort to war, the use of force. Such a method is tragic and cruel, but when there is no other alternative, it must be used. The Union and constitutional law were of a high order, and when they were threatened with destruction, those who offered the threat had either to be co-opted or eliminated. Sherman's thought process was logical and consistent—there were no contradictions. It cannot be said of Sherman that war, with all its cruelty and violence, was his ultimate concern. His words and many of his actions may give that impression to some observers, but for those who fully understand the man, it can only be concluded that Sherman was a man of peace.

It cannot be said of Sherman that it was cruelty, barbarism, or hatred that motivated him to implement his concept of war. He did not, as Walters says, "strip war of all the rules of conduct," nor was he willing to "abandon [all] scruples . . . he might have had at the outset of the war." He did not bring war to the civilian population because of a fear of personal humiliation or a desire to "save his self-esteem," nor were his actions carried out "to exact payment and fulfill . . . long pent-up craving[s] to get back at his enemy [the South]." Personal retaliation and retribution were not his motivation, nor did he feel he might be robbed of the "opportunity to demonstrate his abilities as a soldier."[47] Such conclusions about Sherman are shallow and oversimplified. Those who hold them fail to understand the complexity and wholeness of the man and, therefore, do him injustice.

Walters, although begrudgingly so, is accurate on one point. Sherman was a merchant of terror, and he first implemented this aspect of his theory of war in and around Memphis.[48] Sherman's notion of collective responsibility (although Sherman never used the term) was revolutionary, and this is what justifies his being characterized as the first modern general. He saw the entire South as being collectively responsible for the war, and he determined that the South's will to fight had to be destroyed.[49] Therefore, no one in the South was innocent, and, if it meant that all must suffer in order to bring the war to a close, then all must suffer. On this point Sherman wrote to Rawlins, "I propose to expel ten secession families for every boat fired on, thereby lessening the necessity for fighting boats for their benefit, and will visit on the neighborhood summary punishment. It may sometimes fall on the wrong head, but it would be folly to send parties of infantry to chase these wanton guerrillas."[50] Sherman meant what he said, for on the same day he wrote these words, he issued a special order to the Forty-Sixth Ohio, the troops who had destroyed the town of Randolph. The orders stated: "The Forty-sixth Ohio . . . will embark to-night . . . , and before daybreak drop down to a point on the Arkansas shore about 15 miles below this, near Elm Grove Post-office, and there disembark. [The troops] will then proceed to destroy all the houses, farms and corn-fields from that point up to Hopefield."[51] Sherman understood the civil foundations of armies and became intent on the destruction of that foundation. This meant the demoralization of the Southern people. The "destruction of property, the holding of hostages, and the improper exposure of prisoners to the fire of their own forces"[52] were means to that end. Such tactics did create alarm, dismay, consternation, fear, and terror among noncombatants, but that was exactly his purpose. So, in this sense, Sherman was a merchant of terror.

But to imply as Walters does that Sherman was cruel, unfeeling, bloodthirsty, and barbaric, and that "he had hardened his heart and shut out the voice of conscience . . . ,"[53] is simply false. To conclude that Sherman's reasoning was distorted is to misunderstand the man and the changes taking place in warfare in the nineteenth century.[54] Also, Walters' implication that Sherman had flouted international military law is absurd. Sherman was an astute student, widely read, and a close friend of General Halleck, a contemporary expert on such law. It would be hard to imagine Sherman not having read Halleck's translations and thus being unfamiliar with the laws governing armies invading enemy territory. What Walters fails to admit is that Sherman *expanded* the rules to include the entire South—combatants and noncombatants—as enemies. He did not *disregard* those rules. He broadened them, thus, introducing the idea of collective responsibility. Whether this action is ethical or unethical is an argument that goes beyond the scope of this study. Walters feels comfortable in making such a judgment. For him, Sherman committed an unethical act and, in doing so, opened the door to total war, "a mode of warfare which transgressed all ethical rules and showed an utter disregard for human rights and dignity."[55] If Walters is correct, then every general since Sherman has been unethical and every general before Sherman was ethical. This, seemingly, is a rather simplistic approach to the study of history.

The truth of the matter is, Sherman was an extremely ethical man, one who despised war; yet, he was a realist and knew that there would be times in the history of human affairs that war must be resorted to. War, however, was a means to an end, the end being peace. Although an avid warrior, he was quick to beat his swords into plowshares. He was willing to help the enemy if they would lay down their arms and rejoin the Union. In Memphis he organized a charity drive to feed the poor; he established a bureau of relief; he donated funds to assist the needy. He encouraged his troops to give money and food to sick families,[56] and there is no evidence that a single family was ever expelled from the city as a result of his orders. Sherman knew the psychological effect of threats and was willing to use them. Writing in his *Memoirs* he stated: "It was to me manifest that the soldiers and people of the South entertained undue fear of our Western men, and, like children, they had invented such ghost-like stories of their own inventions. Still this was a power, and I intended to utilize it."[57] What general marching through enemy territory would not gladly embrace such responses if it meant the demoralization of resistance?

Immediately after the war Sherman urged his friends to work together, both North and South, to restore the country to its former prosperity. Even tactically he showed his distaste for violence. The way, therefore, to decide wars and even battles was more by the movement of troops than by fighting. It is interesting that Sherman's directness in speech and manner was, and to some still is, offensive. His indirectness in war was, and to some still is, offensive also. But that is the way it is with paradoxes. They offend easily and are easily misunderstood. Paradoxically, Sherman was both a "merchant of terror" and an "advocate of peace."

The "I" in Sherman had finally emerged. Now he was confident, self-assured, and free. In August 1862, he wrote this curious yet interesting statement to his wife: "Well, at last I hope the fact is clear to their minds [the minds of Lincoln's cabinet] that if the North design to conquer the South, we must . . . reconquer the country. . . . It was this conviction then [in 1861] . . . that made men think I was insane. A good many flatterers now want to make me a prophet."[58]

*General Sherman after the march to the sea, 1865.*

# CHAPTER SIX

# *"They Chose War"*

On November 17, 1862, Sherman received the following dispatch from General Grant: "Meet me at Columbus, Kentucky, on Thursday next. If you have a good map of the country south of you, take it up with you."[1] This conference was to be the first between the two generals that would eventually lead to the fall of Vicksburg and the control of the Mississippi River by the Union. Both men were keenly aware of the importance of this great winding body of water in the defeat of the South. Each understood that whoever won the river would win the war. For Grant, control of the Mississippi River was a military necessity; for Sherman it was much more. Not only did it hold military significance, but it was also "the symbol of geographic unity." Sherman's biographer notes that, to Sherman the Mississippi "was the trunk of the American tree, with limbs and branches reaching to the Alleghenies, the Canadian border, the Rocky Mountains." For Sherman it was "the spinal column of America."[2] Ever since he had first seen it some twenty years earlier, he had been enthralled with its power and its geographical importance to America. The river and its valley were the "heartland binding together the Union in an indivisible whole." For him it was the "center that made America unique and great and worth preserving."[3] It was "the physical refutation of sectionalism."[4] In 1860, he had said, "Were it not for the physical geography of the country it might be that people would consent to divide and separate in peace. But the Mississippi is too grand an element to be divided and all its extent must of necessity be

145

under one government."[5] It was so important to him that he said in
order to secure its safety, "I would slay millions. On that point I am
not only insane, but mad."[6]

Militarily, the river and its valley "took precedence over all other
theaters" of the war.[7] Richmond could fall and Washington could be
destroyed, yet the war would continue, "But let Federal steamers roll
from St. Louis to New Orleans and the Confederacy, cut in two, must
whither and die."[8] In addition, both Sherman and Grant were
rapidly arriving at the conclusion that protecting, holding, and operating the railroads in Grant's area of command was too costly and
was accomplishing little. Further, the energy expended on inland
expeditions against guerrilla bands was an exercise in futility. The
real strategic goal, therefore, ought to be the river. To Grant, Sherman wrote, "Detachments inland can always be overcome or are at
great hazard and they do not convert the people. They cannot be
made to love us, but may be made to fear us, and dread the passage
of troops through their country." Increasingly, he said, "I am . . .
more and more convinced that we should hold the river absolutely
and leave the interior alone." He pressed his point further, "With
the Mississippi safe we could land troops at any point, and by a quick
march break the railroad, where we could make ourselves so busy
that our descent would be dreaded the whole length of the river, and
by the loss of negroes and other property they would in time discover that war is not the remedy for the political evils [of] which they
complained."[9] With Grant he agreed that to continue to "occupy
West Tennessee and keep the railroads operating would tie-up an
inappropriate amount of . . . resources in a defensive stance. . . ."[10]
Such a strategic operation must cease.

In the fall of 1862, the United States controlled this vital waterway
as far south as the mouth of the Arkansas River and as far north
from New Orleans as Port Hudson. Between these two points
stretched more than two hundred miles still held by the Confederacy. Sherman and Grant, close friends now, met in Columbus
and concluded that the key to possession of the river was Vicksburg,
Mississippi. The fall of this heavily fortified city would rescue the
war from stalemate and a possible Northern defeat.

The two generals were on the eve of an experience that would
draw them even closer together, make them a formidable team, and
seal the fate of the Confederacy. By now Grant had come to view
Sherman as his most trusted warrior, and Sherman had a faith in

Grant's abilities and judgments that would never be matched by another person. Writing to Grant he expressed this faith. He spoke of Grant's simple faith in success and how, when he had completed his best preparations, he entered battle without hesitation. "I tell you," Sherman wrote, "that it was this that made me act with confidence."[11] It was Grant's simplicity, his confidence, his willingness to act that made Sherman feel secure. Rear Adm. David Dixon Porter recognized the closeness of the two men and noted how they complemented each other. What was lacking in one, the other made up, and vice versa. Together, Porter said, they make "a very perfect officer."[12] Unconcerned with appearances, both were determined to transcend the military principles of the nineteenth century. Both "were soldiers who saw that their first duty was to command and obey, to wage war with one consideration—victory."[13] Although they approached battle differently, they agreed on strategy and were willing to do whatever was necessary to implement that strategy. As Richard Goldhurst says, "These two soldiers were involved in a psychological romance," an *entente cordiale*, as Sherman described it. Sherman had a respect for authority that bordered on adoration. In Grant he saw "the authoritative figure . . . the man who [would] put things right, who knows always what he is doing. . . ."[14] In Sherman, Grant saw "the perfect general,"[15] the one man he could unquestionably trust. They had come to respect each other because they needed each other. Sherman said of the relationship: "We were as brothers—I the older man in years, he the higher in rank. We both believed in our heart of hearts that the success of the Union cause was not only necessary to the then generation of Americans, but to all future generations. We both professed to be gentlemen and professional soldiers, educated in the science of war . . . for the very occasion which had arisen. Neither of us by nature was a combative man . . . "[16] And upon receipt of his commission as brigadier general in the regular army, Sherman wrote Grant, "I know that I owe this to your favor . . . I beg to assure you of my deep personal attachment, and hope that the chances of war will leave me to serve near and under you till the dawn of that peace for which we are contending. . . ."[17] Vicksburg was to seal the relationship that was less than two years old.

Not only did Sherman recognize the strategic importance of Vicksburg, he was also acutely aware of its strength. It would be a "hard nut to crack," for it was extremely strong "both by nature and art."[18] In early December 1862, Sherman and Grant met again, this time at Oxford, Mississippi, to hammer out the final plans to take the city. From Sherman's point of view, the best approach for success would be to march the army straight south along the railroads that ran south from Grand Junction to Jackson and then west to Vicksburg; push the Confederate Army under Lt. Gen. John C. Pemberton back to Vicksburg; and in the meantime send a second force in transports down the Mississippi River to demonstrate against the city's waterfront. Between the two forces Vicksburg could be captured.[19] Grant agreed with the plan, but due to political pressure and the need for an immediate victory, he did not wholly accept it. Instead, Sherman was ordered to proceed to Memphis, collect some 30,000 men, load them on steamers, and, with the support of gunboats commanded by Admiral Porter, float down the Mississippi to the mouth of the Yazoo River eight miles from Vicksburg. Turning into the Yazoo, Sherman was to storm the bluffs rising above the river and fight his way to the higher plateau in the city's rear. While Sherman was accomplishing this feat, Grant would move on Vicksburg by way of Grenada, Mississippi, keeping Pemberton's army occupied in North Mississippi. This would enable Sherman's forces successfully to capture Vicksburg and prepare the way for Grant's arrival.[20] It was to be a cooperative effort involving both an amphibious and a land maneuver.

Sherman returned to Memphis and began what he later described as "preparations hasty in extreme."[21] To secure the smooth operation of his part of the plan, Sherman issued copies of his own maps, complete with the latest information, to his divisional commanders and ordered them to have copies made for their subordinates. He wanted no mistakes to be made or confusion to delay their march. Over the past year it had become characteristic of Sherman that in his instructions he described the general strategy of a campaign so that his officers would know their action was but one "part—an important one of the great *whole*."[22] Or, as Jomini expressed it, "The whole theatre of operations may be considered as a single field upon which strategy directs the armies for a definite end."[23] Cognizant of the difficulties faced by the Army of the Potomac in Virginia, where four men were issuing the orders (the president, the secretary of war, the general-in-chief, and the commander of the army), Sherman was determined to place his men under one head, all working with a united effort.[24]

Finally, after seeing to most of the details himself, Sherman, and his flotilla of gunboats and transports, left Memphis on December 20. The trip downriver went well, and on December 26 the expedition traveled up the Yazoo River and disembarked in the flat Chickasaw Bayou area several miles from the steep bluffs of the Walnut Hills immediately north of Vicksburg and on which the city rested. For the next few days his troops inched their way closer to the steep hills and hollows and vainly waited to hear of Grant's presence east of the city. Finally, realizing that to wait any longer would mean defeat, Sherman assaulted the bluffs on December 29. Almost immediately he was repulsed. Despite the haphazard preparations, the attack failed and Sherman retreated counting 208 killed, 1,005 wounded, and 563 captured and missing. A second operation was begun on December 30 but had to be canceled because of a dense fog. On January 1, 1863, his disheartened and defeated troops returned to the transports and the entire flotilla retreated to the safety of Milliken's Bend. Sherman's first independent command had ended in failure.

Discouraged and dejected, Sherman that evening visited Admiral Porter on his flagship "drenched to the skin." As Porter recalled, "He looked as if he had been grappling with the mud and had gotten the worst of it." Porter continued, "He sat down and remained silent for some minutes. . . . I said at length 'What is the matter?'" Sherman raised his head and replied, "'I have lost seventeen hundred men and those infernal reporters will publish all over the country their ridiculous stories about Sherman being whipped, etc.'"[25]

Sherman's fear was legitimate, for in a matter of days the newspapers were descending on him for his failure to take Vicksburg. The St. Louis *Missouri Democrat*, among others, called the expedition "a stupid blunder," "a shame," "a national calamity," and pressed for an answer to the question, who is responsible? Of course, as to be expected, the blame was placed on "the mismanagement, incompetence, and insanity of the commanding general [Sherman]." Mocking Sherman, the *Democrat* said, "We came, we saw, and did not conquer." The Cincinnati *Commercial* cried, "We want McClellan!"[26] Sherman would eventually submit that the failure rested in the lack of support, not only from Grant in the north but from one of the brigades participating in the attack. A number of critics assess the reason to have been "the impregnable position of the enemy."[27]

They are probably correct. Sherman, however, always remained firm in his belief that "had . . . [Gen. George W. Morgan] used with skill and boldness one of his brigades, in addition to that of Frank P. Blair's, he could have made a lodgement on the bluff, which would have opened the door for our whole force to follow."[28] Whatever the cause of defeat, Sherman realized two things: 1) frontal assaults were no way to win battles, and 2) it would be futile to continue the attack. To dig in and cling to a tenuous position was rapidly erased from his book of tactics.

But, all of this was to come later. As Sherman sat in Porter's quarters, his more immediate concern was what he should do next. "I must take my boys somewhere and wipe this out," he told the admiral. To this, Porter, looking at the general with complete empathy, said he was ready to go anywhere. Accepting the encouragement, Sherman responded, "Then, let's go and thrash out Arkansas Post."[29]

Before Sherman had a chance to wipe out the defeat of the Chickasaw Bayou campaign, he was faced with his last crisis of a political nature until the surrender of Joseph Johnston in North Carolina. Gen. John A. McClernand, a veteran of the Black Hawk War, Springfield neighbor of President Lincoln's, and former Democratic congressman from Illinois, had conceived a plan in mid-August 1862 that he himself wanted to put into operation. Like Sherman and Grant he had concluded that the key to the war was the Mississippi River and that the key to the river was the city of Vicksburg. By taking Vicksburg the Union would deprive the Confederates of their communications and supply lines running east and west. McClernand "had won a deserved reputation as a hard-fighting division commander under Grant at Donelson and Shiloh,"[30] even though he was not a professional soldier. He was an astute politician and acutely aware "that a political crisis was mounting in the prairie states, which demanded a military remedy."[31] Since April 1861, the professional soldiers had failed to free the Mississippi from Confederate control, and the war had sunk into a stalemate. McClernand reasoned correctly that if the river were not open to trade, the Midwest's will to continue the war would seriously be drained away. In addition, McClernand knew that the person who succeeded in breaking the Confederate stranglehold would be hailed a hero and would gain significant political capital. So, this "swarthy, black-bearded man of slight figure and transparent egotism" and friend of the president, laid a plan before Lincoln in September 1862. He should be commissioned to raise a separate army in the states of Iowa, Illinois, and Indiana, move the newly organized army south for the capture of Vicksburg and the opening of the Mississippi, then head east toward Atlanta or west into Texas. Lincoln was impressed with the plan and told McClernand to present it to Halleck, which he did. Mistrustful of political generals, Halleck disapproved the plan, but Lincoln overruled, and, on October 20, issued McClernand a "Private and Confidential" paper. This document authorized him to organize recruits and enlist regiments and to move them south " . . . to the end that when a sufficient force, not required by the operations of General Grant's command, shall be raised, an expedition may be organized under General McClernand's command against Vicksburg and to clear the Mississippi River and open navigation to New Orleans."[32]

On the morning of January 3, 1863, while hastily making preparations for the move against Arkansas Post, Sherman was informed by Admiral Porter that McClernand had reached the mouth of the Yazoo and was "waiting to take command of your army!"[33] (A major reason Grant had rushed Sherman south to the Chickasaw area was because Halleck had informed him of the Lincoln-McClernand plan.) On January 2, Sherman boarded the steamer *Tigress* and reported to the major general.

McClernand showed Sherman Lincoln's orders and assumed command.[34] He further informed Sherman that Grant's advance had been halted by Confederate forces who had destroyed his supply depot at Holly Springs, Mississippi, and, thus, Grant would not be coming. Finally, he told Sherman that the army would be renamed the Army of the Mississippi and divided into two corps, one to be commanded by Sherman, the other by General Morgan, the same officer Sherman had criticized a few days earlier.

Realizing that his first independent command had ended in failure and that he had been replaced by a politician, Sherman relinquished his position with poise and dignity.[35] He had learned much about himself over the past few years as well as about the world in which he operated. But, without a doubt, this changing of the guard rankled him. He felt insulted not only because he was being replaced by a politician (a hard pill for Sherman to swallow), but also because Lincoln with this act seemed to be favoring citizen-soldiers over professional military men.

The urge to resign and strike out with verbal criticism surged within him, but instead of "sulking Achilles-like in his tent,"[36] Sherman accepted the situation and indicated a complete willingness to cooperate with McClernand. To Ellen, he wrote, "Well we have been to Vicksburg and it was too much for us and we have backed out. McClernand has arrived to supersede me by order of the President himself. Of course I submit gracefully. The President is charged with maintaining the government and has a perfect right to choose his agents."[37] He told John, "I never dreamed of so severe a test of my patriotism as being superseded by McClernand, and if I can keep my tamed (?) spirit and live I will claim a virtue higher than Brutus."[38] With dignity that was rooted in the self-confidence he had gained at Shiloh and Memphis, Sherman announced to his troops: "A new commander is here to lead you. . . . I know that all good officers and soldiers will give him the same hearty support and cheerful obedience they have hitherto given me. There are honors enough in reserve for all and work enough too. Let each do his appropriate part, and our nation must in the end emerge from this dire conflict purified and ennobled by the fires which now test its strength and purity."[39]

Such words could have come only from a man dedicated to his profession and the cause at hand. Had Sherman been self-serving, his response would have been less conciliatory, even belligerent. He was a man who had much at stake. Having just recently overcome the hostility of the press, he had finally made a place for himself in this war. Shiloh had given him the self-confidence he needed to work within the system. He had found a close friend in Grant, one he truly believed understood the direction the war must go. Together they had reached the river that gave the Confederacy life, and they had begun to implement a campaign that would bring the war to a sure close. In spite of the defeat at Chickasaw, he felt confident that, once he and Grant could regroup, all would go well. His hopes were high, his spirits strong, his goals, clear. The road ahead might be bumpy, but the barriers could be overcome. But now, with the entrance of McClernand, all had been taken from him. A lesser man would have sulked his way either to another theater of the war or out of the conflict completely. Sherman, however, chose to stay, and, in doing so, proved his devotion not only to his profession but to the Union as well. Granted, the choice was not easy and to the "significant others" in his life he complained of injustice and insults. To Ellen he spoke of resignation, of returning to St. Louis. And when he learned the Northern newspapers were blaming him for the "butchering" of his men at Chickasaw, he thought, "I ought to get away."[40] He complained to his brother about the constant attacks on his ability. Yet, despite the complaints and threats of resignation, the "I" in Sherman would not allow him to withdraw. Who he was made him stay. Actually, he had no other choice.

During the initial days of McClernand's command of the newly formed Army of the Mississippi, no definite plans were made to open the river. Indeed, it was decided that any further attempt to capture Vicksburg would be futile. Seeing that the troops were rapidly lapsing into a state of immobility, Sherman "suggested to McClernand a new move which would crown the new command with laurels, and leave his own brow the barer by contrast."[41] Hearing nothing from Grant, he proposed that "we should go to the Arkansas [River] and attack the Post [Fort Hindman] from which the enemy threatened our rear and line of communications."[42] After consulting with Admiral Porter and settling some differences with him (Porter was aggravated with McClernand over the manner in which he had treated Sherman during the change of command), McClernand adopted Sherman's suggestion. On January 9, the expedition moved up the White River toward Fort Hindman. The fort mounted eleven heavy guns and garrisoned approximately 5,000 men, but, with little trouble, the Union forces succeeded. Porter attacked with three ironclads and several smaller vessels, managing in three hours to disable all the fort's guns. Sherman's and Morgan's troops landed, drove the enemy into their works, and the garrison surrendered to McClernand on January 11. After partially destroying the fort and sending its prisoners northward, the Federal troops moved south to Young's Point, on the Louisiana side, about five miles west of Vicksburg. At this dog-leg in the Mississippi River, Sherman settled in with the Army of the Mississippi to make preparations for another attempt against Vicksburg.[43] Although of little strategic importance and rather costly in Union troops (800 men were lost to capture a fort manned by 5,000 Confederates), the capture of Arkansas Post "was an inspiring change from the repulse at

Vicksburg"[44] and contributed to restoring the morale and spirits of the men. It also provided further proof of the growing bond between Sherman and Grant. Upon hearing of the expedition Grant wired Halleck that McClernand was on a "wild-goose chase." He wrote to McClernand his disapproval of the move believing "it will lead to the loss of men without a result." But, upon receipt of a letter from Sherman informing him that the move was his idea and not McClernand's (Sherman was incorrect; the attack on Arkansas Post was as much McClernand's as Sherman's), Grant changed his opinion and stated to Halleck that the venture was "very important."[45] As Lloyd Lewis put it, the political general "was, unwittingly, welding the bonds of friendship" between the two men.[46]

The bond was welded together even more when Sherman tested Grant's loyalty by renewing his battle with the press. In complete defiance of orders, Thomas W. Knox, a correspondent of the New York *Herald* had accompanied the Chickasaw expedition. In reporting the results of the expedition Knox charged Sherman with poor leadership and behaving in ways that were totally "unaccountable." Having defied the general's orders, Sherman demanded that Knox be tried as a spy. To Porter, Sherman wrote, "The spirit of anarchy seems deep at work at the North, more alarming than the batteries that shell us from the opposite shore. . . . Reporters print their limited and tainted observations on the history of events they neither see nor comprehend. . . . We cannot prosper in military operations if we submit to it. . . ." And he added a familiar note, "And some one must begin the attack, I must assume the ungracious task."[47] Writing to Ellen he said he could not allow newspaper reporters to come into his camp against his orders. He further stated that he would never again command an American army if it meant carrying "along paid spies." Angrily he told her that he would resign if President Lincoln "attempts to interfere with the sentence of any court ordered by me." He added that Lincoln must "conform to the well-established rules of military nations and not attempt" to conduct war according to the rules of peace.[48]

Eventually, Knox was tried by a military court, found guilty, and sentenced to be removed from the department. Near the end of March, Sherman learned that Knox had been notified by President Lincoln that the sentence would be revoked if Grant agreed. Sherman's temper flared, and he wrote his brother, "I'll tell Lincoln to his face that even he shall not insult me. If Knox comes into my camp he'll never leave it again at liberty. I have soldiers who will obey my orders and Knox shall go down the Mississippi floating on a log if he can find one, but he shall not come into my camp with impunity again."[49]

How would Grant decide? Sherman knew that Grant and Lincoln had developed a great respect for each other and that Lincoln was desirous of pacifying the *Herald* as well as other critical newspapers. Was the bond between Sherman and Grant real? Sherman found out a few days later when he received a letter from Knox which contained Grant's decision. Grant informed the reporter that he supported Sherman's actions and declined to revoke the decision of the court "unless General Sherman first gives his consent. . . ." Grant further informed Knox that "General Sherman is one of the ablest soldiers and purest men in this country. . . ."[50] So, the bond was real and, under test, held firm. Sherman was so confident of Grant's support that he notified Knox that an appeal to him would be useless. He told Knox, "Come with a sword or musket in your hand, prepared to share with us our fate, in sunshine and storm, in prosperity and adversity, in plenty and scarcity, and I will welcome you as a brother and associate; but come as you now do expecting me to ally the reputation and honor of my country and my fellow-soldiers with you, as the representative of the press, which you yourself say makes so slight a difference between truth and falsehood, and my answer is Never."[51] At last, due to his strong ties to Grant, Sherman had won a victory over his archenemy.

The incident over, he promised his wife that in the future he would try to use the newspapers for his advantage and that he would attempt to "endure" them.[52] But more important, the relationship between the two generals was solidified. Each consulted the other and each had come to trust the other implicitly. To Ellen, Sherman confided, "The army is in good condition and if they fight us we will have a desperate one. Grant was delighted to see me, and everything works well. . . ."[53] In Grant, Sherman had found an important role model—almost, at times, a father figure. From Grant he had gained strength and confidence.

In April 1863, Vicksburg and the reaches of the Mississippi River between the Hill City and Port Hudson still lay in the hands of the Confederacy. Within three months four attempts had been made to wrest them from the control of the Rebels. In addition to the

Chickasaw Bayou expedition, two attempts were made to bypass the
city with the construction of canals, as well as through Yazoo Pass,
but all came to naught. Finally, in March, an expedition through the
swamps, creeks, and bayous north of the city was tried, but to no
avail. It was becoming bitterly clear that Vicksburg was indeed a
tough nut to crack. Northerners were growing impatient with what
they felt was incompetence on behalf of Grant. Newspapers were
reviving the old stories concerning his drinking habits and began
demanding a change of command. So concerned was Washington,
and so in need of a victory, that Charles A. Dana was sent west as a
special commissioner for the War Department. His charge? To evaluate the situation and determine if Grant was fit for the job.

In a conversation with Dana, Grant explained a new plan he had
devised. The new attempt would call for Admiral Porter's ironclads,
along with several transports, to sail past the enemy's fortifications at
Vicksburg to a point below the city. There they would be used to
transport the army, which was to march down the Louisiana side of
the Mississippi to a place opposite New Carthage. Once a base was
secure on the Mississippi side of the river, Grant would send a force
to cooperate with Maj. Gen. Nathaniel Banks in the capture of Port
Hudson, and then these combined forces would return and operate
against Vicksburg from the south. It was a bold plan requiring coordination and deception, but Grant, in consultation with Porter, believed it would work.

Sherman, however, did not agree, and he urged Grant to carry out
the plan that they had developed earlier at Oxford. He submitted
that the safest and surest approach would be to return the entire
army to Memphis, then march down the railroads to Vicksburg's
rear. Militarily, Grant knew this was the correct approach, probably
the easiest, as well as the surest. But he also knew such a plan would
take time, more time than he or Lincoln could afford. The war had
settled into a stalemate. It had to be broken, and soon. For political
reasons, a victory was needed. Sherman also objected to the new
plan because it meant that the army would have to depend upon a
precarious line of supply once it crossed the river into Mississippi.
But Grant refused to be deterred, and Sherman was confident that he
was making a serious mistake and that he was buckling under to "the
thunder of popular criticism."[54] He was sure the plan "must fail and
the fault will be on us all. . . ."[55] What Sherman did not realize (although he got a glimpse of it at Shiloh) was that Grant had developed

what Lewis calls "a new psychology for the Federal armies." This psychology was built on the idea "that if two fighters were exhausted the first to revive would be the victor." Lloyd Lewis explains, "Lying at the foot of Vicksburg's cliffs Grant had come to the irrevocable belief that, in the end, triumph would come to that army which never counted its dead, never licked its wounds, never gave its adversary breathing space, never remembered the past nor shrank from the future—the army which dismissed old rules and which ignored rebuffs—the army which held implicit faith in a simple and eternal offensive."[56]

Finally, on the night of April 16, Admiral Porter's fleet of iron-clads and three transports successfully ran the batteries of Vicksburg, and immediately the army began its march through the swamps and bayous of Louisiana. In spite of the success, Sherman remained skeptical. To Ellen he wrote, "I look upon the whole thing as one of the most hazardous and desperate moves of this or any other army."[57] But, it was too late now. All was in motion and could not be stopped.

Once the bulk of the army reached its destination opposite Grand Gulf, Grant was faced with his next problem—that is, how to get his troops to the east side of the Mississippi. There was real danger that Pemberton would oppose the crossing and thus end the campaign prematurely. To prevent this possibility, Grant ordered Sherman and his corps to remain behind to make a feint against Snyder's Bluff on the Yazoo. Grant explained, "My object was to compel Pemberton to keep as much force about Vicksburg as I could until I could secure a good footing on high land east of the river."[58] In a letter to Sherman, Grant said, "The effect of a heavy demonstration in that direction [north of Vicksburg] would be good as far as the enemy are concerned." Aware that such a demonstration would be viewed in the North as an apparent repulse, Grant couched his order in the form of a request. "I therefore leave it to you whether to make such a demonstration. . . ." Quite an act of faith in one of his subordinates on the part of a superior officer. It is even more astonishing because of the tactical importance of the demonstration for the plan. But Grant knew Sherman, and he knew him well. Ever obedient and loyal, Sherman replied, "I will take ten steamers and ten regiments and go up the Yazoo as close to Haynes' [Snyder's] as possible without putting the transports under the rifled guns of the enemy. We will make as strong a demonstration as possible. The troops would understand the purpose and would not be hurt by the repulse." Then he included the theme that had come to be part of his correspondence since the war broke out: "The people of the country must find out the truth as they best can; it is none of their business. You are engaged in a hazardous enterprise, and, for good reasons, wish to divert attention. That is sufficient for me, and it shall be done. . . ."[59]

Immediately he set to work and, with the use of deception and by making every man "look as numerous as possible," the feint was successful. Sherman made his regiments look so numerous that the Confederate commander at Vicksburg, despite reports to the contrary by the officer on site, notified Pemberton that the attack was there rather than at Grand Gulf. "The enemy are in front of me in force such as have never been seen before at Vicksburg," he said, and withheld reinforcements from Grand Gulf until too late.[60]

The demonstration was a success and, on April 30, the Union army crossed the Mississippi and landed at Bruinsburg. The way was clear for Grant, following victory at Port Gibson, to lead his army into the interior of enemy territory. But, still, Sherman remained skeptical. He had received word that Maj. Gen. Banks would not join Grant's force on schedule, if at all, and that Grant had decided to attack Vicksburg without him. His anxiety increased even more when he learned that Grant with a force of 41,000 men was about to enter a region where some 35,000 well-armed enemy troops awaited him. Grant would be faced with a hostile civilian population familiar with the land. Having caught up with Grant south of Vicksburg, Sherman observed that Grant's troops had no wagon trains and no railroad. His men would be dependent on the ammunition and rations they carried on their backs. Sherman could not believe his eyes. This was sheer folly and would undoubtedly lead to ultimate disaster. By courier he sent a message to Grant pleading with him "to stop all troops till your army is partially supplied with wagons. . . ." Grant, however, had no intention of delaying his next move for the purpose of land transports and told Sherman, "I do not calculate upon the possibility of supplying the army with full rations from Grand Gulf. I know it will be impossible without constructing additional roads. What I do expect is to get up what rations of hard bread, coffee and salt we can, and make the country furnish the balance."[61] Sherman was astonished. This was contrary to everything he and Grant had been taught at West Point. Even Jomini in his most bold moments would balk at Grant's plan and upcoming maneuver. But Sherman had come to know Grant well and realized that it was futile to try to change his mind. Once he committed himself, Grant seldom ever turned back. As the army's movement progressed and as Sherman thought about Grant's actions, "the old military world of West Point [began] to spin around beneath him— then disappear." Lewis's comments are classic: "This was a new kind of war—and Grant was making his own rules as he went along. Here was an army caring not a whipstich for a base of supplies. From field, barn, smokehouse, and cellar they were extracting epicurean meals." They ate "fried ham, bacon, pork chops, beefsteak" at noontime, and they "boiled spring chicken, duck, turkey, guinea hens" for supper, and in the mornings for breakfast "they ate the eggs of all kinds of poultry." They had an abundance of black molasses, wine, and whiskey, and "enough cornmeal to supply themselves with corn bread for days."[62] Sherman looked around him, was impressed, and followed Grant like a blind man.

Actually, what Grant was doing was what Sherman had begun to articulate months earlier: Sherman just had not had the courage, or perhaps, the opportunity, to put it into practice. Sherman was also not Grant. He did not possess the confidence Grant did, nor did he see things as simplisticly as Grant. But as he marched along with his troops, living off the enemy's supplies, he was amazed and fascinated, and . . . convinced. Very quickly, whether he wanted to learn it or not, Sherman the theorist learned from Grant the pragmatist a final lesson in the theory of warfare. The lesson? When circumstances demand it, make your own rules.

Grant had organized his army into three corps which were commanded by Sherman, McClernand, and the young and promising James B. McPherson. By mid-May, after defeating a 3,000-man detachment of Confederates near the small town of Raymond, they marched to Jackson. With little difficulty the 12,000 men under Gen. Joseph E. Johnston were dispersed and forced to withdraw from the capital city. In a month's time Grant had run the batteries of Vicksburg, transported much of his army to the eastern side of the Mississippi River, traversed more than fifty miles through enemy territory, and captured a major state capital of the Confederacy. Now he was prepared to take "the final fortress."[63]

As the corps of McClernand and McPherson headed west toward

Vicksburg, Sherman remained in Jackson, but only long enough to destroy the city as a railroad and manufacturing center of the Confederacy. He set two divisions of his corps to work destroying the railroad, the arsenal, the government foundry, and various other military installations. Because of its value to the Rebels, a cotton factory was put to flame and the machinery destroyed.[64] The assistant secretary of war, Charles A. Dana, remained with Sherman and was an eyewitness to the method of warfare Sherman was to bring to the South. He made the observation: "I remained with Sherman to see the work of destruction. I remember . . . that I saw . . . the burning of vast quantities of cotton packed in bales, and that I was . . . astonished to see how slowly it burned."[65]

Since the beginning of the Vicksburg campaign, Sherman had witnessed the effectiveness of destruction brought to the houses of the enemy. What he saw, and in many cases what he was responsible for, was making a lasting impression on his attitude toward war. His observations and actions, however, were at times the source of a dilemma. He was pressed between his emerging theory of war based on destruction and devastation of public and private property, and his strong dedication to law and order. Was it really appropriate to break loose from the tenets of nineteenth-century warfare where army faced army on isolated battlefields? Was it ethically and morally right to bring the horrors of war to the lives of noncombatants? In the spring and early summer of 1863, Sherman found himself living a contradiction. His actions and much of what he had said and written said "yes,—taking war to the front porch steps of private citizens was necessary to defeat an enemy." Yet, at the same time, his words revealed an inner struggle with this issue. There were things he observed that he questioned and of which could not approve. He wrote to Ellen in May, "Of course devastation marked the whole path of the army, and I know all the . . . officers detest the infamous practices as . . . I do. Of course I expect and do take corn, bacon, ham, mules and everything to support an army, and don't object much to the using of fences for firewood. But this universal burning and wanton destruction of private property is not justified in war."[66] There was a repulsion and fascination with what Sherman ordered and observed. Attempting to draw as vivid a picture as possible, he described to Ellen the contrast:

> The trees are now in full leaf, the black and blue-birds sing sweetly, and the mocking bird is frantic with joy. The rose and

violet, the beds of verbena and mignonette, planted by the hands now in exile from their homes occupied by the rude barbarian, bloom as fair as though grim war had not torn with violent hands all the vestiges of what a few short months ago were houses of people as good as ourselves. You may pray that a good God in His mercy will spare the home of your youth the tread of an hostile army. . . .[67]

Bringing total war to the South was important to Sherman. It had grown increasingly so since his experience in Memphis. He had grown fascinated with the idea; he had become dedicated to the concept. He saw it as the only way effectively to defeat the enemy and bring hostilities to a rapid close. But it also repulsed him. Sherman was not simply a theorist, he was as much a pragmatist as Grant—he was a product of the nineteenth-century American environment. Sherman was the next logical step in the evolutionary development of warfare, and had it not been Sherman marching through the South, it would have been someone else, perhaps somewhere else. In other words, total war was inevitable. The Industrial Revolution made it inevitable. For armies to plunder and destroy for the purpose of implementing strategy was one thing, but for men to wreak havoc on people simply for havoc's sake was another. This Sherman could not accept. Granted, a very thin line separated the two and to some the distinction was blurred, but to Sherman the two were quite different. War justified the destruction because war was a means of re-establishing order.

To keep the distinction clear, Sherman took steps to make the difference real through action. To the planters of the Yazoo area Sherman restored farming implements carried off by his soldiers and wrote his division commander, Frederick Steele, "War at best is barbarism, but to involve all—children, women, old and helpless—is more than can be justified. Our men will become absolutely lawless unless they can be checked. . . . I always feel that the stores necessary for a family should be spared and I think it injures our men to allow them to plunder indiscriminately."[68] So, Sherman commanded his troops to forage for such items as corn and meat but to protect private property as much as possible. In this he was no different from all other officers of his day, both North and South. This was in accord with the established rules of warfare. In his eyes, in the summer of 1863, it was still anarchy to burn houses. To appropriate food, to destroy mills and warehouses was the business of war.

Sherman, however, was undergoing a transformation. In earlier years he had been entrenched in the ideas of nineteenth-century warfare. Then there was no contradiction in his life. War was to be fought by armies, and it was against the rules to include noncombatants. Now, due to changes beyond his control, changes that were pressing in on him from all sides, he found himself wedged between the old views and a new and different world. The foundations of traditional society were being shaken, and Sherman, like everyone else, had to adapt. Some held on to the old ways for dear life. They retreated into the values that made them feel secure. Lee, Davis, McClellan are examples. Others attempted to ignore the changes and simply continued to do what they had always done. But Sherman became an innovator. He made a choice, and the choice took him into the twentieth century. He came to the realization that in war the enemy encompassed more than its army and that victory required an attack on both the military and the support systems of that military. The Industrial Revolution, more specifically the development of the railroad and the advancement in weaponry, had made noncombatants and soldiers the same. Both were the enemy. In the summer of 1863, Sherman was on the verge of making the final shift from contradiction to paradox. Indeed, from Vicksburg on he became a man of paradox. In one letter to Ellen he could begin a discussion condemning the plundering and destruction brought about by his army, and finish the same letter with, "Until they [the enemy] lay down their arms and submit to the rightful authority of the government they must not appeal to me for mercy or favors. . . ."[69] Even when it came to death, Sherman was a paradox. In appearance he was completely callous toward death; in reality his nights and days were full of sorrow and pain because of the loss of human life. Speaking after the war, in December 1886, he said to an audience of veterans, "I assure you that we who took part in that war were kindly men. We did not wish to strike a blow. I know that I grieved as much as any man when I saw pain and sorrow and affliction among the innocent and distressed, and when I saw burning and desolation. But these were incidents of war, and were forced upon us. . . ."[70]

Sherman was unable to complete his work of destruction in Jackson. Grant, moving toward Vicksburg, encountered a strong force under Pemberton blocking his path and ordered Sherman to rejoin the army. Sherman immediately dropped what he was doing and headed west. But, before he could join Grant, the Battle of Champion Hill had been fought. With victory for the Federals, the Confederates retreated to the Big Black River just ten miles east of Vicksburg. Sherman arrived, but before his troops bridged and crossed the river, McClernand had routed the Rebels from their bridgehead and sent them scurrying back into the Vicksburg defenses. On May 19 and 22 Grant assaulted the works of the Confederates but failed. Realizing that future attempts would be pointless, Grant settled in for a long siege. The campaign lasted six weeks, and for over forty days the defenses and town were bombarded by both the land forces and Porter's gunboats and mortar scows on the river. Writing home, Sherman told Ellen that "Vicksburg at this moment must be a horrid place. . . ." He continued, "Vicksburg contains many of my old pupils and friends; should they fall into our hands I will treat them with kindness, but they have sowed the wind and must reap the whirlwind. Until they lay down their arms and submit to the rightful authority of government they must not appeal to me for mercy or favors."[71]

Finally, on July 4, General Pemberton surrendered his forces and the city to General Grant. Thus was the end of a brilliant and well-executed campaign. To Sherman it represented the most important gain of the war up to that time. The Union army took possession of valuable public property, consisting of railroads, locomotives, cars, steamers, cotton, guns, rifle-muskets, and ammunition. In addition, there was a tremendous loss of Southern manpower. Sherman was aware, however, that the true value of the fall of Vicksburg could not be measured in terms of men and material lost but by the fact that the Union forces with the surrender of Port Hudson on July 9 had gained control of the Mississippi River "from its source to its mouth."[72] He wrote proudly to his brother that the campaign completed "as pretty a page in the history of war and of our country as ever you could ask my name to be identified with."[73]

Sherman viewed the taking of Vicksburg as both a geographical and psychological victory. Not only did it free the Mississippi River from control by the Confederacy, but coinciding with the victory at Gettysburg on July 3, it hit the South so hard that hope began to fade. To borrow from a future war leader, it was the beginning of the end. Explaining the situation to his brother, Sherman wrote, "I see much of the people here—men of heretofore high repute. The fall of Vicksburg has had a powerful effect. They are subjugated. I even am amazed at the effect. . . ."[74] Sherman understood that loss of hope was much worse than loss of men, land, and material. To him it was the effect on morale "which made Vicksburg the great turning point of the war."[75] Finally, a direct hit had been made on the South's will to fight.

The Vicksburg campaign did not end with the fall of the city and the opening of the river. Grant had to secure his rear against a possible attack by the Confederate forces under General Johnston who had reoccupied Jackson and was using it as a base of operations. Two weeks before Vicksburg surrendered, Grant had ordered Sherman east to mass a second front to guard against an attempt by Johnston to relieve Pemberton. Now Sherman was to prepare a movement against Johnston. Grant instructed Sherman "to break up Johnston's Army . . . and . . . to destroy the rolling stock and everything valuable for carrying on war. . . ." Once this was accomplished he was to return to Vicksburg.[76] Seven weeks earlier Sherman had begun his destruction of Jackson, but before he was able to complete it he had been forced to rejoin the main army and assist in pushing Pemberton back into Vicksburg. Now he could return and finish what he had started. Walters is correct in saying, "This time Sherman was determined to employ his theory of total war to wreck Jackson and cripple that section of Mississippi permanently."[77]

Sherman moved his army east from the camps on the Big Black River and on July 9 invested the former state capital. Detachments of troops systematically destroyed the railroads, and foragers stripped the surrounding countryside of corn, hogs, sheep, and poultry. Reporting to Grant on his progress, Sherman said, "The wholesale destruction to which this country is now being subjected is terrible to contemplate, but it is the scourge of war, to which ambitious men have appealed, rather than the judgment of the learned and pure tribunals which our forefathers had provided for supposed wrongs and injuries."[78]

As Sherman's troops pressured Johnston and threatened his flanks where they anchored on the Pearl, the Confederate general wisely crossed the Pearl River and evacuated the city. In the process of their retreat, the Confederates set fire to a building containing commissary stores, and, in a matter of minutes, the flames spread to one of the wealthiest residential areas of Jackson. Sherman informed Grant that " . . . the city, with destruction committed by ourself in May last, and by the enemy during the siege, is one mass of charred ruins."[79] And to Admiral Porter, he said, "Our men, in spite of guards, have widened the circle of fire [begun by Johnston's men] so that Jackson once the pride and boast of Mississippi, is now a ruined town."[80] When it was all over, soldiers would refer to Jackson as "Chimneyville."

In spite of his efforts to control the devastation of Jackson, Sherman's troops got out of hand and small cadres of men, for various reasons ranging from personal revenge to material gain, looted and sacked the city. Against orders, they entered the homes of residents, destroyed personal belongings, and appropriated whatever they deemed as valuable. Many committed acts of sheer vandalism, removing doors from hinges, knocking out windows, piercing pictures with bayonets, and burning furniture in the streets. The Confederate Hotel and a Catholic church had already been destroyed by Sherman in mid-March, the presses of the Mississippian destroyed, and books from the Mississippi State Library stolen. The destruction was so great that a correspondent of the Chicago *Times* reported: "Finally after every other excess had been committed in the destruction of property, the torch was applied. The entire business portion of the city was in ruins except a few old frame buildings. One residence after another has been burned until none of the really fine ones remain, save those occupied by some of our general officers. Such complete ruin and devastation never followed the footsteps of an army before."[81] Charles E. Wilcox, a captain in an Indiana regiment, confessed that he had never seen "or heard of a city being so thoroughly sacked and burned as this place."[82]

Sherman issued orders that vandals were to be hanged by their thumbs and that courts-martial were to be held, but things were happening too rapidly, In addition, Sherman was so intent on making sure that Jackson would never again be used as a center of military operations that his heart was not in his orders. He was working on the belief that once the Vicksburg campaign was completed the war would soon end. Thoroughness was important, and to let up now would be a mistake, perhaps a drastic one. He wanted this incident to be a warning to the South that, when people resort to war, they must suffer its consequences. To a Warren County citizen's committee who approached him for relief, Sherman said: "General Grant can give you now no permanent assurance or guarantee, nor can I, nor can anybody. Of necessity, in the war the commander on the spot is the judge, and may take your house, your field, your everything, and turn you all out, helpless to starve." He continued, "It may be wrong, but that don't [sic] alter the case. In war you can't help yourselves, and the only possible remedy is to stop war. . . ." And he urged them to look around and "see the wreck. Let your minds contemplate the whole South in like chaos and disorder. . . . Those who die by the bullet are lucky compared to those poor fathers and wives and children who see their all taken and themselves left to perish, or linger out their few days in ruined poverty." In conclusion, he told the citizens that it was not his duty "to build up" but "rather to destroy both the rebel army and whatever wealth or property it has founded its boasted strength upon."[83]

The work of destruction and devastation was producing the desired results. It was bringing havoc to the social organization of the region and, in turn, was having a negative impact on the psychological well-being of citizens and soldiers. The area transportation system was torn from its foundations and the means to plant and harvest crops were made useless. Slaves were either taken from their owners or followed the Union army of their own accord. Families were separated from their homes either forcibly or, by choice, and left to fend for themselves. Some headed eastward, hoping to escape the devastation being heaped on them, while others remained and faced the choice of either perishing or begging for subsistence from the enemy. Any semblance of government left them when the last soldier of Johnston's army evacuated the city. Educational institutions became nonexistent, and the only hope left was their faith in God and the mercy of their invaders. Some were even beginning to wonder if God had decided against them. Sherman had succeeded in bringing sociological warfare to the area by disrupting the basic institutions of that part of the South. And it had the desired impact. A sense of hopelessness began to grow in the hearts and minds of those who had experienced the horror of Sherman's army, and to Sherman it was evident everywhere he looked. Writing to Grant, he said, "We have made fine progress to-day in the work of destruction. Jackson will no longer be a point of danger. . . . The inhabitants are subjugated. They cry aloud for mercy. The land is devastated for 30 miles around."[84]

The Southern armies had been dealt an indirect blow. Initial anger upon hearing of Sherman's activities against the noncombatants soon turned to anxious concern for the safety and welfare of their families. Depression gripped many as they received news "that wives, children and parents were deprived of sufficient food and clothing."[85] Some soldiers began to slip away from their ranks and headed home. Sherman's method of warfare was having its effect. During the siege of Jackson, General Johnston had written to President Davis that his men were deserting in large numbers using the various fords of Pearl River.[86] After the evacuation of Jackson, the general again reported to the Confederate president that the desertion rate was equally high among Mississippians.[87] In his final report to the secretary of war, Johnston regrettably admitted that "desertions during the siege and on the march were . . . frequent."[88] Thus, as evidenced by Johnston's remarks, Sherman's first rehearsal for the march to the sea was a tremendous success.

Of Sherman's part in the Vicksburg campaign Grant made these comments, "The siege of Vicksburg and last capture of Jackson and dispersion of Johnston's army entitle General Sherman to more credit than usually falls to the lot of one man to earn." He commended Sherman's April demonstration at Snyder's Bluff that proved successful in holding "the enemy about Vicksburg, while the army was securing a foothold east of the Mississippi." He praised his " . . . rapid marches to join the army afterwards; his management at Jackson, Mississippi, in the first attack; his almost unequalled march from Jackson to Bridgeport and passage of Black River; [and his] securing Walnut Hills on the 18th of May." All "may attest his great merit as a soldier."[89] Dana also approved of Sherman and his observations of the general in action at Vicksburg increased his admiration of him. Sherman was considered by the assistant secretary of war to be "a brilliant man and an excellent commander of a corps." He was especially impressed with Sherman's unequalled loyalty to Grant. Sherman had criticized the plan of the campaign frankly and openly to Grant, but, as Dana pointed out, he "supported every movement with all his energy. . . ."[90] Even Sherman's old enemy the Cincinnati *Gazette* re-evaluated his abilities as a soldier and commander. From John came the welcome news that Northern newspapers were now especially laudatory.[91]

Up to this time Sherman had passed through various stages of popular misunderstanding and criticism, but his movements around Vicksburg resulted in general and widespread appreciation throughout the country. His abilities, and even his perspective on the war, were at last being recognized and praised. Needless to say, Sherman was conscious of the plaudits, and they enhanced his self-confidence. For the first time he felt secure and independent. Not only had he proven himself in combat, but in Grant and Halleck he had witnessed a change in viewpoint concerning the character and, therefore, the implementation of the war. They were seeing, as he had seen for at least a year and a half, that the war must be directed against the will of the South. The security and independence came also as a result of his being commissioned a brigadier general in the regular army. Now his career was cemented, and he need no longer wander from occupation to occupation.

During these months in Mississippi, Sherman became dedicated to the proposition that strategy is not only the forerunner but the master of tactics; that without a total plan, the simple movement of troops will lead to sure disaster. The miles of rapid marches required of his corps taught him lessons he would apply with skill as he marched through Georgia and the Carolinas. Not only did he learn the value of rapid marches and the element of surprise, he also realized that the use of mobility by an army was highly effective. Such tactics could first disturb the enemy, then upset his balance. He learned the value of deceptive direction and the importance of communication. Although these ideas were not totally new to Sherman, Vicksburg provided the opportunity for him to see and participate in their demonstration. He absorbed them into his philosophy of warfare. Sherman, so cautious earlier in his career, was now understanding that, militarily, there was much more security and success in the unexpected than in reliance on sheer brute force.

He not only learned the value of maneuver in war, he also recognized more than ever the spiritual effect a general has on his soldiers. He once said, "There is a soul of an army as well as to the individual man, and no general can accomplish the full work of his army unless he commands the soul. . . ."[92] Thus, he was determined to let his soldiers see and know that the man who led them was always near. The front lines became the best place to make prompt decisions, and from this campaign on, he was always to choose the roughest quarters among his men, to march with them, and to refrain from demanding too much of them.

He came to cherish mobility and took every opportunity to polish his army's marching ability. From the first, he taught his men that it was futile to beg rides in wagons. None could ride except the desperately ill or wounded, and men found in ambulances or on mules or horses without written permission from a surgeon were dismounted and sent to the ranks. Straggling was seen as intolerable and viewed to be "as much a crime as rebellion." It was punished severely. "Our corps . . . must be compact and strong," Sherman said.[93] Discipline was important for mobility, and he believed it could make or break an army. And always there was that psychological value of example. Sherman constantly made himself visible to his troops; he marched with them and showed them an interest that was genuine. Writing to Ellen, he said, "Soldiers have a right to see and know that the man who guides them is near enough to see with his own eyes. . . ."[94]

As Grant was a significant person in shaping Sherman's life, so Vicksburg was a significant event in shaping his philosophy of war. The experience at Vicksburg fixed permanently his attitude toward war in general and the South in particular. "A logical ruthlessness"[95] captured his mind as he realized even more fully that the principal issue behind the war "rested in the wills of the Southern people and not in the bodies of their troops."[96] Writing to General Halleck in September 1863, Sherman gave expression to his attitude. He wrote, "I would not coax them, or even meet them half way. . . ." Instead, Sherman was intent on making the people of the Southern states so "sick of war that generations would pass away before they would again appeal to it. . . ."[97] The most effective way to defeat the South was to break its morale, and the way to break its morale was to take every opportunity to destroy property that in any way enhanced the military. Such a strategy, he reasoned, would shorten the war and save lives. Thus, destroy the enemy's resources, and you destroy the enemy.

Sherman's demand for respect for the laws of the Constitution intensified as a result of the Vicksburg experience. "Obedience to the law," he wrote to Halleck, "absolute—yea, even abject—is the lesson that this war, under Providence, will teach and enlighten American citizens."[98] In detail he expressed his ideas on government to John. In August 1863, he wrote, "A government resting immediately on the caprice of a people is too instable to last. The will of the people is the ultimate appeal, but constitution, laws of Congress, and regulations of the executive departments subject to the decisions of the Supreme Court are the laws which all must obey without stopping to inquire why. All *must* obey."[99] To Sherman, the law was more important than the whims of people, thus the law must be "independent of man." Whatever it took to bring people outside the law back into its confines was permissible, for the absence of law means the presence of anarchy. Sherman's love and hope for the United States would not allow him to take any other stance. Intent on re-establishing respect for law, Sherman was determined to carry out his ruthlessness to the point of no cessation until the South was willing to beg for mercy. He would not compromise.

But it is easy to misunderstand his ruthlessness. Sherman was not ruthless in the sense that he slaughtered people in cold blood, nor did he maim them or torture them. Such practices would have been abhorrent to him. Sherman was not ruthless for the sake of being ruthless. His form of ruthlessness was contained, yet firm. He was willing to destroy property, set people on the road to the unknown, and create fear in their souls. He was willing also to soften his commands against them and lighten their loads. On one issue, however, he would not budge. He was and would remain ruthless on the issue of breaking the will of the Southerners. He would be harsh until he encountered people who were seriously concerned with ending the war, then he would become compassionate, helpful, and understanding. He viewed Southerners as fellow Americans who had gone astray. In Jackson he was contacted by a group of citizens whom he believed were serious about ending the rebellion. Men whom he knew as "very intelligent and influential" came to him to discuss ways of bringing themselves and their state back into the Union. "This was the moment," Lloyd Lewis writes, "for which Sherman had been waiting since the beginning of the war."[100] The way was simple, Sherman told them. Admit their error in rebelling and cease fighting. For a very complex man, the world in which he lived appeared simple. He had thought things through and the complexities of the world were clear. To him, there was right and wrong, and little room for discussion or debate between the two.

The experience with the citizens in Jackson convinced Sherman that when circumstances warranted, he should carry forth acts of mercy. So he returned to the enemy their family carriages, buggies, and farming tools. He dispatched food and medicine to hospitals and asylums and fed hundreds of women and children with army supplies. But, just as he was not ruthless for the sake of being ruthless, he was not merciful for the sake of mercy. Perhaps he had in mind Jomini's recommendation that the invader should "calm the popular passions in every possible way, exhaust them by time and patience, display courtesy, gentleness, and severity united . . ." when he committed acts of mercy.[101] But there was always a condition. Sherman reasoned that with merciful acts he might gain the respect of the enemy and thus wean them from the Southern cause. Mercy, in other words, like ruthlessness, had a military purpose. It was a tactical act.

But the actions of the Confederate government following the fall of Vicksburg and the destruction of Jackson eliminated mercy as a tactic of warfare. His euphoria over the unprecedented success of a Union army and his tremendous hope for an end to the conflict blinded Sherman to reality. In summer quarters west of the Big Black River, Sherman's logic told him that the war would now end shortly. The Mississippi River flowed freely from its source to the Gulf of Mexico, all around him he saw the subjugation of citizens, Johnston's army had retreated eastward, and the interior of the heartland of the South lay wide open. How could the enemy rationally continue the war? And therein is Sherman's mistake. A highly logical thinker, extremely rational, he expected the enemy to be the same. So, when he read in the newspapers that the Confederate government was conscripting males between the ages of eighteen and forty-five and that Confederate general Braxton Bragg was readying to do battle against a Union force under Gen. William S. Rosecrans in Georgia, he was astounded and angered. It appeared that the various defeats of 1863, instead of making "the enemy collapse with exhaustion" had caused its rage to arise "like a wounded bull."[102]

Sherman also expected logic from his own government. While engaged in rebuilding the Memphis and Charleston Railroad to the east so that the army could be supplied, he began to realize that the success of Vicksburg had brought a general relaxation to the Army of the Tennessee.[103] With the relaxation of effort came a "desire to escape the hard drudging of camp. . . ."[104] Sherman saw danger and foolishness in such a stance. Now that the Union forces were on the move, it was, in his opinion, absurd to relax, even for a moment. To Halleck he wrote, " . . . I contend that the interests of the United states and of the real parties concerned demand the continuance of [the movement against the enemy] till . . . all the organized armies of the South are depressed, conquered, and subjugated."[105] Sherman was sure that now was the time, not to become idle, but to "pile on our blows thick and fast."[106] Loyalty and gratitude kept Sherman from openly criticizing Halleck, yet he did disagree on policy. He disapproved of Halleck's defensive warfare and his policy of scattering Grant's army throughout the Mississippi Valley for the purpose of garrisoning towns. Sherman believed that such a policy would lead to stalemate. Besides, it kept troops exposed to capture and death by making them stationary targets. He also believed it was wasteful to guard so many outlying railroads, which was another of Halleck's practices.

But, with or without Sherman's advice, the Army of the Tennessee settled into a two-and-a-half-month period of idleness. Sherman had no choice but to accept the situation and make it as constructive a time for his troops as possible. He disliked garrison life because of its boredom and the negative effects it had on the health of soldiers.[107] So, he set about the task of training his men in the various areas necessary for campaigning and resupplying them with items of both a personal and military nature.

Training and resupplying his corps, however, brought Sherman little satisfaction. He thought the army must move, take the offensive until the South was willing to lay down its arms. To seize enemy territory and retain it was fine, but there was more to conducting war. The enemy must be kept on the move.

Sherman sought satisfaction by writing letters—to Halleck, to Ellen, and to John. Although written in the guise of a letter, Sherman carefully composed a detailed and enlightened essay to Halleck expressing his views on everything from his dreams for America in the future to how the country should be governed once the war ended. After expressing his belief that "the valley of the Mississippi is America," he turned to thoughts concerning the "State governments of Louisiana, etc." He wrote, "I would deem it very unwise at this time, or for years to come, to revive the [state governments of the southern Mississippi Valley], or to institute in this quarter any civil government in which the local people have much to say." For Sherman they could not be trusted. "They chose war—they ignored and denied all the obligations of . . . government. . . ." They chose to use force to settle their complaints. "I know them well" and they would do the same again. The large planter class was basically responsible for the war and should be replaced rather than reconstructed. The small farmers, storekeepers, and laborers did not understand the war and had little interest in it. Sherman believed that they followed the large planters blindly and were used effectively by them. To seek assistance from the Union people of the South would be a waste of energy. "I account them as nothing in this great game of war." Sherman saw them as submissive and "full of complaints." Finally, there are the "young bloods," those "who never did work and never will." Sherman felt war pleased them. He called them brave and "the most dangerous set of men this war has turned loose upon the world." He advised Halleck that once the war was over the "young bloods" must be controlled. From this group Sherman feared partisan activity after the formal hostilities had ended.

Based on this analysis Sherman suggested that the wisest policy would be "the continuance of . . . military rule till after *all* the organized armies of the South are dispersed, conquered and subjugated." He, therefore, urged that the war be continued with great vigor, holding that all other issues were minor compared to defeating the South, and that to hesitate could lead to disaster.[108]

After much urging from her husband, Ellen and the four oldest of the Sherman children came to Vicksburg for a visit. When they arrived they found a man happy and content with his life. Ellen was pleased and took pride in her husband's accomplishments. Sherman had just been promoted to brigadier general in the regular army which brought increased status and financial security. This, for both Ellen and her husband, was a tremendous relief. They all stayed at the camp on the Big Black River, and it was not long before the family was participating in the various and sundry activities of an idle army. Sherman particularly enjoyed his nine-year-old son Willie. The two were constantly together as Sherman moved among his troops. "The little fellow . . . won all hearts by his winning ways and his fondness for playing soldier," said one trooper.[109] Sherman would recall later that "Willie took the most intense interest in the affairs of the army" and that "he was a great favorite with the soldiers." He rode on horseback with Sherman, learned the manual of arms, and attended parades.[110] Eventually, Willie was made an honorary sergeant in the Thirteenth Battalion, United States Regulars.

While Sherman was enjoying his family in Mississippi, the war was continuing in Tennessee and northwest Georgia. The Army of the Cumberland under the command of Maj. Gen. William S. Rosecrans moved against the Confederates and were mauled and defeated at

Chickamauga. Retreating northward, Rosecrans found himself in a state of siege at Chattanooga. Halleck sent word to Grant to forward immediately as many troops as he could spare to relieve Rosecrans. Grant turned to Sherman for the task and ordered him to take the major part of his corps to the Chattanooga area via Memphis. Sherman's wife and children joined him as his steamer embarked from Vicksburg. Once in Memphis, he would debark and his family would continue northward to Ohio and home. On the slow trip up the Mississippi, Willie fell ill with a high fever. The surgeon diagnosed the illness as typhoid fever. By the time the family arrived in Memphis the illness had become critical and the boy soon died.

The loss was devastating and hurt Sherman deeply. He felt extreme guilt for having urged his family to come South; when he tried to sleep he would awaken seeing Willie, and he wrote his wife, "Why was I not killed at Vicksburg, and left Willie to grow up to care for you?"[111]

The men of the Thirteen Infantry gave Willie a military funeral, and Ellen, along with the other children, took him northward for burial. Writing to the commander of the First Battalion, Thirteenth Infantry, Sherman said, "The child that bore my name . . . now floats a mere corpse, seeking a grave . . . with a weeping mother, brother, and sister clustered about him. For myself I ask no sympathy. On, on I must go, to meet a soldier's fate or live to see our country rise superior to all factions. . . . God only knows why he should die thus young."[112]

But Sherman had little time to grieve. In mid-October, Maj. Gen. George Thomas replaced Rosecrans as commander of the Army of the Cumberland, and Grant was ordered to Chattanooga as commander of the Military District of the Mississippi. The District was to consist of the Armies of the Ohio, the Cumberland, and the Tennessee. Sherman was made commander of the Army of the Tennessee.

# CHAPTER SEVEN

# *"Well-Established Principles of War"*

IN NOVEMBER 1862, SHERMAN HAD CONFERRED with Grant in Columbus, Kentucky, to begin plans for the capture of Vicksburg and the opening of the Mississippi River. Now, a year later, in mid-November 1863, Sherman arrived in the besieged city of Chattanooga to assist Grant in laying plans for, hopefully, another victory against the Confederate forces. Much had happened in that eventful year to harden Sherman's attitude toward the South, and he was prepared mentally to do whatever was necessary to bring victory to the Federals. Six weeks had passed since the death of his son, and he had managed to put his grief behind him and move forward. Except for this tragic event, the year had been a productive and satisfying one. He had sealed his relationship with Grant to the extent that he could say, "With Grant I will undertake anything in reason."[1] He had come to see Grant as "a second self."[2] Indeed he had already proven with the Vicksburg campaign that he would undertake anything Grant proposed, even if it appeared unreasonable. He held no doubts now concerning his own abilities and knew what was needed to defeat the South. His philosophy of war was fixed within him, and with the work he had implemented at Jackson, he had come to see that crushing the morale of the South was the best means of bringing the war to an end. In his mind he had made the transfer from nineteenth-century warfare to twentieth-century warfare, and had settled in his heart all moral scruples concerning the involvement of noncombatants in war. Arriving in Chattanooga to meet with Grant, Sherman

*Lt. Gen. William T. Sherman.*

was a portrait of self-confidence and conviction. He was ready for the next campaign.

To break Bragg's hold on Chattanooga, Grant developed a three-pronged plan of attack. Maj. Gen. Joseph Hooker would assault Lookout Mountain or the left flank of the Confederate army. Sherman would cross the Tennessee River and effect a lodgement upstream from Chattanooga at the northern extremity of Missionary Ridge, the right flank of Bragg's army. The third prong of Grant's plan was a demonstration against the Confederate center by General Thomas.[3]

For three days (November 23, 24, and 25) the two armies clashed with each other until the Union forces were successful in dislodging the Confederates from their heights west, south, and east of Chattanooga. Bragg's troops retreated southeast to the town of Dalton, Georgia, some twenty miles away. Chattanooga now lay in the hands of the Federals. Its loss was yet another devastating blow to the Confederacy, for instead of the South being able to use the city as a route into Tennessee, now Chattanooga "gave the Union a window into Georgia."[4] The Union army held "the keys of the whole central region, and of the gates of Georgia."[5]

Sherman was impressed with the manner in which Grant had conducted the campaign, saying, "It was magnificent in its conception, in its execution, and in its glorious results."[6] Grant, rightfully so, became the North's "man of the hour."[7] Yet, like Shiloh, Chattanooga brought controversy and tended to obscure Sherman's role in the campaign. The common criticism is that Sherman failed to carry out his goal of capturing Missionary Ridge and that he failed to throw the full weight of his troops into the effort. Sherman, in a rather self-serving manner, answered his critics by stating they missed the whole point of his role in the battle. He argued that he did not fail because he deliberately abstained from taking the ridge. All he sought to do was to delude the enemy into the belief that he was trying to take it. In a letter to his brother he provided an analysis of his actions. He wrote, "The whole philosophy of the battle was that I should get, by a dash, a position on the extremity of the Missionary Ridge from which the enemy would be forced to drive me, or allow his depot at Chickamauga Station to be in danger. I expected Bragg to attack me at daylight, but he did not, and to bring matters to a crisis quickly, as time was precious, for the sake of

Burnside in East Tennessee, Grant ordered me to assume the offensive."[8]

In support of Sherman's position is a dispatch he received from Grant praising him for the work he had done, not only in taking "by the forces under your command . . . much of the same range of hills [Missionary Ridge]," but also "in attracting the attention of so many of the enemy as to make Thomas' part certain of success."[9] No doubt, Grant had been misinformed. Although criticisms continued to surround Sherman's part in the battle,[10] they did not have an adverse effect on his morale. He personally felt that he had carried out his part of the plan, and that Grant considered Sherman's actions vital to the outcome.

Now that the sections of Mississippi adjacent to the Vicksburg and Natchez enclaves had been freed from Rebel control with the capture of Vicksburg and the victory at Chattanooga, it became Sherman's task to keep the Rebels at bay. On his return in January from a short leave to celebrate the Christmas holidays in Ohio with his family, he learned that Confederate armies were active in those parts of the state east of the Pearl River. This not only posed a threat to the unimpeded navigation of the Mississippi River, it also meant that a year's work could easily be lost. Writing to Maj. Gen. John A. Logan, Sherman expressed in his exaggerated style his apprehension concerning the safety of Mississippi. He said:

> To secure the safety of the navigation of the Mississippi I would slay millions. On that point I am not only insane, but mad. Fortunately, the great West is with me there. I think I see one or two quick blows that will astonish the natives of the South, and will convince them that, though to stand behind a big cotton-wood and shoot at a passing boat is good sport and safe, it may still reach and kill their friends and families hundreds of miles off. For every bullet shot at a steam-boat, I would shoot a thousand 30-pounder Parrotts into even helpless towns on Red, Ouachita, Yazoo, or even wherever a boat can float or a soldier march. Well, I think in all January and part of February I can do something in this line.[11]

Sherman's plan was to place a number of detachments of his army at various points in the state to observe the movements of the enemy, operate against them when necessary, and then send a powerful force through the heart of the state. Sherman planned a raid of destruction and devastation. The geographical objective was Meridian, Mississippi, a town of less than 1,000 people, but an important stronghold of the Confederacy. Meridian "was the key to the remaining railroads in Mississippi" and housed valuable military stores.[12] Capturing Meridian would mean that the "whole Confederate position west of the Tombigbee River would be untenable."[13] Actually the raid against Meridian had developed in Sherman's mind back in July 1863, when he was bringing devastation to Jackson. As he pushed General Johnston's army out of that city, he had hoped to continue eastward until Johnston and his 32,000 men were completely out of the state. In the process Sherman planned to destroy property useful to the enemy's military efforts and railroads, especially the Mobile and Ohio. However, due to the heat and the lack of adequate provisions for such a long raid, Sherman turned back to Vicksburg and encamped west of the Big Black River. Now, four months later, the opportunity was made available for him to carry out his plan. The strategic importance of the move would be the assurance of the Union's control of Mississippi, and he would accomplish it through the implementation of his concept of total war. This would be, as Walters described it, the first "practical application" of his accumulated ideas of warfare.[14]

Although it has been suggested that the Meridian expedition was part of "a chain reaction of fires and desolation in Mississippi"[15] begun as a result of the death of Sherman's son, the evidence is to the contrary. It is true, as Margie Bearss points out, that Sherman's attitude toward the South hardened following the Vicksburg campaign, and it is also true that Sherman experienced extreme guilt over having his family come South for a visit, especially since it was at his urging.

It was normal for him to have sought an explanation for Willie's tragic illness. Grief and guilt cause all people to enter a stage of projection. Naturally, due to the type of illness—typhoid fever—Sherman blamed "that sickly region" with "so fated a climate at so critical a period of the year." In a letter to Ellen in October 1863, he even went so far as to conclude: "To it [the climate of Vicksburg] must be traced the loss of my child. . . ."[16] But to conclude from this situation that the Meridian expedition was the result of personal grief and revenge borne of guilt is to misunderstand Sherman the soldier. First, it must be remembered that he developed the idea of the raid to Meridian before his family came South, thus it was already in his mind. At the time he was not even sure it would take place. Second, the raid fit perfectly with his developing theory of war. He had come to believe that an indirect attack against the military forces of the Confederacy would be just as effective as an assault on its armies. Such a raid would be a strike against the will of the South. Third, Sherman had never evidenced in his forty-plus years any act of personal revenge. To do so would be a complete deviation from his past patterns of behavior. Sherman had always carried himself with integrity and honesty, even during the roughest times. An attack on Mississippi for personal revenge and inner satisfaction would be abhorrent to him. Fourth, Sherman was a professional. He was, and always had been, dedicated to being a soldier. He was ever aware of his profession and his duty as a member of the military. An act of personal revenge would have been a violation of the oath he had first taken as a cadet at West Point. Sherman did not have it within him to commit such a violation. Fifth, Sherman was a man of great personal control and pride. Although he was highly animated and expressed his frustrations verbally, oftentimes quite exaggeratedly, he never lost that control or compromised his integrity. To commit an act of vengeance as a result of personal grief would be out of character. Sixth, Sherman was highly influenced by Grant and he would not have committed any act contrary to Grant's strategy as he understood it. The two men had become a team and both were dedicated to ending the war. Finally, Sherman was dedicated to the Union and the future of the United States. He wanted this conflict to end as soon as possible, not for personal satisfaction and gain, but for the sake of his country. Sherman knew how to keep separated what the sociologist C. Wright Mills termed personal troubles and public issues.[17] The war was a public issue and, therefore, on a higher plane. It affected his country. That was much more important to Sherman than any personal trouble he would ever experience, even the death of his favorite son. No, the Meridian campaign was not an act of personal vengeance against the South; it was a military expedition planned and executed by a professional for strategic purpose.

Sherman was anxious to begin the expedition, for now he could independently apply his philosophy of war. In a sense, this was what all his previous years of preparation were about. Writing to Ellen about the planned movement, he said, "If I had ten more regiments I would be tempted to try Mobile, but as it is if I break at Meridian and Memphis, I will cut off one of the most fruitful corn supplies of the enemy, and will give Mississippi a chance to rest. The State is now full of conscript gangs carrying to their armies the unwilling, the old and young. We will take all provisions, and God help the starving families; I warned them last year against this last visitation, and now it is at hand. . . ."[18] Informing John of the expedition, he said, "I'll break up those roads so effectively that repairs will cost more time and money than they can afford in a year. The effect of this will be to keep the force in Miss. from receiving prompt reinforcements and supplies and will gradually alienate them from the rest of the Confederacy."[19]

The expedition moved out of Vicksburg on February 3, 1864, "with only a bare minimum of transport."[20] Ahead was 120 miles of enemy territory open to Sherman to do at will what he desired. From the beginning he set the pace by ordering that "the expedition [should] be one of celerity. . . ." Since Bull Run he had emphasized the necessity for marching lightly, and now the emphasis was even greater. From the commander down, the order was given that not a tent "will be carried." The sick would be left behind "and the surgeons can find houses and sheds for all hospital purposes."[21] This was to be a raid, not a leisurely march into the enemy's interior. Sherman was not about to have his movement impeded by his own army. Also, he executed the tactic of delusion by letting it be known that his destination was Mobile, Alabama.[22] Other rumors were spread that he was headed for Selma or Demopolis.

Although Maj. Gen. Stephen D. Lee's Confederate cavalry met Sherman's force near Bolton, fourteen miles east of the Big Black River and continued to harass him most of the way to Meridian,[23] Sherman had little difficulty in reaching Jackson on the evening of February 5. Here a number of buildings were destroyed by runaway slaves as an act of retaliation for the cruelties inflicted on them by their former masters.[24] Others were also torched by Union soldiers. The raid from Jackson to Meridian went as Sherman had planned. The army lived abundantly off the land as it cut its swath through Mississippi. A soldier in Sherman's army recorded in his diary dated February 7, 1864: "Plenty of forage. . . ."[25] As Capt. Andrew Hickenlooper observed passing through the small community of Hillsboro, it is "nearly deserted and now mostly destroyed by fire."[26]

Finally, on February 14, Sherman's army entered Meridian with "the enemy retreating before us." Immediately the Federal forces set to work destroying "an arsenal, immense storehouses, and the railroad in every direction."[27] Every building that had been used by the Confederate government was burned, and a Confederate hospital was destroyed after the few patients were evacuated.[28] Railroads were demolished and the rails twisted and bent so as never to be used again.[29] Sherman said of the destruction, "On the 16th began a systematic and thorough destruction of the railroads centering at Meridian. The immense depots, warehouses, and the length of side-track [all eventually destroyed] demonstrated the importance to the enemy of that place. Through it he has heretofore transported his armies and vast supplies, and by means of the railroads large amounts of corn, bacon, meal, and produce have been distributed to his armies."[30] Reporting to Grant he gave this description, "For five (5) days, ten thousand of our men worked hard and with a will, in that work of destruction, with axes, sledges, crowbars, clawbars, and with fire, and I have no hesitation in pronouncing the work well done. Meridian with its Depots, Storehouses, Arsenals, offices, Hospitals, Hotels, and Cantonments, no longer exist."[31]

Besides supervising the work of destruction in Meridian itself, Sherman sent out raiding parties in all directions for the purpose of destroying whatever might be of benefit to the enemy.[32] On February 16, the Mobile and Ohio Railroad to Marion was uprooted,[33] bridges and culverts outside the city were burned,[34] smokehouses were broken into and contents taken, sawmills and cotton gins put to the torch, and private residences destroyed.[35] From all directions—north, south, east, and west—Sherman received reports from his officers of the results of their work. For example, from Maj. Gen. Stephen A. Hurlbut sixty miles of railroad with ties and iron bent and burned, and from General McPherson 6,075 feet of trestle work below Enterprise burned.[36] The reports kept coming in for five days and Sherman was pleased. The campaign was a success. He had accomplished his goals of driving the enemy from the state and destroying the only remaining rail center in Mississippi. In approximately a month, Meridian, the surrounding area, and a strip 120 miles long and 10 miles wide had been reduced to "fire-charred timbers and ashes."[37] As one Union soldier described it, "Sherman's army left fire and famine in its track. The country was one lurid blaze of fire; burning cotton gins and deserted buildings were seen on every hand."[38]

The last week in February, Sherman turned his army west for the return to Vicksburg and again let loose his troops on villages and the countryside. The destruction was so thorough that it led an officer of Sherman's Signal Corps to report that at Lake Station (destroyed on the way to Meridian), "We went through the town like a dose of salts and just as we were leaving I noticed a man hunting around to get someone to make an affidavit that there had been a town there."[39]

On March 3, Sherman was back in Vicksburg, exactly a month after he had left, and he was reported with pride, "We accomplished all I undertook. Our march out and in from Vicksburg was well accomplished; we beat the enemy whenever he opposed or offered resistance. We drove him out of Mississippi, destroyed the only remaining railroads in the state, the only roads in which he could maintain any army in Mississippi threatening to our forces on the main river." He was happy to report that "we subsisted our army and animals chiefly on his stores, brought away about 400 prisoners and full 5,000 negroes, about 1,000 white refugees, about 3,000 animals (horses, mules, and oxen), and any quantity of wagons and vehicles. . . ."[40] In his final report to General Halleck, Sherman summarized his campaign and offered an evaluation. He stated:

> My movement to Meridian stampeded all Alabama. [Gen. Leonidas] Polk retreated across the Tombigbee and left me to break railroads and smash things at pleasure. . . . Weather and everything favored me . . . [and] the enemy spared me battle. . . . Our loss was trifling, and . . . we broke . . . a full hundred miles of railroad at and around Meridian. . . . We lived off the country and made a swarth of desolation 50 [an exaggeration] miles broad across the State of Mississippi. . . . The destruction of Meridian makes it simply impossible for the enemy to risk anything but light cavalry this side of Pearl River. . . .[41]

Confederate general Stephen D. Lee called the destruction through Mississippi the "Sherman Torch" and asked in later years, "Was this the warfare of the civilization of the nineteenth century?"[42] To which Sherman would have quickly answered, "No." Lee and other critics of Sherman's Meridian raid failed to understand that he had intended to accomplish one thing with his movement— to paralyze the Confederacy so that Mississippi would remain peaceful and free during the rest of the war.[43] He was not in the conflict to fight chivalrous battle, but to bring the war to a victorious conclusion.

Much to Sherman's pleasure, word spread rapidly throughout the country concerning the expedition. The New York *Times* published a letter from Meridian that described the destruction, pointing out that few unoccupied buildings escaped being burned and that most of the private homes of the citizens had been destroyed.[44] Other Northern newspapers wrote of plundering, taking of animals, destruction of fences, and slaves being carried away.[45] The Mobile *Daily Tribune* carried a letter from a citizen who lived outside Meridian. It said, "They have destroyed everything in our neighborhood, all communication by letter or otherwise has stopped. They took nearly all the negroes, horses, mules, hogs, and chickens in our settlement. I do not think you can hear a chicken crow for ten miles around Meridian."[46] Again, as in Jackson, but on a much larger scale, the sociological destruction was enormous. Families were scattered, communication systems destroyed, the means of making a livelihood ripped from its roots, and government annihilated.

A young soldier in Sherman's army wrote home to Cincinnati that foraging had been so thorough that "I think if a mosquito would go over that road now, or in the country for miles each side, he would not find provisions for three days rations."[47] William Pitt Chambers, a Mississippi soldier, wrote the following in his diary:

> The enemy has Meridian. . . . It is a shame!—a stigma on the fair fame of the confederacy that thirty-five thousand hostile men should march entirely through Mississippi . . . and no obstacle be placed in the way to impede their progress!
>
> We are told that the Country is devastated where they go— that their trail is marked by the smouldering ruins of burned dwellings—that crops are destroyed, and that everything that ministers to the necessities of life is laid waste by a remorseless foe.

With a sense of sadness and resignation, Chambers ended his entry with, "Never did I once think that such degradation could come upon my beloved native State, so long as she had one son left whose heart beat true to freedom, home, and God!"[48]

Never before had the country, both North and South, heard of such devastation. To some it was appalling, a crime against humanity, a sin, while to others it was an event to be acclaimed as the only way to bring the South to its knees. To Sherman it was what he hoped for—the psychological and sociological underpinnings of the Confederacy had begun to tumble and fall.

While the news of the Meridian raid traveled up and down the land, Sherman sent messages to his officers to heighten Southern fears of the Federal army. The messages basically carried the content of a letter he had sent in January to Maj. R. M. Sawyer in Alabama, a message he instructed be read to the citizens of that area. His position should be made clear "so as to prepare them for my coming." He wrote, "In Europe whence we derive our principles of war, wars are between kings and rulers through hired armies, and not between peoples. These remain, as it were, neutral, and sell their produce to whatever army is in possession. Therefore, the general rule was and is that war is confined to the armies engaged, and should not visit the houses of families or private interests."[49] But this was not Europe, and the Confederacy was not a king or a ruler. A new era had arrived. This was America, and the Confederacy was people— leaders, soldiers, and civilians.

Sherman warned the South that, if they persisted in rebelling against the United States, they could expect the confiscation of their homes and land. He continued, "So long as non-combatants remain in their homes and keep to their accustomed peaceful business, their opinions and prejudices can in no wise influence the war, and therefore should not be noticed; but if any one comes out into the public streets and creates disorder, he or she should be punished, restrained or banished. . . ."[50] Those who continued "correspondence with parties in hostility" would be treated as spies and punished accordingly. Whereas, to those who submitted to the law all gentleness and forbearance would be given. No tolerance would be shown toward citizens who remained persistent with the secessionist movement. To them death was mercy.

To Sherman these were "well-established principles of war, and the people of the South having appealed to war . . . must abide by its rules and laws. . . ."[51] For women, children, and other noncombatants he established a policy of protecting their houses as long as they remained inside. In response to those who criticized his failure to protect private property, he said, "The people of the South, having appealed to *war*, are barred from appealing for protection under our constitution, which they have practically and publicly defied."[52] Herein is the core of Sherman's justification for total war. The people of the South had selected war as the means to solve their differences with the rest of the country. In doing so, they had relinquished their rights under the Constitution and submitted themselves to the

rules of war. This was the consequence of secession and the firing on
Fort Sumter. Granted, the rules Southerners had appealed to were
nineteenth-century rules, but times change; thus the rules change. It
was not vengeance that stirred Sherman, nor did he "unleash a
horde of destroyers to prowl" the land. Restraints were provided,
policy was established, and there was regard for law and order.[53]
But, a new day had dawned in warfare and Sherman was at its
forefront. The world had ceased being a provincial place to live.

The Meridian experience confirmed Sherman's views concerning
the role of the cavalry in military operations. In coordination with
the march Sherman had intended for Gen. W. Sooy Smith to leave
Memphis with his cavalry, disable the Mobile and Ohio Railroad,
consume the resources of the enemy, break up the connection with
Columbus, Mississippi, and finally "reach me at or near Meridian as
near the date" mentioned as possible.[54] It was hoped that once he
arrived, the joint Union forces could head for Mobile or perhaps
Selma.[55] Much to Sherman's distress, however, Smith did not arrive
at Meridian with his cavalry on or near the date Sherman had selected; in fact, he never got there at all, having met and been bested
by Nathan Bedford Forrest at Okoloma on February 22. Sherman
waited in hopes that he would appear and even sent out parties to
look for him, but to no avail.[56] While waiting for his subordinate,
Sherman remarked, "It will be a novel thing in war if infantry has to
await the motions of cavalry."[57] The novel did not happen, and it
made Sherman even more skeptical concerning the effectiveness of
cavalry. Within the past year he had on occasion been critical of the
traditional use and performance of the cavalry. Now with the failure
of Smith, his criticisms became more frequent and harsh.

Most cavalrymen in both the eastern Union and Confederate armies held to the old European standards of "brilliant thundering
charges, spectacular hurricanes of steel." Sherman knew that such
an attitude was no longer relevant, especially in an industrial age
and a country "as wooded and broken as the South." He remarked,
"Infantry can always whip cavalry and in a wooded or mountainous
country can actually thwart it and even at times capture it. . . . I have
not seen in this war a cavalry command of 1,000 that was not afraid
of the sight of a dozen infantry bayonets, for the reason that the
cavalry to be effective have to have a road or smooth fields, whereas
the infantryman steps into the bushes and is safe, or can block a road

in five minutes and laugh at the man on horseback."[58] (Surely he was impressed with the victories scored by Forrest and Morgan over Union infantry?) From Sherman's point of view the cavalry had two main functions: one, to gather information for an army as to the strength and whereabouts of the enemy, and two, to destroy railroads and lines of supply. Cavalry no longer made any significant contribution as a fighting unit. Believing this to be true, Sherman broke from the generally accepted philosophy concerning horse soldiers. This action, of course, led to complaints from those dedicated to the romance of Sir Walter Scott, but, in spite of the arguments, Sherman held his ground and enforced his views.

The Meridian expedition resulted in little bloodshed and loss of life, and confirmed Sherman's belief that maneuverability was more important and effective than frontal assault. He commented, "Of course I must fight when the time comes, but whenever a result can be accomplished without a battle I prefer it."[59] This would become a trademark with Sherman and he would perfect it as he fought Johnston and Hood northwest of and around Atlanta.

Although the South, as could be expected, was highly critical of Sherman's raid through Mississippi, he received little or no negative remarks from personal or military friends. Indeed, they seemed to have understood what he was accomplishing. Even Halleck approved of the results. He wrote Sherman, "The safety of our armies and a proper regard for the lives of our soldiers, require that we apply to our inexorable foes the severe rules of war. . . . I have endeavored to impress these views upon our commanders for the last two years. You are almost the only one who has properly applied them."[60]

But, exactly what did the expedition mean? Did it have a strategic purpose? Or, was it simply a side maneuver that filled time during a stalemate in the war? The answer is found in Grant's developing new strategy of raids, a strategy he was envisioning for the 1864 campaign, "conceived out of his experience of war as well as his collaboration with . . . Sherman."[61] As pointed out clearly and accurately by Richard Berringer, et al., "Like virtually every other Civil War general, Grant by the end of 1863 perceived that the destruction of an enemy army in battle was practically impossible." He also was aware of the inherent danger and futility of "supplying the Union armies over great distances by railroad." Such a strategy was too costly. Grant also had come to understand that occupying enemy territory was laden with unsolvable problems. He reasoned that since Confederate armies could not be destroyed in battle, that capturing them was of little avail, and that capturing and occupying enemy territory was too costly, he would make "it unnecessary for the Union armies to rely heavily on railroads and impossible for the Confederate armies to do so." He further reasoned that the way to accomplish this goal was to "use water communications where available," and make frequent raids upon enemy territory. Of the two, raids would be the most important. But, unlike the Confederates who had used effectively its cavalry for raids, Grant intended to use armies.[62]

So, the Meridian expedition was not a lark to make time pass more quickly due to the stalemate following Chattanooga. It was an execution of Grant's new strategy of raiding the enemy's territory with fully equipped and fully manned armies. In this conflict, therefore, Sherman's Meridian expedition was "one of the most significant raids of the winter."[63] It was "a large-scale test of [Grant's] . . . concept and a dress rehearsal for the spring campaign in the West."[64] With this raid, both Grant and Sherman knew that their new strategy for the war would be successful and that the armies of the Confederacy could eventually be exhausted, the will of the South destroyed, and the Rebels defeated.

In early March, Sherman traveled to New Orleans to discuss plans for an expedition up the Red River with General Banks. After agreeing to loan Banks 10,000 men for one month, Sherman boarded a steamer and headed north to Memphis. On his return he received word from Grant that Grant had been promoted to lieutenant general and was making preparations to go to Washington. Grant was to become supreme commander of all Union armies and Halleck was to become chief of staff.[65] Grant expressed "thanks to you [Sherman] and McPherson as *the men* to whom, above all others, I feel indebted for whatever I have had of success." He continued by praising their advice and execution of plans, claiming that the reward he was receiving was theirs as well.[66] Sherman responded immediately, saying:

> You do yourself injustice and us too much honor . . . at Donelson
> . . . you illustrated your whole character. I was not near and
> General McPherson in too subordinate a capacity to influence

you. Until you won Donelson, I confess I was almost cowed by . . . anarchical elements. . . . I believe you are as brave, patriotic and just as the great prototype Washington; as unselfish, kind-hearted and honest as a man should be; but the chief characteristic is the simple faith in success you have always manifested. . . .

This faith gave you victory at Shiloh and Vicksburg . . . [and] at Chattanooga—no doubts, no reserves. . . .

My only points of doubt were in your knowledge of grand strategy and of books of science and history, but I confess your common-sense seems to have supplied all this.[67]

The promotion of Grant meant the promotion of Sherman, and by the middle of March he learned he had been made commander of the Military Division of the Mississippi. Of Sherman's ability to hold such a position Brig. Gen. Jacob D. Cox wrote: "His courage and activity had been abundantly proven, but his capacity for the independent command of a large army was to be tested." He had a "nervous and restless temperament," Cox continued, "with a tendency to irritability. . . ." Such characteristics "might have raised a doubt whether he would be successful . . . but experience showed he had the rare faculty of becoming more equitable under great responsibilities and in scenes of great excitement." According to Cox, "At such times his eccentricities disappeared, his grasp of the situation was firm and clear, his judgment was cool and based upon sound military theory as well as upon quick practical judgment, and no momentary complication or unexpected event could move him from the purpose he had based on full previous study of contingencies." Cox was sure that Sherman's mind " . . . seemed never so clear, his confidence never so strong, his spirit never so inspiring, and his temper never so amiable as in the crisis of some fierce struggle. . . ."[68]

Although pleased with his promotion, Sherman wrote to Washington stating that he preferred not to be nominated for another promotion. He said, "I now have all the rank necessary to command, and I believe all here concede to me the ability, yet accidents may happen and I don't care about increasing the distance of my fall. The moment another appears on the arena better than me, I will cheerfully subside. . . . I know my weak points. . . . I will try and hold my tongue and pen and give my undivided thoughts and attention to the military duties devolving on me."[69] Modesty, not fear, provoked such a statement. Sherman was more sure of himself now than he had ever been in his life. Two years earlier he had written a similar letter to President Lincoln, but it was composed out of fear of failure. This time the letter was one of modesty and realism. He had settled his fears, overcome his failures, developed his theory of war and put it to the test—now conditions were right for him to burst forth. Indeed, in a little more than a year Sherman would complete his contribution to the evolutionary development of military theory.

Sherman accompanied Grant from Nashville to Cincinnati on the latter's trip to the East. To Sherman the promotion of his close friend was an important step in the final destruction of the South. He had learned much from this middle-sized man and he considered it fortunate that Grant should decide "to go East, a stranger almost among strange troops . . . a more daring thing was never done by man on earth."[70] Before departing from Cincinnati the two men secluded themselves in a room at the Burnet House and pored over military maps. Grant stated that there were but two objectives: one, Lee's army in Virginia, and two, Johnston's army thirty miles southeast of Chattanooga in Georgia.[71] Both Grant and Sherman knew what they were up against and that the Confederacy had its best and most competent leaders facing them. They knew that ahead was one blow after another, "thick and fast," until it was all over. This was the type of warfare Sherman wanted, the type he had advocated since the beginning. It would be cruel and ugly, "hideous carnage," but in the end it would be the most merciful.[72] Years later, after he and Grant had sat there studying those maps, Sherman would return to the Burnet House. Pointing at the room that must have held so many memories for him, he would say: "Yonder began the campaign . . . we finally settled on a plan. He was to go for Lee and I was to go for Joe Johnston. That was his plan. No routes prescribed. . . . It was the beginning of the end as Grant and I foresaw right here. . . ."[73]

Col. S. M. Bowman of Sherman's army leaves this account of that day in Cincinnati:

> During the journey, they had a full and free conference as to the plan of operation in the approaching campaign, and a complete understanding of the work to be done by each. In the parlor of the Burnet House at Cincinnati, bending over their maps, the two generals, who had so long been inseparable, planned

together . . . the great campaigns of Richmond and Atlanta . . . and, grasping one another firmly by the hand, separated, one to the east, the other to the west, each to strike at the same instant his half of the ponderous death-blow.[74]

Thus plans were made for the longest and most destructive military raid in the history of the North American continent.

# CHAPTER EIGHT

# *"In War All Is Ajar"*

T. HARRY WILLIAMS, IN HIS CLASSIC WORK *McClellan, Sherman and Grant*, has written:

> This man who would lead his army against Atlanta in 1864, was
> . . . an imaginative thinker and a political scientist and a social
> philosopher as well as a soldier.
>   He would prove to be a great engineer and a master of logistics.
>   . . . he introduced engineering as a major factor in modern
> warfare. He introduced other modern devices as well: map coordinates, the photographic duplication of maps, trip wires, and a
> looser and more extended order of infantry attack.[1]

Williams could have added to the description of this complex man "sociologist" and "psychologist" because Sherman had proven by the spring of 1864 his ability to understand the relationship between the human mind and the social structure of society. He knew that by disorienting one, the other could be disrupted and vice versa. Richard McMurry writes that "Sherman was a military intellectual given to thinking deeply about the warfare that he saw going on about him." Of all the high-ranking Civil War generals, Sherman, says McMurry, "was probably the most creative and intuitively brilliant. . . ."[2] Gen. Omar Bradley said that Sherman "was probably the ablest general the Union produced."[3] Earl Schenck Meirs, in his biography of Sherman, provides further insight into this man (who was making preparations to lead an army of 100,000 into Georgia)

193

by comparing him with Maj. Gen. George H. Thomas through the observations of W. F. G. Shanks of *Harper's Magazine*. Meirs writes, " . . . whereas Sherman's strength came from 'the momentum resulting from the rapidity, with which he moves,' Thomas, moving more slowly, accomplished his purposes by 'sheer strength.'" According to Shanks, Meirs continues, "Sherman [was] a nervous man and Thomas a man of nerve; Sherman was 'the dashing leader of light, flying columns,' and Thomas was 'the director of heavily-massed columns'; Sherman's plans were 'original, embracing new rules of war,' and Thomas, while originating nothing, most skillfully directed 'his army on well-defined principles of the art.' Sherman jumped at conclusions where Thomas deliberated; one was quick and positive, the other slow but equally positive." For Shanks, says Meirs, Sherman could be described as "an innovator on the customs not only of the army but of every phase of social life." He was "at least one generation ahead of the American people. . . ." Thomas, on the other hand, "belonged 'to a past generation, and his exceedingly regular habits to the good old times.'"[4] John Chipman Gray, a Sherman aide and then recent graduate of the Harvard School of Law, described the general as

> . . . the most American looking man I ever saw, tall and lank, not very erect, with hair like a thatch, which he rubs up with his hands, a rusty beard trimmed close, a wrinkled face, sharp, prominent red nose, small bright eyes, corse red hands; black felt hat slouched over the eyes . . . dirty dickey with the points wilted down, black, old-fashioned stock, brown field officer's coat with high collar and no shoulder straps, muddy trousers and one spur. He carries his hands in his pockets, is very awkward in his gait and motion, talks continually and with immense rapidity, and might sit to *Punch* for the portrait of the ideal Yankee.[5]

Samuel Carter is correct when he writes that "there seem to be more descriptions of General Sherman than almost any other figure of the war." And he is also correct in saying that "one could take almost any personality—defining adjective, couple it with its antonym, and apply it to this Yankee general."[6] Beyond any doubt, the man was unique among men and he had paid his dues. Now he was ready to move.

While many of the rank and file of the Northern forces could see little advantage to be gained in a conquest of Georgia (many still thought of military objectives in terms of the enemy's army), the necessity was quite clear to Sherman. In Virginia, Lee was constantly harassing the Union high command by his series of brilliant offensive and defensive movements. Lee was successful only as long as he could depend on Georgia to keep vital supplies coming by rail up through the Carolinas to his depots. Sherman believed Lee could be stopped by Grant only if some means were found to bring a halt to the supplies that rolled up on every train from Georgia. Sherman knew the value of this southern stronghold, for virtually every captured wagon on all the campaigns in which he had participated had borne the markings "Made in Atlanta." Wagons, plus other major supplies of war boasted the same brand, including "splendid revolvers, scabbards and swords, shoes and uniforms."[7] It was vitally important to the Union cause that such supplies be destroyed before they reached Lee in Virginia. To do this, Sherman was prepared to move against the Confederate army under Johnston, the hostile civilians of Georgia, and one of that state's wealthiest and strongest fortified cities. Atlanta had to be destroyed, Georgia crushed.

The strategic importance of Atlanta was fourfold. First, it represented a moral symbol to the South. It was located in the heart of the Southland and had come to represent much of the best of Southern life. With its influx of "engineers, mechanics, artisans, salesmen, realtors and opportunists, aggressive in thought and action in contrast to the *dolce vita* of the great plantations,"[8] it also represented the South's future as it moved into the industrial age. Its destruction would mean an important moral victory for the North and a crippling moral defeat for the South. Indeed, "the depression of the people and their desires for peace deepened after the fall of Atlanta. . . ."[9] Second, Atlanta was one of the few remaining manufacturing centers in the agrarian South. It housed a pistol factory, a machine shop for the rifling of guns and cannons, and a foundry that manufactured essentials for an army, such as buttons, spurs, bridles, bits and buckles. Within its confines could be found a sword factory and pike plant, a foundry that produced freight cars and railroad supplies, as well as several gun-making factories. Just east of the center of the city was the Confederate Rolling Mill which turned out vast quantities of cannon, rails, and armor plate. In 1864, Atlanta was producing and manufacturing "a high proportion of the material without which the war could not be maintained."[10] Thus its capture was a necessity for the defeat of the South. Third, Atlanta had become the greatest railroad center of the South. Its "asterisk of railway lines comprised the most important transportation center" of the Confederacy.[11] The system of rails pointed out in every direction connecting and holding together the various parts of the South. In addition, railroads made Atlanta a gateway to the sea and connected the Atlantic seaboard and the Gulf coast with the western part of the Confederacy. As Carter points out, "A strike from that city to Charleston or Savannah or Mobile would more completely, and more mortally, divide the South than had the fall of Vicksburg."[12] Fourth, Chattanooga had been the "outer" gate to the heart of the Confederacy, Atlanta was the "inner" gate. Once it was opened, the path to the Carolinas would be opened and a "mortal thrust" could be made.[13]

Sherman was keenly aware of the strategic importance of Atlanta and this knowledge, no doubt, played a heavy influence on the way in which he interpreted his orders from Grant. There can be no doubt either that the importance of Atlanta fit into his scheme of military objectives. He knew, even before he left Chattanooga, that Atlanta was just as important as was Johnston's army.

On April 10, 1864, Sherman received his orders from Grant. After telling Sherman of movements to be made by Gens. Nathaniel P. Banks and Benjamin F. Butler, Grant spoke of their own operations in Virginia and Georgia. He stated, "I will stay with the Army of the Potomac . . . and operate directly against Lee's army, wherever it may be found . . . you I propose to move against Johnson's army, and to get into the interior of the enemy's country as far as you can, inflicting all the damage you can against their war resources." Consistent with his past pattern of faith and trust which he had established with Sherman, he added, "I do not propose to lay down for you a plan of campaign, but simply to lay down the work it is desirable to have done, and leave you free to execute it in your own way."[14] Sherman responded, saying he understood what was expected of him and paraphrased Grant, "I am to knock Joe Johnston and do as much damage to the sources of the enemy as possible."[15] Liddell Hart claims that "there is a subtle but significant difference" in the purpose of the two assignments. Grant's was completely military, he maintains, while Sherman's was military and economic. Actually there was nothing subtle concerning the "differences." Grant and Sherman had already by March 1864, arrived at an agreement on what war was meant to be. Both were aware that the military objectives no longer could be limited to the enemy's armies and that the Confederacy was the enemy—soldiers and noncombatants. There really was no difference. The economic objective was the military objective. Grant was to exhaust Lee in Virginia, keep him occupied so he could not provide aid to Johnston against Sherman, and Sherman was to keep Johnston from providing assistance to Lee, while, at the same time, bringing destruction to the region. The assignments were quite clear and both fit into the two generals' understanding of how war had to be conducted.[16]

With his promotion as commander of the Military Division of the Mississippi, and the completion of plans with Grant, Sherman found himself on the "threshold of greatness." The prominence and responsibility he had long shunned were no longer avoidable.[17] Activities around Memphis and the siege of Vicksburg, the burning of Jackson and the raid to Meridian were, as it turned out, only experimental. The full application of his philosophy of total war was about to be applied with campaigns through Georgia, South Carolina and North Carolina. These marches were to bring him fame and glory and win for him a high place in the annals of American military history.

In April 1864, Sherman began preparations for the campaign into Georgia. Since he had only five weeks to get everything ready, he worked with one principle in mind, that of "harmonious action without rigid discipline" in which every man would be asked to become a selfless individual.[18] Sherman was prepared himself to abide by such a principle and gave hour upon hour to making his army prepared. Sherman not only had control of himself now, but he also had control over his troops. The confidence of his men is evidenced in the words of Capt. George W. Pepper. "Hat in hand, bowing and smiling, there stood General Sherman, the commander of the military Division of the Mississippi, who shares with General Grant the esteem and confidence of Western armies. . . . [The men] rushed in hundreds to catch a glimpse of their heroic leader and hear what he had to say."[19]

With confidence, self-control and "harmonious action," Sherman began work immediately on the problem of supply for the forthcoming campaign. On his first day as an independent commander he began reorganizing the single line of railroad that was to supply him as he moved against the enemy. With an army of 100,000 men and 30,000 animals, he knew he could not attempt an advance into Georgia without adequate food and ammunition. It was necessary to accumulate supplies and material.

To attain such an end, Sherman, on April 6, issued a general order limiting the use of railroad cars to transporting only the essential articles of food, ammunition and supplies for the army, forbidding any further issues to citizens, and cutting off civil traffic. According to Adj. F. Y. Hedley, Sherman cut "red tape with a stroke of his pen" and "ordered all railroad cars reaching Louisville . . . to be loaded with supplies and sent to the front. . . ." Even under "the angry protests of railroad officials all over the country, his order was obeyed to the letter."[20] As a result, enormous stockpiles of material flowed into Nashville and then onward to Chattanooga—horses and mules by the tens of thousands, corn and oats by the millions of bushels, hay by the tens of thousands of tons, subsistence stores by the hundreds of thousands of tons, and miscellaneous articles in the aggregate proportionately large.[21] Sherman acted as his own chief quartermaster and sent word to his aides in the Northwest to purchase food, grain, saddles, uniforms, and equipment. His tolerance for quartermaster laziness was all but nonexistent and on one occasion he was overheard, after coming upon the head of a commissary napping, "I'm going to move on Joe Johnston the day Grant telegraphs me he is going to hit Bobby Lee; and if you don't have my army supplied, and keep it supplied, we'll eat your mules up, sir— eat your mules up!"[22] Eventually Nashville and Chattanooga became a "vast storehouse—warehouses covering city blocks, one a quarter of a mile long—stables by the ten and twenty acres, repair shops by the fieldful."[23]

Chattanooga was to be Sherman's starting point. It was 120 miles from his primary supply base in Nashville and 235 miles from his principal source of supply in Louisville. Of necessity, therefore, he would have to depend upon a railroad line. Indeed, he wanted to be able to rely as much as possible on the railroad and as little as possible on supply wagons drawn by animals. "Locomotives," he said, "don't eat corn and hay like mules, but a single locomotive will haul 160,000 pounds. A man eats 3 pounds a day, and therefore one train will feed 50,000 men. Animals eat about 15 pounds." Therefore, he estimated, "65 cars a day necessary to maintain an army of 100,000 men and 30,000 animals."[24] He would eventually change the figure to 120 cars a day. The seizure of trains and locomotives was ordered by Sherman and he banned the transportation of civilian goods and passengers. In response, some citizens of East Tennessee appealed to President Lincoln to have Sherman's order modified or repealed. Lincoln telegraphed Sherman concerning the harshness of his order, but Sherman would not change his position. Instead, he replied that the railroads had a limited capacity and they would not provide for the necessities of the army and civilians. One or the other had to be sacrificed and as far as he was concerned his army would not be denied priority "until the army of Jos. Johnston was conquered. . . ."[25] Some even raised the issue of biblical tracts that were to be sent in large quantities to the troops, to which Sherman relied, "Bullets are better than Bibles."[26]

The long line of supply had to be made safe from Confederate attack. To accomplish this objective, Sherman created a moveable railroad base equipped with repair tools and manned by crews skilled "in the art of mending tracks and mending bridges."[27] Hundreds of men were trained in railroad maintenance and would eventually prove their worth as they kept Sherman's line of supply flowing continuously.

Despite the importance of the railroad, Sherman knew that he could not be tied to it at all times. He was aware that no matter how well it was protected and how many repair crews he had, there was always the chance of enemy intervention. Also, he knew that as he moved into enemy territory he would need the freedom to strike in directions the railroad did not travel. So, he organized a cadre of horse and wagon trains that would provide supplies and ammunition, yet remain highly mobile.

Mobility was his chief concern. To be successful he had to move rapidly with a large force, thus he stripped his army to the bare bones. Wagons were not to be used for the carrying of tents or baggage. Troops could sleep in the field and carry their food on their back. They could forage for any extras needed. "The wagons and packs shall carry ammunition and food alone," and to make his point clear, he "set the example" himself.[28] Beef would be transported on the hoof. Troops were to be as self-sustaining as possible. Sherman was set on converting his army into a highly mobile machine that could move with agility and speed.[29] He was determined to have "by May 1st . . . one of the best armies in the world."[30]

No stone was left unturned. He carefully studied the United

States Census reports for the state of Georgia and the tax rolls for the counties through which he would march. The information told him which areas could best provide food for his army. He would say later, "No military expedition was ever based on sounder or surer data."[31]

Clerical work was to be reduced significantly by establishing permanent offices in the rear. This enabled Sherman to condense the size of the various headquarters staffs of his army, and in so doing, reduce the amount of baggage to be transported. In a letter to the War Department he wrote, "My entire headquarters transportation is one wagon for myself, aides, officers, clerks and orderlies. I think that is as low as we can get. . . ." Always in character, he had to add a commentary. He continued, "Soldiering as we have been doing in the past two years with such trains and impediments has been a farce and nothing but absolute poverty will cure it. I will be glad to hear Uncle Sam say 'we cannot afford this and that—you must gather your own grub and wagons. . . .'"[32]

On and on the preparations went, all under the careful eye of the commander, and in five weeks Sherman had succeeded in putting together what would prove to be the largest and most mobile army ever to face an enemy up to that time. General Thomas praised Sherman's work by saying, "In such duty as this, General Sherman had no superior. Quick-eyed, ingenious, nervously active in mind and body, sleeplessly alert on every occasion, with a clear idea of what he wanted and an unyielding determination to have it, he made himself and everybody around him uncomfortable till his demands were gratified. . . ."[33] All things considered, even before the "Army Group" moved out of Chattanooga, Sherman had proven himself to be a master organizer, a brilliant engineer and an incomparable logician. Strategy came to him almost naturally: now all that was left was for him to prove his ability as a leader and tactician.

Even amid all the duties of preparing his army for the move against Johnston, Sherman managed to find time to explain his ideas on war to any and all willing listeners. Angry over a War Department order that permitted a Quaker minister passage into East Tennessee to feed his brethren, Sherman wrote to Assistant Secretary of War Dana explaining his philosophy of war. "In peace there is a beautiful harmony in all the departments of life—they all fit like a Chinese puzzle, but in war all is ajar. Nothing fits, and it is the struggle between the stronger and weaker, and the latter, however it may appeal to the better feelings of our nature, must kick the beam." War, he told Dana, meant the hardening of hearts. "Therefore, when preachers clamor and sanitaries wail, don't join in. . . ." Know that war "like the thunderbolt, follows its laws and turns not aside even if the beautiful, the virtuous and charitable stand in its path." Thus, he informed the assistant secretary, " . . . in the time allotted to me for preparations I must and will be selfish in making those preparations which I know to be necessary."[34]

On the same subject, but to a different party, Sherman wrote, "I believe in fighting in a double sense, first to gain physical results and next to inspire respect on which to build up our nation's power. . . . We saw the beauty of time in the battle of Chattanooga and there is no reason why the same harmony of action should not pervade a continent."[35]

Theory and political philosophy aside, at last all was ready. Sherman in record time had directed the preparations of all departments—infantry, artillery, cavalry (in which he still had little faith), the medical corps, telegraphers, signalmen, engineers, pioneers and laborers. He had done a magnificent job. As Adjutant Hedley would say, "It was this complete system of organization . . . that raised this army to so high a degree of efficiency and gave to its chief such a wonderful mastery over it. Well might he say 'The least part of a general's work is to fight a battle.'" Sherman had accomplished the most difficult task, all was ready. Hedley continues, "The troops were now ready to move out of Chattanooga. 'The pomp and circumstance of glorious war' were to be left behind. . . . The army was at its fighting weight, stripped to the buff, ready and willing to give and take the hard knocks."[36]

Although historians have written abundantly of Sherman's Atlanta campaign, his march to the sea, and the ensuing raids through the Carolinas, it is seldom recognized that, as dramatic as they were, none of these events would have occurred had it not been for the years of preparation and training in Sherman's life preceding 1864. Attention has been focused on his military movements because they were accomplished under Sherman's independent campaign. With these events the military historian can be concerned with tactics and can trace step-by-step the magnificent chess game Sherman played with Johnston and Hood.

It is with these events also that Sherman's tactical errors are the most pronounced and his execution of total war the most dramatic. But, the period from April 1864 to the end of the war a year later was simply a culmination of his experiences since he first entered West Point twenty-eight years earlier. It was an important year in that the strategic moves of Sherman and Grant brought the war to a close. So, in a sense, 1864 was very significant for the future of the country. It was an important time also for Sherman since it gave him the chance to prove his worth as a military commander which would ultimately gain him a high place in the history of warfare. The drama of 1864 cannot cause historians to lose sight of the very fact that Sherman, by May of that year, had already concluded his evolutionary development of war. Nothing profoundly new would enter his thinking about war as a result of his capture of Atlanta and his march through the South. He was simply implementing, with little significant variation, what he had come to see as the proper way to conduct war. For twenty-four years (especially the four years since he had emotionally "preached" to Professor Boyd in Alexandria, Louisiana, about the futility of the South's war effort) Sherman had progressively moved away from the idea that war was a chivalrous activity engaged in by professional armies on an open battlefield. His experiences with the Indians of Florida, the ruffians in California, and the inept military leaders at First Bull Run; his fears in Kentucky; his observations of Grant at Donelson, Vicksburg and Chattanooga and of the devastation of Jackson and Meridian—all had led him to this moment in his life. He had responded to the experiences positively. Philosophically, he had no other choice: this was the moment to which all the other moments in his life had taken him. And he knew it clearly. His excitement was evident. In May 1864, he was on the threshold of the apex of his military career and life. So, the preparation of his army was complete for the move into Georgia, and the preparation of the man was complete for the move into history. There was little else to do but act. This year would be a year of execution; all the previous years were developmental.

On May 8, four days after the Army of the Potomac entered the Wilderness of Virginia, Sherman issued general orders for the advance southeast into Georgia. The long-awaited step was finally taken, the march had begun. Maj. James A. Connolly, after the first day's march, wrote his wife, "I do dread starting out in the dust and hot sun after such a long period of ease, but the rebels must be whipped, and since we can't do it sitting in the house, I suppose we must content ourselves with going out after them. Everybody about me is bustling and hurrying. . . ."[37] A day's marching amid the beauties of spring led the army to the old Chickamauga battlefield and reality. C. E. Benton from New York wrote of their experience, "Soon we came to trees cut down by shell; nearly all of the trees were marked and torn by bullets and shells. Mounds of earth, with the middle sunken in, showed where dozens of men had received scant burial." It was a ghastly reminder of the horrors of war as the marching men passed "a foot protruded; or a hand with the skin dried to the bones" extending from the hurried grave. Eventually they passed a number of bodies that had never been buried.[38] Soon they passed the west fork of Chickamauga Creek and moved back into the glories of spring.

From the beginning Sherman executed the flanking maneuver that would come to be his trademark during the campaign. While General Thomas, commander of the Army of the Cumberland, and Maj. Gen. John M. Schofield, commander of the Army of the Ohio, held Johnston's forces at Dalton, General McPherson, commander of the Army of the Tennessee, was to move to Johnston's left and rear at Resaca to cut off the Confederates' means of supply and retreat. Such a maneuver would force Johnston to stand and fight. Unfortunately, McPherson was not successful in reaching the Confederate rear, and the movement failed. As Stanley Horn has pointed out, "For an operation of tactics rather than combat, this was well thought out." Horn continues, "Resaca commanded the railroad bridge over the Oostanaula River and was vital to Johnston's communications with his Atlanta base. Also, at this particular time the railroad was the only link between Johnston and the reinforcements coming from Alabama with Leonidas Polk. To break it was to break his lifeline."[39] No wonder Sherman looked at his subordinate and said, "Well, Mac, you have missed the opportunity of your life."

Although "well thought out," the execution of the plan fell short, and the blame must be laid at the feet of both McPherson and Sherman. McPherson encountered greater difficulty than he had anticipated because of the rugged country his army had to cross; plus, when he finally reached the outskirts of Resaca, he faced a larger Confederate force than he had expected. So, instead of pressing forward with the agreed plan, he retreated. Sherman has been criticized for the Resaca failure on two counts. One, he worked on

the assumption that McPherson would have little difficulty in reaching the rear of Johnston's army, and two, he failed to initiate a
simultaneous attack against the Confederates and, therefore, was
unable to provide proper support for McPherson.[40] General
Scofield would write later of the Resaca movement that "impartial
history must . . . hold Sherman . . . responsible for the failure." He
submitted that Sherman should have provided more troops to assist
McPherson in his rear movement.[41] In essence, Sherman underan-
ticipated Johnston's ability to defend his position.

Narrowly missing the chance to destroy Johnston's Confederate
army at the outset of the campaign, Sherman came under criticism
for the Resaca failure after the war. For example, "It is well known
among those who participated in it that the prominent officers of
the three [Federal] armies which began the Atlanta campaign considered its opening move at Dalton and Resaca as grave and needless
failures. The feeling was that Sherman with his 100,000 men, should
have brought Johnston's 45,000 to decisive battle in front of Resaca."[42] But Horn comes to Sherman's defense saying, "It is quite
true that Sherman did miss a great opportunity when the odds were
all in his favor. On the other hand, by not precipitating a general
engagement he frustrated any plans Johnston might have been laying for counterattack. The upshot was that Johnston was maneuvered out of an exceedingly strong position and forced to retreat."[43]
Although the tactical conception was sound, its implementation was
a failure. Still, despite the lost chance, Sherman strategically remained on sound ground. His army was intact, the Confederate
army was in retreat, and the Union forces had moved farther into
the South's heartland toward its twin objectives, Johnston's army and
the city of Atlanta. In this first encounter, both generals learned
something about each other. Sherman learned that his adversary was
one of the best defensive artists he had faced, and Johnston learned
that his opponent was artful at flanking. Johnston also realized that
Sherman, in spite of his superiority of numbers, did not intend to
decide the contest by a battle.[44] Indeed, Sherman would eventually
become so efficient with this maneuver that "his men were heard to
boast that their commander could flank the devil out of hell, if
necessary."[45]

On the night of May 16, Johnston took his army across the bridges
south of Resaca, setting fire to them as he retreated. The following
day Sherman entered the little town, arriving too late to join battle

with the Southern force.[46] The first move against the Rebel army had ended, but was only the beginning of the game of strategy and tactics to be played by the two opposing commanders during the summer of 1864, a game that would eventually result in Johnston's gradual and steady surrender of ground without a pitched battle. Years later Hedley would offer this description: Sherman's movements were "marvelous" and he faced "a worthy adversary in General Joseph E. Johnston." Hedley continues, "Move succeeded move, like rook and pawn on the chessboard, one giving a check here, the other there. Sherman maneuvered so as to gain position after position with the minimum lose of men and material; Johnston retreated so skillfully before him that he scarcely lost a tin cup."[47]

Johnston soon learned also that Sherman was a master at logistics and that destroying rails and bridges in his path was of little use. Sherman had brought with him a stock of pre-fabricated bridges and a crew of trained pioneers. The repair gangs under the guidance of engineers worked with efficiency and skill "beyond praise," renewed bridges "as if by magic, and perhaps nothing produced more moral effect upon the enemy than hearing the whistle of locomotives in rear of our armies within a few hours after they had received reports that the railroads had been broken."[48] Bridges and sections of rails torn up by the Confederates were repaired so rapidly that, according to Hedley, " . . . the enemy was convinced that Sherman and his men were omnipotent, and that destructive measures were of little avail to arrest their progress." He tells the story of Johnston's plans to destroy an important railroad tunnel in order to halt the advance of the Federals, "whereupon one of his men remarked, 'There isn't no use in that. . . . Sherman carries along duplicates of all the tunnels.'"[49]

From Resaca, following a number of flanking maneuvers, Sherman backed the Confederate army into a small village called New Hope Church. He had steadily driven his antagonist from the strong positions of Dalton, Resaca, and Cassville, and he had advanced his "lines in strong compact order . . . nearly a hundred [eighty] miles . . ." through extremely difficult country.[50] At New Hope Church Sherman was faced with a fateful decision, to attack or not to attack. Abruptly, he reached the decision to attack Johnston on his flank, a decision years later he admitted he instantly regretted. Actually, "the two armies locked horns in a desultory but violent four days' battle of

disconnected skirmishes, charges and countercharges. . . ."[51] When
the skirmishing ended, the Union counted losses totaling 3,000
men, while Johnston's casualties were about 2,000.[52]

These engagements changed the character of the campaign.
Trench warfare as opposed to fighting in the open became the practice of both armies. They realized quickly the advantage of breastworks, and during the remainder of the Atlanta campaign both
armies became adept at constructing entrenchments wherever they
stopped. Randolph De Bow Keim, a Union correspondent wrote,
"As soon as a command got into position, if the enemy were near,
the work began. In a single night the position was secured. . . . To
this extent every fighting command was its own pioneer corps. General Sherman improved on this system by organizing in each division
a pioneer corps of negroes seeking refuge within his lines. . . . The
scheme acted to a charm. The negroes, worked during the night and
slept when they could during the day, while the soldier took his rest
as he could at night, and was ready, fresh, and fierce for the fray
during the day."[53] So skilled at this task did each become that it was
said of Confederates that they had to carry their breastworks with
them, and of the Federals that "Sherman's men march with a rifle in
one hand and a spade in the other."[54]

The Battles of New Hope Church, Pickett's Mill, and Dallas were
the result of Sherman's attempt to keep from attacking Johnston at
Allatoona Pass. As a young artillery officer back in 1844, Sherman
had reconnoitered the area around Marietta, just northwest of Atlanta. He had noted well the topography of that country and concluded "that the Allatoona Pass was very strong, would be hard to
force. . . ." Recalling his experience he "resolved not even to attempt
it, but to turn the position by moving to Kingston from Marietta *via*
Dallas."[55] The maneuver would be dangerous because it would cut
him loose from his railroad supply line. Now that the fighting along
the New Hope Church-Dallas line had subsided and Johnston was in
retreat once again, Sherman headed back to the railroad at Acworth.
From there he prepared to advance on the Brush Mountain-
Kennesaw-Olley Creek line.

The supply line had been Sherman's major concern since leaving
Chattanooga. The life and success of his vast army depended on the
single thread of rails that stretched miles through the enemy country. He was constantly concerned about its safety. Writing to his
brother John he spoke of how weak this link was: "My long and

single line of railroad to my rear of limited capacity, is the delicate point of my game, as also the fact that all of Georgia . . . is densely wooded, with a few roads, and at any point an . . . enemy can in a few hours with axes and spades, make across our path formidable works, whilst his sharp-shooters, spies, and scouts . . . can hang around us and kill our wagonmen, messengers, and courtiers."[56] Sherman was compelled numerous times during the march to repair the railroads as his army advanced.

After repairing the long railroad to his rear, Sherman began his move against the Confederate army now concentrated on Kennesaw Mountain, four miles in front of Marietta. The range, about two and a half miles in length, and at its highest point about 700 feet, was a formidable barrier. Sherman, knowing the area well as a result of earlier days, knew it formed a formidable military position, yet he made the decision to fight Johnston at this point. His decision was based on a number of reasons, none quite justifiable. First, there was the problem of supplies. As Sherman thrust deeper into the South his line of supply grew longer and longer, and thus more vulnerable. If he lost the railroad at this point in the game, his armies would be as good as beaten. The defeat of Johnston's forces here would ensure the safety of that line and make the entrance into Atlanta a sure move. Second, there was the temptation of a final and quick defeat of the Confederate forces in Georgia. For almost a month now Sherman had been dancing with a potentially deadly enemy. The dance was tiring and costly. To defeat Johnston here would open the door to Atlanta with little or no opposition to hamper his movement. In other words, on his side there was the element of numerical superiority and the unexpected. He felt confident that, with his superior strength, he could break the Confederate line and succeed in scattering Johnston's forces. To attack here would be a change in his pattern of flanking and thus a surprise. His final decision to attack was based on this factor. In his report, he said, "I perceived that the enemy and our own officers had settled down into a conviction that I would not assault fortified lines. All looked to me to outflank. An army to be efficient must not settle down to a single mode of offense, but must be prepared to execute any plan which promises success. I wanted, therefore, for the moral effect to make a successful assault against the enemy behind his breast-works and resolved to attempt it at that point where success would give the largest fruits of victory."[57] Fourth, he reasoned that one dramatic victory would give the North a boast in morale and would more than likely ensure Lincoln's re-election for a second term.[58]

For six days Union cannon bombarded the Confederate position as Sherman made final preparations for the attack. A Confederate soldier remarked, "We would work hard every night to strengthen our breastworks, and the very next day they would be torn down smooth with the ground by solid shots and shells from the guns of the enemy. Even the little trees and bushes which had been left for shade, were cut down as so much rubble. For more than [nearly] a week this constant firing had been kept up against this salient point."[59]

At last all was ready and on Monday, June 27, Sherman sent his troops against the Kennesaw Mountain line. The result was a Federal disaster and the costliest battle of the campaign. While Johnston's losses were put at 808, reports were that Sherman's losses in killed, wounded, and missing were more than three times that number.[60] General Johnston would record later that the Federals "retired—unsuccessful, because they had encountered intrenched infantry unsurpassed by that of Napoleon's Old Guard or that which followed Wellington into France out of Spain."[61] Union Maj. Gen. Oliver O. Howard, whose corps took the heaviest of Confederate fire, remarked, "Our losses in this assault were heavy indeed, and our gain was nothing. We realized now, as never before, the futility of direct assaults upon intrenched lines already well prepared and well manned."[62]

Sherman, after the war, spoke little about the Kennesaw tragedy. Briefly, he said, "I ordered a general assault, with the full cooperation of my great lieutenants, Thomas, McPherson, and Schofield . . . ; but we failed. . . ." He added that it taught his men that they sometimes had to attack fortified lines so as to keep the enemy guessing.[63] He even refused to admit that he had made a mistake.

Critics do not agree with Sherman and one of them referred to the Kennesaw affair as "an utterly needless move . . . an inexcusable slaughter," claiming that Johnston could have been forced out of his position without a battle.[64] Liddell Hart says of the move, "A direct assault on an unshaken enemy in position has no justification in history. . . ." After excusing Sherman for having done this only once, whereas many generals had made it a normal practice, he continues with, " . . . the historical test at Kennesaw is whether Sherman had done enough to unhinge the defense before releasing this assault. And here the answer is that he had done as much as was possible, but hardly enough to assure a justifiable anticipation of success." And finally, Liddell Hart remarks, "Being unsuccessful, the momentary effect was to depress his own troops and fortify the confidence of the enemy."[65]

Alfred H. Burne, on the other hand, defends Sherman by stating briefly and pointedly, "Sherman has been unmercifully blamed for attacking Kennesaw Mountain, but his reasoning seems to me to be perfectly sound. It [assaulting a fortified position] is a fair gamble—once in a while."[66] So, Burne accepts Sherman's keep-your-enemy-guessing justification.

Whatever the case and whoever is correct, the move was a deviation from Sherman's pattern of thinking and behavior. He knew the futility of frontal assaults, especially against a force deeply intrenched behind breastworks. The explanation, although it cannot be proven, most likely lies in impatience. Sherman was a man who demanded action and results. For more than a month he had been flanking and pursuing Johnston's army. The result? Johnston's army was still intact and Sherman's own army was moving deeper and deeper into enemy territory. He was growing more nervous about his line of supply. In addition, he was becoming more anxious about achieving a victory that would enhance both Grant and Lincoln. Thus, his impatience caused him to take a chance. He attacked, it was a gamble, and he lost. Although his strategic thinking remained sound, his tactical move at Kennesaw left much to be desired. But, the issue is academic now, for as Horn points out, "The ultimately successful outcome of Sherman's Georgia campaign overshadowed any regret that too many eggs were broken in the making of the omelet."[67]

Johnston's forces, despite the excellent military position at Kennesaw Mountain, soon saw themselves outflanked and, on the night of July 2, evacuated that position. Flanked in quick succession out of the Smyna and Chattahoochee lines, Johnston's troops retreated into the Atlanta defenses. Sherman immediately followed, and, on July 16, he found time from his responsibilities to respond to a letter he had received from Anne Gilman Bower of Baltimore. He had known her as a young girl in Charleston before the war.

As Barrett says, "This remarkable bit of correspondence, written when his name was fast becoming an anathema in all the South, shows clearly that he still harbored a strong affection for his former friends."[68] He wrote Bower that he never dreamed that when he knew her years ago he would one day be leading a vast army "towards the plains of the South."

> Why, oh, why is this? If I know my own heart, it beats as warmly as ever towards those kind and generous families that greeted us with such warm hospitality in days long past but still present in memory; and today were . . . any or all of our cherished circle, their children, or even their children's children, to come to me as of old, the stern feeling of duty and conviction would melt as snow before the genial sun, and I believe I would strip my own children that they might be sheltered.
>
> And yet they call me barbarian, vandal, and a monster and all the epithets that language can invent that are significant of malignity and hate.

Repeating a theme he had pronounced so many times in the past year, he said, "All I pretend to say, on earth as in heaven, man must submit to an arbiter. He must not throw off his allegiance to his Government or his God without just reason and cause." To him the South had no cause, "not even a pretext." Instead "she [had] bantered and bullied" the North into war. "Had we declined battle, America would have sunk . . . meriting the contempt of mankind. . . ." And again, he presented his conditions for peace.

> I would not subjugate the South in the sense so offensively assumed, but I would make every citizen of the land obey the command, submit to the same that we do—no more, no less— our equals and not our superiors. . . . Even yet my heart bleeds when I see the carnage of battle, the desolation of homes, the bitter anguish of families, but the very moment the men of the South say that instead of appealing to war they should have appealed to reason, to our Congress, to our courts, to religion, and to the experience of history, then will I say peace, peace; go back to your point of error, and resume your places as American citizens, with all their proud heritages.

Sherman did not know if he would live to see peace, but he wanted Bower to know that he did not wish to "efface" the fond memories of the South by having to put "on the armor of war." He was a warrior in the land he loved because he did not want "our common country . . . [to] perish in infamy and disgrace. . . ." He sincerely hoped that all who had known him in earlier years would not be ashamed that they had once been friends.[69]

Although the war had momentarily hardened Sherman, ultimately, as this letter illustrates, in some respects it would make him wise and merciful. It was true that he had a callous streak as a military professional, but Sherman's experiences in the South assisted him in becoming not only a modern general but a man of peace as well. Even at this point in his life the paradox remained.

In early July, Sherman left Marietta and moved his "Army Group" across the Chattahoochee River.[70] Back in May, when he had begun this campaign into Georgia, Sherman had been given two assignments that were interrelated; or to put it more accurately, he had been given an assignment with two parts. The assignment was to bring war to the South by: one, moving "against Johnston's army" and breaking it up and, two, "get[ting] into the interior of the enemy's country as far as possible, inflicting all the damage [possible] against their war resources." Almost two months later he was still in the process of completing his assignment. He had yet to break up Johnston's army, but he had made progress in inflicting damage on the South's resources and was moving deeper and deeper into the enemy's interior. On his long march from Chattanooga to the outskirts of Atlanta, towns and villages had been destroyed, cotton and wool mills wrecked, and the population brought under submission. Writing to Ellen, Sherman said that "all the people retire before us and desolation is behind. To realize what war is one should follow our tracks." The land was being devoured and his animals were eating the wheat and corn.[71] He was in a good position not only to enter Atlanta, a major source of war supplies, but to deal the Confederate army a crippling if not devastating blow. The traditional interpretation offered by historians concerning Sherman's attitude at this time is that he decided to "abandon his first objective, 'to knock Joe Johnston,' in favor of the second, 'to get into the interior of the enemy's country.'"[72] Horn argues, by stating, "Sherman had started out with the military correct idea that the Confederate army was his objective. Now, with that army huddled before him in inferior force, he deliberately turned his back on the supposed goal and marched off 30 miles in the other direction."[73]

The difficulty with such interpretations lies in the writers' understanding, or rather lack of understanding, of Sherman's assignment. He was not given two separate assignments as is traditionally believed but one that had two parts. Further, he was not ordered by

Grant to accomplish one first, then the other. Nor was he given specific instructions on how to carry out his mission. Sherman was left free to decide how he wanted to achieve the desired results. The problem with the traditional interpretations is that the authors are deeply committed to the accepted differences between a military and a geographical objective. Sherman had abandoned this distinction. He saw both as being the same. So, Sherman, on the eve of his capture of Atlanta, was acting consistently with what he had been ordered to do. He had not changed his mind since leaving Chattanooga concerning his objective.

By mid-July, Sherman had crossed the Chattahoochee River, and Johnston had positioned his forces on the south bank of Peachtree Creek, just a few miles outside Atlanta. While determining his next move Sherman received word of a change in the Confederate command. President Davis, under pressure from many quarters to stop Sherman's advance, had removed Johnston and replaced him with Lt. Gen. John Bell Hood. The change pleased Sherman and of it he wrote, "At this critical moment the Confederate Government rendered us a most valuable service. The character of a leader is a large factor in the game of war, and I confess I was pleased with the change."[74] Sherman was confident that he could have eventually outmaneuvered Johnston, but it would have taken time and cost lives. He knew Hood would change the tactics used by Johnston and would stand and do battle. Hood had the reputation of being "a fighting man."

Sherman's generals were also pleased with the change. Gen. Joseph Hooker wrote that the news of Johnston's replacement "was received by our officers with universal rejoicing," and General Cox regarded his removal "as equivalent to victory for us."[75] The new Southern commander had been a classmate of Generals McPherson and Schofield at West Point, and they knew him well. They informed Sherman that the change in command would almost surely lead to a change in tactics, that Hood possessed a bold and ruthless nature.[76] As Burne put it, "Knowing . . . that Johnston had been displaced for failure to arrest his advance, he [Sherman] naturally expected a more resolute attitude by Johnston's successor."[77] Schofield told Sherman, "He'll hit you like hell, now, before you know it."[78] Sherman understood that now he would have to be "unusually cautious, and prepared at all times for sallies and for hard fighting." He knew that " . . . Hood, though not deemed much of a scholar, or of great mental capacity, was undoubtedly a brave, determined and rash man."[79] Sherman was pleased to have beaten Johnston even though he had been assisted by the Confederate government. He had great respect for the man and believed that "he had the most exalted reputation with our old army as a strategist."[80] But he was equally satisfied with the appointment of Hood.

The assessments of the new Confederate commander were accurate, for two days after he replaced Johnston, Hood left his entrenchments to fight a losing battle at Peachtree Creek. He then withdrew to the ramparts outside Atlanta and two days later fought and lost the Battle of Atlanta. With these two defeats Hood evacuated his outer defense lines and withdrew into Atlanta's fortifications. As the last days of July approached, Hood found himself in a siege situation with his rail communications either cut or seriously threatened. In less than ten days the Confederate general had proven Cox correct. The appointment of Hood was "equivalent to a victory. . . ."

As Sherman approached the city of Atlanta, what he observed affirmed the reports he had received concerning its strength. He saw redoubts, breastworks, and rifle pits all strongly revetted with heavy timbers; and, in most cases the outer sides of the breastworks were strewn with abatis and the formidable *chevaux-de-frise*. He wrote to Ellen, "Atlanta is on high ground. . . ."[81] He knew that its fortifications made it suicidal for any enemy to attempt direct assault. So, with no other choice before him, he settled in for a siege.

On August 1, he intensified the bombardment of the city. To General Schofield he issued the following order: "You may fire 10 to 15 shots from every gun you have in position into Atlanta that will reach any of its houses. Fire slowly and with deliberation between 4 p.m. and dark."[82] To General Thomas he issued a similar order on August 7 commanding him to put his cannon in position and "knock down the buildings of the town."[83]

Thus began, and continued for days, the systematic bombardment of Atlanta. Admitting that he was too impatient for a siege. Sherman assured Halleck, "One thing is certain, whether we get inside of Atlanta or not, it will be a used-up community by the time we are done with it."[84] The bombardment was so effective that it caused Mary Gay, a resident, to explain, "The constant roaring of cannon and rattling of musketry; the thousands—yea, tens of thousands of shots blending into one grand continuous whole . . . told in

thunder tones of the fierce contest . . . being waged without inter-
mission for the possession of Atlanta."[85]

Another Atlanta resident, Noble C. Williams, who was a young
boy at the time, described later what he had seen. He wrote, "Shells
were frequently exploding in the main business portion of the city,
and when they would come on contact with the hard paving stones
there was no calculating what course they would take. Both soldiers
and citizens were maimed and killed in the streets. . . ." Williams
continues, "Night and day . . . shells were constantly being thrown
into the city, adding to the death-rate daily, and setting fire to the
houses, which kept the firemen very busy extinguishing the
flames."[86] So effective was the shelling of Atlanta that it brought an
official protest from Hood, who maintained that the barrage was
inhuman and cruel. To this Sherman replied that even Hood must
realize that "war is the science of barbarity."[87]

For six weeks General Hood managed to hold the city and, with
Sherman bombarding it from the outside and Hood holding firm on
the inside, the battle for Atlanta turned into a duel of nerves. It was
Hood, however, who weakened first. He lost the Battle of Ezra
Church on July 28, and on August 31 and September 1, the Battle of
Jonesboro, which cut off railroad communications running south
from Atlanta. He was left with no other choice. On the night of
September 1, General Hood evacuated Atlanta and made it possible
for Sherman to make his long-awaited announcement to the North:
" . . . Atlanta is ours and fairly won."[88] The long advance from
Chattanooga was at last completed, and as a mid-nineteenth-century
city, "Atlanta was dead."[89]

The fall of Atlanta, wrote correspondent David P. Conyngham,
was "the crowning point in Sherman's great campaign." Sherman
had succeeded in outgeneraling, outmaneuvering, and outflanking
Hood.[90] The astonishing success of Sherman's army fixed the eyes
of the world more than ever on its commander. Sherman became an
instant hero and received letters of praise from people all over the
world. The North saw him as a great leader, Europe looked to him
as a strategic genius, and the South condemned him, calling him
vandal and barbarian. In the future, students of warfare would
study his campaign and "haughty professionals of the Old World
would talk less after this, of the American war as merely the scramble of two armed mobs."[91] Grant would say that Sherman "had

accomplished the most gigantic undertaking given any general in the war."[92] In honor of his "great victory" Grant ordered "a salute to be fired, with *shotted* guns, from every battery bearing upon the enemy."[93]

Beyond any doubt Sherman with this campaign displayed imagination, resourcefulness, versatility, boldness, determination, and a genuine power of leadership—all fundamental characteristics of a great commander. He followed many of the orthodox teachings of warfare, yet he also shattered these theories by broadening a military objective to include a geographical destination. He had captured Atlanta and, at the same time, inflicted his unorthodox concept of war upon the people of the South. Although he had not broken up Hood's army *yet*, he had disoriented it. Tactically he had made errors, particularly in execution, but "some eggs have to be broken to make the omelet."

President Lincoln decreed a day of thanksgiving for Sherman's capture of Atlanta and offered the following words for his and the nation's gratitude: " . . . Major-General William T. Sherman and the gallant officers and soldiers of his command before Atlanta, for the distinguished ability and perseverance displayed in the campaign in Georgia, which, under Divine favor, has resulted in the capture of the City of Atlanta. The marches, battles, sieges, and other military operations, that have signalized the campaign must render it famous in the annals of war, and have entitled those who have participated therein to the applause and thanks of the nation."[94]

For two and a half months Sherman would occupy Atlanta, reorganizing his army, directing the operations against the forces of Hood still within fighting distance, and preparing for his next move, the March to the Sea. "I will make the interior of Georgia feel the weight of war," he wrote General Schofield in October.[95] No sudden careless expression of revenge, this was simply the utterance of a long-held belief that until the full weight of war should be felt by the South, the conflict would continue. Mercy lay in hastening its end.

As Sherman's army marched toward the city, Maj. Stephen Pierson wrote:

> For us it was a glorious morning. . . . It meant the end of a campaign of more than a hundred days of almost continuous fighting, upon each of which, somewhere along those lines, could have been heard the sounds of war, the sharp crash of the rifle of the outpost, the rattle of the skirmish, or the roar of a full

line of battle; the end of a campaign of more than a hundred miles of marching, manoeuvering [*sic*], struggling, scarcely one of which was made unopposed; the end of a campaign crowned with victory and honor for the one, closed by defeat, without dishonor, for the other. . . . [96]

CHAPTER NINE

# "War Is Cruelty, and You Cannot Refine It"

SHORTLY AFTER NOON ON SEPTEMBER 2, 1864, the occupying forces under Maj. Gen. Henry W. Slocum of the Army of the Cumberland began their entrance into the city of Atlanta. It was a victory parade as regiment after regiment marched to the tunes of "Yankee Doodle" and "Battle Hymn of the Republic." The city they entered was a city thrown into a state of anarchy. There was no government, nor was there any evidence of military or police protection. Looters of all ages were ransacking and plundering stores, vacant buildings and abandoned homes intent on taking whatever they could before the Federals arrived. There was destruction everywhere. Union surgeon J. C. Patton recorded in his diary: "The City is about the size of Evansville [Indiana] and is terribly shattered. I had often heard of the terror of bombardment of a crowded city, but I never realized it before." Patton saw houses shattered and "torn in every shape that can be imagined." Some were destroyed, while others had hardly been touched. "Some had shells through the doors, some places the shell had burst inside and torn it all to pieces."[1] Correspondent David P. Conyngham examined the city after its bombardment and told his readers of how "the suburbs were in ruins, and few houses escaped without being perforated." Citizens were killed "and many more had hair-breath escapes."[2] Rufus Mead, Jr., a soldier in the Commissary Office of the Fifth Connecticut Volunteers, wrote his family about the effectiveness of the shelling of Atlanta. He noted that Macon Depot, in the center of the city, "has been a good target

217

for all our batteries I should judge by the way things are splintered up. . . ." He spoke of shade trees cut down, fences destroyed, "in short every kind of mischief done by these iron missles."[3] The psychological effect of the sociological devastation was perhaps best described by Wallace Reed, who observed, "In the dread silence of that memorable morning [before Sherman's troops entered at noon] ten thousand helpless people looked at each other's faces for some faint sign of hope and encouragement. . . ."[4] To be sure, Atlanta had become a desolate place, its foundations had been destroyed and now it was at the mercy of its destroyer.

Five days after Slocum entered the city, Sherman arrived, but unlike Slocum's triumphant entry, with bands playing and troops cheering, Sherman rode in quietly and unostentatiously. As Carter describes it, "No guard of honor greeted him, no heralding salute of cannon, no drums or bugles. While the accompanying officers, a handful of them, wore their best regalia, were mounted on handsomely caparisoned prancing steeds, and seemed to relish this moment of glory, the beak-nosed general himself, mounted on a mottled mare, wore only 'a gray flannel shirt, a faded old blue blouse and trousers that he had worn since long, before Chattanooga.'"[5] Fanfare was not for Sherman, at least not yet. He was no McClellan, and besides, the war was not over and there was still much to be done. The cheering would have to wait for a later time. He guided his steed to the house of John Neal on Washington Street, set up headquarters, and immediately began work.

Sherman had reached that point in his life where he no longer needed the praise of others. He was at peace with himself. He was also grateful. Immediately after the capture of Atlanta he composed a personal letter to General Halleck expressing his appreciation of Halleck's faith in him. He wrote, "I owe you all I now enjoy of fame, for I allowed myself in 1861 to sink into a perfect slough of despond [*sic*], and do believe I would have run away and hid from dangers and complications that surrounded us. You . . . opened . . . the first avenues of success and hope, and . . . put me in the way of recovering from what might have proved an ignoble end."[6]

Sherman had finally become his own man. Confident, sure, tried and tested under fire, he knew what needed to be done and how to do it. No doubts plagued his mind, there was no longer any need to please the "significant others" in his life. Now everything was for himself, he became his own standard.

The confidence was also shared by his men. One day as Sherman walked the streets of Atlanta he saw a sign over a door proclaiming the opening of an Indiana Relief Agency that intended to restrict assistance to soldiers from that state only. Turning to Henry Hitchcock, his new military secretary, he very emphatically stated that "I hadn't any *Indiana army* down there, but a U. S. army." The small-mindedness of some people disturbed him greatly, and the presence of this agency was a perfect example of such thinking. Sherman did not want to " . . . have one man nursed because he was from Indiana and his . . . neighbor left to long . . . for what *he* couldn't get because he was from Ohio."[7] He ordered the agency closed and let it be known that sectionalism had no place in an army warring against disunion. He refused to allow a part of his army to be cared for at the expense of the rest.

Such a small affair, in and of itself not very significant, yet coupled with the fame and glory attending the capture of Atlanta and the national recognition such a feat had brought the "Army Group," it made Sherman even more popular among his troops. It was clear evidence to them that their commander cared. In the past Sherman had had his ups and downs with the men he commanded, but not now. This was not First Bull Run or Kentucky or Chickasaw Bayou. With the capture of Atlanta he had gained and would retain their complete and almost unquestioned confidence and respect. Writing to his wife, Hitchcock told her not to worry for his safety, but to "believe in 'Uncle Billy' as his soldiers do. . . ."[8]

Sherman knew the importance of the unquestioned confidence that a commander must have from his men, and he had his own theory about how it should be attained. "The true way to be popular with troops is not to be free and familiar with them, but to make them believe you know more than they do." Confiding to the Arkansas Bishop, Henry C. Lay, he added, "My men believe I know everything; they are much mistaken but it gives them confidence in me."[9] Without a doubt, the completion of the Atlanta campaign had sealed Sherman's confidence in himself and his troops' confidence in him.

It was a healthy confidence. As Liddell Hart has said, "His head rose higher" but "it did not swell." He was quick to give credit to his officers and men and refused to be a braggart like McClellan or Hooker. He delivered a congratulatory address to his troops following the fall of Atlanta that emphasized not his leadership, but the successful efforts of his men. All he asked in return for their sacrifices was that they continue "the cultivation of soldierly virtues" of "courage, patience, obedience to laws." He encouraged them to continue the good feelings they had for each other and to try "to excel the other in the practice of their high qualities." The result of their dedication would be "that our country will in time emerge from this war, purified by the fires of war." Liddell Hart sums up Sherman's newly achieved fame quite well by writing that "Sherman's confidence was of a type which is born of accomplished facts, not of mere conceit of his own qualities. . . ." He never lost sight of his limitations no matter how great his achievements. In other words, he retained his balance.[10]

Even before he entered Atlanta, Sherman had made the decision that the city would be a military post, occupied and controlled by the army. Past experience had taught him that to use a captured city for a permanent garrison was simply another way of giving aid and comfort to the enemy. Sherman explained:

> I peremptorily required that all the citizens and families resident in Atlanta should go away, giving to each the option to go south or north, as their interests or feelings dictated. I was resolved to make Atlanta a pure military garrison or depot, with no civil population to influence military measures. I had seen Memphis, Vicksburg, Natchez, and New Orleans, all captured from the enemy, and each at once was garrisoned by a full division of troops, if not more; so that success was actually crippling our armies in the field by detachments to guard and protect the interests of the hostile population.[11]

Ultimately it was his goal to abandon Atlanta after thoroughly destroying its means of supplies and lines of communication. He had no desire or intention to leave Union troops to garrison it. Temporarily, out of necessity, while he planned and prepared for his next move, it would become a military garrison and all military personnel would have precedence over the civilian population. To accomplish this end, Sherman, in early September, issued this order: "The City of Atlanta belonging exclusively for war-like purposes, it will at once be vacated by all except the armies of the United States. . . . At the proper time full arrangements will be made for a supply to all the troops of all articles they may need. . . . The same military principles will apply to all military posts south of Atlanta."[12]

On the same day, Sherman gave notice to Washington of his drastic order and defended his unprecedented action by telling Halleck, "Atlanta is a fortified town, was stubbornly defended, and fairly captured. As captors we have a right to it. The residence here of a poor population would compel us sooner or later to feed them or see them starve under our eyes. . . . I propose to remove all the inhabitants of Atlanta. . . . If the people raise a howl against my barbarity and cruelty I will answer that war is war and not popularity-seeking. If they want peace they and their relatives must stop war."[13] They could go north or south, but they had to go. Sherman had seen and suffered too long the drain of strength because of the permanent garrisoning of towns.

Sherman had held these views about warfare since the outbreak of the conflict. From the beginning he believed that the South had to be defeated—militarily, psychologically, and sociologically. The conciliatory policy of earlier years had lead him to frustration and doubt concerning Washington's methods. He had tried to conform, but could not do so. Now there was no need for conformity because he was no longer alone, no longer deviant. Washington was conforming to him. His earlier predictions of a long war had come true. "A mild conciliatory policy had failed to bring the South back into the Union. . . ."[14] A stern policy was needed and was even being demanded by many.

Russell Weigley describes this transition which Lincoln, Halleck, and Grant made to a harsher more punitive policy against the South, a policy that Sherman had held since the outbreak of hostilities. Lincoln's warnings to the citizens in Union-held Louisiana in 1862 and his acquiescence to Maj. Gen. John Pope's decree to the civil population of Virginia are illustrative. In response to Louisianians' complaints that the Federal forces were departing from his earlier assurance of protection, Lincoln said: " . . . I never had a wish to touch the foundations of their society, or any right of theirs. With perfect knowledge of this, they forced a necessity upon me to send armies among them, and it is their own fault, not mine. . . . They . . . know the remedy. . . . Remove the necessity. . . . And might it not be well for them to consider whether they have not already had time enough?"[15]

Punishment was, in Lincoln's mind, becoming an element of military strategy, and it was the type of punishment Sherman had advocated all along. Although reluctantly, Lincoln approved the spirit of

Pope's decree in Virginia. Pope directed his forces to live off the land, to requisition supplies from Southerners, and to provide reimbursement to loyal citizens only. He announced stern penalties for those who harassed the rear echelons of his armies, demanded payment for damage done by marauders and guerrillas, and threatened to destroy any house from which a Union soldier was shot. He ordered commanders to "proceed immediately to arrest all disloyal male citizens within their lines or within reach" of their stations. Those willing to take an oath of allegiance to the United States he would permit "to remain at their homes and pursue in good faith their accustomed avocations." He threatened to remove any who remained yet refused to take the oath. And those who returned after expulsion would be faced with a death penalty.[16]

Even General Halleck came to the point of agreement with Sherman's tactics. In 1864, he encouraged Sherman to pursue policies he had earlier found distasteful. " . . . I am fully of opinion that the nature of your position, the character of the war, the conduct of the enemy (and especially of non-combatants and women . . . ), will justify you in gathering up all the forage and provisions which your army will require, both for a siege of Atlanta and for your supply in your march farther into the enemy's country."

He minced no words, left nothing in doubt, as he continued, "Let the disloyal families of the country, thus stripped, go to their husbands, fathers, and natural protectors in the rebel ranks; we have tried three years of conciliation and kindness without any reciprocation; on the contrary, those thus treated have acted as spies and guerrillas in our rear and within our lines. . . . We have fed this class of people long enough. Let them go with their husbands and fathers in the rebel ranks; and if they won't go, we must send them to their friends and natural protectors." How more Shermanesque could he sound than: "I would destroy every mill and factory within reach which I did not want for my own use. . . ."[17]

It was after Shiloh that Grant made the change. Years later, writing his memoirs, Grant described his transition. "Up to the battle of Shiloh I, as well as thousands of other citizens, believed that the rebellion against the Government would collapse suddenly and soon, if a decisive victory could be gained over any of its armies. But when Confederate armies were collected . . . and made a gallant effort to regain what had been lost, then, indeed, I gave up all ideas of saving the Union except by complete conquest."[18] At Vicksburg

Grant ordered Sherman to return to Jackson and "destroy that place as a railroad centre, and manufacturing city of military supplies. He did the work most effectually."[19] He approved of Sherman's Meridian expedition and, to Maj. Gen. Philip A. Sheridan concerning the Shenandoah Valley, he said, "If the war is to last another year, we want the Shenandoah Valley to remain a barren waste."[20]

Thus by 1864 the strategy had changed. Realization had finally come that victory could not be achieved by a grand Napoleonic defeat of the enemy on a specific battlefield. Victory would come only through conquest. At last, the strategy Sherman had been recommending from the start of the war was accepted by his three superiors. So, with approval, Sherman designed his campaign to destroy Atlanta and march through Georgia to Savannah " . . . breaking roads and doing irreparable damage,"[21] and thence proceed northward through the Carolinas carrying destruction in his path.

Sherman's order to the citizens of Atlanta to evacuate the city fell on them "like a thunder-bolt."[22] They had never imagined that the war would reach their city. Sherman knew the measure would be severely criticized, but he "made up his mind to do it with the absolute certainty of its justness and that time would sanction its wisdom." He believed "the people of the South would read in this measure two important conclusions: one, that we were in earnest; and the other, if they were sincere in their common and popular clamor 'to die in the last ditch,' that the opportunity would soon come."[23] As J. G. Barrett has said, "It was not an utter disregard for the people's welfare that made Sherman issue the order, but instead, his conviction that it was an essential war measure."[24] Sherman believed that his operations in the Deep South, if harsh enough, would have a negative impact on the morale of Lee's Army of Northern Virginia presently involved in opposition to Grant near Richmond. The Deep South was, of course, home to many of Lee's soldiers. A threat to their homes and families would have a devastating effect psychologically. The result would be to increase an already rising desertion rate within that army. It would also act as a mortal blow against those who had families in the upper states, realizing that if it could happen in Georgia then it could happen in Virginia too.

The anticipated criticisms and reactions to his order came immediately. The Montgomery *Daily Advertiser* stated that "the proceeding is justly regarded as very extraordinary," that it was inhumane, and "perhaps without a parallel in history."[25] The Macon *Telegraph* in an editorial entitled "The Atlanta Exile" exclaimed: "Modern warfare may be challenged in vain for an edict from a military satrap so utterly and inexcusably barbarian as this." No act, it continued, had a parallel "since the expulsion of the Moors from Grenada." It was an act of horror inflicted "on helpless women and babies" and should call forth "a universal burst of indignation from Christendom. . . ."[26] Mary Gay, a resident of Atlanta, called the order an outrage. "By this order," she wrote, "and by others even more oppressive and diabolical, the Nero of the nineteenth century, alias William Tecumseh Sherman, was put upon record as the born leader of the most ruthless, Godless band ever organized in the name of patriotism—a band which, but for a few noble spirits who, by the power of mind over matter, exerted a restraining influence, would not have left a Southerner to tell the tale of its fiendishness."[27]

Even some present-day writers have continued to criticize Sherman's order, calling it a "crime against the citizens of Atlanta"—"a people who had demonstrated their courage and their love for their homes by the manner in which they had endured the siege of the city." To many, the suffering inflicted was reason enough for condemnation of Sherman's act.[28] Needless to say, Sherman would have disagreed.

As an act of humanity, Sherman wrote General Hood informing him of his order. He said, "I have deemed it to the interest of the United States that the citizens now residing in Atlanta should remove those who prefer it to the south, the rest north. For the latter I can provide food and transportation to points of their election in Tennessee, Kentucky, or further north. For the former I can provide transportation by cars as far as Rough and Ready [just north of Atlanta], and also wagons. . . ." He told Hood that if he consented he would "undertake to remove all the families in Atlanta who prefer to go south" and assist them with "their moveable effects," such as furniture, clothing, trunks, and bedding. He would also permit their personal servants to accompany them, "white or black." He would even be willing to hire men who wanted jobs through his headquarters. Then he concluded, saying, "Atlanta is no place for families or non-combatants, and I have no desire to send them north if you will assist in conveying them south."[29]

Hood was enraged. But, of course, that was the only response he could give. He, like most Confederate officers, were of the nineteenth-century military tradition. War was still a gentlemanly affair to be conducted on a professional basis with little or no involvement of noncombatants. He did not understand that history had passed him by and that a new era had dawned. He wrote to Sherman in reply, "I do not consider that I have any alternative in this matter. I . . . shall render all assistance in my power to expedite the transportation of citizens in this direction. . . ." Then in anger and with a complete lack of understanding as to the new age he was being forced to enter, he added, "And now, sir, permit me to say that the unprecedented measure you propose transcends, in studied and ingenious cruelty, all acts ever before brought to my attention in the dark history of war. In the name of God, and humanity, I protest, believing that you are expelling from their homes and firesides the wives and children of brave people."[30]

Sherman quickly responded with the assertion that one need not look back into the history of war for examples of cruelty. "It is not unprecedented," he said, "for General Joseph E. Johnston himself very wisely and properly removed the families all the way from Dalton down, and I see no reason why Atlanta should be excepted." In addition, Johnston had done the same at Jackson, Mississippi, and Lt. Gen. William J. Hardee the same at Jonesboro. Sherman wrote further, "Modern examples are so handy. You yourself burned dwelling houses along your parapet, and I have seen today fifty houses that you have rendered uninhabitable because they stood in the way of your forts and men. You defended Atlanta on a line so close to town that every cannon-shot and many musket-shots from our line of investment, that overshot their mark, went into the habitations of women and children."

"I say," he continued, "that it is a kindness to these families . . . to remove them now, from scenes that women and children should not be exposed to. . . ." Then with a tinge of sarcasm, he added, these "'brave people' should scorn to commit their wives and children to the rude barbarians who thus, as you say, violate the laws of war, as illustrated in the pages of its dark history." With apparent emotion, Sherman told Hood, "In the name of common sense, I ask you not to appeal to a just God in such a sacrilegious manner. You who, in the midst of peace and prosperity, have plunged a nation into war—dark and cruel war—who dared and badgered us to battle, insulted our flag, seized our arsenals and forts . . . turned loose your privateers to plunder unarmed ships; expelled Union families by the thousands, burned their homes, and declared, by an act of Congress, the confiscation of all debts due Northern men. . . ."

"If we must be enemies," Sherman wrote, "let us be men, and fight it out as we propose to do, and not deal in such hypocritical appeals to God and humanity." He concluded his letter with, "God will judge us in due time, and he will pronounce whether it be more humane to fight with a town full of women and the families of a brave people at our back, or to remove them in time to places of safety among their own friends and people."

Sherman eventually terminated the exchange with Hood by saying, "I was not bound by the laws of war to give notice of the shelling of Atlanta, a 'fortified town with magazines, arsenals, foundries and public stores'; you were bound to take notice. See the books."[31] As Lloyd Lewis puts it, Sherman perhaps by "the books" meant *Instructions for the Government of Armies of the United States*, issued by the War Department in April 1863. Article 19 stated: "Commanders whenever admissible [should], inform the enemy of their intention to bombard a place, so that the non-combatants and especially the women and children, may be removed before the bombardment commences. But it is no infraction of the common law to omit thus to inform the enemy. Surprise may be a necessity."[32] Privately, to Bishop H. C. Lay, Sherman said of the Hood correspondence, "To be sure, I have made war vindictively. War is war, and you can make nothing else of it. But Hood knows as well as anyone, I am not brutal or inhuman."[33]

The Hood-Sherman exchange is important because it epitomized the clash of two ages, the warfare of the nineteenth century with its romantic view of martial splendor, and the warfare of the twentieth century, with its pragmatic emphasis on achieving a clear defeat of the enemy. Sherman understood both and rejected one for the other. Hood was too deeply rooted in the nineteenth century to understand the coming of the twentieth, thus his attack on Sherman. Hood simply was incapable of understanding. The culture of the South did not provide him with the necessary conceptualizations.

On the 11th of September, the mayor of Atlanta and two members of the city council wrote and presented a formal and impassioned appeal to Sherman, hoping he might rescind his order. The letter delineated the sufferings and hardships his forced evacuation was causing the citizens of Atlanta:

Many poor women are in advanced state of pregnancy, others now having young children, and [others] whose husbands . . . are either in the army, prisoners, or dead.

Some say: 'I have one sick at my house. . . .'

Others say: ' . . . We have no house to go to, and no means to buy, build, or rent any. . . .'

This is but a feeble picture of the consequences of their measure.

. . . In conclusion, we must earnestly and solemnly petition you to reconsider this order. . . .

There were no accommodations for the refugees traveling south, and people were forced to stay in churches and other buildings that were unoccupied. Even worse, winter was coming and would be devastating to those unable to find shelter and food.[34]

In answer to their appeal, Sherman presented a clear and succinct statement of the causes of the war, his philosophy of war, and his desire for peace. The people of Atlanta, he said, had to understand that evacuation of the city was a military necessity. "I . . . give full credit to your statements of . . . distress," but he could not revoke his orders. The order was "not designed to meet the humanities of the case but to prepare for the future struggles in which millions of good people outside of Atlanta have a deep interest. . . ." Military plans made the evacuation necessary. And once again, with words similar to ones he had used on other occasions, he tried to make the Atlantans understand war: "You cannot qualify war in harsher terms than I will. War is cruelty, and you cannot refine it; and those who brought war into our country deserve all the curses and maledictions a people can pour out. I know I had no hand in making this war, and I know I will make more sacrifices today than any of you to secure peace."

The war, as he had said so often, was the result of the violation of law. He told the mayor and city council members:

You might as well appeal against the thunder-storm as against these terrible hardships of war. They are inevitable and the only way the people of Atlanta can hope once more to live in peace and quiet at home is to stop the war, which can only be done by admitting that it began in error and is perpetuated in pride.

We don't want your negroes or your houses or your lands, or anything you have. But we do want, and will have a just obedience to the laws of the United States . . . and if it involves the destruction of your improvements, we cannot help it.

The South was to be blamed for the war. It was the South that had seized "forts, arsenals, mints, custom-houses, etc. . . ." As far as cruelty was concerned, Sherman wrote that he himself had seen "hundreds and thousands of women and children fleeing from your armies and desperadoes, hungry and with bleeding feet. . . ." The people of Atlanta and the entire South must arrive at the realization that war is cruelty and destruction. For many the war had been experienced only at a distance, but, no longer. "Now that war comes home to you, you feel very different. You deprecate its horrors, but did not feel them when you sent car-loads of soldiers and ammunition, and moulded shells and shot, to carry war into Kentucky and Tennessee, to desolate the homes of hundreds and thousands of good [Union] people who only asked to live in peace at their old homes and under the Government of their inheritances."

And finally, he expressed his desire for peace: "I want peace, and believe it can only be reached through union and war, and I will ever conduct war with a view to perfect an early success. But, my dear sirs, when peace does come, you may call on me for anything. Then will I share with you the last cracker, and watch with you to shield your houses and families against danger from every quarter."[35] Sherman had warned the people of Atlanta of his coming seven months earlier; if they had not heeded his notice it was not his fault. He could not, would not, stop now. He must continue onward. In time of war the military must take precedence over civilian affairs. That was his rule since Shiloh and would remain his rule until Johnston's surrender in North Carolina. War was inconceivable to Sherman without the principle of military superiority over civilian authority. Civil authority would regain its dominance once the war ended.

With Atlanta secure, Sherman turned to planning his next move. His philosophy of war and entire personality would not permit him to remain idle, to rest on the laurels of one victory, no matter how glorious. The objective of the war was the conquest and defeat of the South. Simply because Atlanta, one of the citadels of the South, had fallen, this did not mean the war was over. He would not fall into the belief that now the Confederate armies would cease their resistance and the Rebel government would sue for peace. He had fallen into that trap following the victory at Vicksburg, but would not do so now. He knew that this war must be fought to the bitter end, that the will of the South had to be conquered.

He decided it would be futile to pursue or even attempt to interfere with the movements of Hood's army. To Maj. Gen. George H. Thomas he would eventually write, "To pursue Hood is folly, for he can twist and turn like a fox, and wear out an army in pursuit; to continue to occupy long lines of railroads simply exposes our small detachments to be picked up in detail and forces me to make counter-marches to protect lines of communication. I know I am right in this. . . ."[36]

Col. Horace Porter, an aide to Grant, recalled Sherman's thinking at this time. After lunching together Sherman and Porter retired to a house the general was using as headquarters, and there Sherman elaborated on his next move. He felt it vital that a definite "objective point or points" should be established. To march in a general manner "through Georgia for the purpose of inflicting damage would not be good generalship." Instead, he had settled on a definite point. "I want to strike out for the sea. . . ."[37] The idea was not new to Sherman. At least as far back as May 1864, he had contemplated such a raid. Col. Willard Warner, then recently assigned as inspector general, recalls an interesting conversation with Sherman. After Sherman had explained his intentions to march from Chattanooga to Atlanta, Warner inquired as to what Sherman would do if and when he was in Atlanta. He pointed out to the general that his army would be 450 miles from its main supply base and that he would be dependent on a single line of railroad to provide materiel for his army. Warner describes Sherman's response, "Stopping short in his walk and snapping the ashes off his cigar in a quick, nervous way he replied in two words—'Salt water.'" At first Warner did not fully understand, until he gave a map a more thorough examination. Then he asked Sherman if he meant Savannah or Charleston, to which Sherman replied, "yes."[38]

There were serious dangers in such a plan, however. As long as Sherman could keep his army moving he could subsist off the land, " . . . but if I should have to stop and fight battles the difficulty would be greatly increased." There was also the matter of Hood and the lingering Army of Tennessee. What would Hood do? Would he follow and attempt to interfere, or would he move north or northwest? Then in one jerky statement, Sherman told Porter, "I don't care much what he does." He felt sure he would never succeed in bringing Hood to battle, and he had no intention of following him all over Georgia and/or Tennessee, or wherever he might choose to go. Hood really did not interest him. Sherman said that he preferred that the Confederate general move north. Indeed, he told Porter, " . . . I would be willing to give him a free ticket and pay his expenses if he would decide to take that horn of the dilemma." That way Sherman " . . . could send enough of his army to delay his progress . . ." and eventually " . . . destroy him. . . ." This would free " . . . the bulk of my army . . ." to " . . . cut a swath through to the sea. . . ." Once there, Sherman believed he could move north to the rear of Lee, " . . . or do almost anything else that Grant might require of me."[39] Whatever the case, Sherman had concluded that a slow pursuit of Hood would only add to the strength of the enemy.

Sherman has been criticized for not pursuing Hood and forcing him into a showdown that might destroy the Confederate army. The criticisms, all from armchair generals who never heard a shot fired in battle, basically take the form of his failure to get at the Army of Tennessee and "break it up."[40] For example, Lloyd Lewis, a Sherman biographer, states, "He had, after all, failed in his primary purpose, the ruin of the Confederate Army. He had taken Atlanta and kept his opponent from reinforcing Grant, but Hood still faced him. . . ."[41] The historian J. C. Ropes states that not only had Sherman not destroyed the Confederate army, " . . . he had done practically nothing towards carrying out his intention."[42] For Stanley Horn, "there was no sound military reason for pulling his army from Hood's front backward into the city and permitting Hood to pursue unmolested whatever plans he might have to rest and recruit."[43] E. M. Clauss writes, "Despite his successful seizure of the strategically important Confederate city, Sherman failed to achieve his primary objective in the Atlanta Campaign, the destruction or capture of Hood's army."[44] "As a matter of fact," writes Bruce Catton, "Sherman had done less than he set out to do. Hood's army had escaped. . . . He had been told to destroy the Confederate army and had not done it. . . ."[45]

All these criticisms appear to be based on the assumption that Sherman's primary objective was the Confederate army and that his secondary objective was Atlanta, or the interior of the enemy's territory. "There could have been no difference of opinion as to the first duty of the armies of the Military Division of the Mississippi," Grant would write in 1884. "[Hood's] army was the first objective, and that important railroad center, Atlanta, the second."[46] The problem with using this statement for an interpretation of Sherman's moves in 1864 is that: one, the statement was made twenty years after the event, and two, it cannot be supported with similar statements made by Grant at the time Sherman was in and around Atlanta or even prior to his Atlanta campaign. As stated in the previous chapter, to assume, even based on Grant's later statement, that Sherman's primary objective was Hood is to open oneself to serious question. A close examination of Grant's orders to Sherman on April 4, 1864, gives no support for such an assumption, There was no indication as to a timetable given by Grant's order either. The order simply stated that Sherman was to break up Johnston's army and get into the enemy's interior. In war it can be assumed that the orders should be carried out as quickly as possible unless otherwise stated. In addition, as has already been pointed out, Grant gave Sherman freedom to accomplish the two objectives in any manner he saw fit. If Grant had intended otherwise, he should not have waited twenty years to clarify his order. Sherman did exactly what Grant ordered him to do. Not only did he get into the interior of the South, but, through General Thomas, an army leader in the Military Division of the Mississippi, he succeeded in destroying Hood's army. Thus, there was no failure on Sherman's part.

The criticisms are also based on the assumption that there is a difference between a military objective and a geographical objective. For example, Clauss states that "Sherman failed to achieve Clausewitz's primary objective in war: 'To conquer and destroy the armed power of the enemy.'"[47] Such criticisms fail to take into account two things: one, that Sherman had already redefined war and viewed geography as much of a military objective as the enemy's army, and two, that his strategy included accomplishing two tasks at the same time, which he did. Further, the criticisms fail to note that Sherman could not separate the activities of an army from those of that army's government. Thus, his military goal not only entailed geographical objectives but political ones as well. He knew politically the importance of Atlanta. He also knew that Atlanta would fall more rapidly and with the loss of fewer lives if he occupied it than if he fought Hood's army. So, he turned his back, momentarily, on Hood's forces and ensured the re-election of Lincoln with the capture of Atlanta.

Finally, Castel submits that although Sherman can perhaps be criticized for being too cautious, "In all likelihood the Confederates would have fallen back farther south if pressed. . . ." This would have placed Sherman in the position of experiencing supply problems.[48] Thus, Sherman concluded it would be folly to pursue Hood. The error of most critics of Sherman's decision at Atlanta is that they measure his performance based on Jominian and Clausewitzan principles. Therefore, from that point of view, "Sherman's handling of the Atlanta Campaign was at most a qualified success."[49] The truth of the matter is, Sherman defied those principles, and that is what made him a success, and that is what entitles him to be labeled "one of the first modern generals."

With the fall of Atlanta and the retreat of Hood's army, the Army of the West was entrusted with tremendous power. Sherman had to determine what to do with this power, and he knew it had to be used effectively and successfully. He knew that he must apply it in such a manner as to "produce the result—the end of war—which was all we desired; for war is only justifiable among civilized nations" if it produces peace.[50]

Knowing that Georgia was now open to him and having fairly adequate knowledge of the enemy's positions, Sherman set out to convince Grant of the need for Sherman to march to Savannah.[51] Throughout the month of September and into October they debated the issue. On October 1, Sherman telegraphed Grant, raising the question: " . . . why will it not do to leave Tennessee to the forces Thomas has, and the reserves soon to come to Nashville, and for me to destroy Atlanta and march across Georgia to Savannah or Charleston, breaking roads and doing irreparable damage?"[52] Grant was skeptical of the move because it would take Sherman farther away from his base of supply into a hostile country with an enemy army at his rear.[53] But Sherman was determined, arguing that, "The possession of the Savannah River is more fatal to the possibility of Southern independence. They may stand the fall of Richmond, but not all Georgia. . . . I admire your dogged perseverance and pluck more than ever. If you can whip Lee, and I can march to the Atlantic, I think Uncle Abe will give us twenty days' leave of absence to see the young folks."[54] He pressed his point even further, declaring that no longer could his army remain on the defensive; no longer did he want to guess at what his enemy might do. Cutting loose from Atlanta and heading east could place him on the offensive and would force his enemy into guessing "at my plans."[55] If Grant would approve his proposal then he felt sure he could "make this march, and make Georgia howl!"[56]

Finally, after serious deliberation and raising such issues as the inability to prepare a coastal base, fear of being attacked by hostile citizens, and the strength of Thomas's army, Grant wired Sherman from City Point, Virginia, that he approved of the plan. Since Sherman had left a strong force under the command of Thomas to keep watch over Hood, Grant felt it would indeed be better for Sherman to move south rather than north. He told Sherman, "Hood's army now that it worked so far north, ought to be looked upon as the 'object.' With the force, however, that you have left with General Thomas, he must be able to take care of Hood and destroy him. I do not see that you can withdraw from where you are to follow Hood, without giving up all we have gained in territory. I say, then, go on as you propose."[57] Sherman answered Grant immediately, assuring his commander that his proposed march "would produce fruits more compensating for the expense, trouble, and risk."[58]

Writing to Chief of Staff Halleck, Sherman said, "I now consider myself authorized to execute my plans. . . ." He told him to "have look-outs at Morris Island, S. C., Ossabaw Sound, Ga., Pensacola and Mobile Bays" because "I will turn up somewhere." He had to have "alternatives," be they "Charleston, Savannah, or the mouth of the Appalachicola [on the Gulf]." He could not be "confined to one route" because "the enemy might so oppose that delay and want would trouble me." With alternates "I can take so eccentric a course that no general can guess my objective." He felt confident that he could take "Macon and Milledgeville, Augusta and Savannah, Ga., and wind up with closing the neck back of Charleston so that they will starve out." With emphasis on his view of warfare, he told Halleck, "This war differs from European wars in this particular: we are not only fighting hostile armies, but a hostile people, and must make old and young, rich and poor, feel the hard hand of war."[59] To General Thomas he wrote, "I propose to demonstrate the vulnerability of the South and make its inhabitants feel that war and individual ruin are synonymous terms."[60] He was intent on bringing together personal troubles and social issues, psychology and sociology, with the result being the conquest of the Southerner and the South. As Merrill puts it, "Sherman wanted to show the world that the Confederacy was a hollow shell. Watching his army move through Georgia unhampered would create a sense of helplessness not only for Georgians but for troops in Hood's and Lee's armies and plantation owners in the Carolinas. They must realize that there was no hope for the Confederacy."[61]

With the agreement reached between Grant and Sherman a profound change took place in the American Civil War. Total war had officially been sanctioned and supported by Lincoln and Halleck. Grant and Sherman had ascended to the two most powerful positions in the United States Army, the war had descended into a "remorseless revolutionary struggle," and Lincoln "had had to abandon nearly all his hopes for reconciliation. . . ." Therefore, the possible "dangerous effects of military means upon the ultimate ends of postwar sectional understanding had to be sacrificed to the immediate quest for victory. . . ." Nothing short of total war seemed to offer complete victory and thus reunion. Two strategies of war were being combined to form a grand strategy. Sherman's strategy was to wage war against "the enemy's mind," while Grant's was to bring complete destruction to the enemy's armies. "The Northern generals were pulled toward both methods because their aim was the utter and complete conquest of the South."[62] As of November 1864, the Civil War ceased being a war of reconciliation and became officially a war of conquest. The move was made to take the historical development of war into a new era, and Sherman was in the lead.

The transition had not been easy, except for Sherman. Lincoln, Halleck, and Grant had perceived the concept of total war early, however, they had feared implementing it. Yet, it was inevitable. The Industrial Revolution, democracy, even nationalism had swept the military institution into a new age. It was absurd to expect certain aspects of the social structure to change while other aspects remained the same. In order to function effectively in a nation that had become an industrial democracy, the military had to change. Its very survival depended on it. When order in a society becomes disorder, and diplomacy, discussion, debate, compromise—all the nonviolent means of re-establishing order—fail, war is the inevitable result. The role of the military is to wage war for the purpose of re-establishing order. If the military, with its methods, fails to bring peace, then it ceases to have meaning; its function is of no value. Therefore, the military, like all things in a society if they are to survive, must adapt. Under the leadership of Lincoln, Halleck,

Grant and Sherman a new military tradition was inaugurated. Whether it was liked or not was not at issue. The United States Army adapted.

Adaptation the leaders of the Confederacy could never grasp, and their inability to do so was partially responsible for their defeat. With Lee it was his narrowness. He could see little beyond the war in Virginia and in the East. He was never able to grasp the significance and importance of the West. But, of course, his conceptualization of the world made it impossible for him to understand. He was too entrenched in the mores and values of the early nineteenth century. Thomas Connelly and Barbara Bellows have presented a clear picture of the dilemma Lee never managed to resolve. They write:

> He was the man of basic American values of decency, duty, and honor, the devotee of unionism trapped in 1861 by conflicting loyalties. Lee was the post-war nationalist, driven by an unswerving determination to help restore the old Union.[63]
>
> Lee's greatness—duty, honor, and loyalty to his people—were products of his environment.
>
> The tragedy was that in 1861 a grief-stricken Lee was entrapped by his upbringing. His adherence to the duty principle warred against his strong devotion to the Union.[64]
>
> Robert E. Lee probably saw no inconsistency in this rapid conversion from the sorrowful Unionist to the ardent Confederate. In fact he may have never pondered the matter. In essence he was a non-reasoning individual who abdicated decisions to forces beyond his control. By the 1850s his pattern of life was well established—to move almost mechanically, governed by the unseen force of Divine Providence and an unanswering devotion to his concept of duty.[65]

He had made a "commitment to noncommitment." Connelly and Bellows continue, "By the 1850's Robert E. Lee had become an exaggeration of . . . [the] classical—Christian view."[66] He was "an exaggeration of the southern norm."[67] Indeed, he had been over-socialized by a culture that was rapidly dying.

Connelly and Bellows, however, seem to be off the mark when they conclude that "Lee is the greatest paradox of a paradoxical South."[68] If paradox is defined as "a statement or proposition [or action] seemingly self contradictory or absurd but in reality expressing a possible truth,"[69] then a paradox Lee is not. In actuality, Lee, like the South, was and to a degree still is a contradiction. Lee in his thoughts and actions was logically incongruous and inconsistent. And this was the truth he expressed. He found himself straddling two eras of a changing world and could only make the commitment not to make a commitment. As Connelly and Bellows have described, "He was the advocate of the Union who led an army of secessionists; and the man who described slavery as 'a moral and political evil' but who fought for the slavocracy. Lee was one of almost incredible gentleness, Christian piety, and sensitivity for the feelings of others. He was also the greatest artist of violence possessed by the Confederacy, and a man whose calm spirit could be transformed into high excitement by battle."[70] In essence Lee was a contradiction who said one thing and did just the opposite. He was never able to resolve the inconsistencies, and they plagued him to his death. He wanted both worlds and ended up losing both. Because of his contradictions Lee did not possess the ability to become a modern general.

It was the same with Pres. Jefferson Davis. His inability to grasp what was happening in the world was evident in his hope that Lee could bring the Federals to their knees. Even after Atlanta had fallen Davis wrote to Herschel Johnson of Georgia, "I think Atlanta can be recovered; that Sherman's army can be driven out of Georgia, perhaps utterly destroyed."[71] He, like Lee, never fully understood the importance of the West. He was operating in a totally different world from Grant and Sherman. To illustrate this point, while Sherman was considering what his next move should be after the fall of Atlanta, Davis was in Macon, Georgia, attempting, rather belatedly, to revitalize the spirits of the masses he never really understood. In one of his speeches, he said, "Sherman cannot keep up his long line of communication, and he must retreat. [Had he forgotten Vicksburg so soon?] And when that day comes, the fate that befell the army of the French Empire in its retreat from Moscow will be reenacted. Our cavalry and our people will harass and destroy his army as did the Cossacks that of Napoleon, and the Yankee general, like him, will escape with only a body-guard."[72] Grant's remarks upon hearing of Davis's speech show clearly the gulf between the two worlds. He said, "Mr. Davis has not made it quite plain who is to furnish the snow for this Moscow retreat."[73] Davis, in essence, no matter the circumstances or present crisis, continued to live in a different age and world that was rapidly dying at his feet. As Bell I. Wiley states, "Perhaps the greatest of all Davis's shortcomings was his lack of capacity for growth."[74]

Even before Sherman received official approval of the march to Savannah he had begun preparations. As early as October 19 he had issued this order: "I want to prepare for my big raid. On the 1st of November I want nothing in Atlanta but what is necessary for war. Send all trash to the rear at once, and have on hand thirty days food and but little forage. I propose to abandon Atlanta, and the railroad back to Chattanooga, to sally forth to ruin Georgia and bring up on the seashore. Make all dispositions accordingly."[75] F. Y. Hedley, adjutant of the Thirty-Second Illinois Infantry Regiment, recalled: "Events during the last week in October and the first ten days in November, 1864, were stirring enough. The railroad . . . was repaired from Chattanooga to Atlanta, where the bulk of Sherman's army was assembling. Every train going north was loaded to its utmost capacity with the wounded and infirm; [and with] almost everything that the men could not carry on their backs. Returning trains brought only the most needed articles—hard bread, pork, coffee, sugar, and ammunition. It was evident even to those in the ranks that some important, if not desperate, undertaking was at hand."[76] Now that Grant had approved the campaign, Sherman stepped up his preparations. He issued orders making it clear that men, during marches and in camps, must keep their places and not scatter about to be picked up by the hostile people; it was of the utmost importance that "our wagons should not be loaded with anything but provisions and ammunition."[77] There was to be no general train of supplies because the army was to forage "liberally" off the country during the march; and, to the corps commanders alone "is entrusted the power to destroy mills, houses, cotton-gins, etc."[78]

Determined to make as great a psychological and sociological impression on the people of Georgia as possible, Sherman decided not to start his march until the presidential election of 1864 was over. He felt sure the news of Lincoln's victory would add to Southern consternation and to the damage he proposed as a military move. Sherman, unlike many of his soldiers, did not bother to vote. Instead, he spent the time studying the latest United States Census statistics regarding those counties in Georgia through which he proposed to pass in order to determine where he should march and what he should destroy.[79] He was determined "not to stand on the defensive," and was confident that his wife would soon "hear of me on a bigger road than that of Meridian."[80]

Finally, on November 9, from Kingston, Georgia, Sherman issued orders dividing his army into two wings—the right under Maj. Gen. Oliver O. Howard (Howard had replaced McPherson as commander of the Army of the Tennessee after the latter's death at the Battle of Atlanta), the left under Maj. Gen. Henry W. Slocum. On November 12, Sherman ordered the Western and Atlanta Railroad, his line of communication and supply, torn up all the way from Atlanta to Dalton. "Thus," as William Key put it, "he crosses his Rubicon, [and] commits his big armies to live off the land."[81]

The last order to be carried out before the march began was the destruction of the city of Atlanta. Sherman assigned Chief Engineer Orlando Poe to this special task and the "cataclysm . . . began November 12 [and] increased in fury over four volcanic days of flame, smoke, and exploding dynamite. . . ."[82] The depot, roundhouse, and machine shops of the Georgia Railroad, plus a number of houses and shops were leveled to the ground.[83] Carrie Berry recorded in her diary:

> Sun. Nov. 13. The federal soldiers have been coming to day and burning houses and I have been looking at them come in nearly every day.
>
> Mon. Nov. 14. They came burning Atlanta to day. We all dred it because they say that they will burn the last house before they stop. We will dred it.
>
> Tues. Nov. 15. This has been a dreadful day. Things have ben burning all around us. We dread to night because we do not know what moment that they wil set our house on fire. We have had a gard a lttle while after dinner and we feel a little more protected.[84]

The newsman, David P. Conyngham, reported, "Winship's iron foundary and machine shops were early set on fire. An oil refinery nearby next got on fire and was soon in a fierce blaze. Next followed a freight warehouse. . . . The depot, turning-table, freight sheds, and stores . . . were soon a fiery mass. . . ." Churches were burned and hotels, "and all the square around the railroad depot, were soon in one sheet of flame." Nothing was spared the torch. "Drugstores, drygood stores, hotels, negro marts, theatres, and grog shops were all . . . feeding the fiery element. Worn-out wagons and camp equipage were piled up in the depot and added to the fury of the flames."[85]

Maj. George Ward Nichols, an aide-de-camp to Sherman, wrote of the burning, "A grand and awful spectacle is presented to the beholder in this beautiful city, now in flames. . . . The heaven is one expanse of lurid fire; the air filled with flying, burning cinders; buildings covering two hundred acres are in ruins or in flames; every instant there is the sharp detonation or the smothered booming sound of exploding shells and powder concealed in buildings, and then the sparks and flames shoot up . . . scattering cinders far and wide."[86] Capt. George Pepper, as he marched through the city, recalled, "Clouds of smoke, . . . were bursting from several princely mansions. Every house of importance was burned on Whitehall street. Railroad depots, rebel factories, foundaries and mills were destroyed."[87] And as one officer put it, the final hours of Atlanta's life was filled with horror. He wrote:

> No darkness—in place of it a great glare of light from acres of burning buildings. This strange light, and the roaring of the flames that licked up everything habitable, the intermittent explosions of powder, stored ammo. and projectiles, streams of fire that shot up here and there from heaps of cotton bales and oil factories, the crash of falling buildings, and the change, as if by a turn of the kaleidoscope, of strong walls and proud structures into heaps of desolation; all this made a dreadful picture of the havoc of war, and of its unrelenting horrors.[88]

Naturally, there was much criticism against Sherman alleging that his actions were unnecessary and inhumane. But, such criticism, according to the British military lawyer, J. M. Spaight, was, and is, unwarranted. "A commander," he said, "has an undoubted right to destroy such places if he cannot hold them and if they would otherwise be used by the enemy." In Spaight's view, Atlanta had been unquestionably "specialized for war."[89] To Sherman this was total war.

Others, however, viewed the burning as an act of depraved people,[90] and the Canton *American Citizen* ran the following editorial:

> The vandalism of the enemy exceeds belief, and were it not authenticated by an official report, could hardly be credited. The destruction of property, private as well as public, was almost universal. . . . For this barbarous conduct on the part of Sherman there is neither palliation nor excuse. No military necessity

whatever, can be pleaded in extenuation of it. During the whole time the Federals occupied Atlanta, the town was not even threatened by our forces. It was not even menaced with attack. Therefore the burning of a large city and the destruction of millions of dollars of private property, stands forth before the world as an act of monstrous and wanton wickedness, for which no apology can be made. It was done through sheer, un-adulterated malice.[91]

Still, to Sherman, this was total war.

A few days before the beginning of the burning of Atlanta, Sher-man sat down and wrote his farewell letter to Grant. It was a restate-ment of why the march to the sea had to be made. He wrote:

> I propose to act in such manner against the material resources of the South as utterly to negative Davis' boasted threat. . . . If we can march a well-appointed army right through his territory, it is a demonstration to the world, foreign and domestic, that we have a power which Davis cannot resist. This may not be war but rather statesmanship, nevertheless it is overwhelming to my mind that there are thousands of people abroad and in the South who reason thus: If the North can march an army right through the South it is proof positive that the North can pre-vail. . . .[92]

Not only would such an act give proof to the world of the power of the Union, but more important, and perhaps more practical, was the fact that it "was a direct attack upon the rebel army and the rebel capital at Richmond, . . . it would end the war."[93]

On November 16, about 7 A.M., Sherman, unquestionably the most unwelcome visitor Atlanta was ever to experience, rode out of the blazing city, leaving behind his line of supply and communica-tion and a hostile army.[94] "Behind us," he said, "lay Atlanta, smouldering and in ruins, the black smoke rising high in the air, and hanging like a pall over the ruined city." As a band struck up "John Brown's Body Goes Marching On," Sherman further remarked, " . . . we turned our horses' heads to the east. Atlanta was soon lost behind the screen of trees, and became a thing of the past."[95]

Sherman was taking an enormous risk. Not only was he turning his back on a hostile army, he was breaking his lifeline. With this action he was taking a step into the future and abandoning a long history of warfare. As a result, the world would never be the same.

But, he did so with confidence. Not only was he sure of what he was doing, he wanted to do it, and knew it would succeed. He had learned a year ago from one of the best in the military world. At Vicksburg he had seen Grant make a similar move. Now he was confident enough to do the same thing but on a much larger scale. Moving three-fourths of his army to another objective while the enemy's power was so close at hand was a move that entailed not only a risk, but nerve and boldness. It was a decision that proved successful and showed on Sherman's part "a refreshing combination of shrewdness and willingness to take risks that are the hall mark of a great commander."[96]

The point of least resistance became Sherman's goal. While Grant held the main forces of the Confederacy under Lee in Virginia, and Thomas kept Hood's army occupied in Tennessee, Sherman marched south and southeast into the enemy's rear. Grant's force became the massive body of the Union—Sherman and his forces became the swinging, long-reaching arms which destroyed the Confederacy's stores, railways, and food, reducing it to impotency by the use of the incendiary torch as much as by the weapons of war. Grant " . . . practiced naked attrition while his lieutenant practiced wholesale slaughter of cattle and pigs and, in South Carolina, marched day after day under the clouds of black smoke."[97] This was the grand strategy arrived at by Grant and Sherman to bring the Civil War to a rapid close, and it worked.

The criticisms make little difference, the tactical errors are basically unimportant. The fact remains, the fall of Atlanta had significant results for both the North and the South, and they were more psychological and sociological than military. Perhaps no one has presented more accurately the importance of Atlanta as a turning point in the war than Beringer, et al., in their valuable work *Why the South Lost the Civil War*. Of the fall of Atlanta they say: "The Fall of Atlanta changed the entire complexion of events, for Sherman had provided a needed victory . . . that indicated the beginning of substantial progress." Prior to the fall "it appeared to the weary Union that the war was likely to drag on for several more years. . . ." Then came from an unexpected area a victory and, "as a result, in 1864 the Union voters reelected the administration [of Lincoln]" and, in doing so, made the commitment to carry the war to its ultimate conclusion. In a sense, Atlanta was the Union's Rubicon.

The fall of Atlanta produced "exactly the opposite effect" on the Confederacy. Beringer, et al., write, "Desertion rates, already serious, now multiplied as the needs of destitute families at home were reinforced by a soldier's presumption of the inevitable outcome of the war to persuade him that there was no more point in risking his life for a lost cause." The will of the Southerners had been struck a fatal blow. "It was no longer possible to augment military power by the strength of national will, nor was it possible to stiffen civilian determination by exciting victories in the field." The psychological and sociological underpinnings of the Confederate society were being severely weakened. The blow was so devastating that thousands of soldiers and civilians were asking the question, "Why, then, a Confederacy?" The answer came more and more frequently after the fall of Atlanta, that the Union could serve them best. From Atlanta on "they waged war with less enthusiasm than heretofore. After Atlanta, the bottom was about to drop out of the Confederate tub."[98]

*Sherman and his generals, 1865. From left to right: Maj. Gen. O. O. Howard, Maj. Gen. John A. Logan, Maj. Gen. William B. Hagen, Maj. Gen. William T. Sherman, Maj. Gen. Jefferson C. Davis, Maj. Gen. Henry W. Slocum, Maj. Gen. Joseph Mower, and Maj. Gen. Francis P. Blair.*

# CHAPTER TEN

# *"The Hard Hand of War"*

THE REMAINING IS SIMPLY DESCRIPTIVE HISTORY and has been told numerous times by both participants and historians. The key actor holding the narrative together is Sherman, admired and despised. From West Point in 1836 to Atlanta in 1864, he had come a distance, geographically and mentally. In those twenty-eight years he had experienced a number of events and each had left its mark. Now he was at the beginning of the full implementation of his concept of total war. Some twenty years later, after the march through Georgia and the Carolinas was long behind him, Sherman would describe the major change that had occurred in his thinking:

> I know that in the beginning, I too, had the old West Point notion that pillage was a capital crime, and punished it by shooting, but the Rebels wanted us to detach a division here, a brigade there, to protect their families and property while they were fighting. . . . This was a one-sided game of war, and many of us . . . kindhearted, fair, just and manly . . . ceased to quarrel with our own men about such minor things and went in to subdue the enemy, leaving minor depredations to be charged up to the account of the rebels who had forced us into the war, and who deserved all they got and *more*.[1]

T. Harry Williams says of Sherman on the eve of his famous march, "The plan which Sherman now put into action had evolved slowly, but the germ of it had long been with him. It could have come only from a mind like his, a mind that nourished mystic concepts of authority and natural unity and was capable of indulging in the most

245

violent excesses of thought and of translating these excesses into action."[2] So, this paradoxical man, dedicated to order and peace, was on the verge of bringing disorder and total war to the people of the South.

Before striking out, he sat down and wrote his children. To his daughters Minnie and Lizzie he said, " . . . I am going to make another campaign that I hope will prove as successful as that of Atlanta, and after it is over I will try and come to see you. I want to see you very much—indeed I cannot say how much—and then I can tell you all about the things of which you hear so much but know so little." He told them, "War is something about which you should not concern yourself . . . ," and he emphasized that he was "fighting now that you may live in peace." He assured them that he was not "fighting for myself, but for you and the little children, who have more to live for than we older people."[3] To his son Tommy he wrote, "People write to me that I am now a Great General, and if I were to come home they would gather round me in crowds & play music and all such things. That is what people call fame and Glory, but I tell you that I would rather come down quietly and have you and Willy meet me at the car than to have the shouts of the People."[4]

If Sherman had been thorough in his preparations for the Atlanta campaign, then he was now meticulous. When possible, the troops would march by four roads and each corps would carry its own ammunition and provision trains. They were ordered to "forage liberally on the country during the march."[5] Each brigade was to organize its own foraging party. Only corps commanders were given authority to destroy mills, houses, cotton gins, and other structures. The cavalry would be permitted to appropriate horses, mules, and wagons. Blacks were to be put to work when possible. Sherman ordered that artillery and wagon trains be reduced to the minimum. Wagon loads were to be kept light, and each soldier would carry forty rounds of ammunition. Beef would be driven on the hoof, and oats were to be supplied through foraging. The point of Sherman's preparations, of course, was to "develop the mobility of his army to such a pitch that it should be a huge 'flying column' of light infantry."[6] He knew the great risk he was taking and had to be sure he was fully prepared, for as he put it, "Success would be accepted as a matter of course, whereas, should we fail, 'this march' would be adjudged the wild adventure of a crazy fool."[7]

From the beginning the tactic of delusion was used as a means of confusing the enemy and keeping it off balance. The right wing of Sherman's army headed south toward Jonesboro, while the left marched east through Madison. These were divergent lines designed to threaten both Macon and Augusta simultaneously so as to prevent a concentration of the enemy at his intended destination, Milledgeville, the capital of Georgia.[8] The move proved to be so effective that Sherman continued to use it throughout Georgia and into the Carolinas.

Sherman's 62,000 men marched out of Atlanta "into the fat fields of Georgia . . . like locusts devouring a land."[9] Indeed, it was "probably the finest army of military 'workmen' the modern world has seen."[10] A soldier of the 100th Indiana wrote, "Such an Army as we have I doubt if ever was got together before: all are in the finest condition. We have weeded out all the sick, feeble ones and all the boys are ready for a meal or a fight and don't seem to care which it is."[11] "A remarkable body of men," is how Adj. F. Y. Hedley described it. It was an army of young men, all veterans, "who had served an apprenticeship of more than three years at their profession. . . ." Many were too young to vote, yet they could be counted on "to carry their load." Each was "practically a picked man," resourceful and self-sufficient.[12]

Spreading his columns to a width of more than sixty miles, Sherman tore up every mile of railroad track and almost every station. "Bridges were destroyed, railroad cars burned, wheels broken, axles bent, boilers punctured, and cylinder heads cracked and dumped into deep water."[13] Miles upon miles of railroad track were ripped from the ground. The ties were arranged in piles and burned. Sections of rails were heated over the ties, then twisted around trees to form what the men called "Sherman's neckties" and "Sherman's hairpins." Maj. James Connolly reported that "every 'Gin House' we pass is burned; every stack of fodder we can't carry along is burned; every barn filled with grain is destroyed; in fact everything that can be of use to the Rebels is either carried off by our foragers or set on fire and burned." The separated columns of the army were able to determine each other's progress, route and location by watching "smoke by day and 'pillars of fire' by night. . . ."[14]

"The march became a wild excursion of an army in a holiday spirit,"[15] and at certain points the men got out of hand as they looted town dwellings and farms of provisions of a private nature. Though under his orders to limit their seizures to necessary items, Sherman's "bummers," as the more enthusiastic foragers were commonly called, stole silver, jewelry, and personal knickknacks; bayoneted tapestried furniture, and battered magnificent pianos and spinets; slaughtered cattle, and carried off pigs, sheep and poultry.[16] David P. Conyngham has left a graphic picture of the bummer and the rather criminal work he did. He pried open chests to take the personal valuables of families; knocked to pieces tables, pianos and chairs; tore bed clothing in strips and scattered them about the yard. "Color is no protection from these roughriders. They go through a negro cabin, in search of diamonds and gold watches, with just as much freedom and vivacity as they 'loot' the dwelling of a wealthy planter. . . ." The bummer would return to camp "loaded down with silver ware, gold coin, and other valuables. I hazard nothing in saying that three-fifths (in value) of the personal property of the counties we passed through was taken."[17]

In Covington, just a few miles out of Atlanta, Federal troops invaded the plantation of Dolly Sumner Lunt. She provided in her diary the following description: " . . . like demons they rushed in! To my smokehouse, my Dairy, Pantry, Kitchen and Cellar, like famished wolves they come, breaking locks and whatever is in their way. The thousand pounds of meat in my smoke-house is gone in a twinkling, my flour, my meat, my lard, butter, eggs, pickles of various kinds, both in vinegar and brine, wine, jars, and jugs are all gone. My eighteen fat turkeys, my hens, chickens, fowls, my young pigs, are shot down in my yard and hunted as if they were rebels themselves."[18] Ten days later she would, after assessing her losses, record that she was "poorer by thirty thousand dollars."[19] It causes wonder as to who was causing the greatest amount of suffering, or who was committing the real crime, the Federal soldiers or Dolly Lunt. For sure, her sacrifice to the Confederate cause had been great, but not voluntary.

Just out of Atlanta, Sherman's troops realized why they had been ordered to travel so lightly. It was not for speed alone, for instead of the scheduled fifteen miles a day they were averaging ten, two-thirds the rate at which Sherman had trained them to march. Now they understood that the reduction had been made to enable them to lay waste the resources of the region through which they were marching. In his official report Sherman at the end of the march would write, "This may seem a hard species of warfare, but it brings the sad realities of war home to those who have been directly or indirectly instrumental in involving us in its attendant calamities."[20]

The impact of Sherman's march on the civilians in its path was devastating. At first, word was out in the form of rumor that only a large raiding party was approaching. However, as refugees from Atlanta came into contact with other Georgians, the truth was revealed. Sherman's army was headed to the sea! A. C. Cooper, one of the refugees, exclaimed, "Then we learned the truth, the fateful truth! We were not threatened by a mere raiding party. It was Sherman—Sherman on his 'march to the sea', and we lay in the course of his march."

"We were . . . paralyzed," Cooper said. "Had we not all heard of him?" she cried. She described Sherman as being "like a huge octopus" that had "stretched out his arms and gathered everything in." He left nothing behind except "ruin and desolation." Cooper went on to ask, "Had not the very heavens glowed with the reflection of the fires lit by his orders? Were there not among us, even then, those whose homes had been laid in ashes by his soldiers, and they themselves turned out without a second suit of clothing? There was not a place to which we could flee, for that army would spread for miles. . . ."[21]

To the people of Georgia, Sherman had become a terrorist, one to be feared, and it was exactly the psychological effect he intended.

For the blacks, the effect was just the opposite. They flocked to his columns by the thousands and greeted him as a messiah. Sherman forbade his armies to take refugees unless they were able-bodied and could work. Some freed slaves heeded his warnings and returned home, but many others continued to attach themselves to the long blue columns. But Sherman was insistent. He did not want them along because they hampered his movement, and, on occasion, he would take up his bridges at a river crossing leaving the blacks on the opposite side. He could not care for them and his own men as well. As J. P. Austin, a Confederate cavalry office observed, "When the crowd became too burdensome the Federals would take up their bridges at the crossing of some river and leave their poor, deluded followers on the opposite bank, to ponder over the mutability of human plans and to cast a longing look at the receding forms of their supposed deliverers."[22]

The closer Sherman got to Milledgeville the more evident was the success of his delusion tactic. "The fright of the honorable body of legislators must have been amusing," wrote Conyngham. Because Sherman had marched his different columns in such a manner as to create confusion amid those in his path, the legislators "scarcely knew where to run or what to do." At first they heard Sherman was headed for Augusta so "they felt secure." Then they received word that he was headed directly to Milledgeville "and they shivered again." Then they received reports that the destination was Macon "and they became valiant again and made their fiery speeches. . . ." Finally, news reached them that Sherman was moving "right on the capital, and [that] the cavalry were right in the city." This was too much so "the Falstaff heroes . . . fled in . . . confusion. . . ."[23]

The delusion tactic also played havoc with the Confederate army. Up until November 21, General Hardee was convinced that Macon was the Federals' destination. Then he changed his mind, believing that Augusta was the objective. He attempted to shift his forces only to discover that the railroad and telegraph had been destroyed, "and that Sherman had interposed between the two places." The Georgia militia, under orders from Hardee, marching from Macon to Augusta, "bumped into the rear guard of Sherman's right wing . . . and fell back to Macon badly bruised." They were eventually sent south on a long route and arrived in Savannah on November 23. Maj. Gen. Joseph Wheeler's cavalry, by swimming the Ocmulgee River, managed to get out of Macon and place itself in Sherman's front. "Meantime, Bragg, sent posthaste from Wilmington with a handful of reinforcements, had arrived at Augusta to take supreme charge of the campaign, only to find himself cut off from the rest of the Confederate forces and for some days completely in the dark as to what was happening. He and his force of about 10,000 were to remain idle and ineffective at Augusta while Sherman tranquilly pursued his path to the sea."[24]

On November 23, Sherman reached Milledgeville. He had traveled almost a third of the way to Savannah and had left behind a sixty-mile-wide swath of destruction. Everything had gone according to his plans. The weather had been perfect and the enemy had presented no threat at all. Roads, for the most part, had been good, food abundant, streams and rivers easy to cross, and his men exhilaratingly happy.

At Milledgeville, however, a number of events occurred that affected the rather carefree attitude of the troops. First, they witnessed firsthand evidence of the horror and inhumanity of Andersonville Prison when a small band of escapees wandered into camp and told all in hearing distance of that dreadful place.

Second, rumors began to spread of barbarities committed by Wheeler's cavalrymen. Supposedly, Wheeler had captured a number of Federals and had given them a choice: death or pledge an oath of allegiance to the Confederacy. The rumors were that some had remained loyal and, as a result, had had their throats slashed.

Third, soldiers read in newspapers that Confederate leaders, both military and civilian, were urging noncombatants to harass and attack the invading army at every chance available to them. For example, they learned that Sen. Benjamin Hill and six Georgia congressmen had urged the people of Georgia to rebel. "Every citizen with his gun, and every negro with his spade and axe, can do the work of a soldier," it was declared. "Remove your negroes, horses, cattle and provisions and burn what you cannot carry—Assail the invader. . . ."[25] While occupying the deserted mansion of Gov. Joseph E. Brown (which had been hastily stripped of practically everything), Sherman received word that Gen. P. G. T. Beauregard at Corinth, Mississippi, had wired the people of Georgia the following impassioned plea: "Arise for the defense of your native soil! Rally round your patriotic Governor and gallant soldiers! Obstruct and destroy all roads in Sherman's front, flank, and rear, and his army will soon starve in your midst!"[26]

These events brought Sherman's troops back to the world of reality. This was not a holiday, the war was real and it hardened the soldiers' attitudes. And the hardening boded ill for Milledgeville. Buildings that would have otherwise escaped official condemnation were leveled. To halt any noncombatant resistance that might arise due to "patriotic" appeals, Sherman simply reissued his order of November 9.[27] Harshness, as Sherman interpreted it, meant that if the enemy burned corn and other forage on his route, then houses, barns, and cotton gins must be destroyed in return. He could not and would not be hindered by mere civilians.

Maj. Henry Hitchcock observed the workings of Sherman's order on the day the army marched out of Milledgeville, heading for Savannah. Finding a bridge in ashes at Buffalo Creek, Sherman ordered the destruction of a nearby house belonging to the farmer charged with the offense. Hitchcock argued that the owner should be proved guilty before suffering punishment. Sherman answered curtly, "Well, let him look to his people, if they find that their burning bridges only destroys their own citizens' houses they'll stop it, etc." He went on to say, "In war everything is right which prevents anything. If bridges are burned I have a right to burn all houses near it."[28] The collective responsibility of all Southerners in rebellion gave him that right.

Since coming to Sherman's army Hitchcock had disliked Sherman's philosophy of war. In Milledgeville on November 23, he wrote in his diary: "I am bound to say I think Sherman lacking in enforcing discipline. Brilliant and daring, fertile, rapid and terrible, he does not seem to me *to carry out things* in this respect."[29] But Sherman's words at the Buffalo Creek bridge opened Hitchcock's eyes, and that same night he wrote again in his diary that there was nothing to do now but to make war "so terrible that when peace comes it will *last*."[30] At the end of two weeks as Sherman's aide, Hitchcock recognized his leader's purpose as one that would "produce among the *people of Georgia* a thorough conviction of the personal misery which attends war, and of the utter helplessness and inability of their 'rulers' . . . to protect them."[31] Thus, within two weeks' time, Sherman had made a believer out of his aide.

Despite the changing temper of the troops, the anticipated destruction of Milledgeville never occurred. The burning of private structures was rare, and only two plantation residences were destroyed, and these were on the outskirts of the city. The only known fatality was Patrick Kane, a gardener and caretaker of a local plantation. Only two private homes were destroyed in the town itself, although a number of the houses of state officials were severely damaged. The warehouses of the two richest cotton merchants of Milledgeville were spared and a large flour mill was left standing. Two textile mills and an iron and brass foundry went undamaged, and, despite the rumor that all public buildings in the city were to be torched, only two were destroyed—the arsenal and the magazine. The Central of Georgia Railroad station and the toll bridge over the Oconee River were both burned.

The most blatantly irresponsible act of vandalism occurred on the day Sherman's troops entered Milledgeville. Some of the younger officers staged a mock session of the Georgia legislature and things got out of control. The capitol building was ransacked, including the state library. Most of the books were thrown into the street and trampled over by the soldiers, both on foot and horseback.[32] The scene was so disgusting that it led Major Connolly to write in his diary, "It is a downright shame. Public libraries should be sacredly respected by all belligerents, and I am sure General Sherman will, some day, regret that he permitted this library to be destroyed and plundered."[33] Despite Sherman's leniency, and "although Milledgeville escaped the general destruction which befell the younger city of Atlanta, it did witness in great measure the suffering and tragedy of war."[34]

During the latter days of November, an Indian summer fell upon Sherman's troops. Happy, healthy, and enthusiastic, the columns of his army left Milledgeville and headed toward Savannah. Their approach to Sandersville, just twenty-five miles southwest, has been graphically captured by a seventeen-year-old girl. Peering from the front window of her home, she was taken aback by what she saw:

> Looking out, I screamed in horror. It seemed to me the whole world was coming.
>
> Here came the "woodcutters" clearing the way before the army. Men with axes . . . men with spades. . . . Men driving herds of cattle—cows, goats, hogs, sheep. Men on horseback with bunches of turkeys, bunches of chickens, ducks and guineas swinging on both sides of the horses like saddle-bags. Then the wagons—oh, the wagons! In every direction, wagons, wagons!
>
> "What do [sic] it mean? Have they stripped the whole country?" I thought. "Oh, we will perish!"
>
> Now came the soldiers—cavalry and infantry. . . .
>
> . . . Now the rush of Yankee ruffians![35]

Nothing hampered their approach, and, if anything got in the way, it was rapidly eliminated. The troops were free to roam the land and take everything on it. And . . . they did.

Just outside Sandersville, Sherman encountered something horrible to him in the way of warfare. He passed a group of men standing around a young officer whose foot had been blown to pieces by a mine planted in the road. The device had been loaded with a percussion primer so as to explode when stepped on. Immediately Sherman ordered a group of Rebel prisoners to be brought from the provost-guard. They were given spades and picks and made to "march in close order along the road, so as to explode their own torpedoes, or to discover and dig them up."[36] Six years after the incident, Sherman would declare that " . . . prisoners should be protected, but mercy is not the legitimate attribute of war. Men go to war to kill and to get killed if necessary and should expect no tenderness. . . . But it was, I think a much better show of tenderness for me to have the enemy do this work than to subject my own soldiers to so frightful a risk. . . ."[37] Sherman's action had two immediate results: one, it gave his enemies new proof of his firmness in prosecuting war, and two, it gave his men dramatic evidence that he would protect them at all possible points.

No one was immune from Sherman's determination and intensity. Even ministers of the Gospel felt the heavy hand of Sherman's warfare. Writing in his diary, Maj. George Ward Nichols recalled Sherman's singlemindedness. He wrote, " . . . General Sherman is terribly in earnest in his method of conducting war. . . . He once said to a Methodist preacher in Georgia who had, by voice and example, helped to plunge the nation into war: 'You sir, and such as you, had the power to resist this mad rebellion; but you chose to strike down the best government ever created, and for no good reason whatsoever. You are suffering the consequences, and have no right to complain.'" As Sherman preached to the preacher, Nichols records, his soldiers emptied "the preacher's barns of their stores of corn and forage."[38]

By December 1, Sherman's march was two weeks old and had become "the most dramatic and suspenseful episode of the war."[39] What would be the outcome? Where would his army strike and reappear next? Would he be stopped and repulsed? Speculation was heard not only in the North but in Europe as well. The London *Times* said of the march, "That it is a most momentous enterprise cannot be denied; but it is exactly one of those enterprises which are judged by the event. It may either make Sherman the most famous general of the North, or it may prove the ruin of his reputation, his army, and even his cause altogether."[40] The British *Army and Navy Gazette* said: "It is clear that, so long as he roams about with his army inside the Confederate States, he is more deadly than twenty Grants, and that he must be destroyed if Richmond or *anything* is to be saved."[41] The London *Herald* was confident that his campaign would result in either "the most tremendous disaster that ever befell an armed host" or "the very consummation of the success of sublime audacity." If he failed, the *Herald* predicted, "he will become the scoff of mankind and the humiliation of the United States." But, if he succeeded, it was noted, his name would "be written upon the tablet of fame side by side with that of Napoleon and Hannibal. He will either be a Xerxes or a Xenophon."[42]

Of course the North was apprehensive and seriously concerned about Sherman and his army, and newspapers wrote encouraging words about his success and the glory to come. On the streets, in the shops, at the dinner tables, and in government circles, the conversation was about Sherman and where he would emerge next. In Washington, John Sherman anxiously awaited news of his brother, and, on one occasion when a newspaper ran a Southern claim that Sherman had been stopped, John asked President Lincoln if it were true. Lincoln replied, "Oh no, I know the hole he went in at, but I can't tell you what hole he will come out of."[43] On and on the suspense went, day after day, and week after week. How were things going? When would he appear? Would he succeed?

As to be expected, Southern papers were bitter and continued to talk of the "retreat" of the Army of the West. For example, the Richmond *Whig* exclaimed, "Where is he now? We leave it to the Yankee papers to guess, supplying them only with the information that he has not found sweet potatoes very abundant in Georgia and that hog and hominy have not been served up for the entertainment of his bedeviled troops."[44]

Reality, however, was quite different, for on December 11, Sherman's army approached the outskirts of Savannah. As his troops inched ahead he moved against Fort McAllister guarding the Ogeechee River. Two days later the fort fell and Sherman established contact with a nearby Federal fleet. Rejoicing filled the streets of Northern cities as news arrived by telegraph that "Sherman has reached Savannah!" In a matter of hours the news spread across the land. People danced in the streets and sang victory songs amid the peals of church bells. At last, after three and a half long, painful years, the foundations of the Confederacy were crumbling.

Four days later, on December 17, Sherman sent a dispatch to Lt. Gen. William J. Hardee whose troops defended Savannah, asking for unconditional surrender of the city. It was an ultimatum which read, "Should you entertain the proposition, I am prepared to grant liberal terms to the inhabitants and garrison; but should I be forced to resort to assault, and the slower and surer process of starvation, I shall then feel justified in resorting to the harshest measures, and shall make little effort to restrain my army. . . ." Sherman informed

Hardee that he would not hesitate to "avenge the national wrong" attached to Savannah by burning it.[45]

Hardee replied, saying he refused to surrender, and added a threat: "I have hitherto conducted the military operations intrusted to my direction in strict accordance with the rules of civilized warfare, and I should deeply regret the adoption of any course by you that may force me to deviate from them in the future."[46] Exactly what Hardee had in mind will never be known, for on the 19th and 20th of December his 10,000-man army slipped out of the city leaving it open for occupation by the Federal forces.[47]

On the morning of the 21st Sherman entered the city and immediately dispatched a telegram to President Lincoln: "I beg to present you as a Christmas gift, the city of Savannah, with 150 heavy guns and plenty of ammunition, and also about 25,000 bales of cotton."[48]

The day after Christmas, Lincoln sent his letter of thanks to Sherman: "Many, many thanks for your Christmas gift, the capture of Savannah." Then he told Sherman of the anxieties he had experienced concerning the march, saying, "When you were about to leave Atlanta for the Atlantic coast, I was anxious, if not fearful; but feeling you were the better judge, and remembering that 'nothing risked, nothing gained,' I did not interfere." Finally, he included a small paragraph that must have pleased Sherman more than any compliment he had ever received. "Not only does it afford the obvious and immediate military advantages, but in showing to the world that your army could be divided, putting the stronger part to an important new service, and yet leaving enough to vanquish the old opposing forces of the whole—Hood's army—it brings those who sat in darkness to see a great light."[49] Lincoln recognized what Sherman had done, that he had broken up the enemy's army and gotten into the interior and done irreparable damage to its resources—just as he had been ordered to do by Grant. Upon hearing of Thomas's defeat of Hood in middle Tennessee at the Battle of Nashville, Sherman summed it all with these words of praise for Thomas: "His brilliant victory . . . was necessary to mine at Savannah to make a complete whole. . . ."[50]

David P. Conyngham wrote that with the capture of Savannah, Sherman had fulfilled "his covenant with his troops" by leading "them to a new base. . . ." Then he summarized the march.

> The results of our campaign were more glorious than the most
> sanguine could anticipate. We had passed through in our march

over forty of the wealthiest counties of Central Georgia; occupied over two hundred depots, county seats, and villages; captured about fifteen thousand negroes . . . about ten thousand
head of cattle, horses, and mules; destroyed nearly two hundred
miles of railroad; burned all the gins, cotton mills, and government property throughout the country; also about fifty millions
worth of cotton and Confederate bonds and currency, besides
supporting our army . . . on the country.[51]

Sherman, in his official report, stated: "I estimate the damage done
to the State of Georgia and its military resources at $100,000,000
dollars, at least $20,000,000 of which has inured to our advantage,
and the remainder is simple waste and destruction."[52]

In less than a month after leaving Atlanta, Sherman arrived at his
destination, completing the first leg of his campaign. By this time he
was the most popular general in the North and the most hated in the
South. He was no longer the nervous "gone in the head" man of
earlier years. Through constant study, valuable experience, and
careful planning he had become superior in leadership. Indeed, so
much popularity came to him that people were beginning to be
highly critical of Grant in his campaign against Lee in Virginia. At
one point there was talk of replacing Grant with Sherman, but to
such a suggestion Sherman said, "It won't do; it won't do. . . . General Grant *is a great General.* I know him well. He stood by me when I
was crazy and I stood by him when he was drunk; and now, sir, we
stand by each other always."[53] A bill was introduced in Congress to
raise Sherman to Grant's rank of lieutenant general. When Sherman
heard of the bill he shot off a letter to his brother John, saying, "I
will accept no commission that would tend to create a rivalry with
Grant. I want him to hold what he has earned and got. I have all the
rank I want."[54] The future president of the United States had
taught Sherman too many lessons in the art of war for him to be
tossed aside in a quest for greater fame and glory. In addition,
Sherman's character was not of that mold.

Although the popularity came to Sherman and, there is no reason
to doubt he savored it, he kept one principle ever present in his
mind: a common plan to end the war. He was eager to make it clear,
not only to the higher officials of the government and the military
but to the rank and file of his troops, that the past month of campaigning was not simply a move isolated from other areas of the war.
His strategy was not that narrow. On the contrary, the march to the

sea was closely and directly related to Grant's campaign in Virginia and it was simply "one step in the direction of Richmond, a movement that had to be. . . ."[55] To ensure such unity of his army with Grant's, Sherman wrote on December 24 to the lieutenant general, "I wish you [would] run down and see us; it would have a good effect, and show to both armies that they are acting on a common plan."[56]

Looking back over the damage done by his marching army, Sherman was pleased. To Montgomery C. Meigs, the quartermaster general in Washington, he tried to make sense of it. He wrote, "My marches have demonstrated the great truth that armies even of vast magnitude are not tied down to bases. . . ." He knew now that "more animals are lost to your department whilst standing idle, hitched to their wagons, than during the long and seemingly hard marches into the interior." Sherman felt sure that he had "personally aided your department more than any general officer in the service, by drawing liberally from the enemy, thereby injuring him financially and to the same extent helping ourselves. . . ."[57] To Maj. Henry Hitchcock outside Milledgeville he had proven the need for harshness in war, now to General Meigs in Washington, Sherman was proving the effectiveness of a new principle of economic warfare.

Sherman's occupation of Savannah resembled that of Memphis rather than Atlanta. To maintain law and order he kept civil officers at their posts, strengthened the hand of the mayor, shipped tons of rice to Boston in exchange for meat and flour, and fostered charitable gifts from citizens of the North. He provided assistance in holding town meetings and even permitted Episcopal churches to omit prayers for the president of the United States. Although he made the city a base of military operations, he permitted its 20,000 people to remain in their homes. In addition, because the city contained large numbers of people in need, Sherman provided food for them from his own supplies.[58] The cooperation that existed between the Federals and the citizens of Savannah led one soldier to comment, "The citizens of Savannah seemed well pleased with their change of rulers. They . . . displayed sociability that we didn't usually get in the South."[59] The occupational period was, according to Adjutant Hedley, "a continual round of merry-making." He said, "If the few male inhabitants remaining were somewhat formal and distant, ample amend was made by the ladies, who were generally cordial; and each little knot of soldiers made acquaintance with fair ones, glad to entertain and be entertained with cards, dance, and song."[60]

But, there were harsh moments. Some women, for example, would leave the sidewalk and walk in the streets rather than pass under the United States flag. Others refused to attend any functions where Union officers were present. These were the very women who had sent their men off to war and were continuing to urge them to keep fighting. Col. William D. Hamilton of the Ninth Ohio Cavalry recorded the following: "You, in wild enthusiasm, urge young men to the battlefield where men are being killed by the thousand, while you stay at home and sing 'The Bonnie Blue Flag;' but you set up a howl when you see the Yankees down here getting your chickens. Many of your young men have told us that they are tired of war and would quit, but you women would shame them and drive them back."[61] While on the street one day, Sherman was approached by one of these women: "General," she said, "you may conquer, but you can't subjugate us." He looked at the woman and sharply replied, "I don't want to subjugate you; I mean to kill you, the whole of you, if you don't stop this rebellion."[62]

On another occasion he came into conflict with a consul of the British government. Riding through Savannah, Sherman noticed a number of buildings flying the British flag. Thinking it odd that that nation's consul had so many offices, he investigated and discovered that the flags were flying on buildings where cotton was stored. He seized "all of it," at once, "in the name of my government," and the following exchange transpired:

"But sir," said the consul indignantly, "there is scarcely any cotton in Savannah that does not belong to me."

"There is not a pound of cotton here, sir, that does not belong to *me*, for the United States," responded Sherman.

"Well, sir," said the consul . . . , "my government shall hear of this. I shall report your conduct to my government."

"Ah! Pray, who are you, sir?" [Sherman asked].

"Consul to Her British Majesty," [came the response].

"Oh, indeed!" responded the general. "I hope you *will* report me to your government. You will please say for me that I have been fighting the English Government all the way from the Ohio River to Vicksburg and thence to this point. At every step I have encountered British goods of every description. And now, sir, I find you claiming all the cotton. I intend to call on my government to order me to Nassau [the capital of England's Bahama Islands and a major port of exchange for the Confederacy] at once."

"What do you propose to do there?" asked the consul. . . .

"I will," replied the general, "take with me a quantity of picks and shovels, and throw that cursed sand hill into the sea, sir! You may tell that to your government. . . . Good day, sir!"

Sherman was not bothered again by any representative of the British government.[63]

The paradox was real, the consistency never flagging. Sherman knew what had to be done to accomplish his goal and was unwilling to compromise. To some, his lenient policy toward Savannah and his harsh treatment of certain women and the British consul was a contradiction in behavior. Such critics, however, do not understand Sherman's philosophy of war. What seemed a contradiction was in the context of his method of warfare, consistency—paradoxical.

The march was acclaimed by many to be the greatest movement of the entire war. Amid the words of praise even Sherman revealed a hint of wonder and bewilderment. Writing to Ellen on December 23, he said, "Like one who has walked a narrow plank, I look back and wonder if I really did it."[64] His doubt, however, was only fleeting. In a dispatch to General Halleck the next day he explained the consequences of his campaign. He proudly wrote, "We are not only fighting hostile armies, but a hostile people, and must make old and young, rich and poor, feel the hard hand of war, as well as their organized armies." He was sure "that this recent movement of mine through Georgia has had a wonderful effect in this respect." He wrote, "Thousands who had been deceived by their lying papers into the belief that we were being whipped all the time realized the truth, and have no appetite for a repetition of the same experience. To be sure, Jeff. Davis has his people under a pretty good state of discipline, but I think faith in him is much shaken in Georgia. . . ."[65]

The march to the sea was over. But what did it mean? First, as pointed out by Beringer, et al., this great raid broke the stalemate that had settled in after Chattanooga.[66] The combined raids of Sherman, then Sheridan and Sherman again, pulled the war out of a standstill and, as a result, left "the rebellion nothing to stand upon."[67] Many in the South either did not understand this fact or were unwilling to accept it. For example, the Richmond *Whig* voiced the naive opinion of many in the South, except, of course, those who had experienced Sherman's march. The *Whig* stated, "Sherman is simply a great raider. His course is that of a bird in the air. He is conducting a novel military experiment and is testing the problem whether or not a great country can be conquered by raids."[68] No doubt the "experiment" was successful, the "test" was passed, and the country "conquered." The stalemate had been broken.

Second, the march dealt a severe blow to the Rebels' economic support of the war. Sherman's troops "had destroyed the resources of one of the most productive sections of the Confederacy and had erased Georgia as a possible source of supply for General Lee's army in Virginia."[69] By Sherman's estimates the damages were $100,000,000. Almost 300 miles of track from Atlanta to Savannah were destroyed, along with bridges, trestles, and stations. Rolling stock was damaged beyond repair and locomotives dismantled and made immobile. Cotton was torched, and mills and factories made useless. The list goes on. Without a doubt, Sherman's raid hurt the Southern armies dramatically from an economic point of view. And the individual soldiers felt it. In January 1865, a soldier in Lee's army wrote: "There are a good many of us who believe that this shooting match has been carried on long enough. A government that has run out of rations can't expect to do much more fighting. . . . Our rations are all the way from a pint to a quart of cornmeal a day, and occasionally a piece of bacon large enough to grease your palate."[70]

In addition, as Richard Goff points out, the destruction of Southern railroads resulted in "dissolving armies [that] wandered about the country while factories produced and storehouses held supplies that could not be moved to the troops. Shortages had hamstrung the armies."[71] Also, Sherman was probably correct when he told Quartermaster General Meigs that he had saved the Union enormous sums by living off the country, thus freeing materials that were in turn made available to Grant's forces. Finally, as Herman Hattaway and Archer Jones have said, "Organized resistance in terms of major armies in the field [with the exception of Lee's Army of Northern Virginia] came virtually to an end. The strategy of exhaustion through raids had succeeded."[72]

Third, the march caused a dramatic decline in the morale of Confederate soldiers, especially those from Georgia. Desertions increased in all armies. Between February 15 and March 18, while

Sherman was marching through the Carolinas, nearly eight percent of Lee's army was lost due to soldiers walking away. Douglas Southall Freeman states, "Desertion continued to sap the man-power of the army. After Christmas, when the winter chill entered into doubting hearts, and every mail told the Georgia and Carolina troops of the enemy's nearer approach to their houses, more and more men slipped off in darkness."[73] Rebel soldiers were rapidly becoming aware of the futility of continuing the rebellion, and as each day passed more and more of them gave in to the lost cause. Sherman's indirect attack on them by bringing war to their families was proving successful.

Fourth—and this is closely tied to the third item—the march, along with the fall of Atlanta and the re-election of Lincoln, severely crippled Confederate will to win. The Southern civilian's morale was devastated so that, by the time Sherman reached Savannah, most of the citizens were ready to rejoin the Union. "Thus," as Beringer, et al., have stated, "Sherman's Georgia raid was a political as well as a military maneuver, and it was aimed as much at Confederate morale and will as at her railroads and granaries."[74] And, it proved successful. Sherman knew what he was doing and was confident in the result.

Fifth, by marching almost unopposed through the heart of the South, creating havoc and confusion, Sherman demonstrated the growing weakness and vulnerability of the Confederacy. He wanted to "pierce the shell of the Confederacy and all its hollow inside" and, indeed, he did just that.[75]

Sixth, and last, more than punishment, more than a strategy to bring war to an end, Sherman's march contributed to the creation of a social revolution in the South. Although Sherman was aware of the numerous effects of his march, it is doubtful if he was cognizant of this result. Without question he was an extremely perceptive person in possession of a quick mind; yet, like so many of his contemporaries, he did not want to let go of much of the old world. Capable of being a revolutionary in war, he always held firmly to the accepted views of the Old South. End the war, kill the possibility of future secession, bring the rebel states back into the Union; then continue, almost as if civil war had never occurred. But, of course, the world does not operate that way. When one area of society changes, it always creates change in other areas of society. Thus, Sherman did not see the revolutionary impact his march was having on the South.

Of all the accounts that describe the results of Sherman's march as a social revolution, perhaps none is more graphic and telling than Charles Coffen's. A correspondent for the Boston *Journal*, Coffen wrote that "the people of Savannah generally were ready to live once more in the Union. The fire of Secession had died out. . . ." Things were different now and would never be the same. Secession and the war had made it impossible to go back to the way things were. "Society in the South, and especially in Savannah, had undergone a great change." Prior to the war "the extremes of social life were very wide apart. . . ." This gulf had been held in place up to "the night before Sherman marched into the city." With the entrance of Sherman's army came the revolution. "[T]he morning after [Sherman entered Savannah], there was a convulsion, an upheaval, a shaking up and a settling down of all the discordant elements." Almost with a touch of sadness, Coffen continued, "The tread of that army of the West, as it moved in solid column through the streets, was like a mortal earthquake, overturning aristocratic pride, privilege, and power." Coffen's sociological perception was keen. He wrote, "Old houses, with foundations laid deep and strong in the centuries, fortified by wealth, name, and influence, went down beneath the shock. The general disruption of the former relations of master and slave, and forced submission to the Union arms, produced a common level. . . . On the night before Sherman entered the place, there were citizens who could enumerate their wealth by millions; at sunrise the next morning they were worth scarcely a dime." Everything was overturned. Wealth had been counted in "cotton, Negroes, houses, land, Confederate bonds and currency, railroad and bank stocks." Now it was gone. "Government had seized their cotton; Negroes had possession of their lands . . ." and were free. Troops occupied their houses. "Confederate bonds were waste paper; their railroads were destroyed, their banks insolvent." Finally, Coffen concludes, "They had not only lost wealth, but they had lost their cause."[76] Upon hearing of the fall of Savannah, a clerk in the Confederate war office in Richmond recorded in his diary, "Men are silent, and some dejected. It is unquestionably the darkest period we have yet experienced."[77] The revolution had come, there would be attempts to stop it, but the attempts would fail—America would never be the same.

There are, of course, some issues that will never be settled. The first, and perhaps the easiest with which to deal, is that of violence.

No doubt, violence can be psychological as well as physical. Fear for one's life or fear for the lives of loved ones has lasting effects. It cannot be argued that Sherman's march did not produce such violence. But, it could have been worse had Sherman's character been different. As it was, "the remarkable feature of the campaign is perhaps that violence to property was accompanied by so little personal violence, and that homicide and rape were almost unknown."[78]

After the war, when a full report was made, it was revealed that physical violence against persons was almost nonexistent. According to Lloyd Lewis, "Sherman knew of but two cases of rape among his soldiers in 1864–65. . . ." Hitchcock was aware of no evidence of rape or murder, and Brig. Gen. Jacob Cox thought rape "nearly unknown." Says Lewis, "Many other responsible officers, as well as that of any number of private soldiers, supported this view."[79]

E. Merton Coulter, a scholar often accused of pro-Southern sympathies in his work, has described Sherman quite accurately. Here are some examples that assist in placing the issue of violence in its proper perspective: "Cruelty was not remotely concerned with his makeup; it was the great American god efficiency which Sherman was serving. . . . Some defense for Sherman rests in [the] weakness of his for making extravagant statements; . . . he announced policies he did not act upon, and said things he did not believe, though he did not realize it at the time. . . ." Actually Coulter is half correct. It is true, Sherman did have a proclivity for making extravagant statements: whether this is a weakness can be debated. Sometimes his statements got him into trouble, but at other times they produced the desired effect. Coulter is also correct in saying that Sherman made announcements and set policies that he never acted on and said things he did not believe. But he knew he had said them; he had intended to say them. He knew the power and influence of extravagance in speech and the written word, and he used them effectively. But, all this aside, Coulter is accurate in his defense of Sherman concerning the issue of violence. Sherman's bark was much louder than his bite. Coulter continues, "Plainly enough he was not an enemy of the South apart from the four years of warring against it to preserve the Union." Finally, Coulter argues that Sherman's war record "was not nearly so cruel as some of his widely expressed intentions would indicate." There is no evidence that he permitted his army to "slay non-combatants or that his army ever desired to do so. . . ." Coulter continues, " . . . it was not inborn cruelty that prompted Sherman in his war measures; it was his idea of effective warfare. It was his conception of the best method by which to perform a given duty." Sherman "firmly believed that his system would win the war in the shortest time. . . ."[80] Finally, "Many Southern scholars, examining the evidence one and two generations later, agreed. . . ."[81] It has been more than 125 years since that fateful march and no evidence has been produced to contradict Lewis or the others.

A second issue is that of abuses in the foraging parties of Sherman's troops. There is ample evidence supporting such activity. Looting and plundering of citizens' personal belongings existed. Despite Sherman's orders that "foraging must be limited to the regular parties properly detailed,"[82] there were abuses. As James M. Merrill has pointed out, "The only effective deterrent—death, to men who were caught—could not be applied without Washington's sanction." Sherman, however, could not "secure consent from the higher authorities in the War Department"[83] because he was cut off from communication with Washington. Still, Sherman was guilty. He was lax in his discipline of violators, and his attitude even encouraged plundering. Many believed that their commander approved of their actions. The question that will never be settled is: When does foraging end and plundering begin? The issue is even more complex in the context of Sherman's concept of total war. His intent was to subjugate the Southerner by bringing war to the front door of the noncombatant. Can that be interpreted to mean the parlor, bedroom, dining room, and study as well? Sherman never provided any explanation to assist in the settling of this question.

The third issue is more difficult. John Bennett Walters states the problem well: "The acts of terror committed against the civilian populace of the South by Sherman's troops indeed planted seeds of hatred which bore bitter fruit and postponed a sense of unity and understanding between the United States far longer than might otherwise have been the case."[84] This is more than likely an issue that will never be resolved. The main difficulty is the inability in this instance to measure the lasting effect of an event on subsequent events. So, the debate is full of speculation. It cannot be denied that Sherman became a hated figure among most people in the South and that the actions of his army created great bitterness. That the hatred and bitterness were long-lasting and prevented the re-establishment of unity between the people of the United States can be questioned. Sherman was enamored with the South. He liked both the geography and its people. After the war he let it be known that he held no resentment toward the section and, indeed, was welcomed with great respect by the people of Atlanta when he returned to that city in 1879. The same thing was true when he traveled to Chattanooga, Dalton, Rome, and Savannah. At each place crowds of whites and blacks thronged to the railroad depots to see the general. His old college associates from Louisiana "remembered him with feelings of friendship" and even requested a portrait to hang in the college library. Not only did he provide them with a painting but sent books for the library. Coulter has enumerated the following:

> He returned from Mexico in 1866 through the Mississippi Valley and visited the scenes of some of his recent raids. Many people met him "in the most friendly spirit." Even amongst the bleak chimney stacks and broken railways of Jackson, Mississippi, grim reminders of his recent visit, many people pressed to see him "and evinced natural curiosity, nothing more." In 1869 he was received with warm cordiality in New Orleans and at other places in Louisiana. The friendly feeling extended to the point of refusing to permit the General to pay his steamer fare or hotel bills. So rapid and complete a healer was time that when he passed northward, he was invited by Jackson and Canton, towns he had once laid waste, to pay them a visit.[85]

Sherman's post-war behavior was a healing factor rather than a reminder of the destruction he had wrought. If Sherman's march was a factor in the postponement "of a sense of unity," it was a very minor one. When held up to the harsh (according to Southerners) policies of the Radical Republicans, it pales in importance. The South also never forgot the surrender terms Sherman offered to Gen. Joseph E. Johnston, the surrender terms rejected by the post-Lincoln reconstructionists. All in all, the evidence, although speculative, tilts the scales against the "postponement of unity" argument. More than likely, the present bitterness among some Southerners stems not from the facts concerning Sherman but from a constant effort to keep the "lost cause" alive. Needless to say, this is an exercise engaged in by those who are purely unwilling to examine reality.

The fourth issue is: Did the march help shorten the war? This is probably unsolvable too. One side argues that, if Sherman had pursued General Hood after Atlanta and forced him into battle, he would have defeated him. Then Sherman could have transferred his forces by land to Virginia to assist Grant. According to this argument, Lee could have been defeated in early spring, 1865.[86] The argument is weak because it assumes that Sherman could have quickly forced Hood into battle and that he would have destroyed his army. Such assumptions are without foundation. Even if this had happened, the war would have only been shortened, at best, by a couple of months. The argument also assumes that Lee could have been easily defeated with Sherman's presence in Virginia. This assumption is probably correct, but Lee's army would not have been as weak because of desertions and the lack of supplies. As Albert Castel has said, Sherman's selecting the march rather than Hood's army was "his best alternative under the circumstance." Castel writes, "Not only did it rescue him from the military impasse created by Hood's northern movement but it also (and this was the advantage he emphasized) made it possible, once he secured a new base of operations at Savannah, to carry the war into the Carolinas and threaten Lee's rear in Virginia."[87]

The other side states simply that Sherman's march was equal to a great victory in battle.[88] It led to desertions, the shattering of the Southerners' will to continue the war, and the cutting off of essential Confederate war materials. In addition, Hood's army was taken out of the picture anyway by his own decision to head for Nashville. All things considered, the issue is still up in the air, and evidence supports both positions. What cannot be argued is that Sherman's movement was a necessity for the defeat of the South.

Issues aside, Sherman was satisfied that he had accomplished more by attacking the South's economic, psychological, and sociological resources than by concentrating directly on its military power. Granted, his methods were unorthodox and cruel; yet the fact remains that, whether he shortened the war or not, his methods saved lives on both sides.

Sherman was not a naive man. He may not have appreciated the full revolutionary impact his march was having on the South, and ultimately on the United States, but he knew his actions would be misunderstood and long debated. It was inevitable that his contemporaries, as well as future generations all over the world, would most certainly regard him as a barbarian and a ruthless vandal, the leader of a mob of bummers and criminals. But he never allowed such criticisms to deter him, and it has always remained a curiosity that a general who destroyed property rather than lives would be looked upon as more cruel and inhumane than one who led men into bloody, deadly battle. In a sense, Sherman was not a Lee nor a Grant. The heart of his paradoxical character was that to others he appeared cruel, yet, in reality, he was a man of compassion.

# CHAPTER ELEVEN

# "See War Such as They Never Dreamed of Before"

AFTER THE CAPTURE OF SAVANNAH, Grant had intended that Sherman would come by sea to Virginia,[1] and on December 15, Sherman received such an order. Sherman immediately replied that he would come as soon as adequate transport was made available for his troops. He added a note of disappointment, saying he "had expected, after reducing Savannah, instantly to march to Columbia, South Carolina; thence to Raleigh, and thence to report to you."[2] Realizing that Grant was asking him to abandon his "strategic task [and leave it] uncompleted,"[3] Sherman sent a plea to Halleck, saying: "I think the time has come now when we should attempt the boldest moves, and my experience is, that they are easier of execution than the more timid ones. . . . I think our campaign of the last month, as well as every step I take from this point northward is as much a direct attack on Lee's army as though we are operating within the sound of his artillery."[4] Hoping to change his mind, Sherman sent another letter to Grant two days later. He said, "With Savannah in our possession, at some future time if not now, we can punish South Carolina as she deserves. . . . I do sincerely believe that the whole United States, North and South, would rejoice to have this army turned loose on South Carolina, to devastate that State in the manner we have done in Georgia, and it would have a direct and immediate bearing on your campaign in Virginia."[5] Sherman was convinced that the more damage he did in the heart of the South, the weaker Lee's army would be in Virginia.

*General Sherman, astride his horse Sam, on the outskirts of Atlanta, 1864.*

Upon hearing the news that General Thomas had defeated General Hood's army at Nashville, Grant began to reconsider. In addition, Sherman had succeeded in convincing Chief of Staff Halleck of the importance of his march through the Carolinas. Halleck, in turn, began to pressure Grant to give his approval. Realizing that it would take Sherman two months to arrive in Virginia by sea, Grant finally rescinded his order. Writing to Sherman, he stated, "I did think the best thing to do was to bring the greater part of your army here, and wipe out Lee. The turn affairs now seem to be taking has shaken me in that opinion. I doubt whether you may not accomplish more toward that result where you are than if brought here. . . ."[6]

On Christmas Eve Sherman received permission to begin his march through the Carolinas. He could not have been more pleased with Grant's decision. He now had the chance to complete his plan of devastation. Responding to Grant's dispatch, Sherman said, "In about ten days I expect to be ready to sally forth again. I feel no doubt whatever as to our future plans. I have thought them over so long and well that they appear as clear as daylight."[7] For the first time since the beginning of his long march through the heartland of the South, Sherman spoke of revenge openly and without shame. To Halleck he wrote, " . . . the truth is, the whole army is burning with an insatiable desire to wreck vengeance upon South Carolina. I almost tremble at her fate, but feel that she deserves all that seems in store for her." He told Halleck that "many a person in Georgia asked me why we did not go to South Carolina," and when he told them that that was his next move, "the invariable reply was, 'Well, if you will make those people feel the utmost severities of war, we will pardon you for your desolation of Georgia.'"[8] South Carolina was the state that had started the rebellion, and Sherman was to show he had no patience with its citizens. He believed they should be punished, and punished firmly, so as to kill forever the thought of secession. Sherman never made an apology for such an attitude. This was war. All the South had to do was surrender, and he would gladly cease his acts of destruction. He justified his desire to punish South Carolina the same way he had justified his destruction of Georgia—it would have an immediate effect on Lee's army in Virginia and bring the war to an end.

Although Sherman spoke of revenge and punishment, he never allowed them to blind him from his purpose. Granted, he shed no tears over the destruction brought to South Carolina, his purpose was never revenge for the sake of revenge. His actions were geared to putting an end to secession and bringing about a rapid close to the war.

After a month of preparation, Sherman was ready to march out of Savannah. The weather was rainy and uncooperative, and to Sherman it seemed that "the terrible energy of the [enemy forces]" that "had been displayed in the earlier stages of the war was beginning to yield to the slower but more certain industry and discipline of our Northern men." He felt, as he moved farther into South Carolina, that "the soldiers and people of the South entertained an undue fear of our Western men, . . ." and they " . . . had invented such ghostlike stories of our prowess in Georgia that they were scared by their own inventions."[9] Even Mary Boykin Chesnut began to lose her courage and on January 14 recorded in her diary, "Yesterday I broke down and gave way to abject terror under the news of Sherman's advance."[10] A seventeen-year-old Columbia, South Carolina, girl wrote in her journal, " . . . They are planning to hurl destruction upon the State they hate most of all, and Sherman the brute avows his intentions of converting South Carolina into a wilderness."[11] Sherman wrote to Grant, "I observe the enemy has some respect for my name." He further observed that they retired "when they heard the attacking force belonged to my army. I will, try to keep up that feeling which is a real power."[12] Sherman preserved this fear as power and intended to utilize it to his advantage. He understood clearly that power meant the ability to get others to do what he wanted them to do even if they did not want to do it.

Having previously been stationed in South Carolina during his first years out of West Point, Sherman was familiar with the treacherous topography of the region he was about to enter. He knew that heavy rainfall would make the existing roads impassable and that his army would encounter streams, rivers, and swamps at every turn. Indeed, the northward march experienced a two-week delay at the very start due to heavy winter rains that swelled the low country rivers and swamps. The success of the campaign, therefore, would depend largely on the efficiency of his pioneer corps whose duty it was to build and repair roads and bridges. The pioneers proved to be so efficient that one Confederate soldier remarked, "If Sherman's army had gone to hell and wanted to march over and there was no other way, they would corduroy it and march on."[13] As during the march to Savannah, the army was divided into two wings and would advance in a "Y" formation, "the two wings well forward pointing to two different objectives, the center . . . held back to reinforce either wing hit by the enemy."[14]

Since Sherman planned to cut himself off from his base in Savannah, he knew he could expect no support until he reached the Cape Fear River in North Carolina. Once again, his wagons would travel with limited provisions, therefore, his army of 60,000 men would have to forage liberally on the country during the march. Concerning the preparations, Maj. George Ward Nichols recorded in his diary, "General Sherman has reduced the army to its simplest and most effective fighting and marching conditions, rejecting as superfluities all that is not essential to its health, or that may clog its movements." Nichols was also impressed with Sherman's example to his men, saying, "In all these personal sacrifices General Sherman demands nothing of his soldiers which he does not himself share. His staff is smaller than that of a brigade commander in the army. He has fewer servants than the military regulations allow; his baggage is reduced to the smallest possible limit. . . ." Finally, Nichols recorded, "When we left Atlanta we thought the army had been stripped to the lowest possible point, but our experiences thus far prove that we can go several steps lower, and that a man may have but little and still be contented, if not comfortable."[15] Besides ordering his forces to gather supplies for the army and destroy property valuable to the enemy, Sherman expected them to secure maps, newspapers, and letters. Such material would provide valuable information on Confederate operations.[16]

No, this would not be "the picnic hike that had prevailed in Georgia. To go north across the lowlands, Sherman had to cross a flat swampy country crossed by many rivers, most of which were in flood."[17] But Sherman would succeed with such speed that the movement would cause General Johnston to say, "When I learned that Sherman's army was marching through the Salk swamp [Chatchie of South Carolina] making its own corduroy roads at the rate of a dozen miles a day and more, and bringing its artillery with it, I made up my mind that there had been no such army in existence since the days of Julius Caesar."[18] As Bruce Catton has pointed out, "Johnston was right, in a way." The army was unusual and in many ways "was not actually an army. . . ." More specifically, " . . . it was just a collection of western pioneers on the march—men with axes who could cut down a forest and corduroy a road without breaking step, men who would flounder for miles through floodwaters armpit-deep, making nothing of it except for casual high-private remarks to the effect that 'Uncle Billy seems to have struck this river end-ways.'" This army "plowed across the bottom lands as if they were on parade. . . ." They built bridges that had been destroyed, cut roads that never existed, marched in ice-cold water, "casually burned towns and looted plantations and set fire to pine forests. . . ."[19]

Once again, as with his march from Atlanta, Sherman employed the tactic of delusion. He planned on keeping the Confederates from concentrating forces by making feints on both Augusta and Charleston, then march directly to Columbia and thence to Goldsboro, North Carolina. Goldsboro was selected as his ultimate destination because it was connected to the North Carolina coast by two rail lines. By this route Sherman could destroy the chief railroads of the Carolinas and devastate the heart of the two states.[20]

During his days as an educator in Louisiana, Sherman had realized the importance of having only one head in the undertaking of any particular enterprise. Now, in Savannah, as he prepared for his final march, he put the lesson to good use. With so much to be done and so many plans to be made, Sherman limited as much decision-making by his subordinates as possible. Decisions had to be made quickly and to have to depend on proper chains of command would end up hampering preparation.[21]

Although Sherman looked upon his march through South Carolina as "one of the most horrible things in the history of the world . . . ," he was determined to apply total war in its fullest to the region.[22] The policy of utter destruction was the keystone of his strategy, and he intended to make it felt by the South Carolinians. In later years he wrote of this campaign:

> I consider this march as a means to an end, and not as an essential art of war. Still . . . the march to the sea was generally regarded as something extraordinary . . . something out of the usual order of events; whereas, in fact, I simply moved from Atlanta to Savannah, as one step in the direction of Richmond. . . .
>
> Were I to express my measure of the relative importance of the march to the sea, and of that from Savannah northward, I

would place the former at one and the latter at ten, or the maximum.[23]

The march to the sea had been simply a change of base, whereas the march from Savannah was an attack on Richmond.

By January 31 Sherman's army was on the move, beginning a campaign that he considered his greatest military achievement.[24] The major objective was Lee's army in the vicinity of Richmond, and Sherman's Westerners intended to have the honor of taking the Confederate capital themselves.[25] And they moved swiftly. Sherman's insistence on the value of marching light paid off. So swift and deceptive were his movements in South Carolina that General Beauregard and his lieutenants did not have time to defend the interior of the state against the invading Union forces.[26] Not that it would have mattered.

Thus, with the movement of Sherman's army northward, South Carolina "commenced," as Major Nichols put it, "to pay an instalment, long overdue, on her debt to justice and humanity." Continuing, Nichols said, "With the help of God, we will have principal and interest before we leave her borders. . . . Little did she dream that the hated flag would again wave over her soil. . . ." To Nichols it was glorious that "the ground [trembled] beneath the tramp of thousands of brave Northmen, who [knew] their mission, and [performed] it to the end."[27]

The army Sherman commanded in South Carolina march was the same one he had led through Georgia with one exception. John Bennett Walters puts it well. He writes, "The veteran soldier of Sherman's corps followed the same practices of devastation and destruction in South Carolina that they had in Georgia, with one outstanding exception—they destroyed and wrecked South Carolina with a thoroughness and deliberation that arose out of pure hatred for that state. It was not an impersonal feeling directed against the enemy in general, but rather a personal hatred felt by the soldiers in the ranks as well as the officers. . . ."[28] Major Connolly could sense the different feeling that the men "had it in" for South Carolina. Staff officer Hitchcock spoke "of all mean humbugs 'South Carolina's Chivalry' is the meanest."[29] And Chaplain John J. Hight of the Fifty-Eighth Indiana would write: "Poor South Carolina must suffer now. None of the soldiers are storing up mercy for her. Her deluded people will

. . . reap the full folly and crimes."[30] Conyngham wrote, "There can be no denial of the assertion that the feeling among troops was one of extreme bitterness towards the people of the State of South Carolina." The men, according to Conyngham were "eager to commence the punishment of 'original secessionists.'"[31] Capt. Julian Hinkley of the Third Wisconsin Infantry, said of the possibility that their destination might be Charleston. "I wanted the people of South Carolina who started the war to feel its effects and to reap their share of the horrors."[32]

Sherman's troops set to work immediately, and from the beginning it was called "the Smoky March."[33] As in Georgia, railroad cars, stations, depots, ties and rails were destroyed. Lloyd Lewis provides an itemized list: bales of cotton, bins of cottonseed, acres of pine trees, barrels of resin, factories, public buildings, rail fences, barns, and houses.[34]

Conyngham observed that "In Georgia few houses were burned, here few escaped. . . . The middle of the finest day looked black and gloomy, for a dense smoke arose on all sides."[35] And the towns— Lawtonville, Hardeeville, Grahamsville, Gallisonville, McPhersonville, Barnwell, Blackville, Midway, Orangeburg, and Lexington—all were burned and left in ruin.[36]

One soldier of the 103rd Illinois in the XV Corps wrote on February 7, "I never saw so much destruction before. Orders are strict as ever but our men understand they are in South Carolina and are making good their old threats."[37]

Finally, there was the plundering and stealing of private property. Homes were robbed of jewelry, silverware, and other personal items. Stores and shops were looted and items destroyed by vandals. As in Georgia, attempts were made to control the activities of the plunderers, but due to the hostile spirit that prevailed, little was accomplished. Even Sherman himself seemed less concerned with this activity than he had been on the March to the Sea. Indeed, he attempted to justify the actions of his soldiers by referring to the Duke of Wellington's condoning of plundering in France. He also rationalized his lack of discipline over his men with, "Fighting is the least and easiest part of war, but no General ever was or will be successful who quarrels with his men, who takes the part of citizens against the petty irregularities or who punishes them unduly for gathering firewood, using wells and springs of water, and even taking sheep, chickens and food when their regular supplies are insufficient."[38] Sherman never spent much time explaining his lack of discipline in this area, nor did he expend much effort on justifications and rationalizations. He viewed such plundering and pillaging as part and parcel of his concept of total war. Indeed, the work of his foragers and bummers was having the intended effect. They were doing their part in ripping apart the psychological and sociological foundations of the enemy.

As in Georgia, diehard Southerners in South Carolina attempted to rally civilians to come out and halt the Union forces. Now, however, few were to be found, and Sherman credited this lack of response to his harshness in implementing war. Savannah had provided evidence of Southern subjugation, and there was even greater evidence in South Carolina. The following comments, from a letter, are a perfect example of how the will to fight had been beaten out of the Southerners: "It will be a . . . disgrace to Carolina that 'she' forced old men for the hardships of wars . . . and children 16 years of age to be butchered in opposing strong and well disciplined Veteran troops under command of such a General as Sherman and for what? To save the life of a few aristocrats, who deserve to be hung. All we have to say is that if you execute that order [an order to civilians to report for duty], know that a bullet is prepared for you and your house will be razed to the ground."[39] The social-psychological foundations of the Confederacy were crumbling. This was Sherman's plan, and it was working. The will of the South to continue fighting was dying a rapid death.

Columbia, the capital city of South Carolina, fell to the Union forces on February 17. By noon Sherman had made his entrance and was greeted with jubilation by the black population. One officer wrote, "The welcome given to Sherman by the Negroes was touching. They greet his arrival with exclamation of unbounded joy. 'Tank de Almighty God, Mister Sherman has come at last. We knew it; we prayed for de day, and de Lord Jesus heard our prayer. Mr. Sherman has come wid his company.'"[40]

Such jubilation did not last, however. That evening, as Sherman was dining, a fire began to rage out of control in the business district of Columbia, and by the next day much of the city had been burned to the ground.

Immediately, a controversy arose as to who was responsible for the destruction. The Confederates, of course, blamed Sherman and his army, arguing that not only had they started the fire but had allowed it to burn out of control, making little or no effort to put it out. Sherman and many of his officers, on the other hand, denied the accusations, saying that the blame should be placed on Confederate Gen. Wade Hampton who had hurriedly evacuated the city on the 16th. In the process of leaving he had ordered and encouraged soldiers and civilians to place bales of cotton in the streets and set them on fire so as to keep them out of the hands of the Yankees. Both sides were able to provide witnesses to support their positions.

The most comprehensive study of the controversy surrounding this incident can be found in *Sherman and the Burning of Columbia* by Marion Lucas. He concludes that the burning was the result of a number of factors, and that there was not one fire but a series of fires. According to Lucas's research, the fires began with bales of cotton being ignited by Southerners under the leadership of General Hampton as they evacuated the city. Although Federal troops and city firefighters attempted to bring the fire under control, they were hampered in their efforts because of extremely high winds. The winds carried particles of burning cotton to other parts of the business district and set other buildings ablaze. New fires were also started by prisoners recently released from jail. Glad to be free, and vindictive over their imprisonment, they attacked the city with fire. Still other fires were set as a form of celebration by blacks who were rejoicing over their new-found freedom from their Columbian masters. Other fires were begun by poorly disciplined and irresponsible Union soldiers. To complicate the situation, many of the culprits were intoxicated as a result of liquor either seized from shops or distilleries in the city, or given out to them by citizens in Columbia.

So the evidence points not to Sherman or Hampton but to a number of factors ranging from people to natural elements. Eventually, as a result of cooperation between Federals and local citizens (including Sherman himself), and the dying of the winds, the fires were brought under control. When the smoke lifted, the destruction was not as great as many had initially thought. Lucas's research shows that only 458 buildings, or about one-third of the total, were actually destroyed.

Although Lucas exonerates Sherman, his final conclusion is that no individual or group can be blamed. As Bell Irvin Wiley states in his foreword to Lucas's work, "The principle demons in the drama were cotton, whiskey, and wind."[41]

John Bennett Walters, of course, places all the blame on Sherman, and concludes that "no one can follow the record of Sherman's lawless troops in South Carolina without the conviction that Columbia was a doomed city even before it was taken."[42] Unfortunately, Walters is so intent on making Sherman into a senseless amoral terrorist that he fails to take into account some important variables. The first error is his failure to adequately research the Columbia fires incident. Therefore, he draws his conclusions based on inadequate information. He, in his subjectivity, presents the Columbia burning in such a way as to fit appropriately his preconceived assumptions about Sherman as a barbarian. Second, Walters leaves the impression that the entire city was burned—that it was another Atlanta, if not worse. Third, he is reluctant to record the efforts by Sherman himself, as well as his troops, to bring the fire under control. Fourth, he works on the assumption that somehow Columbia had been declared an open city. Finally, Walters is led to his erroneous conclusions because of his lack of an understanding of the character of Sherman and his concept of warfare. Although Sherman, like his men, had gotten caught up in the spirit of revenge against South Carolina, Sherman never ceased being professional nor did he abandon his purpose of bringing the war to an end. If Sherman had been a vengeful person, he would have left Savannah and marched straight for Charleston. His men were hopeful that this would be their destination, and even Halleck, Sherman's superior, indirectly urged him to march on that city. Prior to his leaving Savannah, Halleck had said to him: "Should you capture Charleston, I hope that by some accident the place may be destroyed, and if a little salt should be sown upon its site, it may prevent the growth of future crops of . . . secession."[43] Easily, Sherman could have marched on Charleston, burned it, and, in doing so, increased his popularity not only among his troops, but among civilians at home and his superiors as well. Quite a temptation! But Sherman did not see Charleston as being strategically as important as Columbia. (The advance on Columbia was strategically sound. By moving inland, Sherman's columns cut the Charleston defenders off from the hinterland, compelling General Hardee's army to evacuate Charleston on the night of February 17 and 18.) General Lee's Army of Northern Virginia depended on supplies passing through that city and its environs. Also, since Charleston was not in the "heart" of South Carolina, heading there would not have enabled Sherman to cut as wide a swath through the state as he felt necessary. To have advanced on Charleston would have been an act of revenge, and thus a complete contradiction of who Sherman was and what he was trying to accomplish.

Consistent with his purpose, Sherman made the following comment concerning the partial destruction of Columbia: "Though I never ordered it and never wished it, I have never shed many tears over the event, because I believe it hastened what we all fought for, the end of the war."[44]

The Union army remained in Columbia for two more days destroying property deemed valuable to the enemy. As Major Nichols recorded in his diary on February 19, "General Sherman has given orders for the further destruction of all public property. . . ." Nichols continues, "The arsenal, railroad depots, storehouses, magazines . . . , and cotton to the amount of twenty thousand bales . . . [are destroyed]. There is not a rail upon any of the roads within twenty miles of Columbia. . . ."[45]

On the day Sherman and his army left Columbia, Emma Le Conte, a resident of the city, wrote with apathy and despondency, " . . . How desolated and dreary we feel—how completely cut off from the world. No longer the shrill whistles of the engine—no daily mail—the morning brings no paper with news from the outside— there are no lights—no going to and fro. It is as if a city in the midst of business and activity were suddenly smitten with some appalling curse." Two days later, after having walked through the city, she recorded:

> I have seen it all—I have seen the "Abominations of Desolation."
> It is even worse than I thought. The place is literally in ruins.
> The entire heart of the city is in ashes—only the outer edges
> remain. On the whole length of Sumter Street not one house
> beyond the first block after the campus is standing. . . . Standing
> in the centre of town, as far as the eye can reach nothing is to be
> seen, but heaps of rubbish, tall dreary chimneys and shattered
> brick walls. . . . Poor old Columbia—where is all her beauty—so
> admired by strangers, so loved by her children! . . .[46]

On February 20, Sherman marched out of Columbia and pursued a northerly course. From Winnsboro to Camden to Cheraw he left a track marked with fire and destruction. While in camp at Cheraw, Lt. George Wise overheard a conversation taking place between

Sherman and a number of generals. The issue was secession and the need for immediate use of force against violators of the law. Lieutenant Wise remembered Sherman saying that "when the rebels took Sumter an army ought to have been sent against Charleston and every building burned & leveled to the ground, more than this I would have killed every man, woman, and child found in it." Sherman, according to Wise, also stated: "This people are possessed with devils and when we fight the devil we must fight him with fire. . . . Let South Carolina take warning for if it ever becomes necessary to come here again to put down the rebellion of her people they will see war such as they never dreamed of before." Writing to his brother, Wise tried to provide a sense of meaning to what had happened in South Carolina. He said that he knew Sherman's actions in South Carolina would "be severely condemned by many in the North." Almost in a pleading manner he urged his brother: "If you hear any condemning us for what we have done, tell them for me and for Sherman's Army that *'we found here the authors of all the calamities that have befallen this nation & the men & women whose hands are red with all the innocent blood that has been shed in this war, and that their punishment is light when compared with what justice demanded.'"*[47]

In early March, Sherman crossed the line into North Carolina and on the 11th entered Fayetteville. South Carolina was left behind. Immediately the conduct of the soldiers changed. George Ward Nichols saw no evidence of plundering, "The men keep their ranks closely; and more remarkable yet, not a single column of the fire or smoke which a few days ago marked the positions of heads of columns, can be seen upon the horizon."[48] Brig. Gen. Manning Force noticed the change also and remarked, "When we crossed the boundary line into North Carolina, destruction ceased. Not a house was burned, and the army gave to the people more than it took from them."[49] It was obvious the men knew they were marching into a state whose citizens had been hesitant to leave the Union. Maj. Gen. Henry Slocum seemed to express the feelings of everybody when he stated that the people of North Carolina had made sacrifices for the Union and that there existed a strong Northern sentiment among the majority of its citizens. On March 7, he issued General Order No. 8 which, among other things, expressed the hope that "every effort will be made to prevent any wanton destruction of property, or any unkind treatment of citizens."[50]

Just before Sherman entered North Carolina he received word

that his old adversary, General Johnston, had been recalled to duty and to the state to consolidate all available troops for a final attempt at stopping Sherman. His first and last opportunity would come in less than a week.

Sherman left Fayetteville and headed for Goldsboro. On March 19, Johnston confronted Sherman at Bentonville, a small town west of Goldsboro, and came close to isolating and defeating the Federal Fourteenth Corps led by Brig. Gen. Jefferson C. Davis. The fighting continued intermittently until March 21 when Johnston withdrew to Smithfield. Sherman refused to pursue the Confederate army and moved eastward to Goldsboro where Federal troops from the coast raised his total force to 90,000. The march had come to an end. Sherman was now less than two hundred miles south of Richmond and was prepared to join General Grant.

Writing to his wife, Sherman quickly evaluated his march. He said, "The last March from Savannah to Goldsboro, with its legitimate fruits, the capture of Charleston, Georgetown and Wilmington, is by far the most important in conception . . . of any act of my life. . . ."[51] He had made the entire South feel the weight of war. With an army of 60,000 he had marched through a hostile country, inflicting his concept of war on its inhabitants. He had brought total war to the South in the form of economic depression, psychological disturbance, sociological disorganization, and material destruction. The North, the South, Grant, Lincoln, Halleck and the world knew he had succeeded, but it was not until he read a letter written by General Lee to Gov. Zebulon Vance of North Carolina that Sherman was satisfied. The letter read, "The state of despondency that now prevails among our people is producing a bad effect upon the troops. Desertions are becoming very frequent and there is good reason to believe that they are occasioned to a considerable extent by letters written to soldiers by their families at home . . . that our cause is hopeless, and that they had better provide for themselves."[52] What is tragic is, Lee did not act accordingly and lived to kill another day— with Pres. Jefferson Davis's blessing, of course.

On March 25, Sherman boarded a fast steamboat and headed for City Point, Virginia, to consult with President Lincoln, General Grant, and Admiral Porter. On board the president's floating White House—the *River Queen*—the four held two conferences on March 27 and 28. After discussing past operations, they turned to the approaching end of the war. It was decided that Grant should not delay his offensive against Lee by waiting for Sherman's arrival in Virginia. Therefore, Sherman was to return to North Carolina and ensure the surrender of Johnston as quickly as possible. It was important that Johnston be prevented from joining up with Lee. The talks eventually turned to peace terms. Lincoln was not interested in a vindictive peace and wanted to reunite the nation with as little bitterness as possible.[53] Sherman was instructed that, once the Confederate armies had surrendered, he should assure Gov. Zebulon B. Vance that Southerners would be protected in accordance with civil law. In addition, state governments were to remain in existence and be recognized as *de facto* governments until Congress decided otherwise. According to Sherman, Lincoln did not "name any special terms of surrender" nor did he issue definite instructions for negotiating a peace.[54]

Sherman returned to Goldsboro on March 30 and, except for some minor skirmishing, his army did no further fighting. On April 11 at Smithfield, the day after the "army group" left Goldsboro, Sherman received word that Grant had obtained Lee's surrender at Appomattox Court House. On April 14, Sherman, having entered Raleigh the previous day, was contacted by Johnston and informed that he was prepared to talk surrender terms. For the next four days, the two generals met and discussed the details of the surrender. Finally, on April 18, at Bennett's farmhouse, outside Durham Station, Sherman presented his final document of surrender.

Consistent with his promise—made time and time again for the past year and a half—to befriend the people of the South once they ceased fighting, Sherman's terms were generous. As historian Barrett puts it, "Through the Carolinas he had reiterated this statement and at Bennett's farmhouse he had proved his words."[55] Indeed, the defeated general could not have asked for more lenient terms than those offered by Sherman. The terms even exceeded Lincoln's conceptions. They included an orderly disbandment of the Confederate Army; the re-establishment of Federal courts in the rebellious states; the recognition of state governments by the executive branch of the Federal government; the guarantee of political, property, and personal rights "as defined by the Constitution of the United States and of the States respectively"; freedom from molestation due to participation in the war; adjudication by the United States Supreme Court of the legitimacy of rival state governments, where they existed; and a general amnesty "so far as the Executive can command."[56] In essence, these terms "restored the South a large measure of its *status quo* ante-bellum."[57] Sherman had gone beyond his responsibilities as a member of the military. Lincoln had not given him the authority for such terms, and (Lincoln was dead now) probably would not have approved them. The general had negotiated civil terms that were beyond his purview. But Sherman was motivated by two ideas. First, he did not have a full understanding and appreciation of what the rebellion had actually done to this country. He was naive and in many ways innocent. He believed that the country could return to its previous state prior to the war, and that, under the mechanisms of government, guided by the Constitution, differences could be worked out without reference to secession or war. Second, Sherman's terms were motivated by a sincere desire to reunite the country as quickly and as easily as possible. Further, he wanted to help the South recover. His love for both the Union and the South prevented him from being a ruthless victor. The end of the war and the establishment of peace through union were Sherman's goals, and the meetings at David Bennett's farmhouse convinced Sherman that he had attained them. As Barrett points out, "the generosity of his terms . . . were in complete harmony with his design for reconstruction of the South."[58]

So, the negotiations were completed and, they would become official with Pres. Andrew Johnson's approval.

Years later Sherman would write that he was confident the peace terms would be acceptable to the president and his administration. "I believed," he said, that the terms "contained what would ultimately result if the people of the South accepted and acted in prompt and willing acquiescence." He believed the fulfillment of his terms "would produce instantaneously a condition of reason and lawful fidelity consistent with the Constitution . . . and the laws then in existence. . . ." As far as he was concerned, "the only thing in April, 1865, left for us to combat was prejudice and habits of thought." For him, this could not be accomplished "by force of arms, but must be left to time's influence."[59]

Sherman had tried to create a peace settlement that would enable the North and South to exist side by side. Having completed this task, Sherman returned to Raleigh prepared for a few days' rest.

The peace terms reached Washington on April 21 and were immediately rejected by President Johnson and his cabinet. On April 24, General Grant arrived in Raleigh and informed Sherman of the rejection of the terms and of the fact that Sherman was authorized to offer only the terms Grant had given Lee at Appomattox Court House. Thus, a second meeting between Sherman and Johnston was necessary. On April 26, once again at Bennett's farmhouse, Sherman presented the new terms of surrender to Johnston, who, "without difficulty" agreed, and signed the document. From this meeting on, General Johnston's troops were to cease all acts of war; all arms and public property were to be delivered to the United States Army; and Confederate soldiers were obligated not to take up arms against the government of the United States unless duly exchanged. Sidearms of officers were to be retained by them, and all officers and men were permitted to return to their homes " . . . not to be disturbed by the United States authorities."

Although Sherman disagreed with the terms, he saw to their execution until he left for Wilmington. Even though disheartened, he left Raleigh knowing he had honestly endeavored to shorten the road to reunion, for he believed that the terms first offered to Johnston, if they had been accepted, would have returned the Southern people to their original place in the Union. He desired a stronger unified country, not a humbled and subjugated South. He foresaw future difficulty if harsh terms were imposed. Although he had brought hell to the South, Sherman was basically a man of mercy and compassion. He had said at one time during the war that when the "war is over, let us all go and do what seems honest and just to restore our country to its former prosperity—to its physical prosperity."[60] Now that the war was over, he wanted to make his words reality.

There are two issues emerging from this last campaign that reflect on the complexity of Sherman's character and his theory of war. They have been touched on, but need more detailed examination. The first has to do with the impact his march through the Carolinas had on ending the war, more specifically on Lee's decision to surrender, and the second is the controversy over the surrender terms at the Bennett farmhouse.

The first issue centers around the question: Did the march through the Carolinas have an influence on the final defeat of Lee in Virginia? There are basically two camps, one arguing no, the other yes. According to James Merrill, "the destructiveness of that march was to have little bearing on General Lee's eventual decision to surrender."[61] J. C. Ropes, the historian, submits that Sherman was "entirely mistaken in thinking that to devastate the state of S. Carolina would have a direct and immediate bearing on Grant's campaign in Virginia."[62] Even Maj. Gen. John M. Schofield would write later that "Sherman's destruction of military supplies and railroads . . . did not materially hasten the collapse of the Rebellion, which was due to Grant's capture of Lee's army."[63] Finally, Alfred Burnes states that "one thing is certain: Sherman's marches had no appreciable effect upon Lee's surrender." Burnes justifies his conclusion by stating that Sherman's army did not influence Lee's army through "hostile action, i.e., bullets, shells, and cold steel," or through "shortage of food, munitions or numbers." He does admit, however, that Sherman's march did have an impact in the form of "mental action, i.e., hostile propaganda, solicitude for family, etc." Perhaps the strongest point made by Burnes is that there is no way to measure the severity of the impact.[64]

Those in the opposing camp concentrate their arguments on the indirect influence Sherman's march had on Lee's army. They see no reason at all to argue for the direct impact, for there was none. For example, Herman Hattaway and Archer Jones write, "The march through the Carolinas produced a devastating effect on Confederate logistics." They quote Richard Goff's study of Confederate supply to support their contention. They write, "Sherman's 'movements in South Carolina in . . . February nailed the lid on Lee's coffin by cutting Lee off from his Deep South supply sources.'" They add, "Lee had continued to meet some of his needs by means of the railroad which ran east through Augusta, but Sherman cut this." Finally, they state, "In spite of Sherman's march, Lee had miraculously been provisioned to the end, but it would not have continued long."[65] Hattaway and Jones could have added that the quality of provisions, as well as the quantity, dropped significantly.

Lloyd Lewis argues through the use of letters and diaries that the march did indeed have the intended effect. He quotes Robert E. Lee's letter of February 24 to Governor Vance saying that "the despair of North Carolinians was threatening to break up his army. . . ." He presents Col. Archer Anderson's statement that Lee's army was living for months "on less than one-third rations . . . was demoralized not by the enemy on its front [Grant], but by the enemy in Georgia and the Carolinas." And, he turns to Sherman himself, quoting a letter the general wrote to Maj. Gen. Quincy A. Gillmore.

Sherman noted, "The simple fact that a man's home has been visited by an enemy makes a soldier in Lee's . . . army very, very anxious to get home to look after his family and property."[66]

Liddell Hart states, "Sherman's rays were melting the rear of the military ice-barrier which had so long blocked Grant's advance." He turns to Grant himself to justify the impact Sherman was having on Lee's army. " . . . Grant was able to tell Sherman that Lee's 'army is now demoralized and deserting very fast, both to us and to their homes.'"[67]

Finally, John Barrett contends that the march accomplished its purpose. In addition to referring to Lee's letter to Governor Vance, Barrett presents the diary of Samuel Hoey Walkup of the Forty-Eighth North Carolina Infantry Regiment, and the statement written by six North Carolina regimental commanders to Sen. William Alexander Graham of the Confederate Congress. The theme in both documents is that Sherman's march was causing increasing desertions in Lee's army.[68]

Looking at the arguments, what can be concluded? First, both camps have good arguments for their positions. For example, Burnes is correct when he concludes that Sherman's marches did not have a direct effect on Lee as far as "hostile action" is concerned. Obviously, Sherman's army never reached the rear of Lee's army and thus never entered into combat. He is probably correct in his concern about being able to measure the exact impact of "mental action" on the enemy in Virginia. But to state absolutely, as he does and as others in the same camp have done, that a similar result would have occurred (that is, Lee's defeat) had Sherman never made his marches, is unfounded and offers a narrow view of the grand strategy Grant and Sherman had planned and implemented—a strategy based on battle in Virginia and devastating deep penetrating raids in the Southland. Lewis, Liddell Hart, and others present convincing evidence that the "mental action" was effective and that desertions increased significantly after Atlanta and continued to do so to the end of the war. Yet, they are weak on the issue of supplies. It is doubtful that Sherman's march was successful in hurting Lee's flow of supplies significantly. But, the impact was present and, as pointed out earlier, Sherman, along with the breakdown of the Virginia transportation system, did affect the quality of supplies. Lee's soldiers made this admission, and Lee himself saw his army dwindle by at least eight percent. Second, after all the arguments are considered, it can be concluded that Sherman had succeeded in fulfilling his mission. He broke up Johnston's (Hood's) army, and he advanced into the interior of the enemy's territory, destroying its war resources. That was the plan as far back as Chattanooga. In doing so, he made a major contribution, probably more than Grant, to the destruction of the South's will to continue the war. The effect was to take men directly from Lee's army in Virginia. He fulfilled Grant's plan of a successful raid, a vital part of the strategy to defeat the South. Perhaps part of the answer to the question of Sherman's effectiveness in weakening Lee in Virginia can be found in Grant. At City Point he made the decision that the Army of the Potomac could force Lee to surrender without the presence of Sherman's army on the battlefield. Granted, the decision was partially political. Grant wanted to save the pride of the Eastern forces—but Grant was a soldier first and a politician second. He would have used Sherman's forces if he had believed they were needed. Grant would not have risked defeat to save an army's face. By 1865 the Confederacy was its armies—without them the Confederacy was nothing more than paper. Defeat of the armies meant the collapse of the Confederacy. Sherman had not only dismantled the Western forces he had also destroyed the will of the South to fight. This left Grant with a clean-up action, which he accomplished in early April 1865.

What all the arguments fail to take into account is this: Grant and Sherman had developed a symbiotic relationship; they needed each other. Out of that relationship came a symbiotic strategy that needed for success the actions and movements of each of the two generals' armies. Sherman's march could have never taken place had it not been for Grant's holding action, and Grant would have never defeated Lee had it not been for Sherman's long, sweeping movements. That was the plan of commitment, and it worked. It is only in this light that Sherman's theory of war had meaning.

Finally, there is the issue of the surrender terms and Sherman's actions at the Bennett farmhouse. This issue is much easier to resolve, and, when all the arguments about Lincoln's influence on Sherman at City Point are put aside, the only conclusion that can be drawn is that Sherman did not want the South to be treated as a vanquished foe. Specific instructions were not provided him as to terms, so he acted according to his own heart and mind. Had Lincoln given specific guidelines or rules, more than likely this incident of history would have never occurred. But Sherman was left free to decide, and he did so based upon his own view of the South and the war. The conflict was over, therefore, the rebellious states should be accepted back in the Union, and the country should immediately get about the business of healing its wounds. He had always believed that the aim of war is to establish peace. Now that war had ended, peace must begin. His mistake was making decisions of a civil nature. Finally, he had an undying faith in the Constitution and felt confident that, under its laws, all differences could be resolved. In May 1865, in a letter, he wrote, "I confess, without shame, I am sick and tired of fighting—its glory is all moonshine; even success the most brilliant is over dead and mangled bodies, with the anguish and lamentations of distant families, appealing to me for sons, husbands, and fathers. You too, have seen these things, and I know you also are tired of the war, and are willing to let the civil tribunals resume their place. And, so far as I know, all the fighting men of our army want peace. . . ." With a feeling of tragedy, he continued. " . . . and it is only those who have never heard a shot, never heard the shriek and groans of the wounded and lacerated (friend and foe), that cry aloud for more blood, more vengeance, more desolation." He concludes, "I *know* the rebels are whipped to death, and I declare before God, as a man and a soldier, I will not strike a foe who stands unarmed and submissive before me, but would rather say—'Go, and sin no more.'"[69] With childlike hope, all Sherman wanted was to "maintain peace and good order, and let law and harmony grow up naturally."[70]

From Raleigh, Sherman traveled by way of Wilmington and Richmond to Washington where on May 24, his army—65,000 strong—took part in the Grand Review. On May 30, he issued general orders taking leave of his troops, and with the final words of these orders the record of William Tecumseh Sherman's part in the Civil War was concluded. He told his troops, "Our work is done. Your general now bids you farewell, with the full belief that, as in war you have been good soldiers, so in peace you will make good citizens; and if, unfortunately, new war should arise in our country 'Sherman's Army' will be the first to buckle on its old armor, and come forth to defend and maintain the Government of our inheritance."[71]

*General Sherman, 1888, five years after his retirement
as general-in-chief of the United States Army.*

# *Epilogue*

In 1905, SHERMAN WAS HONORED with election to the Military Hall of Fame. His movements through Georgia and the Carolinas were recognized as being innovative, daring, imaginative, bold, and masterfully executed. From the moment the war began in the spring of 1861, Sherman's chief concerns had been to end the war, destroy the idea of secession, establish peace, and reunite the country.

To accomplish this objective, he destroyed railroad communications, ruined enormous quantities of supplies, and brought home to the people of the South the severe realities of war. Never had the United States experienced such destruction. By his actions and the movements of his army, over a two-year period Sherman put into practice a rather unique mode of warfare, one that would eventually be called "total war." Sherman, by directly attacking the economic, psychological, and sociological aspects of the Confederacy, accomplished his purpose. As he marched through the heart of the South with his force of 60,000, his foragers and bummers destroyed both public and private property that was deemed valuable to the enemy's war effort. The destruction contributed significantly to the weakening of the Confederacy's economic foundations and proved to the world the effectiveness of economic warfare. The destruction also had a tremendous impact on the hearts and minds of Southern noncombatants, the spiritual and material foundations of the Confederacy. As Sherman began his destruction outside Chattanooga en route to Atlanta, their response was one of shock and anger. They retaliated with even a greater determination to rid their land of

291

Federals. Partisan activities and hostile—at times ugly and cruel—propaganda was used in an attempt to thwart the movement of Sherman's army and keep Southern spirits high. Such retaliation was expected by Sherman, and he met it with even more destruction and devastation. He was just as determined to remain in the South until his task was complete. Subjected to renewed harshness and the realization that their own government could not help them, the people of the South passed from a state of anger and determination to a condition of depression and hopelessness. By the time Sherman marched out of Atlanta, the will of the South to continue the war with much dedication was gone. Sherman had beaten it out of them. Savannah was proof of the noncombatants' lack of determination. They all but welcomed his entrance. From Savannah to the end of the war, the Rebels were incapable of putting together any semblance of resistance to Sherman's rolling military machine. When they did manage to place an army of any size in front of him, it was too late. For all intents and purposes the war had ended.

Sherman's experience convinced him he had been right, that with the use of economic warfare he had proven the importance of psychological warfare. He had not only destroyed the purse strings of the South, he had also reached into the minds of Southerners and convinced them that their course was futile. Individually, thousands of noncombatants experienced the pathological traumas of alienation, estrangement, and normlessness that accompany dramatic disruption of human lives. All that had been sound and permanent to them was gone, and it was doubtful if such security would ever return. Sherman had effectively destroyed the social cohesiveness that individuals must have for stability in their lives. Sociologically, his march created disorganization out of an already precarious organization among all aspects of the social fabric. Families were disrupted, religious institutions weakened, government devastated, education non-existent, and financial security ended. All the elements of society—institutions, rules, norms, customs—were attacked, and the result was the disintegration of social solidarity. The glue that had held the South together was ceasing to hold. Successfully combining into his theory of war these three elements—the economic, the psychological, and the sociological—Sherman made the South and much of the Western world realize the effectiveness of "total war." For his day his methods were unorthodox, and they defied the traditional theories and practices of warfare. But, they worked.

In a sense, Sherman's marches were similar to a flood raging through a community, destroying everything in its path. Kai Erikson, in his award-winning analysis of the Buffalo Creek flood that occurred in West Virginia in 1972, provides insight that is applicable to the destruction produced by Sherman's army in 1864–65. Erikson states that the flood produced "individual trauma: [a] state of shock," which, in turn led to "depression, anxiety, phobia, emotional lability, hypochondria, apathy, insomnia; and the broader syndrome into which these symptoms naturally fall . . . post-traumatic neurosis, or . . . post-traumatic psychosis." What all this means, Erikson says, is that the flood's devastation produced confusion, despair, and hopelessness.[1] It is not difficult to see the parallel between the Buffalo Creek flood and Sherman's marches through the South. Hundreds of diaries, letters, journals, and newspapers attest to such trauma. Everywhere he led his army, from Chattanooga to Goldsboro, like a flood, he created individual trauma that produced psychological pathology among those in his path.

But, his marches were also sociological, an important point overlooked by historians who have studied Sherman. His marches created what Erikson has called "collective trauma: loss of communality." Erikson writes, "I use the term 'communality' . . . rather than 'community' in order to underscore the point that people [victims of the flood] are not referring to particular village territories when they lament the loss of community but to the network of relationships that make up their general human surround. The persons who constitute the center of that network are usually called 'neighbors,' the word being used . . . to identify those with whom one shares bonds of intimacy and a feeling of mutual concern."[2] As Erikson points out, Ferdinand Toennes called it *"gemeinschaft,"* Charles Cooley "primary," Emile Durkheim "mechanical," and Robert Redfield "folk." Sherman's marches, like the flood in West Virginia, disrupted and, in many instances, destroyed networks of relationships and the common bonds shared by Southerners. In doing so, he created collective trauma and the loss of communality. The social bonds were cut, and people were set adrift.

This, perhaps more than anything else, is the legacy Sherman left—he introduced to the modern world, and established its legitimacy—psychological and sociological warfare.[3]

But, of course, Sherman's marches, and therefore, his legacy, could not have occurred without Grant. These two were dependent on each other. The strategy of the North's approach to the war from Vicksburg on was dependent upon the relationship between these two men. They saw in one other their own individual failures and, as a result, were immediately drawn to each other. They were sources of strength to one another when dangers threatened new failures. They trusted each other, and they agreed on the direction the war should take. The war had to be ended, and defeat of the South meant a combined effort, a cooperative venture, based on orthodoxy and unorthodoxy. Similar in purpose, they were different enough in tactics to produce the desired result. As already stated, they not only had a symbiotic relationship on the personal level, they created a symbiotic plan on the professional level that brought the long war to a close. The legacy they left was the cooperation between two armies to bring about the agreed-upon result.

Sherman can be called a number of things, but one thing he cannot be called is orthodox. Personally and professionally, he marched to the beat of a different drum. The shift to unorthodoxy in war came early for Sherman, and he never turned his back on his way of doing things. Although he had been taught the traditional methods of warfare at West Point—the importance of defense, fortifications, defeat of the enemy's main army, and protection of the rights of noncombatants—he let go of those traditions with little inner struggle. He had learned early in his life the value of efficiency, the importance of defining a goal and immediately establishing means to achieve that goal.

In addition, Sherman understood clearly the importance of psychology and sociology, and they led him to his theory of war—a theory which Liddell Hart has termed the "indirect approach."[4] Sherman saw the value of attacking the military indirectly through its civil foundations. It is important to understand (and this is the weakness in Liddell Hart's presentation) that Sherman was much aware of the fact that ultimately the enemy's army must be made inoperative. Sherman, however, felt it could be done indirectly. As Jay Luvaas states, according to Liddell Hart, the Vicksburg campaign alerted Sherman "to the possibilities of a strategy which minimized fighting by upsetting the opponent—both mentally and physically—and by substituting mobility and deception for force."[5] For Liddell Hart, Sherman's indirect approach involved mobility, the technique of "a wide loose grouping or net," the "baited gambit," and "alternative objectives."[6]

The individual tactics were not new to Sherman; they had been used in varying degrees by armies of the past. What is probably unique with Sherman's usage of them is that he combined them together and made them, not tactics to do battle against the enemy's army, but tactics to defeat the enemy without battle. As Sherman's army, light and efficient, rapidly marched through Georgia and the Carolinas, it spread itself over a sixty-mile-wide area, remaining cohesive all the while and preventing the opposing Confederates from "attacking and defeating sections in detail." At the same time, the scattered, but highly organized army, pulled everything into its "net." From May 1864 till he reached Raleigh, Sherman fought a frontal battle only once, at Kennesaw Mountain. The rest of the time he used the "baited gambit," whereby he would maneuver "so skillfully as to lure the Confederates time after time into vain attacks, their repulse being ensured by the skill of his troops in rapid entrenching after gaining a vantage point."[7]

Finally, with the use of alternative objectives, Sherman kept the Confederate forces in doubt as to his destination. He was effective in keeping the enemy on the defensive at all times and, in doing so, was able to remain mobile. There is little question that Liddell Hart has succeeded in systematically explaining Sherman's tactics and strategy. Sherman created a highly mobile army that remained intact and cohesive over hundreds of miles through hostile enemy territory. He constructed a net that gathered into its confines everything within a sixty-mile-wide area. Except for one time when John Bell Hood took the offensive to no avail, Sherman kept the Confederate army on the defensive. He created confusion as to his ultimate destinations. These were the tactics he used to implement his strategy of economic, psychological, and sociological warfare.

A major fact remains, however, and Sherman probably never lost sight of its reality: Wars are won by defeating armies. This does not always hold true, but it did for the Civil War. Once the war broke out, the only thing that gave the Confederacy its legitimacy was its armed might. Its right of secession was not recognized; its government was given no legitimacy; its leaders were rebels. But its armies—they could not be ignored. They were legitimate. Thus, to defeat the Confederacy, its armies had to be defeated. Upon this fact rests the legitimacy of Sherman's indirect approach. As Russell Weigley has pointed out, Sherman "could adopt the strategy of the indirect approach only after a direct approach had decisively weakened the armed forces initially in front of him." This Sherman did when he "almost swept the rival army opposing him from the board" on his campaign from Chattanooga to Atlanta. Had it not been for Hood's assistance and eventually Thomas's defeat of Hood at Nashville, had it not been for the narrow views of President Davis and General Lee who failed to recognize the strategic importance of the West, Sherman's marches would have never been possible.[8]

Despite the success Sherman achieved in waging "total war," he was at the time, and has been ever since, harshly criticized for his actions. The literature seems to concentrate on basically two areas: his pursuit of a geographical rather than a military objective—specifically the enemy's army—and his avoidance of the element of risk—meaning that he never risked his army in battle. In considering the first, it is clear that Sherman had three main phases in his campaigns. Each of these was terminated by the seizure of a geographical point. In the first, the objective was Atlanta. By selecting this city as a goal, he permitted Hood's army to "escape" and move against Union forces under Thomas at Nashville. In the second. the destination was Savannah, and, once again, he selected the city and allowed Hardee to "escape" and later join Johnston in North Carolina. In the third, his objective was Goldsboro, which he selected after fighting but not defeating Johnston's forces at Bentonville. Johnston was able to reorganize and build his force to a strength of 45,000. In considering the second criticism, it is evident that, by avoiding the risk of battle, Sherman enabled Johnston to retreat to Resaca and finally into the Atlanta defenses, Hood to move on Nashville, and Hardee to hover around Bentonville and Raleigh. It appeared that Sherman did not have it in him to risk his army in major confrontation on the battlefield. But those who make such criticisms as these are judging Sherman from a strictly traditional military position, the military tradition prevalent during the nineteenth century. From that perspective, if the enemy army is indeed the avowed objective, then Sherman can be marked off as a failure. However, the claim that Sherman's military performance was a failure because he never fought a battle and supposedly allowed his enemy to "escape," is sheer absurdity and demonstrates a lack of understanding of the nature and purpose of Sherman's part in the grand plan against the Confederacy. It is Sherman's lack of adherence to orthodoxy that opens him to criticism. What the critics fail to admit is that Sherman changed tradition and, therefore, the rules. The situation made it possible to do so. Instead of conducting war as it had always been conducted (particularly since the French Revolution), he decided to fight in a different way. He changed his objectives because he knew the situation would allow him to do so and because he knew the situation required that he do so. With Grant in agreement—indeed, it was partially Grant's idea—Sherman conducted a raid like no other raid had been conducted before. At the same time, he saw to it, when the opportune time arose, to "break up" Johnston's (Hood's) army. By the time he faced Johnston at Bentonville, Sherman had close to 60,000 men, and the war was all but over. If necessary (and he was prepared to do it), he could have defeated Johnston. As it turned out, it was not necessary. The two criticisms are not valid. The "if he had done this" exercise is purely academic.

Along with these criticisms is the issue of Sherman's operations having little direct bearing on Grant's movements against Lee in Virginia. This has already been examined in greater detail in the previous chapter. Suffice it to say, the war in that theater came to a close as a result of Grant's direct, and stubborn and persistent, pursuit of the Confederate forces. Where Sherman's march through the South was effective was in its indirect results. He kept the Army of Tennessee occupied and out of Virginia. He cut off many of Lee's sources of supply—Atlanta and Columbia, Savannah and Augusta. And he devastated the spirit of the Confederacy. Just as the civilian sector is dependent upon the military in time of war, so is the military dependent upon the civilian sector in time of war. The destruction of one inevitably leads to the destruction of the other. Finally, it is doubtful that Grant would have succeeded as soon as he did had it not been for Sherman's campaign.

Where does Sherman's eminence as a great military general lie? He was not the first to lead a massive army on a long march through enemy territory. Napoleon had accomplished this years before. He was not the first to recognize the importance of psychological warfare. Jomini and Clausewitz had both written about its value and impact in their treatises on war. Nor was he the first to break with tradition and plow a new path in the annals of war. Once again, Napoleon is an excellent example. What makes Sherman important is that he did all these things on a much larger scale and at a time when the world, or at least the Western world, was beginning to perceive itself as modern. He also accomplished his successes with the simultaneous advent of more sophisticated weapons and means of mass transportation. It was almost as if he had perceived the impact such weapons and advancements in transportation would ultimately have on warfare itself. It is as if he knew that they would, in less than a hundred years, lead to a complete rethinking of how war must be fought or if it was to be fought at all. Sherman is important also because he understood that an army need not depend on a long line of supply; he proved that an army could live off the enemy's resources. His eminence also rests in his determination to assist a traditional approach to war with a non-traditional operation. Finally, the importance of Sherman lies in the fact that "he moved the art of warfare significantly forward." T. Harry Williams writes, "More than any other general of his time [and in advance of his time], he understood that the will of a nation to fight rests on the economic and psychological [and sociological] security of its people and that if these supporting elements are destroyed all resistance may collapse."[9]

Sherman has not been ignored. His marches have been avidly studied in both the United States and Europe. Attention has been given to his supply system, and Europeans have been impressed with his efficiency in getting food, clothing, and ammunition to his troops in the field. His method of mobility has been fascinating to military professionals on both sides of the Atlantic, and the Germans displayed the influence of Sherman during both World Wars. His achievement of freedom and flexibility have become part and parcel of many armies since the Civil War, and his flanking actions, although not uniquely his own invention, have been closely examined.

In addition, attempts have been made to draw lines of influence from Sherman to twentieth-century military events. The German *blitzkrieg* and the bombings of Hiroshima and Nagasaki are just two examples. Such analyses as these, however, must be taken cautiously, for as T. Harry Williams so aptly points out, "There is too much easy exaggeration in . . . these ascriptions" and "it is dangerous . . . to push too far a parallel between Sherman and later ways and weapons." The result can often lead to "a false perspective." Sherman's military record and his explosive and fascinating personality lend themselves to "extravagant evaluations."[10] It is probably best to leave the parallels to late-night "what if" sessions. It is probably more accurate in the light of day to say that Sherman, unbeknown to him, left a legacy of "total war" that indeed became *total*. With his use and justification of economic, psychological, and sociological warfare, he opened the door to its fullest development in the form of dropping atomic bombs on the noncombatant cities of Japan. Although James Reston, Jr., speaks out of bitterness, and although he does not understand the character of Sherman, his comments do well in documenting the result of Sherman's legacy. Reston writes, "This is Sherman's legacy: not so much his practice of 'total war' as his intellectual justification of it, his lack of remorse at it. . . . Similar justifications, without remorse, are now put forward for American practices in Vietnam, and the rules of warfare that existed before that war have similarly ceased to exist."[11] There is one difference. Sherman did not permit the slaughter of human life. But Reston is correct; the "total war" Sherman practiced did lead to the "total war" of a Vietnam with its horrible additions.

An extremely complex man, Sherman proved himself to be a combination of Machiavelli, Vauban, Frederick the Great, Jomini, and Clausewitz. He was all of them and yet fully none of them. But elements of each were a part of Sherman. Manifest Destiny was his vision for America, and he viewed secession as a danger to its fulfillment. A fanatical believer in law and order, he was willing to die for the preservation of the Constitution. He understood the complexities of the Black-White issue, and, although he remained a white supremacist all his life, he knew that time, under the law, would resolve this issue for the good of the country. He was a family man, dedicated to his wife and children. Efficiency in everything was of utmost importance to him. And he had a compassion for people that made him loved even by his most ardent enemies. A strategist of top rank, he always managed to see the whole and understand the relationship of the parts to it. Perhaps his greatest shortcoming was that he never really took the time fully to explain himself; thus to some he remains a contradiction, while to others a paradox.

At various periods in Sherman's life, people described him as being crazy, prophetic, barbaric, brilliant, and unethical. But more than anything, he was a paradox. That is why even today he is difficult to understand. His life was wrapped up in a very simple belief that " . . . war must be fought effectively or not at all. An enemy in war, in peace a friend."[12] On his statue in Washington, D.C., are inscribed these appropriate words: "The legitimate object of war is a more perfect peace."

# *Notes*

## CHAPTER ONE

1. Rachel Sherman Thorndike (ed.), *The Sherman Letters, Correspondence Between General and Senator Sherman From 1837 to 1891* (New York, 1894), 1.
2. *Ibid.*
3. Sherman's father, Charles Sherman, died in 1829. Although a member of the Ohio State Supreme Court, he left his wife with a meager income and eleven children. To provide for them, her only recourse was to distribute some of the children among relatives, friends, and neighbors. William was sent to live with the Ewing family. Thomas Ewing, a neighbor and fairly wealthy attorney and businessman, had been a close friend of Charles Sherman.
4. Ellen Ewing was the daughter of Thomas Ewing. William and Ellen had grown close to one another during their childhood and they would marry in May 1850.
5. William Sherman to Ellen Ewing, May 4, 1839, Mark Antony DeWolfe Howe (ed), *Home Letters of General Sherman* (New York, 1909), 7.
6. Samuel Millard Bowman and Richard Bache Irwin, *Sherman and His Campaigns: A Military Biography* (New York, 1865), 10.
7. Lloyd Lewis, *Sherman, Fighting Prophet* (New York, 1932), 56.
8. *Ibid.*
9. William Tecumseh Sherman, *Memoirs of General William Sherman*, 2 vols. (New York, 1931), I, 17.
10. Lewis, *Fighting Prophet*, 55.
11. *Ibid.*, 52.

12. Basil Henry Liddell Hart, *Sherman: Soldier, Realist, American* (New York, 1958), 10.
13. *Ibid.*
14. Bowman and Irwin, *Sherman and His Campaigns*, 11.
15. *Ibid.*, 12.
16. Lewis, *Fighting Prophet*, 52–57.
17. William Sherman to John Sherman, August 31, 1839, *The Sherman Letters*, 9.
18. William Sherman to Ellen Ewing, March 10, 1839, *Home Letters*, 6.
19. Lewis, *Fighting Prophet*, 53.
20. James M. Merrill, *William Tecumseh Sherman* (Chicago, 1971), 31.
21. Sherman, *Memoirs*, I, 17.
22. *Ibid.*
23. Merrill, *Sherman*, 31.
24. Lewis, *Fighting Prophet*, 54.
25. George H. Mead, *Mind, Self, and Society* (Chicago, 1934).
26. Lewis, *Fighting Prophet*, 64.
27. William Sherman to Ellen Ewing, February 8, 1844, *Home Letters*, 24.
28. Sherman, *Memoirs*, I, 17–18.
29. Merrill, *Sherman*, 47.
30. Bowman and Irwin, *Sherman and His Campaigns*, 14.
31. Merril, *Sherman*, 47.
32. Lewis, *Fighting Prophet*, 68.
33. Sherman, *Memoirs*, I, 27–28.
34. Merrill, *Sherman*, 49.
35. *Ibid.*, 52.
36. William Sherman to Ellen Ewing, April 7, 1842, *Home Letters*, 19–20.
37. Merrill, *Sherman*, 53.
38. William Sherman to Ellen Ewing, February 8, 1844, *Home Letters*, 25.
39. *Ibid.*, April 7, 1842, 20.
40. Liddell Hart, *Sherman*, 15.
41. John G. Barrett, *Sherman's March Through the Carolinas* (Chapel Hill, 1956), 5.
42. Merrill, *Sherman*, 54.
43. William Sherman to John Sherman, May 23, 1843, *The Sherman Letters*, 23.
44. Merrill, *Sherman*, 55.
45. "The Prospects and Policy of the South, as They Appear to the Eyes of a Planter," *Southern Quarterly Review*, 26 (1854), 431–32.
46. Merrill, *Sherman*, 56.
47. William Sherman to John Sherman, January 4, 1846, *The Sherman Letters*, 29.
48. Merrill, *Sherman*, 56–57.

49. *Ibid.*, 57.
50. Sherman, *Memoirs*, I, 30–32.
51. Willis Fletcher Johnson, *Life of William Tecumseh Sherman, Late Retired General, U.S.A.* (Philadelphia, 1891), 34.
52. Sherman, *Memoirs*, I, 32.
53. Merrill, *Sherman*, 60; Sherman, *Memoirs*, II, 42.
54. William Sherman to John Sherman, January 4, 1846, *The Sherman Letters*, 29.
55. William Sherman to Ellen Ewing, February 8, 1844, *Home Letters*, 24.
56. Johnson, *Sherman*, 46.
57. Sherman, *Memoirs*, I, 168.
58. William Sherman to Ellen Ewing, September 17, 1844, *Home Letters*, 26.
59. Liddell Hart, *Sherman*, 20.
60. Sherman, *Memoirs*, I, 38.
61. Merrill, *Sherman*, 64.
62. Sherman, *Memoirs*, I, 39.
63. William Sherman to Ellen Ewing, June 30, 1846, *Home Letters*, 34.
64. Sherman, *Memoirs*, I, 41–45.
65. Lewis, *Fighting Prophet*, 76.
66. Liddell Hart, *Sherman*, 23.
67. William Sherman to Ellen Ewing, November 10, 1847, *Home Letters*, 109.
68. *Ibid.*, April 25, 1847, 102.
69. *Ibid.*, August 28, 1848, 116.
70. Sherman, *Memoirs*, I, 85.
71. Lewis, *Sherman*, 77.
72. *Ibid.*, 77–78.
73. William Sherman to Ellen Ewing, July 11, 1847, *Home Letters*, 107.
74. Merrill, *Sherman*, 69.
75. Sherman, *Memoirs*, I, 110.
76. Liddell Hart, *Sherman*, 22.
77. William Sherman to H. S. Turner, August 25, 1848, *The Sherman Letters*, 43–46.
78. Robert K. Merton, *Social Theory and Social Structure*, 2nd. ed. (New York, 1968), 230–46.
79. Bowman and Irwin, *Sherman and His Campaigns*, 19.

## CHAPTER TWO

1. Merrill, *Sherman*, 76.
2. *Ibid.*
3. Lewis, *Fighting Prophet*, 80.
4. Merrill, *Sherman*, 83.

5. *Ibid.*
6. *Ibid.*
7. *Ibid.*, 84.
8. *Ibid.*, 87.
9. *Ibid.*, 92.
10. Lewis, *Fighting Prophet*, 85–97.
11. Merrill, *Sherman*, 97.
12. *Ibid.*, 100.
13. *Ibid.*
14. *Ibid.*, 103.
15. William Sherman to Ellen Sherman, July 29, 1857, *Home Letters*, 148.
16. *Ibid.*, September 18, 1857, 151.
17. Merrill, *Sherman*, 122.
18. *Ibid.*, 123.
19. William Sherman to Ellen Sherman, July 29, 1857, *Home Letters*, 149.
20. Lewis, *Fighting Prophet*, 97.
21. Sherman, *Memoirs*, I, 148–61.
22. Liddell Hart, *Sherman*, 43.
23. William Sherman to John Sherman, April 30, 1859, *The Sherman Letters*, 70.
24. Liddell Hart, *Sherman*, 48–49.
25. William Sherman to Ellen Sherman, April 15, 1859, *Home Letters*, 159.
26. Don C. Buell to William Sherman, June 17, 1859, W. T. Fleming (ed.), *General W. T. Sherman as a College President* (Cleveland, 1912), 23.
27. Sherman, *Memoirs*, I, 172.
28. William Sherman to Ellen Sherman, February 10, 1860, *Home Letters*, 175.
29. January 5, 1861, *Ibid.*, 189.
30. George W. Pepper, *Personal Recollections of Sherman's Campaigns in Georgia and the Carolinas* (Zanesville, 1866), 514.
31. William Sherman to Minnie Sherman, January 22, 1860, Minnie Ewing Sherman, "My Father's Letters," *The Cosmopolitan*, vol. 12 (1891), 65.
32. David French Boyd, "General W. T. Sherman as a College President," *University Bulletin*, Louisiana State University (1910), vol. 1, no. 10, 2–3.
33. *Ibid.*, 1–4.
34. *Ibid.*, 1; Merrill, *Sherman*, 139.
35. Boyd, "Sherman as College President," 4.
36. T. Harry Williams, *McClellan, Sherman and Grant* (New Jersey, 1962), 50.
37. Boyd, "Sherman as College President," 2.
38. William Sherman to Ellen Sherman, February 13, 1860, *Home Letters*, 177.

39. *Ibid.*
40. Merrill, *Sherman*, 141.
41. *Ibid.*, 140.
42. William Sherman to G. Mason Graham, February 8, 1860, Fleming, *A College President*, 152.
43. Sherman, *Memoirs*, I, 176–77.
44. *Ibid.*
45. William Sherman to Thomas Ewing, Jr., December 23, 1859, Fleming, *A College President*, 89.
46. William Sherman to Ellen Sherman, October 29, 1859, *Home Letters*, 163.
47. *Ibid.*, December 12, 1859, 168.
48. William Sherman to John Sherman, January 16, 1861, *The Sherman Letters*, 105.
49. Merrill, *Sherman*, 149.
50. William Sherman to D. F. Boyd, September 16, 1860, Fleming, *A College President*, 280.
51. William Sherman to G. Mason Graham, January 5, 1861, *Ibid.*, 329.
52. Merrill, *Sherman*, 149.
53. Lewis, *Fighting Prophet*, 126–39.
54. Merrill, *Sherman*, 150.
55. William Sherman to G. Mason Graham, Fleming, *A College President*, 329.
56. William Sherman to Ellen Sherman, January 5, 1861, *Home Letters*, 189.
57. Bowman and Irwin, *Sherman and His Campaigns*, 22.
58. Sherman, *Memoirs*, I, 181.
59. David French Boyd, "General William T. Sherman as a College President," *The American College* (New York, 1909–10), II, 6–7.
60. Lewis, *Fighting Prophet*, 139.
61. William Sherman to G. Mason Graham, Christmas, 1860, Fleming, *A College President*, 319.
62. William Sherman to Ellen Sherman, February 1, 1861, *Ibid.*, 360.
63. William Sherman to Ellen Sherman, n.d., *Home Letters*, 188.
64. Sherman, *Memoirs*, 180–81; William Sherman to Thomas Ewing, Jr., December 23, 1859, Fleming, *A College President*, 89.
65. *Ibid.*
66. Sherman, *Memoirs*, I, 183.
67. Bowman and Irwin, *Sherman and His Campaigns*, 23.
68. Sherman, *Memoirs*, II, 504.
69. Boyd, "Sherman as College President," 7.
70. William Sherman to G. Mason Graham, January 16, 1861, Fleming, *A College President*, 339.

71. William Sherman to Minnie Sherman, December 15, 1860, "My Father's Letters," 65.

72. Earl S. Miers, *The General Who Marched to Hell: William Tecumseh Sherman and His March to Fame and Infamy* (New York, 1951), 4.

73. Liddell Hart, *Sherman*, 66.

74. Sherman, *Memoirs*, I, 194–95.

75. *Ibid.*, 194–96.

76. *Ibid.*, 195.

77. *Ibid.*, 196.

78. William Sherman to John Sherman, March, 1861, *The Sherman Letters*, 109.

79. Sherman, *Memoirs*, II, 382.

80. *Ibid.*

81. *Ibid.*, 195–96.

82. Liddell Hart, *Sherman*, 69–70.

83. William Sherman to Simon Cameron, May 8, 1861, *The Sherman Letters*, 118.

84. William Sherman to Ellen Sherman, January 8, 1861, *Home Letters*, 190.

85. Sherman, *Memoirs*, I, 199–200.

86. William Sherman to John Sherman, April 8, 1861, *The Sherman Letters*, 109.

87. Sherman, *Memoirs*, I, 199.

88. William Sherman to John Sherman, April 1861, *The Sherman Letters*, 111.

89. *Ibid.*, 111–12.

90. Bowman and Irwin, *Sherman and His Campaigns*; Miers, *Marched to Hell*; and Manning Ferguson Force, *General Sherman* (New York, 1899).

91. Lewis, *Fighting Prophet*.

92. John B. Walters, *Merchant of Terror: General Sherman and Total War* (New York, 1973).

93. *Ibid.*, 16.

94. Merrill, *Sherman*, 161.

95. *Ibid.*

96. Liddell Hart, *Sherman*, 71.

97. William Sherman to John Sherman, April 22, 1861, *The Sherman Letters*, 113–14.

98. Liddell Hart, *Sherman*, 73.

99. William Sherman to Thomas Ewing, Jr., June 3, 1861, *The Sherman Letters*, 198.

## CHAPTER THREE

1. Thorndike, *Home Letters*, 122.

2. Lewis, *Fighting Prophet*, 161.

3. *Ibid.*, 162.

4. Sherman, *Memoirs*, I, 206.

5. Lewis, *Fighting Prophet*, 166.

6. William Sherman to Ellen Sherman, July 16, 1861, *Home Letters*, 200–201.

7. William Sherman to Minnie Sherman, July 14, 1861, "My Father's Letters," 66.

8. Special Orders No. 81, October 14, 1861, *The War of the Rebellion, A Compilation of the Official Records of the Union and Confederate Armies*, 130 vols. (Washington, D.C., 1880–1901), ser. I, vol. II, 472–78; hereinafter cited as *OR*. Unless otherwise indicated, all citations are to series I.

9. Sherman, *Memoirs*, I, 207.

10. Lewis, *Sherman*, 171.

11. Merrill, *Sherman*, 165.

12. Report No. 25, July 25, 1861, *OR*, II, 368–71.

13. Richard Wheeler, *Sherman's March* (New York, 1978), 8.

14. Report No. 25, July 25, 1861, *OR*, II, 368–71.

15. Lewis, *Fighting Prophet*, 178.

16. Merrill, *Sherman*, 166.

17. William Sherman to Ellen Sherman, July 24, 1861, *Home Letters*, 209.

18. Johnson, *Life of William Tecumseh Sherman*, 87.

19. William Sherman to Ellen Sherman, July 24, 1861, *Home Letters*, 203.

20. Report No. 25, July 25, 1861, *OR*, II, 371.

21. Report No. 16, July 17, 1861, *Ibid.*, 351.

22. William Sherman to Ellen Sherman, July 28, 1861, *Home Letters*, 208.

23. Lewis, *Fighting Prophet*, 175.

24. Report No. 6, August 4, 1861, *OR*, II, 323.

25. Report No. 39, August 3, 1861, *Ibid.*, 398.

26. Sherman, *Memoirs*, 221.

27. William Sherman to Ellen Sherman, July 28, 1861, *Home Letters*, 209.

28. *Ibid.*

29. *Ibid.*, n.d., 214.

30. T. Harry Williams, "The Military Leadership of North and South," in David Donald (ed.), *Why the North Won the Civil War* (New York, 1960), 45.

31. Williams, *McClellan, Sherman and Grant*, 53.

32. William Sherman to Ellen Sherman, July 28, 1861, *Home Letters*, 210.

33. Liddell Hart, *Sherman*, 91.

34. *Ibid.*, 85.

35. William Sherman to John Sherman, August 19, 1861, *The Sherman Letters*, 127.

36. William Sherman to Ellen Sherman, August 3, 1861, *Home Letters*, 212.

37. *Ibid.*, August 17, 1861, 216.

38. *Ibid.*, August 3, 1861, 213.

39. General Orders No. 57, August 15, 1861, *OR*, IV, 254.

40. Sherman, *Memoirs*, I, 220–21.

41. Merrill, *Sherman*, 170.

42. William Sherman to Ellen Sherman, n.d., *Home Letters*, 219.

43. Sherman, *Memoirs*, I, 221.

44. Liddell Hart, *Sherman*, 97.

45. Lewis, *Fighting Prophet*, 182.

46. William Sherman to John Sherman, September 9, 1861, *The Sherman Letters*, 128.

47. *Ibid.*, October 5, 1861, 132–33.

48. Sherman, *Memoirs*, I, 227.

49. *Ibid.*

50. William Sherman to Garrett Davis, October 8, 1861, *OR*, IV, 297.

51. Lewis, *Sherman*, 191.

52. Sherman, *Memoirs*, I, 227; L. Thomas to S. Cameron, Sec. of War, October 21, 1861, *OR*, IV, 314.

53. W. T. Sherman to L. Thomas, October 22, 1861, *Ibid.*, 316.

54. Lewis, *Fighting Prophet*, 194–95. *See also* John F. Marszalek, *Sherman's Other War: The General and the Civil War Press* (Memphis, 1981), 58–62.

55. Chicago *Tribune*, November 5, 7, 1861.

56. R. E. Dupey and R. N. Dupey, *The Compact History of the Civil War* (New York, 1961), 66.

57. Thorndike, *The Sherman Letters*, 133.

58. Shelby Foote, *The Civil War, A Narrative*, 3 vols. (New York, 1958), I, 148.

59. Sherman, *Memoirs*, I, 243.

60. Stephen E. Ambrose, "William T. Sherman, A Personality Profile," *American History Illustrated*, January, 1967, 11. *See also* Cincinnati *Commercial*, November 9, 11, 16, 1861.

61. William Sherman to John Sherman, March 14, 1863, *The Sherman Letters*, 193.

62. Wheeler, *Sherman's March*, 9.

63. *Ibid.*, 9–10.

64. Sherman, *Memoirs*, I, 243–44.

65. Henry W. Halleck to George McClellan, December 2, 1861, *OR*, VII, Part 2, 198.

66. Cincinnati *Commercial*, December 11, 1861.

67. Sherman, *Memoirs*, I, 242–43.

68. Lewis, *Fighting Prophet*, 200.

69. *Ibid.*, 189.

70. Williams, *McClellan, Sherman and Grant*, 56; Walters, *Merchant of Terror*, 25–41; and, Paul E. Steiner, *Medical-Military Portraits of Union and Confederate Generals* (Philadelphia, 1968), 54–118.

71. Ambrose, "William T. Sherman, A Profile," 5–6; Otto Eisenschimel, "Sherman: Hero or War Criminal?" *Civil War Times Illustrated*, no. 2 (January 1964), 7–29.

72. Williams, *McClellan, Sherman and Grant*, 55.

73. Adam Badeau, *Military History of Ulysses S. Grant, from April, 1861, to April, 1865*, 3 vols. (New York, 1882), II, 19.

74. Williams, *McClellan, Sherman and Grant*, 49–50.

75. Badeau, *Military History of Grant*, II, 19.

76. Henry Stone, "The Atlanta Campaign," *Papers of the Military Historical Society of Massachusetts* (Boston, 1910), VII, 348.

77. E. Merton Coulter, "Sherman and the South," *The Georgia Historical Quarterly*, XV, no. 1 (1931), 29.

78. *Ibid.*

79. Erving Goffman, *The Presentation of Self in Everyday Life* (New York, 1959).

80. Liddell Hart, *Sherman*, 105.

81. Ambrose, "William T. Sherman, A Profile," 7.

## CHAPTER FOUR

1. Lewis, *Fighting Prophet*, 204

2. *Ibid.*, 200.

3. Special Orders No. 87, December 23, 1861, *OR*, VIII, 459.

4. Louisville *Journal*, December 17, 1861.

5. William Sherman to John Sherman, n.d., *The Sherman Letters*, 138.

6. Antoine-Henri Jomini, *The Art of War*, G. H. Mendell and W. P. Craighill (Westport, Connecticut, 1862), 29–35.

7. Carl von Clausewitz, *On War* (Princeton, 1976), 340.

8. Walter Millis, *Arms and Men: A Study in American Military History* (New York, 1956), 122, 124.

9. William Sherman to John Sherman, September 9, 1861, *The Sherman Letters*, 128.

10. Merrill, *Sherman*, 192.

11. General Orders No. 37, February 14, 1862, *OR*, VIII, 555.

12. Lewis, *Fighting Prophet*, 211.

13. Liddell Hart, *Sherman*, 118.

14. Lewis, *Fighting Prophet*, 211.

15. U. S. Grant, *Personal Memoirs of U. S. Grant*, 2 vols. (New York, 1892), I, 325–29.

16. Williams, *McClellan, Sherman and Grant*, 58.

17. Lewis, *Fighting Prophet*, 212.

18. L. P. Walker to J. P. Benjamin, February 17, 1862, *OR*, VII, 889.

19. Liddell Hart, *Sherman*, 72.

20. Sherman, *Memoirs*, I, 257.

21. W. P. Johnson, *Life of General Albert Sidney Johnston* (New York, 1878), 342.
22. Sherman, *Memoirs*, I, 257.
23. William Sherman to William McMichael, March 17, 1862, *OR*, X, Part 1, 25.
24. Merrill, *Sherman*, 195–96.
25. Lewis, *Fighting Prophet*, 214.
26. *Ibid.*
27. *Ibid.*; Stanley F. Horn, *The Army of Tennessee: A Military History* (New York, 1941), 124.
28. Addenda A, April 8, 1862, *OR*, X, Part 1, 396–97.
29. Lewis, *Fighting Prophet*, 217.
30. Wiley Sword, *Shiloh, Bloody April* (Dayton, 1983) Introduction to the Morningside Edition.
31. Liddell Hart, *Sherman*, 126.
32. Sword, *Bloody April*, 433.
33. Lewis, *Fighting Prophet*, 223.
34. Jacob Cox, *Atlanta* (New York, 1882), 21.
35. Sword, *Bloody April*, 189.
36. *Ibid.*, 209.
37. *Ibid.*, 211.
38. William Sherman to Ellen Sherman, April 11, 1862, *Home Letters*, 220.
39. Grant, *Memoirs*, I, 343.
40. U. S. Grant to N. H. McLean, April 9, 1862, *OR*, X, Part 1, 110.
41. Bowman and Irwin, *Sherman and His Campaigns*, 70.
42. H. W. Halleck to E. M. Stanton, April 13, 1862, *OR*, X, Part 1, 98.
43. Bowman and Irwin, *Sherman*, 59.
44. A. D. Richardson, *The Secret Service: the Field, the Dungeon and the Escape* (Hartford, 1866), 248.
45. Cincinnati *Commercial*, April 1862.
46. C. E. Macartney, *Grant and His Generals* (New York, 1953), 292.
47. Badeau, *Military History of Grant*, II, 22.
48. Macartney, *Grant and His Generals*, 292.
49. Oliver Otis Howard, *Autobiography of Oliver Otis Howard, Major General United States Army*, 2 vols. (New York, 1907), I, 474–76.
50. Macartney, *Grant and His Generals*, 292.
51. Sherman, *Memoirs*, I, 225.
52. Williams, *McClellan, Sherman and Grant*, 58–59.
53. *Ibid.*
54. Macartney, *Grant and His Generals*, 282.
55. *Ibid.*, 294.
56. William Sherman to John Sherman, January 22, 1865, *The Sherman Letters*, 245.

57. William Sherman to Ellen Sherman, April 11, 1862, *Home Letters*, 222.

58. Lewis, *Fighting Prophet*, 232.

59. William Sherman to Ellen Sherman, June 6, 1862, *Home Letters*, 226–27.

60. *Ibid.*, April 24, 1862, 225.

61. William Sherman to Thomas Ewing, April 27, 1862, *Home Letters*, 225–26.

62. William Sherman to Ellen Sherman, June 6, 1862, *Home Letters*, 227.

63. *Ibid.*, 228–29.

64. Sherman, *Memoirs*, I, 297–98.

65. William Sherman to Ellen Sherman, April 11, 1862, *Home Letters*, 222.

66. Lewis, *Fighting Prophet*, 238.

67. William Sherman to John Sherman, May 12, 1862, *The Sherman Letters*, 148–49.

68. William Sherman to Ellen Sherman, August 3, 1861, *Home Letters*, 211.

69. Lewis, *Sherman*, 238.

70. General Orders No. 65, April 10, 1862, *OR*, X, Part 1, 251.

71. *Ibid.*, 252.

72. Lewis, *Fighting Prophet*, 238.

73. Sherman, *Memoirs*, I, 282.

74. *Ibid.*, 227.

75. William Sherman to Ellen Sherman, May 26, 1862, *Home Letters*, 226.

76. William Sherman to Thomas Ewing, April 24, 1862, *Ibid.*, 226.

## CHAPTER FIVE

1. Henry W. Halleck to William Sherman, July 16, 1862, *OR*, XVII, Part 2, 100.

2. *Ibid.*, 100–101.

3. Barrett, *Sherman's March Through the Carolinas*, 14–15.

4. Sherman, *Memoirs*, I, 293.

5. Merrill, *Sherman*, 205; Sherman, *Memoirs*, I, 293–95.

6. *Ibid.*, 293, 298–99.

7. General Orders No. 90, October 25, 1862, *OR*, XVIII, Part 2, 294–96.

8. Merrill, *Sherman*, 205.

9. Lewis, *Fighting Prophet*, 244.

10. Merrill, *Sherman*, 206.

11. William Sherman to John Sherman, September 22, 1862, *The Sherman Letters*, 162.

12. Sherman, *Memoirs*, I, 293.

13. *Ibid.*, 293–94.

14. Wheeler, *Sherman's March*, 13.

15. William Sherman to John Sherman, September 3, 1862, *The Sherman Letters*, 161.

16. Bowman and Irwin, *Sherman and His Campaigns*, 74–75.

17. Sherman, *Memoirs*, I, 295.

18. *Ibid.*, 294.

19. *Ibid.*, 294–96.

20. Lewis, *Fighting Prophet*, 247.

21. *Ibid.*

22. Merrill, *Sherman*, 206.

23. Special Orders No. 254, September 27, 1862, *OR*, XVII, Part 2, 240.

24. Merrill, *Sherman*, 207.

25. William Sherman to Col. C. C. Walcutt, September 24, 1862, *OR*, XVII, Part 2, 235–36.

26. Liddell Hart, *Sherman*, 146.

27. William Sherman to U. S. Grant, October 4, 1862, *OR*, XVII, Part 2, 261–62.

28. William Sherman to John Rawlins, October 18, 1862, *Ibid.*, 279–80.

29. Sherman, *Memoirs*, I, 294.

30. Walters, *Merchant of Terror*, 64.

31. William Sherman to U. S. Grant, October 4, 1862, *OR*, XVII, Part 2, 261.

32. William Sherman to P. A. Fraser, October 22, 1862, *Ibid.*, 287–88.

33. William Sherman to John Sherman, September 22, 1862, *The Sherman Letters*, 162–63.

34. *Ibid.*, October 1, 1862, 166.

35. Jomini, *The Art of War*, 72–74.

36. William Sherman to John Sherman, October 1, 1862, *The Sherman Papers*, 166.

37. William Sherman to Ellen Sherman, July 31, 1862, *Home Letters*, 230.

38. Walters, *Merchant of Terror*.

39. *Ibid.*, 65.

40. Sherman, *Memoirs*, I, 306.

41. William Sherman to Minnie Sherman, August 16, 1862, "My Father's Letters," 67.

42. William Sherman to U. S. Grant, October 4, 1862, *OR*, XVII, Part 2, 260.

43. Liddell Hart, *Sherman*, 151.

44. Sherman, *Memoirs*, II, 126.

45. Barrett, *Sherman's March Through the Carolinas*, 16.

46. William Sherman to H. W. Halleck, September 4, 1863, *OR*, XXXVIII, Part 5, 794.

47. Walters, *Merchant of Terror*, 58–63.

48. *Ibid.*, 67–83.

49. For an excellent discussion of the need to destroy the will of the South, see Richard E. Beringer, Herman Hattaway, Archer Jones, and William N. Still, Jr., *Why the South Lost the Civil War* (Athens, 1986).

50. William Sherman to John Rawlins, October 18, 1862, *OR*, XVII, Part 2, 279–80.

51. Special Orders No. 283, October 18, 1862, *OR*, XVII, Part 2, 280–81.

52. Walters, *Merchant of Terror*, 69.

53. *Ibid.*, 74.

54. *Ibid.*, 71.

55. *Ibid.*, 82.

56. Lewis, *Fighting Prophet*, 248–49.

57. Sherman, *Memoirs*, II, 184.

58. William Sherman to Ellen Sherman, August 10, 1862, *Home Letters*, 231.

## CHAPTER SIX

1. Sherman, *Memoirs*, I, 307.

2. Lewis, *Fighting Prophet*, 252.

3. Williams, *McClellan, Sherman and Grant*, 64.

4. Lewis, *Fighting Prophet*, 252.

5. Williams, *McClellan, Sherman and Grant*, 65.

6. *Ibid.*

7. *Ibid.*

8. Lewis, *Fighting Prophet*, 252.

9. William Sherman to U. S. Grant, October 4, 1862, *OR*, XVII, Part 2, 260–61.

10. Edwin Cole Bearss, *The Campaign for Vicksburg*, 3 vols. (Dayton, 1985), I, 24.

11. Merrill, *Sherman*, 231.

12. *Ibid.*

13. Richard Goldhurst, *Many Are the Hearts: The Agony and Triumph of Ulysses S. Grant* (New York, 1975), 132.

14. *Ibid.*, 134.

15. *Ibid.*

16. Wheeler, *Sherman's March*, 13.

17. Merrill, *Sherman*, 231.

18. William Sherman to John Sherman, January 6, 1863, *The Sherman Letters*, 180.

19. Sherman, *Memoirs*, I, 342.

20. Order No. 1, U. S. Grant to William Sherman, December 8, 1862, *OR*, XVII, Part 1, 601.

21. Sherman, *Memoirs*, I, 313.

22. Headquarters, Right Wing, Thirteenth Army Corps., December 23, 1862, *OR*, XVII, Part 1, 616–17.

23. Jomini, *The Art of War*, 75.

24. Lewis, *Fighting Prophet*, 254.

25. David Porter, *Incidents and Anecdotes of the Civil War* (New York, 1886), 129.

26. Merrill, *Sherman*, 216.

27. George W. Morgan, "The Assault on Chickasaw Bluffs," in Robert Underwood Johnson and Clarence Clough Buel (eds.), *Battles and Leaders of the Civil War*, 4 vols. (New York, 1884), III, 468.

28. Sherman, *Memoirs*, I, 320.

29. Porter, *Incidents and Anecdotes*, 129.

30. Bearss, *Campaign for Vicksburg*, I, 26.

31. Merrill, *Sherman*, 212.

32. Lewis, *Fighting Prophet*, 255, 260.

33. Porter, *Incidents and Anecdotes*, 130.

34. Sherman, *Memoirs*, I, 321–22.

35. Official Report of W. T. Sherman, January 4, 1863, *OR*, XVII, Part 1, 612.

36. Liddell Hart, *Sherman*, 266.

37. William Sherman to Ellen Sherman, January 4, 1863, *Home Letters*, 235.

38. William Sherman to John Sherman, January 17, 1863, *The Sherman Letters*, 182.

39. Liddell Hart, *Sherman*, 165.

40. William Sherman to Ellen Sherman, January 28, 1863, *Home Letters*, 237.

41. Liddell Hart, *Sherman*, 166; Sherman, *Memoirs*, I, 324–25.

42. William Sherman to John Sherman, January 25, 1863, *The Sherman Letters*, 183.

43. Thomas L. Snead, "The Conquest of Arkansas," *Battles and Leaders*, III, 452–53.

44. Merrill, *Sherman*, 218.

45. U. S. Grant to John McClernand, January 11, 1863, *OR*, XVII, Part 2, 553; Liddell Hart, *Sherman*, 169–70.

46. Lewis, *Fighting Prophet*, 262.

47. *Ibid.*, 264.

48. William Sherman to Ellen Sherman, January 28, 1863, *Home Letters*, 238–39.

49. Merrill, *Sherman*, 222. *See also* Marszalek, *Sherman's Other War*, 127–49.

50. U. S. Grant to Thomas Knox, April 6, 1863, *OR*, XVII, 894–95.

51. William Sherman to Thomas Knox, April 7, 1863, *OR*, XVII, 894–95.

52. William Sherman to Ellen Sherman, February 26, 1863, *Home Letters*, 239–40.

53. *Ibid.*, May 9, 1863, 260.
54. Merrill, *Sherman*, 223.
55. *Ibid.*, 223–24.
56. Lewis, *Fighting Prophet*, 271–72.
57. William Sherman to Ellen Sherman, April 23, 1863, *Home Letters*, 254.
58. Grant, *Memoirs*, I, 470.
59. William Sherman to U. S. Grant, April 28, 1863, *OR*, XXIV, Part 3, 242–43.
60. Lewis, *Fighting Prophet*, 272; Sherman, *Memoirs*, 347.
61. U. S. Grant to William Sherman, May 4, 1863, *OR*, XXXVIII, Part 1, 285.
62. Lewis, *Fighting Prophet*, 273–74.
63. Samuel Carter, III, *The Final Fortress: The Campaign for Vicksburg, 1862–1863* (Wilmington, 1988).
64. Official Report No. 2, May 24, 1863, *OR*, XXIV, Part 1, 754.
65. Charles A. Dana, *Recollections of the Civil War with the Leaders at Washington and in the Field in the Sixties* (New York, 1898), 53.
66. William Sherman to Ellen Sherman, May 6, 1863, *Home Letters*, 260.
67. *Ibid.*, April 10, 1863, 249.
68. William Sherman to Frederick Steele, April 19, 1863, *OR*, XXIV, Part 3, 209.
69. William Sherman to Ellen Sherman, June 27, 1863, *Home Letters*, 268–69.
70. W. T. Sherman, "A Reminiscence of the War," in Thomas B. Reed (ed.) *Modern Eloquence* (Philadelphia, 1900), 1055.
71. William Sherman to Ellen Sherman, June 11, 1863, June 27, 1863, *Home Letters*, 267, 269.
72. Sherman, *Memoirs*, I, 360.
73. William Sherman to John Sherman, July 19, 1863, *The Sherman Letters*, 208.
74. *Ibid.*, August 3, 1863, 213.
75. Liddell Hart, *Sherman*, 196.
76. U. S. Grant to William Sherman, July 13, 1863, *OR*, XXIV, Part 3, 507.
77. Walters, *Merchant of Terror*, 89.
78. William Sherman to U. S. Grant, July 14, 1863, *OR*, XXIV, Part 2, 526.
79. William Sherman to John A. Rawlins, July 28, 1863, *OR*, XXIV, Part 2, 536.
80. William Sherman to David Porter, July 19, 1863, *Ibid.*, Part 3, 531.
81. The New York *World*, August 14, 1863.
82. Edgar L. Erickson (ed.), "With Grant at Vicksburg. From the Civil War Diary of Charles E. Wilcox," *Journal of the Illinois State Historical Society*, vol. XXX (April 1937-January 1938), 501.
83. Merrill, *Sherman*, 231.

84. William Sherman to U. S. Grant, July 18, 1863, *OR*, XXIV, Part 2, 529.

85. Bell Irvin Wiley, *The Life of Johnny Reb, The Common Soldier of the Confederacy* (Indianapolis, 1943), 135.

86. Joseph Johnston to Jefferson Davis, July 11, 1863, *OR*, XXIV, Part 1, 200.

87. *Ibid.*, July 23, 1863, 209.

88. Joseph Johnston to J. A. Seddon, November 1, 1863, *Ibid.*, 246.

89. Johnson, *Sherman*, 248.

90. Dana, *Recollections*, 57–58.

91. John Sherman to William Sherman, July 18, 1863, *The Sherman Letters*, 207.

92. Sherman, *Memoirs*, II, 397.

93. Lewis, *Fighting Prophet*, 275.

94. William Sherman to Ellen Sherman, February 22, 1863, *Home Letters*, 239.

95. Liddell Hart, *Sherman*, 202.

96. *Ibid.*

97. William Sherman to W. H. Halleck, September 17, 1863, *OR*, XXX, Part 3, 698.

98. *Ibid.*, 699.

99. William Sherman to John Sherman, August 3, 1863, *The Sherman Letters*, 211.

100. Lewis, *Fighting Prophet*, 296.

101. Jomini, *The Art of War*, 33.

102. Clausewitz, *On War*, 573.

103. Sherman, *Memoirs*, I, 362.

104. *Ibid.*

105. William Sherman to H. W. Halleck, September 7, 1863, *OR*, XXX, Part 3, 695, 697.

106. Sherman, *Memoirs*, I, 371.

107. Lewis, *Fighting Prophet*, 312.

108. Sherman, *Memoirs*, I, 363–66.

109. Wheeler, *Sherman's March*, 14.

110. Sherman, *Memoirs*, I, 373.

111. William Sherman to Ellen Sherman, October 10, 1863, *Home Letters*, 276.

112. Sherman, *Memoirs*, I, 377.

## CHAPTER SEVEN

1. William Sherman to Ellen Sherman, October 24, 1863, *Home Letters*, 280.

2. William Sherman to John Sherman, December 30, 1863, *The Sherman Letters*, 220.

3. Grant, *Memoirs*, II, 52–54.

4. Merrill, *Sherman*, 237.

5. Bowman and Irwin, *Sherman and His Campaigns*, 146.

6. Merrill, *Sherman*, 237.

7. Wheeler, *We Knew William Tecumseh Sherman* (New York, 1977) 59.

8. William Sherman to John Sherman, December 29, 1863, *The Sherman Letters*, 217.

9. U. S. Grant to William Sherman, November 25, 1863, *OR*, XXXI, Part 2, 45.

10. Liddell Hart, *Sherman*, 218–22.

11. William Sherman to John A. Logan, December 21, 1863, *OR*, XXXI, Part 3, 459.

12. M. R. Bearss, *Sherman's Forgotten Campaign, The Meridian Expedition* (Baltimore, 1987), 5.

13. Robert C. Black, III, *The Railroads of the Confederacy* (Chapel Hill, 1952), 240.

14. Walters, *Merchant of Terror*, 87–127.

15. Bearss, *Sherman's Forgotten Campaign*, 9.

16. William Sherman to Ellen Sherman, October 6, 1863, *Home Letters*, 275.

17. C. Wright Mills, *The Sociological Imagination* (London, 1959), 130–31.

18. William Sherman to Ellen Sherman, January 28, 1863, *Home Letters*, 283.

19. Merrill, *Sherman*, 241.

20. Liddell Hart, *Sherman*, 225.

21. Special Field Orders No. 11, January 27, 1864, *OR*, XXXII, Part 1, 182.

22. Sherman, *Memoirs*, I, 419–21.

23. Stephen D. Lee, "Sherman's Meridian Expedition and Sooy Smith's Raid to West Point," *Southern Historical Society Papers*, vol. VIII (January to December 1880), Richmond, Virginia, no. 2, 54–58.

24. Johnson, *Sherman*, 288.

25. Wirt Armistead Cate (ed.) *Two Soldiers, The Campaign Diaries of Thomas J. Key, C.S.A., and Robert J. Campbell, U.S.A.* (Chapel Hill, 1936), 235.

26. Report of Captain Andrew Hickenlooper of Expedition to Meridian, March 25, 1864, *OR*, XXXII, Part 1, 216.

27. Sherman, *Memoirs*, I, 420.

28. Bearss, *Sherman's Forgotten Campaign*, 165.

29. Report of M. M. Crocker, March 6, 1864, *OR*, XXXII, Part 1, 238.

30. Report of W. T. Sherman to John Rawlins, March 7, 1864, *Ibid.*, 176.

31. Walters, *Merchant of Terror*, 116.

32. Sherman, *Memoirs*, I, 420.

33. Report of James C. Veatch, March 4, 1864, *OR*, XXXII, Part 1, 204.

34. Report of J. M. Rusk, March 4, 1864, *Ibid.*, 206.

35. Bearss, *Sherman's Forgotten Campaign*, 173.
36. William Sherman to John A. Rawlins, March 7, 1864, *OR*, XXXII, Part 1, 176.
37. Bearss, *Sherman's Forgotten Campaign*, 190.
38. Lucius Barber, *15th Illinois Diary* (Chicago, 1894), 138.
39. Merrill, *Sherman*, 242.
40. William Sherman to John A. Rawlins, March 7, 1864, *OR*, XXXII, Part 1, 177.
41. Bearss, *Sherman's Forgotten Campaign*, 239–40.
42. Lee, "Sherman's Meridian Expedition," 55.
43. Sherman, *Memoirs*, I, 422.
44. The New York *Times*, March 27, 1864.
45. The New York *World*, March 14, 1864: The New York *Herald*, March 15, 1864.
46. Mobile *Daily Tribune*, March 5, 1864.
47. Canton *American Citizen*, April 4, 1864.
48. William Pitt Chambers, *Publications of the Mississippi Historical Society*, vol. V (1925), 303.
49. William Sherman to R. M. Sawyer, January 31, 1864, *The Sherman Letters*, 229.
50. *Ibid.*, 230.
51. *Ibid.*
52. *Ibid.*
53. Walters, *Merchant of Terror*, 119.
54. William Sherman to W. S. Smith, January 27, 1864, *OR*, XXXII, Part 1, 181.
55. William Sherman to H. W. Halleck, January 27, 1864, *OR*, XXXII, Part 2, 260.
56. Official Report of William Sherman, March 7, 1864, *OR*, XXXII, Part 1, 176–77.
57. Lewis, *Fighting Prophet*, 336.
58. *Ibid.*
59. Wheeler, *Sherman's March*, 15.
60. Merrill, *Sherman*, 243.
61. Beringer, et al., *Why the South Lost*, 309.
62. *Ibid.*, 309–10.
63. Herman Hattaway and Archer Jones, *How the North Won: A Military History of the Civil War* (Athens, 1983), 506.
64. *Ibid.*
65. General Orders, No. 98, March 12, 1864, *OR*, XXXII, Part 3, 58.
66. Sherman, *Memoirs*, I, 427.
67. *Ibid.*, 427–28.
68. Cox, *Atlanta*, 21.

69. William Sherman to H. W. Halleck, April 2, 1864, *OR*, XXXII, Part 3, 222.

70. Lewis, *Fighting Prophet*, 345.

71. Grant, *Memoirs*, II, 118–19.

72. Lewis, *Fighting Prophet*, 345.

73. *Ibid.*

74. Bowman and Irwin, *Sherman and His Campaigns*, 168.

## CHAPTER EIGHT

1. Williams, *McClellan, Sherman and Grant*, 67, 68.

2. Richard McMurry, *Two Great Rebel Armies: An Essay in Confederate Military History* (Chapel Hill, 1989), 34.

3. Omar N. Bradley, *A General's Life* (New York, 1983), 53–54.

4. Miers, *Marched to Hell*, 44; The original article is W. F. G. Shanks, "Recollections of General Thomas," vol. XXX, *Harper's Magazine*, 754–59.

5. Samuel Carter, III, *The Seige of Atlanta*, 1864 (New York, 1973), 99.

6. *Ibid.*, 98–99.

7. William Key, *The Battle of Atlanta and the Georgia Campaign* (New York, 1958), 14.

8. Carter, *The Seige of Atlanta*, 26.

9. Beringer, et al., *Why the South Lost*, 335.

10. Liddell Hart, *Sherman*, 233.

11. Carter, *The Seige of Atlanta*, 16.

12. *Ibid.*

13. Liddell Hart, *Sherman*, 233–34.

14. U. S. Grant to William Sherman, April 4, 1864, *OR*, XXXII, Part 3, 246.

15. William Sherman to U. S. Grant, April 10, 1864, *Ibid.*, 313.

16. Liddell Hart, *Sherman*, 232.

17. Barrett, *March Through Carolinas*, 118–19.

18. Lewis, *Fighting Prophet*, 345.

19. Pepper, *Recollections*, 44.

20. F. Y. Hedley, *Marching Through Georgia, Pen-Pictures of Every-Day Life* (Chicago, 1884), 99; Sherman, *Memoirs*, II, 10.

21. *Ibid.*, 11.

22. Merrill, *Sherman*, 246.

23. Lewis, *Fighting Prophet*, 351.

24. Merrill, *Sherman*, 245.

25. Sherman, *Memoirs*, II, 10.

26. Carter, *The Seige of Atlanta*, 106. *See also* Lemuel Moss, *Annals of the United States Christian Commission* (Philadelphia, 1868), 496.

27. Lewis, *Fighting Prophet*, 351.

28. William Sherman to Ellen Sherman, January 28, 1864, *Home Letters*, 283.

29. Sherman, *Memoirs*, II, 31.

30. Merrill, *Sherman*, 247.

31. *Ibid.*, 246.

32. Lewis, *Fighting Prophet*, 353–54.

33. Liddell Hart, *Sherman*, 236.

34. Dana, *Recollections*, 167.

35. William Sherman to C. B. Cormstock, April 5, 1864, *OR*, XXXII, Part 3, 242.

36. Hedley, *Marching Through Georgia*, 79, 83.

37. James Connolly to his wife, May 6, 1864, "Major Connolly's Letters to His Wife," *Transactions of the Illinois State Historical Society for the Year 1928* (Springfield, 1928), 329.

38. Wheeler, *We Knew Sherman*, 67.

39. Horn, *The Army of Tennessee*, 323.

40. Alfred H. Burne, *Lee, Grant and Sherman* (New York, 1939), 78–81.

41. J. M. Schofield, *Forty-Six Years in the Army* (New York, 1897), 126.

42. H. V. Boynton, *Sherman's Historical Raid* (Cincinnati, 1875), 96.

43. Horn, *The Army of Tennessee*, 325–26.

44. Joseph Eggleston Johnston, *Narrative of Military Operations, Directed, During the Late War Between the States, by Joseph E. Johnston, C.S.A.* (New York, 1874), 317.

45. Barrett, *March Through the Carolinas*, 18. *See also* Andrew Boies, *Record of the Thirty-Third Massachusetts Volunteer Infantry from August 1862-August 1865* (Fitchburg, 1880), 118.

46. Sherman, *Memoirs*, II, 36.

47. Wheeler, *We Knew Sherman*, 67–68.

48. Cox, *Atlanta*, 61.

49. William W. Calkins, *The History of the One Hundred and Fourth Regiment of Illinois Volunteer Infantry. War of the Rebellion* (Cincinnati, 1865), 284.

50. Sherman, *Memoirs*, II, 46.

51. Horn, *The Army of Tennessee*, 329.

52. Key, *The Battle of Atlanta*, 27.

53. De Bow Randolph Keim, *Sherman: A Memorial in Art, Oratory, and Literature by the Society of the Army of the Tennessee, with the aid of the Congress of the United States of America* (Washington, D.C., Government Printing Office, 1904), 265–66.

54. Horn, *The Army of Tennessee*, 331.

55. Sherman, *Memoirs*, II, 42.

56. William Sherman to John Sherman, June 9, 1864, *The Sherman Letters*, 236.

57. Report of W. T. Sherman, September 15, 1864, *OR*, XXXVIII, Part 1, 68.
58. Key, *The Battle of Atlanta*, 30–31.
59. Carter, *The Seige of Atlanta*, 155.
60. Bowman and Irwin, *Sherman and His Campaigns*, 202.
61. Johnston, *Narrative*, 343.
62. O. O. Howard, "The Struggle for Atlanta," *Battles and Leaders*, IV, 311.
63. W. T. Sherman, "The Grand Strategy of the Last Year of the War," *Ibid.*, 252.
64. Boynton, *Sherman's Historical Raid*, 107. *See also* J. F. C. Fuller, *The Generalship of Ulysses S. Grant* (Bloomington, 1977), 313–15.
65. Liddell Hart, *Sherman*, 267.
66. Burne, *Lee, Grant and Sherman*, 95.
67. Horn, *The Army of Tennessee*, 337.
68. Barrett, *March Through the Carolinas*, 18.
69. Columbia *Phoenix*, May 2, 1865.
70. Sherman, *Memoirs*, II, 65.
71. William Sherman to Ellen Sherman, June 26, 1864, *Home Letters*, 298.
72. Burne, *Lee, Grant and Sherman*, 95.
73. Horn, *The Army of Tennessee*, 367.
74. Sherman, "The Grand Strategy," *Battles and Leaders*, IV, 253.
75. Carter, *The Seige of Atlanta*, 193.
76. Sherman, *Memoirs*, II, 75.
77. Burne, *Lee, Grant and Sherman*, 101.
78. Carter, *The Seige of Atlanta*, 194.
79. Sherman, *Memoirs*, II, 75.
80. William Sherman to Ellen Sherman, July 29, 1864, *Home Letters*, 304.
81. *Ibid.*, August 2, 1864, 306.
82. William Sherman to J. M. Schofield, August 1, 1864, *OR*, XXXVIII, Part 5, 324.
83. William Sherman to George H. Thomas, August 7, 1864, *Ibid.*, 412.
84. William Sherman to Henry W. Halleck, August 7, 1864, *Ibid.*, 409.
85. Mary Gay, *Life in Dixie During the War* (Atlanta, 1897), 122.
86. Noble C. Williams, *Echoes from the Battlefield; or, Southern Life During the War* (Atlanta, 1902), 32–33.
87. Key, *The Battle of Atlanta*, 68–69.
88. William Sherman to Henry W. Halleck, September 3, 1864, *OR*, XXVIII, Part 5, 777.
89. Key, *The Battle of Atlanta*, 76.
90. David P. Conyngham, *Sherman's March Through the South with Sketches and Incidents of the Campaign* (New York, 1865), 213.
91. Lewis, *Fighting Prophet*, 420.

92. Sherman, *Memoirs*, II, 113.

93. *Ibid.*, 110

94. *Ibid.*

95. William Sherman to J. M. Schofield, October 17, 1864, *OR*, XXXIX, Part 3, 335.

96. Stephen Pierson, "From Chattanooga to Atlanta in 1864—A Personal Reminiscence," New Jersey Historical Society, *Proceedings* 16 (1931), 324–56.

## CHAPTER NINE

1. Merrill, *Sherman*, 256.

2. David P. Conyngham, *March Through the South*, 218.

3. Walters, *Merchant of Terror*, 129.

4. Wallace Reed, *History of Atlanta, Georgia* (Syracuse, 1889), 173–99.

5. Carter, *The Seige of Atlanta*, 329. *See also* Conyngham, *March Through the South*, 216.

6. Liddell Hart, *Sherman*, 312.

7. Mark Antony DeWolfe Howe (ed.), *Marching with Sherman, Passages from the Letters and Campaign Diaries of Henry Hitchcock, Major and Assistant Adjutant General of Volunteers, November 1864-May 1865* (New Haven, 1927), 34–35.

8. *Ibid.*, 22.

9. Henry C. Lay, "Sherman in Georgia," *Atlantic*, no. 141 (1932), 149.

10. Liddell Hart, *Sherman*, 311–12.

11. Sherman, *Memoirs*, II, 111.

12. Johnson, *Sherman*, 349.

13. William Sherman to Henry W. Halleck, September 4, 1864, *OR*, XXXVIII, Part 5, 794.

14. Russell F. Weigley, *The American Way of War: A History of United States Military Strategy and Policy* (Bloomington, 1973), 138.

15. Abraham Lincoln to Reverdy Johnson, July 26, 1862, Roy P. Basler (ed.), *The Collected Works of Abraham Lincoln*, 9 vols. (New Brunswick, 1953), V, 342–43.

16. General Orders No. 7 by command of Pope, July 10, 1862, *OR*, XII, Part 2, 51; General Orders No. 18 by command of Pope, August 6, 1862, *OR*, XII, Part 2, 52.

17. Sherman, *Memoirs*, II, 128.

18. Grant, *Memoirs*, I, 368–69.

19. *Ibid.*, 507.

20. Grant to Sheridan, August 26, 1864, *OR*, XLIII, Part 1, 917.

21. Sherman, *Memoirs*, II, 145.

22. Bowman and Irwin, *Sherman and His Campaigns*, 221.

23. Sherman, *Memoirs*, II, 111–12.

24. Barrett, *Marching Through the Carolinas*, 20.
25. Montgomery *Daily Advertiser*, September 15, 1864.
26. Mobile *Daily Advertiser and Registar*, September 15, 1864.
27. Gay, *Life in Dixie*, 137.
28. Walters, *Merchant of Terror*, 131.
29. Sherman, *Memoirs*, II, 118.
30. *Ibid.*, II, 119.
31. *Ibid.*, 120–21, 128.
32. Lewis, *Fighting Prophet*, 418.
33. Lay, "Sherman in Georgia," 152.
34. James M. Calhoun, E. E. Rawson, and S. C. Wells to William Sherman, September 11, 1864, Sherman, *Memoirs*, II, 124–25.
35. William Sherman to James M. Calhoun, E. E. Rawson, and S. C. Wells, September 12, 1864, *Ibid.*, 125–27.
36. Liddell Hart, *Sherman*, 324.
37. Horace Porter, *Campaigning With Grant* (Secaucus, New Jersey, 1897), 292.
38. Liddell Hart, *Sherman*, 313.
39. Porter, *Campaigning With Grant*, 293.
40. Foote, *Civil War Narrative*, III, 603.
41. Lewis, *Fighting Prophet*, 414.
42. Burne, *Lee, Grant and Sherman*, 125.
43. Horn, *The Army of Tennessee*, 367.
44. E. M. Clauss, "Sherman's Failure at Atlanta," *The Georgia Historical Quarterly*, vol. 53, no. 3, 321.
45. Bruce Catton, *Never Call Retreat* (New York, 1965), 387.
46. U. S. Grant, "Preparing for the Campaigns of '64," *Battles and Leaders*, IV, 99.
47. Clauss, "Failure at Atlanta," 327.
48. Albert Castel, "The Life of a Rising Son, Part III: The Conqueror," *Civil War Times Illustrated* (October, 1979), 15.
49. Clauss, "Failure at Atlanta," 329.
50. Lewis, *Fighting Prophet*, 424.
51. William Sherman to Abraham Lincoln, September 28, 1864, *OR*, XXXIX, Part 2, 501.
52. Sherman, *Memoirs*, II, 145.
53. U. S. Grant to William Sherman, September 12, 1864, *OR*, XXXIX, Part 2, 364–65.
54. William Sherman to U. S. Grant, September 20, 1864, *Ibid.*, 412–13.
55. October 11, 1864, Part 3, *Ibid.*, 202.
56. October 9, 1864, *Ibid.*, 162.
57. U. S. Grant to William Sherman, November 2, 1864, *Ibid.*, 595.
58. William Sherman to U. S. Grant, November 6, 1864, *Ibid.*, 660.

59. Merrill, *Sherman*, 265–66.

60. *Ibid.*

61. *Ibid.*

62. Weigley, *American Way of War*, 150.

63. Thomas L. Connelly and Barbara L. Bellows, *God and General Longstreet, The Lost Cause and the Southern Mind* (Baton Rouge, 1982), 86.

64. *Ibid.*, 88.

65. *Ibid.*, 100.

66. *Ibid.*, 101.

67. *Ibid.*, 103.

68. *Ibid.*, 105.

69. *The Random House Dictionary of the English Language* (New York, 1966).

70. Connelly and Bellows, *God and Longstreet*, 105.

71. Carter, *The Seige of Atlanta*, 342.

72. Wheeler, *Sherman's March*, 49–50.

73. Porter, *Campaigning With Grant*, 313.

74. Bell Irvin Wiley, *The Road to Appomattox* (Memphis, 1956), 40.

75. Sherman, *Memoirs*, II, 159.

76. Hedley, *Marching Through Georgia*, 245.

77. Special Field Orders No. 119, November 8, 1864, *OR*, XXXIX, Part 3, 701.

78. Special Field Orders No. 120, November 9, 1864, *Ibid.*, 713–14.

79. Lewis, *Fighting Prophet*, 432.

80. William Sherman to Ellen Sherman, October 19, 1864, *Home Letters*, 312.

81. Key, *The Battle of Atlanta*, 82.

82. Carter, *The Seige of Atlanta*, 358.

83. Sherman, *Memoirs*, II, 177.

84. Carter, *The Seige of Atlanta*, 358.

85. Conyngham, *March Through the South*, 237–38.

86. George Ward Nichols, *The Story of the Great March From the Diary of a Staff Officer* (New York, 1865), 38.

87. Pepper, *Personal Recollections*, 239.

88. Carter, *The Seige of Atlanta*, 361.

89. J. M. Spaight, *War Rights on Land* (London, 1911), 307–8.

90. The Columbus *Times*, December 23, 1864.

91. The Canton *American Citizen*, December 26, 1864.

92. William Sherman to U. S. Grant, November 6, 1864, *OR*, XXXIX, Part 3, 660.

93. Sherman, *Memoirs*, II, 170.

94. Key, *Battle of Atlanta*, 83.

95. Sherman, *Memoirs*, II, 178–79.

96. Burne, *Lee, Grant and Sherman*, 80–81.

97. Cyril Falls, *The Art of War, From the Age of Napoleon to the Present Day* (London, 1961), 76.

98. Beringer, et al., *Why the South Lost*, 326–27.

## CHAPTER TEN

1. Lewis, *Sherman*, 442.

2. Williams, *McClellan, Sherman and Grant*, 72.

3. William Sherman to Minnie and Lizzie Sherman, November 9, 1864, "My Father's Letters," 192–93.

4. Merrill, *Sherman*, 268.

5. Special Field Orders, No. 120, November 9, 1864, *OR*, XXXIX, Part 3, 713.

6. Liddell Hart, *Sherman*, 331.

7. Sherman, *Memoirs*, II, 179.

8. *Ibid.*, II, 177.

9. Lewis, *Fighting Prophet*, 442.

10. Liddell Hart, *Sherman*, 331.

11. Merrill, *Sherman*, 270.

12. Hedley, *Marching Through Georgia*, 258–59.

13. Merrill, *Sherman*, 269.

14. Connolly, "Major Connolly's Letters to His Wife," 406.

15. Merrill, *Sherman*, 270.

16. Official Report of William Sherman, January 1, 1865, *OR*, XLIV, 7–14.

17. Conyngham, *March Through the South*, 314.

18. Dolly Sumner Lunt, *A Woman's Wartime Journal, An Account of the Passage over a Georgia Plantation of Sherman's Army on the March to the Sea, as Recorded in the Diary of Dolly Sumner Lunt* (Macon, 1927), 34–46.

19. *Ibid.*

20. Official Report of William Sherman, January 1, 1865, *OR*, XLIV, 7–14.

21. A. C. Cooper, "Days That Are Dead," *Our Women in the War: The Lives They Lived; the Deaths They Died* (Charleston, 1885), 435.

22. J. P. Austin, *The Blue and the Gray* (Atlanta, 1899), 138.

23. Conyngham, *March Through the South*, 255.

24. Liddell Hart, *Sherman*, 337–38.

25. Sherman, *Memoirs*, II, 191–92.

26. P. G. T. Beauregard to the People of Georgia, November 18, 1864, *OR*, XLIV, 867.

27. Sherman, *Memoirs*, II, 174–76.

28. Hitchcock, *Marching With Sherman*, 92–93.

29. *Ibid.*, 86–87.

30. *Ibid.*, 93.

31. *Ibid.*, 125.

32. James C. Bonner, "Sherman at Milledgeville in 1864," *Journal of Southern History* 22 (1956), 280–84.

33. Connolly, "Major Connolly's Letters to His Wife," 408.

34. Bonner, "Sherman at Milledgeville," 290.

35. Katharine M. Jones (ed.), *When Sherman Came: Southern Women and the "Great March"* (New York, 1964), 40–41.

36. Sherman, *Memoirs*, II, 194.

37. Lewis, *Fighting Prophet*, 462.

38. Nichols, *The Story of the Great March*, 119.

39. *Ibid.*, 121.

40. Wheeler, *Sherman's March*, 121

41. *Ibid.*

42. Lewis, *Fighting Prophet*, 457.

43. *Ibid.*, 457–58.

44. *Ibid.*

45. William Sherman to William J. Hardee, December 17, 1864, *OR*, XLIV, 737.

46. William J. Hardee to William Sherman, December 17, 1864, *Ibid.*, 737–38.

47. *Ibid.*

48. William Sherman to President Lincoln, December 22, 1864, *Ibid.*, 783.

49. Abraham Lincoln to William Sherman, December 26, 1864, *Ibid.*, 809.

50. Sherman, *Memoirs*, II, 219.

51. Conyngham, *March Through the South*, 286, 288.

52. Report from William Sherman, January 1, 1865, *OR*, XLIV, 7–14.

53. Linus Pierpont Brockett, *Our Great Captains. Grant, Sherman, Thomas, Sheridan, and Farragut* (New York, 1965), 175.

54. William Sherman to John Sherman, January 22, 1865, *The Sherman Letters*, 245.

55. Sherman, *Memoirs*, II, 221.

56. William Sherman to U. S. Grant, December 24, 1864, *OR*, XLIV, 797–98.

57. William Sherman to M. C. Meigs, December 25, 1864, *Ibid.*, 807.

58. Lewis, *Fighting Prophet*, 474.

59. Merrill, *Sherman*, 275.

60. Hedley, *Marching Through Georgia*, 337.

61. Lewis, *Fighting Prophet*, 453.

62. Wheeler, *Sherman's March*, 142–43.

63. *Ibid.*

64. William Sherman to Ellen Sherman, December 23, 1864, *Home Letters*, 318–19.

65. William Sherman to H. W. Halleck, December 24, 1864, *OR*, XLIV, 798–800.

66. Beringer, et al., *Why the South Lost*, 332.
67. U. S. Grant to Phillip Sheridan, February 20, 1865, *OR*, XLVI, Part 2, 605–6.
68. Lewis, *Fighting Prophet*, 468.
69. Merrill, *Sherman*, 273.
70. Douglas S. Freeman, *R. E. Lee, A Biography*, 4 vols. (New York, 1936), III, 542.
71. Richard D. Goff, *Confederate Supply* (Durham, 1969), 240–41.
72. Hattaway and Jones, *How the North Won*, 670.
73. Freeman, *Lee*, 541.
74. Beringer, et al., *Why the South Lost*, 329.
75. Lewis, *Fighting Prophet*, 442.
76. Charles Carleton Coffin, *The Boys of '61* (Boston, 1884), 145.
77. *Ibid.*, 150.
78. Liddell Hart, *Sherman*, 335.
79. Lewis, *Fighting Prophet*, 452.
80. Coulter, "Sherman and the South," 28–45.
81. Lewis, *Fighting Prophet*, 452–53.
82. Merrill, *Sherman*, 270.
83. *Ibid.*
84. Walters, *Merchant of Terror*, 207.
85. Coulter, "Sherman and the South," 44.
86. Burne, *Lee, Grant and Sherman*, 147.
87. Castel, "Rising Son," 16.
88. Burne, *Lee, Grant and Sherman*, 147.

## CHAPTER ELEVEN

1. Grant, *Memoirs*, II, 401.
2. Liddell Hart, *Sherman*, 356.
3. *Ibid.*
4. William Sherman to H. W. Halleck, December 24, 1864, *OR*, XLIV, 799.
5. Sherman, *Memoirs*, II, 213.
6. *Ibid.*, 223–24.
7. *Ibid.*, 225.
8. *Ibid.*, 227–28.
9. *Ibid.*, 254.
10. C. Vann Woodward (ed.), *Mary Chesnut's Civil War* (New Haven, 1981), 702.
11. Diary of Emma A. Florence Le Conte, December 31, 1865, *Southern Historical Collection*, University of North Carolina Library (Chapel Hill).
12. Lewis, *Fighting Prophet*, 489.
13. Calkins, *One Hundred and Fourth Regiment*, 284.
14. Barrett, *March Through the Carolinas*, 41.

15. Nichols, *The Great March*, 130.

16. Barrett, *March Through the Carolinas*, 38.

17. Bruce Catton, *This Hallowed Ground* (New York, 1955), 460.

18. Wheeler, *Sherman's March*, 165–66.

19. Catton, *Hallowed Ground*, 460.

20. William Sherman to U. S. Grant, January 29, 1865, *OR*, XLIV, Part 2, 671.

21. Daniel Oakey, "Marching Through Georgia and the Carolinas," *Battles and Leaders*, IV, 671.

22. John C. Gray, Jr., to John C. Rogers, December 14, 1864, John C. Gray, Jr., and John C. Rogers, *War Letters 1862–1865 of John Chipman Gray and John Codman Rogers* (New York, 1927), 428.

23. Wheeler, *Sherman's March*, 160.

24. William Sherman to Ellen Sherman, April 5, 1865, *Home Letters*, 340.

25. Barrett, *March Through the Carolinas*, 47.

26. Johnson, *Sherman*, 429.

27. Nichols, *The Great March*, 131–32.

28. Walters, *Merchant of Terror*, 187–88.

29. Yates Snowden, *Marching with Sherman* (Columbia, 1929), 14.

30. Miers, *Marched to Hell*, 292.

31. Conyngham, *March Through the South*, 310.

32. Julian Wisner Hinkley, *A Narrative of Service with the Third Wisconsin Infantry* (Madison, 1917), 146.

33. Lewis, *Fighting Prophet*, 493.

34. *Ibid.*

35. Conyngham, *March Through the South*, 311.

36. Yates Snowden (ed.), *History of South Carolina*, 2 vols. (Chicago, 1920), II, 801.

37. Lewis, *Fighting Prophet*, 494.

38. *Ibid.*, 495.

39. Barrett, *March Through the Carolinas*, 65.

40. Merrill, *Sherman*, 282.

41. Marion Lucas, *Sherman and the Burning of Columbia* (College Station, 1976), foreword. *See also* James Ford Rhodes, "Who Burned Columbia?" *The American Historical Review* (April, 1902), 485–93.

42. Walters, *Merchant of Terror*, 196.

43. Merrill, *Sherman*, 279.

44. *Ibid.*, 283.

45. Nichols, *The Great March*, 169.

46. Miers, *Marched to Hell*, 318–19.

47. Merrill, *Sherman*, 284.

48. Nichols, *The Great March*, 222.

49. Manning Force, "Marching Across Carolina," *Sketches of War History,*

*1861–1865. Papers Read before the Ohio Commandery of the Military Order of the Loyal Legions of the United States, 1883–1906,* 6 vols. (Cincinnati, 1888–1908).

50. Pepper, *Personal Recollections,* 342–43.
51. William Sherman to Ellen Sherman, April 5, 1865, *Home Letters,* 340.
52. Robert E. Lee to Z. B. Vance, February 24, 1865, *OR,* XLVII, Part 2, 1270.
53. Sherman, *Memoirs,* II, 326–27.
54. William Sherman, "The Surrender of General Johnston, Letter from General Sherman," *The Historical Magazine and Notes and Queries Concerning the Antiques, History, and Biography of America,* XV, 333–34.
55. Barrett, *March Through the Carolinas,* 241.
56. Sherman, *Memoirs,* II, 356–57.
57. Barrett, *March Through the Carolinas,* 241.
58. *Ibid.,* 243.
59. *Ibid.,* 241–44.
60. *Ibid.,* 267–72.
61. Merrill, *Sherman,* 285.
62. Burne, *Lee, Grant and Sherman,* 201.
63. Schofield, *Forty-Six Years,* 341.
64. Burne, *Lee, Grant and Sherman,* 200.
65. Hattaway and Jones, *How the North Won,* 669.
66. Lewis, *Fighting Prophet,* 510–11.
67. Liddell Hart, *Sherman,* 369, 380.
68. Barrett, *March Through the Carolinas,* 118.
69. Liddell Hart, *Sherman,* 402.
70. *Ibid.*
71. Sherman, *Memoirs,* II, 379–80.

## EPILOGUE

1. Kai T. Erikson, *Everything in Its Path, Destruction of Community in the Buffalo Creek Flood* (New York, 1976), 157.
2. *Ibid.,* 186.
3. John Bigelow, *The Principles of Strategy: Illustrated Mainly from American Campaigns* (New York, 1968), 224–33.
4. Basil Henry Liddell Hart, *Strategy, The Indirect Approach* (New York, 1954), 145–54.
5. Jay Luvaas, *The Military Legacy of the Civil War, The European Inheritance* (Chicago, 1959), 220.
6. Basil Henry Liddell Hart, *Thoughts on War* (London, 1944), 241–42.
7. *Ibid.*
8. Russell Weigley, "American Strategy from Its Beginning through the

First World War," *Makers of Modern Strategy from Machiavelli to the Nuclear Age*, Peter Paret (ed.), (Princeton, 1986), 436.

9. Williams, *McClellan, Sherman and Grant*, 77.

10. *Ibid.*

11. James Reston, Jr., *Sherman's March and Vietnam* (New York, 1984), 51.

12. Coulter, "Sherman and the South," 45.

# *Bibliography*

## PRIMARY SOURCES
### Manuscripts

James Beale Papers: Massachusetts Historical Society Library.
Carrie Berry Papers: Atlanta Historical Society.
Mary Ann Bickerdyke Papers: Library of Congress.
David French Boyd Papers: Louisiana State University Library.
Jacob C. Cox Papers: Kennesaw Mountain National Military Park Library.
Hugh Boyle Ewing Papers: Ohio Historical Society.
Philemon Beecher Ewing Papers: Ohio Historical Society.
Thomas Ewing Family Papers: Library of Congress.
U. S. Grant Papers: United States Military Academy Library.
Hiram Gray Papers: Duke University Library.
Oliver O. Howard Papers: Bowdoin University Library.
Emma A. Florence Le Conte Diary: Southern Historical Collection, University of North Carolina.
John A. Logan Papers: Library of Congress.
John A. McClernand Papers: Illinois State Historical Library.
James B. McPherson Papers: Library of Congress.
David Dixon Porter Papers: Library of Congress.
John M. Schofield Papers: Library of Congress.
John Sherman Papers: Library of Congress.
William T. Sherman Papers: Library of Congress, Ohio Historical Society, Duke University Library, United States Military Academy Library, and the Henry E. Huntington Library.
Sherman Family Papers: University of Notre Dame Archives.
"Sherman's Foragers and Bummers": Chemung County Historical Society, Elmira, New York.

Samuel Hoey Walkup Diary: Southern Historical Collection, University of North Carolina.

## Books

Badeau, Adam. *Military History of Ulysses S. Grant, from April, 1861 to April, 1865*. 3 vols., New York, 1882.

Barber, Lucius. *15th Illinois Diary*. Chicago, 1894.

Basler, Roy P., ed, *The Collected Works of Abraham Lincoln*. 9 vols. New Brunswick, 1953.

Boies, Andrew. *Record of the Thirty-Third Massachusetts Volunteer Infantry from August 1862-August 1865*. Fitchburg, 1880.

Bowman, Samuel Millard and Richard Bache Irwin. *Sherman and His Campaigns, A Military Biography*. New York, 1865.

Boyd, David French. *General W. T. Sherman As a College President*. Baton Rouge, 1910.

Boyd, James Penny. *The Life of William T. Sherman*. Philadelphia, 1891.

Brockett, Linus Pierpont. *Our Great Captains. Grant, Sherman, Thomas, Sheridan and Farragut*. New York, 1965.

Cate, Wirt Armistead, ed. *Two Soldiers, The Campaign Diaries of Thomas J. Key, C.S.A. and Robert J. Campbell, U.S.A.* Chapel Hill, 1936.

Calkins, William Wirt. *The History of the One Hundred and Fourth Regiment of Illinois Volunteer Infantry. War of the Great Rebellion 1862–1865*. Cincinnati, 1865.

Chase, Edward. *The Memorial Life of General William Tecumseh Sherman*. Chicago, 1891.

Chambers, William Pitt. *Publications of the Mississippi Historical Society*, vol. V, 1925.

Coffin, Charles Carleton. *The Boys of '61*. Boston, 1884.

Commager, Henry Steele, ed. *The Blue and the Gray. The Story of the Civil War as Told by Participants*. 2 vols., New York, 1950.

Cox, Jacob Dolson. *Atlanta*. New York, 1882.

Cox, Jacob Dolson. *Military Reminiscences of the Civil War*. 2 vols., New York, 1900.

Dana, Charles A. *Recollections of the Civil War with the Leaders at Washington and in the Field in the Sixties*. New York, 1898.

Fleming, W. T. *General W. T. Sherman as a College President*. Cleveland, 1912.

Fletcher, Thomas Clement, ed. *Life and Reminiscences of General William T. Sherman by Distinguished Men of His Time*. Baltimore, 1891.

Foote, Corydon E. *With Sherman to the Sea*. New York, 1960.

Force, Manning Ferguson. *General Sherman*. New York, 1899.

Gage, Moses D. *From Vicksburg to Raleigh*. Chicago, 1865.

Gay, Mary. *Life in Dixie During the War*. Atlanta, 1897.

Gibbes, James Guiguard. *Who Burnt Columbia?* Newberry, 1902.

Harwell, Richard and Philip N. Racine, eds. *The Fiery Trail: A Union Officer's Account of Sherman's Last Campaigns.* Knoxville, 1986.

Headley, Joel Tyler. *Grant and Sherman: Their Campaigns and Generals.* New York, 1865.

Headley, P. C. *Facing the Enemy: The Life and Military Career of Gen. William Tecumseh Sherman.* Boston, 1865.

Hedley, F. Y. *Marching Through Georgia, Pen-Pictures of Every-day Life.* Chicago, 1884.

Hinkley, Julian Wisner. *A Narrative of Service with the Third Wisconsin Infantry.* Madison, 1917.

Howe, Mark Antony DeWolfe, ed. *Home Letters of General Sherman.* New York, 1909.

Johnson, W. P. *Life of General Albert Sidney Johnston.* New York, 1878.

Johnson, Willis Fletcher. *Life of William Tecumseh Sherman, Late Retired General, U.S.A.* Philadelphia, 1891.

Jomini, Antoine-Henri. *The Art of War*, trans. by G. H. Mendell and W. P. Craighill. Westport, Connecticut, 1862.

Jones, Katharine M. *When Sherman Came: Southern Women and the "Great March."* New York, 1964.

Journal of Emma A. Florence Le Conte, December 31, 1864 to August 6, 1865. *Southern Historical Collection.* University of North Carolina Library, Chapel Hill.

Keim, De Bow Randolph. *Sherman, A Memorial in Art, Oratory, and Literature, by the Society of the Army of the Tennessee with the aid of the Congress of the United States of America.* Washington, D.C., 1904.

LeConte, Joseph. *Ware Sherman. A Journal of Three Months Experience in the Last Days of the Confederacy.* Berkeley, 1937.

Lunt, Dolly Sumner. *A Woman's Wartime Journal, An Account of the Passage over a Georgia Plantation of Sherman's Army on the March to the Sea as Recorded in the Diary of Dolly Sumner Lunt.* Macon, 1927.

Martin, Isabella D. and Myrta Locket Avery, eds. *A Diary From Dixie as Written by Mary Boykin Chesnut.* New York, 1929.

McArthur, Henry Clay. *Capture and Destruction of Columbia, South Carolina, February 17, 1865.* Washington, 1911.

McKeever, Elliot B. *He Rode with Sherman.* Aberdeen, S.D., 1947.

Moss, Lemuel. *Annals of the United States Christian Commission.* Philadelphia, 1868.

Moulton, Charles William. *The Review of General Sherman's Memoirs Examined Chiefly in the Light of Its Own Evidence.* Cincinnati, 1875.

Nichols, George Ward. *The Story of the Great March From the Diary of a Staff Officer.* New York, 1865.

Northrop, Henry Davenport. *Life and Deeds of General Sherman.* Waukesha, Wis., 1891.

Pepper, George W. *Personal Recollections of Sherman's Campaigns in Georgia and the Carolinas*. Zanesville, 1866.

Porter, David Dixon. *Incidents and Anecdotes of the Civil War*. New York, 1886.

Porter, Horace. *Campaigning With Grant*. Secaucus, New Jersey, 1897.

Reed, Wallace. *History of Atlanta, Georgia*. Syracuse, 1889.

Richardson, A. D. *The Secret Service: the Field, the Dungeon and the Escape*. Hartford, 1866.

Senour, Fauntleroy. *Major General William T. Sherman and His Campaigns*. Chicago, 1865.

Sherman, William Tecumseh. *General Sherman's Official Accounts of His Great March Through Georgia and the Carolinas*. New York, 1865.

Snowden, Yates, ed. *History of South Carolina*. 2 vols. Chicago, 1920.

Snowden, Yates. *Marching with Sherman*. Columbia, 1929.

*The War of the Rebellion: A Compilation of the Official Records of the Union and Confederate Armies*. 130 vols., Washington, D.C., 1880–1901.

Thorndike, Rachel Sherman, ed. *The Sherman Letters, Correspondence Between General and Senator Sherman from 1837 to 1891*. New York, 1894.

von Clausewitz, Carl. *On War*. Princeton, 1976.

Williams, Noble C. *Echoes from the Battlefield; or Southern Life During the War*. Atlanta, 1902.

Winther, Oscar Osburn, ed. *With Sherman to the Sea. The Civil War Letters, Diaries, and Reminiscences of Theodore F. Upson*. Baton Rouge, 1934.

Wise, John Sergeant. *End of a Era*. New York, 1899.

Woodward, C. Vann, ed. *Mary Chesnut's Civil War*. New Haven, 1981.

## Articles

Boyd, David French. "General William T. Sherman as a College President," *The American College*, II (New York, 1909–1910), 6–7.

Boyd, David French Boyd. "General W. T. Sherman as a College President," *University Bulletin*, Louisiana State University, I, 10, 1910.

Byers, Samuel Hawken Marshall. "Some Personal Recollections of General Sherman," *McClure's Magazine*, III (August, 1894), 212–224.

Cohen, Fanny. "Fanny Cohen's Journal of Sherman's Occupation of Savannah," edited by Spencer B. King, Jr., *Georgia Historical Quarterly*, no. 41, 407–416.

Connolly, James Austin. "Major James Austin Connolly's Letters to his Wife, 1862–1865," *Transactions of the Illinois State Historical Society*, no. 35 (Springfield, 1928), 215–438.

Cooper, A. C. "Days That Are Dead," *Our Women in the War: The Lives They Lived; the Deaths They Died* (Charleston, 1885).

Eaton, Clement, ed. "Diary of an Officer in Sherman's Army Marching Through the Carolinas," *The Journal of Southern History*, IX (May, 1943), 238–254.

Erickson, Edgar L., ed. "With Grant at Vicksburg. From the Civil War Diary of Charles E. Wilcox," *Journal of the Illinois State Historical Society*, vol. XXX (April 1937-January 1938).

Ewing, Charles. "Sherman's March Through Georgia: Letters from Charles Ewing to His Father Thomas Ewing," edited by George C. Osborn, *Georgia Historical Quarterly*, no. 18, 97–112.

Force, Manning. "Marching Across Carolina," *Sketches of War History, 1861–1865. Papers Read before the Ohio Commandery of the Military Order of the Loyal Legions of the United States, 1883–1906*, 6 vols. (Cincinnati, 1888–1908).

Grant, Ulysses Simpson. "Preparing for the Campaigns of '64," *Battles and Leaders of the Civil War*, edited by Robert Underwood Johnson and Clarence Clough Buel, IV, New York, 1888, 97–118.

Howard, O. O. "The Struggle for Atlanta," *Battles and Leaders of the Civil War*, edited by Robert Underwood Johnson and Clarence Clough Buel, IV, New York, 1888.

Lay, Henry C. "Sherman in Georgia," *Atlantic*, no. 141, 166–172.

Lee, Stephen D. "Sherman's Meridian Expedition and Sooy Smith's Raid to West Point," *Southern Historical Society Papers*, VIII, no. 2 (January to December 1880), 54–58.

Lee, Stephen D. "The War in Mississippi after the Fall of Vicksburg, July 4, 1863," *Mississippi Historical Society Publications*, no. 10, 47–62.

Mead, Rufus, Jr. "With Sherman Through Georgia and the Carolinas: Letters of a Federal Soldier," edited by James A. Padgett, *Georgia Historical Quarterly*, no. 33, 49–81.

Morgan, George W. "The Assault on Chickasaw Bluffs," *Battles and Leaders of the Civil War*, edited by Robert Underwood Johnson and Clarence Clough Buel, 4 vols., New York, 1884.

Oakey, Daniel. "Marching Through Georgia and the Carolinas," *Battles and Leaders of the Civil War*, IV, New York, 1888, 671.

Padgett, James A., ed. "With Sherman Through Georgia and the Carolinas: Letters of a Federal Soldier," *The Georgia Historical Quarterly*, XXXIII (March, 1949), 49–81.

Pierson, Stephen. "From Chattanooga to Atlanta in 1864—A Personal Reminiscence," *New Jersey Historical Society, Proceedings* 16 (1931).

Shanks, William Franklin Gore. "Recollections of General Sherman," *Harper's New Monthly Magazine*, XXX (April, 1865), 640–646.

Shanks, William Franklin Gore. "Recollections of General Thomas," *Harper's Magazine*, XXX.

Sherman, Minnie Ewing. "My Father's Letters," *The Cosmopolitan*, vol. 12 (1891), 64–69, 187–194.

Sherman, William T. "A Reminiscence of the War," *Modern Eloquence*, edited by Thomas B. Reed, Philadelphia, 1900.

Sherman, William T. "Sherman and the San Francisco Vigilantes," *Century*, no. 43, 296–309.

Sherman, William T. "Sherman's Estimate of Grant," *Century*, no. 70, 316–318.

Sherman, William T. and John Sherman. "Letters of Two Brothers," edited by J. D. Cox, *Century*, no. 45, 88–101, 425–440, 689–699, 892–903.

Sherman, William Tecumseh. "The Surrender of General Johnston, Letter from General Sherman," *The Historical Magazine and Notes and Queries Concerning the Antiques, History, and Biography of America*, XV (May, 1869), 333–334.

Sherman, William Tecumseh. "The Grand Strategy of the Last Year of the War," *Battles and Leaders of the Civil War*, edited by Robert Underwood Johnson and Clarence Clough Buel, IV, New York, 1888, 247–259.

Slocum, Henry Warner. "Final Operations of Sherman's Army," *Battles and Leaders of the Civil War*, edited by Robert Underwood Johnson and Clarence Clough Buel, IV, New York, 1888, 754–759.

Slocum, Henry Warner. "Sherman's March From Savannah to Bentonville," *Battles and Leaders of the Civil War*, edited by Robert Underwood Johnson and Clarence Clough Buel, IV, New York, 1888, 681–696.

Snead, Thomas L. "The Conquest of Arkansas," *Battles and Leaders of the Civil War*, III, 452–453.

"The Prospects and Policy of the South, as They Appear to the Eyes of a Planter," *Southern Quarterly Review*, 26, 1854.

Stone, Henry. "The Atlanta Campaign," *Papers of the Military Historical Society of Massachusetts*, VII (Boston, 1910).

## Memoirs

Boynton, H. V. *Sherman's Historical Raid*. Cincinnati, 1865.

Grant, U. S. *Personal Memoirs of U. S. Grant*. 2 vols., New York, 1892.

Hood, John Bell. *Advance and Retreat. Personal Experiences in the United States and Confederate Armies*. New Orleans, 1880.

Howard, Oliver Otis. *Autobiography of Oliver Otis Howard, Major General United States Army*. 2 vols., New York, 1907.

Johnston, Joseph Eggleston. *Narrative of Military Operations, Directed, During the Late War Between the States, by Joseph E. Johnston, General, C.S.A.*. New York, 1874.

Schofield, John M. *Forty-Six Years in the Army*. New York, 1897.

Sherman, William Tecumseh. *Memoirs of W. T. Sherman By Himself*. 2 vols., New York, 1931.

## Newspapers

Canton *American Citizen*, April 4, 1864; December 26, 1864.

Chicago *Tribune*, November 5, 7, 1861; December, 1861.

Cincinnati *Commercial*, November 9, 11, 16; December 11, 1861; April 1962.
Cincinnati *Gazette*, July 1862.
Columbia *Phoenix*, May 2, 1865.
Columbus *Times*, December 23, 1864.
Louisville *Journal*, December 17, 1861; 1862.
Mobile *Daily Advertiser and Registar*, September 15, 1864.
Mobile *Daily Tribune*, March 5, 1864.
Montgomery *Daily Advertiser*, September 15, 1864.
New York *Herald*, March 15, 1864.
New York *Times*, March 27, 1864.
New York *World*, August 14, 1863; March 14, 1864.
Richmond *Whig*, 1864.
St. Louis *Missouri Democrat*, December 1862.

## Recollections

Arbuckle, John C. *Civil War Experiences of a Foot-Soldier Who Marched with Sherman*. Columbus, 1930.
Austin, J. P. *The Blue and the Gray*. Atlanta, 1899.
Bradley, George S. *The Star Corps: or, Notes of an Army Chaplain During Sherman's Famous March to the Sea*. Milwaukee, 1865.
Calkins, William W. *The History of the One Hundred and Fourth Regiment of Illinois Volunteer Infantry. War of the Rebellion*. Cincinnati, 1865.
Conyngham, David P. *Sherman's March Through the South with Sketches and Incidents of the Campaign*. New York, 1865.
Gray, John C., Jr., and John C. Rogers. *War Letters, 1862–1865 of John Chipman Gray and John Codman Rogers*. New York, 1927.
Howe, Mark Antony DeWolfe, ed. *Marching With Sherman, Passages from the Letters and Campaign Diaries of Henry Hitchcock, Major and Assistant Adjutant General of Volunteers, November 1864-May 1865*. New Haven, 1927.
Slocum, Charles Elihu. *Life and Services of Major-General Henry Warner Slocum, Officer in the United States Army*. Toledo, 1913.

## SECONDARY SOURCES

### Books

Barrett, John G. *Sherman's March Through the Carolinas*. Chapel Hill, 1956.
Bearss, Edwin Cole. *The Campaign for Vicksburg*. 3 vols., Dayton, 1986.
Bearss, M. R. *Sherman's Forgotten Campaign, The Meridian Expedition*. Baltimore, 1987.
Beringer, Richard E., Herman Hattaway, Archer Jones, and William N. Still, Jr. *Why the South Lost the Civil War*. Athens, 1986.

Bigelow, John. *The Principles of Strategy: Illustrated Mainly from American Campaigns*. New York, 1968.

Black, Robert C., III. *The Railroads of the Confederacy*. Chapel Hill, 1952.

Bradley, Omar N. *A General's Life*. New York, 1983.

Burne, Alfred Higgins. *Lee, Grant, and Sherman. A Study in Leadership in the 1864–65 Campaign*. New York, 1939.

Carpenter, John A. *Sword and Olive Branch: Oliver Otis Howard*. Pittsburg, 1964.

Carter, Samuel, III. *The Seige of Atlanta, 1864*. New York, 1973.

Carter, Samuel, III. *The Final Fortress: The Campaign for Vicksburg, 1862–1863*. Wilmington, 1988.

Catton, Bruce. *Never Call Retreat*. New York, 1965.

Catton, Bruce. *This Hallowed Ground*. New York, 1955.

Connelly, Thomas L., and Barbara L. Bellows. *God and General Longstreet, The Lost Cause and the Southern Mind*. Baton Rouge, 1982.

Connelly, Thomas Lawrence. *Army of the Heartland, The Army of Tennessee, 1861–1862*. Baton Rouge, 1967.

Connelly, Thomas Lawrence. *Autumn of Glory, The Army of Tennessee, 1862–1865*. Baton Rouge, 1971.

Cook, Harvey Toliver. *Sherman's March Through South Carolina in 1865*. Greenville, 1938.

Donald, David, ed, *Why the North Won the Civil War*. New York, 1960.

Davis, Burke. *Sherman's March*. New York, 1980.

Dupey, R. E. and R. N. Dupey. *The Compact History of the Civil War*. New York, 1961.

Erikson, Kai T. *Everything in Its Path, Destruction of Community in the Buffalo Creek Flood*. New York, 1976.

Falls, Cyril. *The Art of War, From the Age of Napoleon to the Present Day*. London, 1961.

Fleming, Walter Lynwood. *W. T. Sherman as a History Teacher*. Baton Rouge, 1910.

Foote, Shelby. *The Civil War, A Narrative*, 3 vols. New York, 1958.

Freeman, Douglas S. *R. E. Lee, A Biography*. 4 vols. New York, 1936.

Fuller, J. F. C. *The Generalship of Ulysses S. Grant*. Bloomington, 1977.

Gibbs, James G. *Who Burnt Columbia?* Newberry, 1902.

Glatthaar, Joseph T. *The March to the Sea and Beyond: Sherman's Troops in the Savannah and the Carolinas' Campaigns*. New York, 1985.

Goff, Richard D. *Confederate Supply*. Durham, 1969.

Goffman, Erving. *The Presentation of Self in Everyday Life*. New York, 1959.

Goldhurst, Richard. *Many Are the Hearts: The Agony and Triumph of Ulysses S. Grant*. New York, 1975.

Hattaway, Herman, and Archer Jones. *How the North Won: A Military History of the Civil War*. Urbana, 1983.

Horn, Stanley F. *The Army of Tennessee: A Military History*. New York, 1941.

Key, William. *The Battle of Atlanta and the Georgia Campaign*. New York, 1958.

Lewis, Lloyd. *Sherman, Fighting Prophet*. New York, 1932.

Liddell Hart, Basil Henry. *Defense of the West*. New York, 1950.

Liddell Hart, Basil Henry. *Strategy, The Indirect Approach*. New York, 1954.

Liddell Hart, Basil Henry. *Sherman: Soldier, Realist, American*. New York, 1958.

Liddell Hart, Basil Henry. *Sherman, The Genius of the Civil War*. London, 1930.

Liddell Hart, Basil Henry. *Thoughts on War*. London, 1944.

Lucas, Marion. *Sherman and the Burning of Columbia*. College Station, 1976.

Luvaas, Jay. *The Military Legacy of the Civil War, The European Inheritance*. Chicago, 1959.

Macartney, C. E. *Grant and His Generals*. New York, 1953.

Marszalek, John F. *Sherman's Other War: The General and the Civil War Press*. Memphis, 1981.

McAllister, Anna. *Ellen Ewing, Wife of General Sherman*. Chicago, 1936.

McDonough, James Lee. *Schofield: Union General in the Civil War and Reconstruction*. Tallahassee, 1972.

McDonough, James Lee, and James Pickett Jones. *War So Terrible: Sherman and Atlanta*. New York, 1987.

McMurry, Richard. *John Bell Hood and the War for Southern Independence*. Lexington, 1982.

McMurry, Richard. *Two Great Rebel Armies: An Essay in Confederate Military History*. Chapel Hill, 1989.

Mead, George H. *Mind, Self, and Society*. Chicago, 1934.

Merrill, James M. *William Tecumseh Sherman*. Chicago, 1971.

Merton, Robert K. *Social Theory and Social Structure*. New York, 1968.

Miers, Earl Schenck. *The General Who Marched to Hell: William Tecumseh Sherman and His March to Fame and Infamy*. New York, 1951.

Miles, Jim. *Fields of Glory*. Nashville, 1989.

Miles, Jim. *To the Sea*. Nashville, 1989.

Millis, Walter. *Arms and Men: A Study in American Military History*. New York, 1956.

Mills, C. Wright. *The Sociological Imagination*. London, 1959.

Nevins, Allan. *The War for the Union: Volume VI, The Organized War to Victory, 1864–1865*. New York, 1971.

Reston, James, Jr. *Sherman's March and Vietnam*. New York, 1984.

Robins, Edward. *William T. Sherman*. Philadelphia, 1905.

Ropp, Theodore. *War in the Modern World*. Durham, 1959.

Spaight, J. M. *War Rights on Land*. London, 1911.

Steiner, Paul E. *Medical-Military Portraits of Union and Confederate Generals*. Philadelphia, 1968.

Sword, Wiley. *Shiloh, Bloody April*. Dayton, 1983.

Waley, Elizabeth J. *Forgotten Hero: General James B. McPherson*. New York, 1955.

Walker, Peter F. *Vicksburg: A People at War 1860–1865*. Wilmington, 1987.

Walters, John Bennett. *Merchant of Terror: General Sherman and Total War*. New York, 1973.

Weigley, Russell F. *The American Way of War: A History of the United States Military Strategy and Policy*. Bloomington, 1973.

Wheeler, Richard. *Sherman's March*. New York, 1978.

Wheeler, Richard. *We Knew William Tecumseh Sherman*. New York, 1977.

Wiley, Bell Irvin. *The Life of Johnny Reb, The Common Soldier of the Confederacy*. Indianapolis, 1943.

Wiley, Bell Irvin. *The Road to Appomattox*. Memphis, 1956.

Williams, T. Harry. *McClellan, Sherman and Grant*. New Jersey, 1962.

Wirt, Armistead Cate, ed. *Two Soldiers, The Campaign Diaries of Thomas J. Key, C.S.A. and Robert J. Campbell, U.S.A.* Chapel Hill, 1936.

# Articles

Ambrose, Stephen E. "William T. Sherman, A Personality Profile," *American History Illustrated* (January, 1967), 11.

Ambrose, Stephen E. "William T. Sherman," *American History Illustrated*, no. 1, 5–12, 54–57.

Barnwell, Robert Woodward, "Bentonville—The Last Battle of Johnston and Sherman," *Proceedings of the South Carolina Historical Association*, XIII (Annual, 1943), 42–54.

Barrett, John G. "Sherman and Total War in the Carolinas," *North Carolina Historical Review*, no. 37 (1960), 367–381.

Bearss, Edwin C., "Sherman's Demonstration Against Snyder's Bluff," *Journal of Mississippi History*, no. 27, 168–186.

Bonner, James C., "Sherman at Milledgeville in 1864," *Journal of Southern History*, XXII, no. 3 (August, 1956), 273–291.

Brown, John Mason, "Man and the Myth," *Saturday Review of Literature*, no. 36 (January 17, 1953), 25–28.

Burt, Jesse C., Jr. "Sherman, Railroad General," *Civil War History*, no. 2 (1956), 45–54.

Castel, Albert, "The Guerrilla War, 1861–1865," *Civil War Times Illustrated* (October, 1974).

Castel, Albert, "Life of a Rising Son, Part III: The Conqueror," *Civil War Times Illustrated* (October, 1979), 15.

Clauss, E. M. "Sherman's Failure at Atlanta," *The Georgia Historical Quarterly*, LIII, no. 3, 321.

Connolly, James A., "Major Connolly's Letters to His Wife," *Transactions of the Illinois State Historical Society for the Year 1928* (Springfield, 1928), 410.

Coulter, E. Merton, "Sherman and the South," *North Carolina Review*, no. 8, 41–54.

Cox, Jacob D., "The Sherman-Johnston Convention," *Scribner's*, no. 28, 489–505.

Cresto, Kathleen M. "Sherman and Slavery," *Civil War Times Illustrated*, no. 17 (November, 1978), 13–21.

DeLaubenfels, D. J., "Where Sherman Passed By," *Geographical Review*, no. 47 (1957), 381–395.

Detzler, Jack J. "The Religion of William Tecumseh Sherman," *Ohio History*, no. 75 (1966), 26–34, 68–70.

Drago, Edmond L. "How Sherman's March Through Georgia Affected the Slaves," *Georgia Historical Quarterly*, no. 57 (Fall, 1973), 361–375.

Dyer, John Percy. "Northern Relief for Savannah During Sherman's Occupation," *The Journal of Southern History*, no. 19 (November, 1953), 457–472.

Eisenschiml, Otto. "Sherman: Hero or War Criminal?" *Civil War Times Illustrated* (January, 1964).

Force, Manning Ferguson. "Marching Across Carolina," *Sketches of War History 1861–65. Papers Read Before the Ohio Commandery of the Loyal Legion of the United States*, vol. I (Cincinnati: R. Clarke and Company, 1888–1908), 1–18.

Freeman, John C. "Address on the Civil and Military Career of General William Tecumseh Sherman," *War Papers Read Before the Commandery of the State of Wisconsin, Military Order of the Loyal Legion of the United States*, vol. 3 (Milwaukee: Burdick, Armitage, and Allen, 1903), 296–316.

Gray, Tom S., Jr., "The March to the Sea," *Georgia Historical Quarterly*, XIV, no. 2 (June, 1930), 111–138.

Hale, Edward Jones, Jr., "Sherman's Bummers and Some of Their Work," *Southern Historical Society Papers*, XII, (July-August-September, 1884), 427–428.

Hay, Thomas R. "The Atlanta Campaign," *Georgia Historical Quarterly* (1923).

Hughes, N. C., Jr. "Hardee's Defense of Savannah," *Georgia Historical Quarterly*, no. 47 (1963), 43–67.

James, Josef C. "Sherman at Savannah," *Journal of Negro History*, no. 39 (1954), 127–137.

Kite, Elizabeth S. "Genius of the Civil War," *Commonweal*, no. 27 (1938), 541–543.

Liddell Hart, Basil Henry, "Sherman-Modern Warrior," *American Heritage*, no. 13, 21–23, 102–106.

Luvaas, Jay, "Bentonville—Johnston's Last Stand," *North Carolina Historical Review*, XXXIII, no. 3 (July, 1956), 332–358.

Marszalek, John F., "Was Sherman Really a Brute?" *Blue and Gray Magazine* (December, 1989), 46–51.

McMurry, Richard M. "Confederate Morale in the Atlanta Campaign of 1864," *Georgia Historical Quarterly*, LIV, no. 2 (Summer, 1970), 226–243.

McMurry, Richard M. "Sherman's Meridian Campaign," *Civil War Times Illustrated*, no. 14 (May, 1975), 24–34.

McNeill, William J., "A Survey of Confederate Soldier Morale During Sherman's Campaign Through Georgia and the Carolinas," *Georgia Historical Quarterly*, LV, no. 1 (Spring, 1971), 1–25.

Murray, Robert K., "General Sherman, The Negro and Slavery: The Story of An Unreconstructed Rebel," *Negro History Bulletin*, no. 22, 125–130.

Naroll, Raoul S., "Lincoln and the Sherman Peace Fiasco—Another Fable?" *Journal of Southern History*, XX (November, 1954), 459–483.

O'Conner, Richard, "Sherman: Imaginative Soldier," *American Mercury*, no. 67, 555–564.

Pfang, Harry W., "The Surrender Negotiations Between General Johnston and General Sherman," *Military Affairs*, XVI (Summer, 1952), 61–70.

Pickett, William D., "Why General Sherman's Name is Detested," *Confederate Veteran*, XIV (September, 1906), 397–398.

Rhodes, James Ford. "Who Burned Columbia?" *The American Historical Review* (April, 1902), 485–493.

Rhodes, James Ford, "Sherman's March to the Sea," *American Historical Review*, no. 6, 466–474.

Scaife, William R. "Sherman's March to the Sea," *Blue and Gray Magazine* (December, 1989), 11–42.

Smalley, E. V. "General Sherman," *Century*, no. 5 (1884), 450–462.

Walters, John Bennett, "General William T. Sherman and Total War," *Journal of Southern History*, XIV, no. 4 (November, 1948), 447–480.

Weigley, Russell, "American Strategy from Its Beginning through the First World War," *Makers of Modern Strategy from Machiavelli to the Nuclear Age*, edited by Peter Paret, Princeton, 1986.

Williams, T. Harry, "The Military Leadership of North and South," *Why The North Won the Civil War*, edited by David Donald, New York, 1960.

Wilson, Edmond. "Uncle Billy," *New Yorker*, No. 34 (1958), 114–144.

# *Index*